Java 25 and Beyond

Michael Inden

Java 25 and Beyond

Modern Java Made Easy

Apress®

Michael Inden
Zurich, Zürich, Switzerland

ISBN 979-8-8688-2384-8   ISBN 979-8-8688-2385-5   (eBook)
https://doi.org/10.1007/979-8-8688-2385-5

This Apress imprint is published by the registered company APress Media, LLC, part of Springer Nature.
The registered company address is: 1 New York Plaza, New York, NY 10004, U.S.A.

If disposing of this product, please recycle the paper.

Dedicated to my little princess, my sunshine, and my beloved daughter, Sophie. I am endlessly grateful that you are here.

Preface

First of all, I would like to thank you for choosing this book. Inside, you will find a wealth of information about the new features in the current Java version, 25 LTS (Long-Term Support), as well as all the significant features introduced in its predecessors, Java 21 LTS and Java 17 LTS. Additionally, an outlook on Java 26 is included, highlighting refinements and new features that offer a glimpse of the platform's ongoing evolution.

Target Audience

This book is not intended for novice programmers, but rather for readers who already have a solid familiarity with Java and are seeking concise information on the most important new features in Java versions 12 through 25 LTS, as well as an impression of what is coming in Java 26.

This book is specifically aimed at the following target groups:

1. On the one hand, these are **dedicated hobby programmers and computer science students**, but also **young professionals** who are proficient in Java and are interested in the new features in the current Java versions.
2. On the other hand, the book is intended for **experienced software developers and architects** who want to supplement or refresh their knowledge to be able to evaluate whether and, if so, for which requirements the new Java versions can be a profitable alternative for future projects.

What Does This Book Teach?
In addition to theoretical knowledge, this book provides readers with practical examples to deepen their understanding, enabling them to successfully master the transition to Java 17 LTS, Java 21 LTS, or even the most modern Java 25 LTS in their own projects. The transition is made easier by a variety of exercises, including sample solutions for the most essential features.

To keep the examples in the book as precise and elegant as possible, I use various features from Java 8 LTS, 9, 10, and 11 LTS. Therefore, it is helpful if you already have experience with these versions. For those who need a concise and sound refresher, Chap. 15 provides a crash course on some of the key features included in Java versions 8 LTS to 11 LTS to help you get started.

Structure of This Book

In the following, I will briefly introduce the topics covered in each chapter. I often categorize new features into syntax, APIs, and JVM, where JVM encompasses all topics related to the JVM, the compiler, and other tooling.

Chapter 1: Introduction The introduction prepares you for modern Java in versions 17 LTS, 21 LTS, and 25 LTS, providing an overview of what you can expect to find in this book. I also discuss programming style and highlight the requirements for using the latest Java versions with build tools and IDEs.

Chapter 2: Key Features in JDK 12 to 17 LTS This chapter provides a concise introduction to essential syntax changes, API extensions, and JVM improvements included in Java 17 LTS. First, we will focus on various changes to the Java syntax. These range from multi-line strings and so-called pattern matching in `instanceof` to significant enhancements in `switch` and records as a highly compact notation for defining data container classes.

There are various features in the APIs of the JDK. These include additions to the `String` class and the Stream API. Finally, we will look at changes to the JVM in the form of an improvement in processing and information enrichment in the case of `NullPointerExceptions`.

Chapter 3: Key Features in Java 21 LTS at a Glance This chapter provides an overview of the enhancements in Java 21 LTS, allowing you to quickly familiarize yourself with the new features and then proceed to read the relevant subsequent chapters according to your interests. Otherwise, it is recommended that you read the chapters in order from start to finish.

Chapter 4: Syntax Innovations in JDK 18 to 21 LTS Record patterns enable the breakdown of records into their components, allowing for easy access. Pattern matching also works in `switch` in modern Java and has been enhanced in terms of functionality. Finally, unnamed patterns and variables allow marking certain elements in a record pattern or a variable as unused with a single underscore ("_").

Chapter 5: API Extensions in JDK 18 to 21 LTS Java 21 LTS includes various API innovations. Two highlights are Sequenced Collections and Virtual Threads. Sequenced Collections provide a uniform, mature interface for processing collections from both the front and back. Virtual Threads simplify multithreading, with a particular focus on scaling. Mainly, there are no longer any restrictions on the number of Virtual Threads, unlike for platform threads.

Chapter 6: JVM Innovations in JDK 18 to 21 LTS In this chapter, we will examine the Simple Web Server and explore improvements in specifying code snippets in JavaDoc, among other topics. Finally, we will discuss the feature Unnamed Classes and Instance Main Methods.

Chapter 7: Exercises on the Features in JDK 18 to 21 LTS This chapter contains various exercises on the new features in JDK 18 to 21 LTS, along with brief descriptions of sample solutions.

Chapter 8: New Features in Java 25 LTS at a Glance This chapter provides an overview of the enhancements in Java 25 LTS. This allows you to familiarize yourself quickly and, depending on your interests, continue reading in the relevant subsequent chapters. Otherwise, it is recommended that you simply read the chapters in order.

Chapter 9: Syntax Innovations in JDK 22 to 25 LTS Java 25 LTS offers many exciting innovations, such as primitive types in patterns, `instanceof`, and `switch`, as well as module import declarations. In the area of record patterns in particular, unnamed variables and patterns provide greater clarity and a more concise notation. Additionally, flexible constructor bodies enable increased flexibility in initialization actions.

Chapter 10: API Extensions in JDK 22 to 25 LTS The APIs were also expanded in Java 25 LTS, for example, with Structured Concurrency, an elegant way to describe multithreading at a higher level of abstraction. Although Structured Concurrency has already undergone several preview iterations, it remains in its fifth preview in Java 25 LTS. In the context of multithreading and information exchange, Scoped Values can simplify the transfer of values between different parts of an application. Another fundamental change is the introduction of Stream Gatherers, which allow the definition of custom intermediate operations for the Stream API.

Chapter 11: JVM Innovations in JDK 22 to 25 LTS In the area of the JVM, there are Markdown Documentation Comments and Compact Source Files to make it easier to get started with Java.

Chapter 12: Exercises on the New Features in JDK 22 to 25 LTS This chapter contains various exercises and sample solutions for the new features in JDK 22 to 25 LTS.

Chapter 13: Outlook: What's New in Java 26 Java 26 focuses less on eye-catching syntax changes and more on strengthening stability, security, and performance. By further restricting deep reflection, the language moves closer to ensuring that final truly means immutable. At runtime, applications benefit from improvements such as higher throughput in the G1 garbage collector and HTTP/3 support in the HTTP (Hypertext Transfer Protocol) client. At the same time, key language and API features continue to mature. Structured Concurrency and

Lazy Constants advance further toward finalization, providing clearer concurrency models and more efficient initialization patterns. Overall, Java 26 lays a solid foundation for future releases.

Chapter 14: Summary and Conclusion This chapter begins with some thoughts on migrating to the latest Java versions. It then briefly summarizes the topics related to the many new features presented, especially those from Java 25 LTS.

Chapter 15: Essentials from Java 8 LTS to 11 LTS This chapter summarizes the key additions to Java versions 8 LTS to 11 LTS. This will help you understand the various new features in the more recent Java versions, especially if you are not yet familiar with Java 8 LTS, 9, 10, or 11 LTS. In addition to introducing functional programming with lambdas, we also focus on streams. These are significant new features in JDK 8 LTS for processing data. Chapter 15 concludes with a brief overview of the JShell and how to execute Java programs using Launch Single-File Source Code Programs (Direct Compilation).

Source Code and Executable Programs

To avoid exceeding the scope of this book, the listings sometimes only show excerpts from executable programs. On demand, essential passages are occasionally highlighted in bold for better understanding. The accompanying material is available for download on the website https://github.com/Apress/Java-25-and-Beyond. The project provided contains all essential source files and executable programs. In the text, the respective program name is given in small caps, for example, DATETIME-EXAMPLE, so that it is more easily recognizable as an executable.

Additionally, the project includes the files `build.gradle` and `pom.xml`, which describe the build processes for Gradle and Maven, respectively.

Java Version(s) Used
In Part I, all examples are based on Java 17 LTS. Part II relies on Java 21 LTS, which contains numerous interesting enhancements. Finally, Part III describes the new features of Java 25 LTS. As an outlook Chap. 13 on novelties in Java 26 then covers state-of-the-art Java 26.

After reading this book, you will be well-equipped for modern Java and be able to use the new features in your own experiments and hobby projects or (hopefully even) professionally.

Conventions
Fonts Used
The following conventions apply to fonts in this book: In addition to the font used here, important passages are marked in *italics* or ***italics and bold***. Names

of programs and design patterns are written in SMALL CAPS. Listings with source code are set in the font `Courier` to make it clear that this is an excerpt from a Java program. This font is also used for names of classes, methods, constants, and parameters in standard text.

Practical Tips and Advice

This book is peppered with various practical tips. These present interesting background information or point out pitfalls.

> Boxes formatted in this way can be found throughout the book, providing valuable tips and additional information to supplement the main text.

Classes Used from the JDK

Whenever classes from the JDK are mentioned for the first time in the text, their fully qualified name, that is, including the package structure, is provided: the class `String` would therefore be noted as `java.lang.String`—all further mentions omit the package name. This rule makes it easier to find your way around and locate items in the JDK and also prevents the subsequent text from becoming too bloated. The fully qualified specification is particularly helpful, as `import` statements are rarely shown in the listings.

Method calls described in the text sometimes include the types of the passed parameters, such as `substring(int, int)`. If the parameters are not crucial in a given context, they are often omitted for reasons of readability—this is especially true for methods with generic parameters.

Abbreviations Used

In this book, I use the abbreviations shown in Table 1. Other abbreviations are mentioned in parentheses after their first definition in the text and then used as needed.

Table 1 Abbreviations used

Abbreviation	Meaning
API	Application Programming Interface
ASCII	American Standard Code for Information Interchange
(G)UI	(Graphical) User Interface
IDE	Integrated Development Environment
JDK	Java Development Kit
JEP	JDK Enhancement Proposal
JLS	Java Language Specification
JRE	Java Runtime Environment
JSR	Java Specification Request
JVM	Java Virtual Machine

Suggestions and Criticism

Despite great care and multiple proofreading, ambiguous wording or even errors cannot be completely ruled out. If you notice anything of this nature, please do not hesitate to let me know. I am also happy to receive suggestions or ideas for improvement. Please get in touch with me by email at:

```
michael_inden@hotmail.com
```

Zurich, Zürich, Switzerland   Michael Inden
February 2026

Acknowledgments Writing a book is a wonderful but laborious and time-consuming task. It is almost impossible to accomplish this alone. I want to thank everyone who contributed directly or indirectly to the success of this book. In particular, I was able to rely on a strong team of proofreaders during the manuscript preparation. It is beneficial to gain insight from different perspectives and experiences.

For the current Java 25 LTS version of this book, I was able to count on three proofreaders in particular: Sven Woltmann, Dr. Clemens Gugenberger, and Dennis Woithe.

First of all, I would like to thank Sven, known for his excellent blog at https://www.happycoders.eu/. Sven's expertise has led to valuable improvements in the content and language of many chapters.

I would also like to extend my heartfelt thanks to Clemens for his helpful suggestions and insightful questions, which prompted me to think critically and improve specific passages—not to mention the many minor corrections he pointed out.

I would also like to thank Dennis, who read the manuscript with great attention to detail and uncovered even the most hidden potential for improvement. Additionally, he repeatedly offered suggestions on how to make the examples even more concise.

In the area of multithreading, Marwan Abu-Khalil supported me this time and contributed several improvements and suggestions—many thanks for that and for our interesting discussions at JAX 2025 in Mainz.

In the past, Michael Kulla, a well-known trainer for both Java SE and Jakarta EE, has been highly committed. I want to thank him for his thorough review of many chapters and his insightful comments.

In previous versions, Prof. Carsten Kern and Sven Friederichs also ensured greater linguistic consistency in various places and made different suggestions for improving the content. Thank you!

Finally, I would like to thank Ursula Zimpfer for her eagle eyes during copyediting. This allowed me to eliminate a few minor errors in previous (German) editions.

Contents

Part II   Key Features in Java 18 to 21 LTS

Part V   Appendix

About the Author

Michael Inden is a Java and Python enthusiast with over twenty-five years of professional experience. He has worked for various international companies in multiple roles, including software developer, software architect, team leader, CTO, Head of Development, trainer and freelance consultant. Currently, he works a lecturer in software engineering. In addition, he speaks at conferences and writes specialist books, such as the pairings "Java Challenges"/"Python Challenges", as well as numerous books in German, including "Der Weg zum Java-Profi" and "Einfach Java"/"Einfach Python".

About the Technical Reviewer

 **Andres Sacco** is a Technical Leader at TravelX and has experience with many languages, including Java, PHP, and Node.js. In his previous job, Andres helped identify alternative approaches to optimize data transfer between microservices, reducing infrastructure costs by 55%. Before introducing these optimizations, he investigated alternative testing methods to improve coverage beyond the microservice unit tests. Andres is a co-author of the books Beginning Scala 3 and Practical Spring LDAP, published by Apress.

Chapter 1
Introduction

This book introduces you to all the key new features in the LTS (Long-Term Support) releases Java 17 LTS, Java 21 LTS, and the brand-new Java 25 LTS. An outlook on Java 26 is also included, highlighting its refinements and new features.

Readers who like a refresher or still rely on the older Java 8 LTS or Java 11 LTS release find a compact quick-start guide to the most outstanding and significant changes from these releases in Chap. 15, allowing them to prepare themselves for the extensions in modern Java in terms of content and syntax.

Before we delve into the topics covered in this book, I would like to outline the changes in Oracle's release policy over the past few years, as there have been several notable developments in this area.

1.1 Release Policy

Before Java 9, there was no fixed schedule or release cycle. Instead, the release of a new Java version was linked to the completion of essential features. Many people remember this well: in the past, Java releases were frequently postponed due to unfinished features.

For example, Java 6 was released in December 2006, while its successor, Java 7, did not appear until July 2011, almost 5 years later. Java 8 LTS, released in March 2014, was delayed several times, mainly due to unfinished major features. Even Java 9 was postponed more than once from its original schedule—primarily because of the complexity of the modularization effort.

These long and unpredictable release intervals made planning difficult for both users and tool vendors. To counteract this, Oracle switched to a biannual release cycle after releasing Java 9 in September 2017. Since then, a new Java version has been released every 6 months, independent of whether all originally

M. Inden, *Java 25 and Beyond*, https://doi.org/10.1007/979-8-8688-2385-5_1

planned features are finished. This change allows the functionality that has been implemented up to that point to be released in a timely fashion.

However, obviously, not all features are always ready for final release. Therefore, since Java 9, two special kinds of features exist: preview and incubator features.

Preview Features

So-called preview features are fully specified and implemented. However, they are integrated into the JDK as previews to gather experience and feedback. Based on the input, the implementation, including the types used and method signatures, may still change. Overall, the aim is to refine the functionality in subsequent releases based on the experience gained and feedback received. In exceptional cases, the insights may also lead to the discontinuation of further development or a reorientation of the feature.

Preview features are not accessible by default and must be explicitly enabled by specifying `--enable-preview` during both compilation and execution to use them in your own programs. When compiling, a source version must also be specified with `--source`. Since Java 23, the latter is optional.

Incubator Features

In addition to preview features, there are also incubator features, which are implemented and provided in the form of corresponding modules. Here, too, the aim is to gather experience and feedback, but based on a preliminary implementation. With incubator features, things will change fundamentally, or functionalities may be completely removed later in the final JDK at all. Because incubator features, or, more precisely, the modules that provide them, are not an official part of the JDK, they must be integrated separately. For this purpose, the JVM parameter `--add-modules` is used. It must be specified both during compilation and execution.[1]

Release Cadence in Transition and Its Effects

Let's return to the release cadence. Up to and including Java 9, new Java versions were always released feature-based. This often resulted in considerable delays to the planned release date, namely, whenever essential features had not yet been completed. This was the main reason why Java 8 LTS and Java 9 were delayed by several months or even over a year. Worse still, at that time, it was impossible to predict or plan when a new Java version would actually be released.

The switch to a time-based release strategy counteracts such delays. It increases predictability because a new Java version is released every 6 months, containing all the features completed by that date. Additionally, an LTS (Long-Term Support) version should be released every 3 years. This duration was applied between Java 11 LTS and 17 LTS. With the latter, Oracle decided to shorten the LTS cycle to 2

---

[1] Interestingly, this does not apply to compilation within Eclipse. There, only the run configuration needs to be parameterized appropriately.

years, meaning that even users who prefer upgrading from LTS to LTS can benefit from the new features more quickly.

Although the rapid, biannual release cycle can be a greater challenge for tool manufacturers, for us as developers, it is often positive because we don't have to wait as long for new features, which tends to be quite demoralizing.

However, the positive aspects primarily apply to personal hobby projects, as you can experiment with the new features there and are less restricted by limitations. In professional use, the focus is more on continuity and the availability of security updates, which is why only LTS versions are likely to be considered in this context—just to keep migration costs calculable and more manageable to plan.

> **On a Side Note …**
> For every developer (amateur or professional), the biannual release cycle has another advantage: you can deal with new features bit by bit as they appear, rather than having to work through a huge chunk of new features every two or three years, where the sheer volume of changes means that you may overlook some relevant things or have to postpone caretaking them until later due to time constraints.

Changing Licensing Policy and Its Effects

There have been a few surprises in recent years, not only in terms of the release cycle, but also in particular with regard to licensing policy. Anyone who wanted to download Java 11 LTS was alerted to the changes in licensing policy by a prominent notice (Fig. 1.1).

Java SE Development Kit 11 Downloads

Thank you for downloading this release of the Java™ Platform, Standard Edition Development Kit (JDK™). The JDK is a development environment for building applications, and components using the Java programming language.

The JDK includes tools useful for developing and testing programs written in the Java programming language and running on the Java platform.

Important changes in Oracle JDK 11 License

With JDK 11 Oracle has updated the license terms on which we offer the Oracle JDK.
The new Oracle Technology Network License Agreement for Oracle Java SE is substantially different from the licenses under which previous versions of the JDK were offered. Please review the new terms carefully before downloading and using this product.

Oracle also offers this software under the GPL License on jdk.java.net/11

Fig. 1.1 Note on new license terms, exemplary for Java 11 LTS

It stated that the licensing terms were changing. This has an impact if you distribute your software commercially or plan to do so: *prior to Java 8 LTS, the Oracle JDK could always be used free of charge, even in production systems; however, it became subject to a fee with Java 11 LTS*. An alternative is provided by the OpenJDK (https://openjdk.org/). Nevertheless, the Oracle JDK stays free of charge during development.

The move to force users to purchase a license has caused anger among the developer community. And it got even worse: shortly after the restriction for Java 11 LTS, the licensing terms for Java 8 LTS were also changed retroactively to require payment. As a result, many companies decided not to update to newer versions for the time being.

Overall, there was a massive counter-reaction. This was facilitated by the fact that, since Java 11 LTS, OpenJDK has been based on the same sources as Oracle JDK and can be obtained free of charge. Based on this, various companies and consortia have developed and provided free versions of Java. Azul Zulu, AdoptOpenJDK (now Eclipse Adoptium), and Amazon Corretto are just a few examples of many others.

Oracle capitulated with the release of Java 17 LTS, and the Oracle JDK is now available for commercial purposes again at no charge. Incidentally, the associated license is called No-Fee Terms and Conditions (NFTC).

However, it is somewhat incomprehensible that Java 11 LTS is still subject to a paid license. This makes it even less attractive and means that it is unlikely to be used as an intermediate step on the way to Java 17 LTS, Java 21 LTS, or even Java 25 LTS—unless you use a JDK other than Oracle's.

1.2   Overview of Contents

This book covers various enhancements that are bundled in Java 17 LTS, Java 21 LTS, and the brand-new Java 25 LTS. These LTS versions are each described in separate parts of the book, giving you a quick, concise, and well-founded overview of the key new features in the Java version you use or prefer.

1.2.1   Part I: Key Features in Java 12 to 17 LTS

In this part, the new features are described in a slightly more concise form, with only a selection covered, as Java 17 LTS should now be widely adopted.

Part I focuses on various changes to the syntax of Java, such as "Text Blocks," which allow multi-line strings. There have also been some improvements to `switch`. The new syntax makes it easier to specify and evaluate conditions, ensuring greater clarity and comprehensibility. In addition, modern Java offers an exciting feature with records, which provides a highly compact notation for declaring special classes with immutable data. Some features are less relevant in practice, but some of which form the basis for further innovations in future Java versions: in the context of `instanceof`, it is possible to avoid artificial helper variables and unsightly casts.

Let's move on to the APIs. Here, we find additions to the `String` class. Furthermore, the Stream API contains some noteworthy innovations, including the teeing collector and the methods `toList()` and `mapMulti()`. We also find a helpful improvement for error analysis in `NullPointerExceptions`, a notable JVM innovation.

1.2.2   Part II: Key Features in Java 18 to 21 LTS

In terms of syntax, we find various significant new features in Java versions 18 to 21 LTS—some of which are only available as preview features. String Templates simplified the concatenation of variable and fixed text components into a result string in Java 21 LTS and Java 22. This preview feature was removed from the JDK in Java 23. Therefore, I will not discuss it further.

Record Patterns extend Pattern Matching for `instanceof` and make it easy to break down records into their components and access them. Pattern matching was initially integrated into the language in the context of `instanceof`. In modern Java, it also works in `switch` and has been functionally enhanced. The combination with record patterns is particularly noteworthy. Finally, Unnamed Patterns and Variables make it possible to replace various elements in a record pattern or variable with a single underscore ("_") to mark them as unused and unusable.

Java 21 LTS includes several API innovations, such as minor enhancements to Reflection with Method Handles and Internet Address Resolution. However, there are also two highlights: Sequenced Collections and Virtual Threads. Sequenced Collections enable easy processing of collections from both the front and the back. Virtual Threads simplify multithreading and allow you to create several thousand threads, even hundreds of thousands or more threads, to ease scalability. This characteristic will enable you to follow the thread-per-request approach.

Additionally, we will examine some changes, enhancements, and new features in the JVM that are cumulatively included in Java 18 to 21 LTS. These include the Simple Web Server and an improvement in the specification of code snippets in JavaDoc. Finally, we will discuss the feature Unnamed Classes and Instance Main Methods, which, in particular, changes the way applications are started and also simplifies getting started with Java by eliminating the need for classes and some boilerplate code in smaller Java programs.

1.2.3 Part III: New Features in Java 22 to 25 LTS

There are several significant new syntax features in Java versions 22 to 25 LTS. However, some of these are only available as preview features.

The final feature, called "Unnamed Variables and Patterns," is used to mark variables or parts within record patterns as unused and unusable with an underscore ("_"). Another final feature is the integration of Markdown for commenting source code. It allows you to define documentation that is more readable and concise than with the previous JavaDoc HTML snippets. Other final features include Module Import Declarations and Flexible Constructor Bodies: Module imports make the imports at the beginning of a Java file tidier and clearer. Flexible Constructor Bodies facilitate initialization actions. The new Primitive Types in Patterns feature enables patterns for primitive types to be specified in `instanceof` and `switch`, although it is still in a preview state.

In terms of API enhancements, Java 25 LTS introduces the Foreign Function and Memory (FFM) API. It provides an API for accessing functionalities and memory areas outside the JVM. The Stream Gatherers are also a handy addition. These extend the Stream API with the ability to provide user-defined intermediate operations. Conveniently, a few Stream Gatherers are already predefined. One highlight that should not go unmentioned is Structured Concurrency. It represents a significant simplification in the context of multithreading, allowing tasks to be split into subtasks, processed in parallel, and their results merged. There are various strategies for handling the combination of subtask results, for example, in cases where all or only one result is relevant.

Among other things, Launch Multi-File Source Code Programs has been implemented as a JVM improvement. It offers the possibility of executing several individual Java files directly without explicit prior compilation. In addition, Compact Source Files and Instance Main Methods make it easier to get started with Java.

In addition to Parts III, and IV contains an outlook on Java 26: this latest Java release largely forgoes spectacular syntax innovations, instead focusing on strengthening stability, security, and performance, including further restrictions on deep reflection. At the runtime level, applications benefit from higher throughput of the G1 garbage collector and HTTP/3 support in the HTTP client, while structured concurrency and lazy constants continue to mature toward finalization, providing a solid foundation for future releases.

1.3 Basic Structure of the Sample Project

The structure of the supplied sample project is based on that of the book and offers a separate package for each chapter, for example, `ch04_syntax_java_18_21` or `ch05_api_java_18_21`. In this case, I am deviating from the naming convention for packages because underscores make the notation more readable.

The project adheres to the standard Maven directory structure, where sources are located under `src/main/java` and tests are stored under `src/test/java`.

Sources: `src/main/java` An excerpt is shown below in Fig. 1.2.

Fig. 1.2 Structure of the sample project

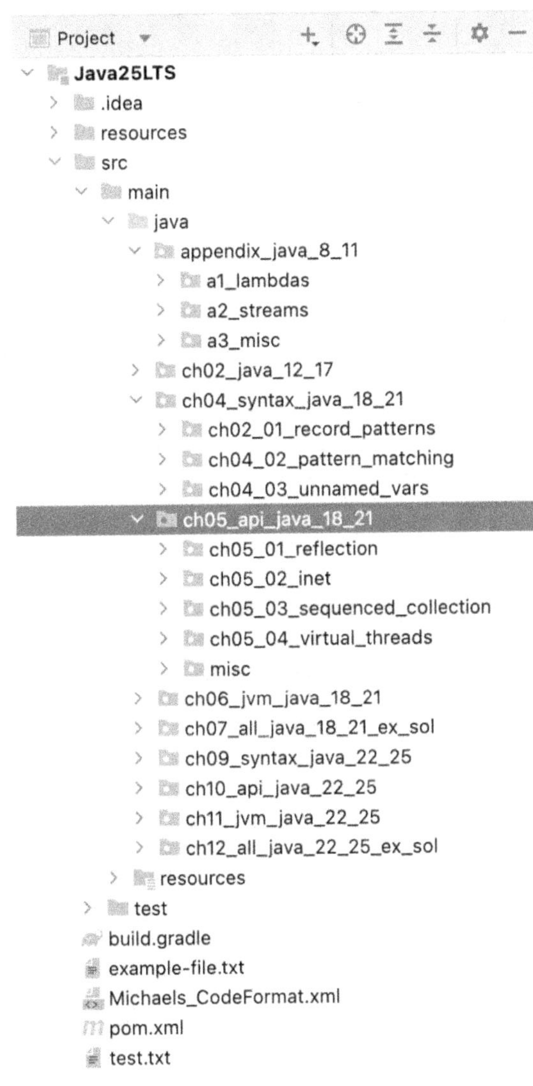

Test Classes: `src/test/java` Since this book primarily develops smaller examples to demonstrate the new features, I have decided not to use unit tests, which are otherwise recommended in practice. Therefore, the test directory is empty.

1.4 Note on Programming Style

In this section, I would like to discuss programming style, as you may occasionally wonder whether certain aspects could be made more compact.

1.4.1 Thoughts on Source Code Compactness

As a rule, when programming, especially for the implementations in this book, ease of comprehension and a clear structure are fundamental, as this simplifies modifications later on; that is why the implementations shown are programmed to be as understandable as possible. As a result, not every construct is as compact as it could be, but it should be generally easier to understand. I want to prioritize this aspect in this book. In practice, too, this is often more acceptable than poor maintainability in exchange for a more compact implementation.

Example

For clarification, let's consider a readable, easy-to-understand, recursive implementation for reversing the contents of a string, which also nicely demonstrates the two essential elements of recursive termination and descent:

```java
public String reverseString(final String input)
{
    // recursive termination
    if (input.length() <= 1)
        return input;

    final char firstChar = input.charAt(0);
    final String remaining = input.substring(1);

    // recursive descent
    return reverseString(remaining) + firstChar;
}
```

The following, significantly more compact variant does not offer these advantages:

```java
public String reverseStringShort(final String input)
{
    return input.length() <= 1 ? input :
        reverseStringShort(input.substring(1)) + input.charAt(0);
}
```

Think briefly about which of the two methods you feel confident about using to make subsequent changes. And what if you want to add unit tests: how do you find suitable value assignments and checks?

It should also be noted that the first, more wordy variant is automatically converted into something similar to the second variant, either during compilation (conversion to bytecode) or later during execution and optimization, with the advantage of improved readability when programming.

1.4.2 Thoughts on `final` and `var`

I usually prefer to mark variables as `final` to indicate that they are immutable. In this book, I sometimes refrain from doing so. One reason is that the interactive command-line application JShell (see Sect. 15.4) does not support the keyword `final` everywhere.

Local Variable Type Inference: `var`

Since Java 10, there has been the so-called *Local Variable Type Inference*, better known as var (see Sect. 15.3.3). It allows the explicit type specification on the left side of a variable definition to be omitted, provided that the concrete type for a local variable can be determined by the compiler based on the definition on the right side of the assignment:

```
var name = "Peter";                     // var => String
var chars = name.toCharArray();         // var => char[]
var mike = new Person("Mike", 47);      // var => Person
var hash = mike.hashCode();             // var => int
```

Local Variable Type Inference shows its advantages particularly in combination with generic containers:

```
// var => ArrayList<String>
var names = new ArrayList<String>();
names.add("Tim");
names.add("Tom");
names.add("Jerry");

// var => Map<String, Long>
var personAgeMapping = Map.of("Tim", 47L, "Tom", 12L,
                              "Michael", 47L, "Max", 25L);
```

Convention: var If Readable Provided that comprehensibility does not suffer, I will use `var` where appropriate to keep the source code shorter and clearer. However, if a type specification is of greater importance for understanding, I prefer the concrete type and avoid `var`—but the boundaries are fluid.

Convention: `final` or `var` One more note: Although you can combine `final` and `var`, I don't find this stylistically appealing because it loses the brevity of `var`. Therefore, I use either one or the other.

1.4.3   Block Comments in Listings

Sometimes listings occasionally contain block comments (comments above a block or sequence of statements, such as `// Create process` below) for orientation and better understanding. In practice, such comments should be used with caution, and sections of source code should preferably be extracted into methods. However, these comments serve as a guide for the examples in this book, as the concepts introduced or described are likely to be new and unfamiliar to you as a reader.

```java
// Create process
Process sleeper = Runtime.getRuntime().exec("sleep 60s");
// ...

// Convert process to ProcessHandle via its Id
ProcessHandle sleeperHandle = ProcessHandle.of(sleeper.pid()).
                                orElseThrow(IllegalStateException::new);
// ...
```

1.4.4   Thoughts on Formatting

The formatting used in the listings differs slightly from the coding conventions of Oracle.[2] I prefer those of Scott Ambler,[3] because he recommends explicitly placing opening curly brackets on their own lines. I have created a special format called `Michaelis_CodeFormat` for this purpose. It is integrated into the project download and is demonstrated below for a class:

```java
import java.util.Arrays;
import org.apache.log4j.Logger;

public final class FormattingExample
{
    private static final Logger log = Logger.getLogger("FormattingExample");

    public static String asHex(final byte[] telegram)
    {
        log.info("asHex(" + Arrays.toString(telegram) + ")");

        final StringBuffer sb = new StringBuffer("0x");

        for (int i = 0; i < telegram.length; i++)
        {
            final String hex = Integer.toHexString(telegram[i]);
            sb.append(hex);
        }

        return sb.toString();
    }
    // ...
}
```

---

[2] https://www.oracle.com/java/technologies/javase/codeconventions-introduction.html.
[3] http://www.ambysoft.com/essays/javaCodingStandards.html.

1.5   Installing Java 25 LTS

To run the Java programs described in this book, you must install or already have installed a current JDK (Java Development Kit). So let's start with the installation of Java.

1.5.1   Java Download

Java is available free of charge on the Oracle website: https://www.oracle.com/java/technologies/downloads/ (see Fig. 1.3).

At the bottom of the website, you will find various links for different operating systems. Select the link that applies to you and download the corresponding installation file, as shown in the example above for macOS.

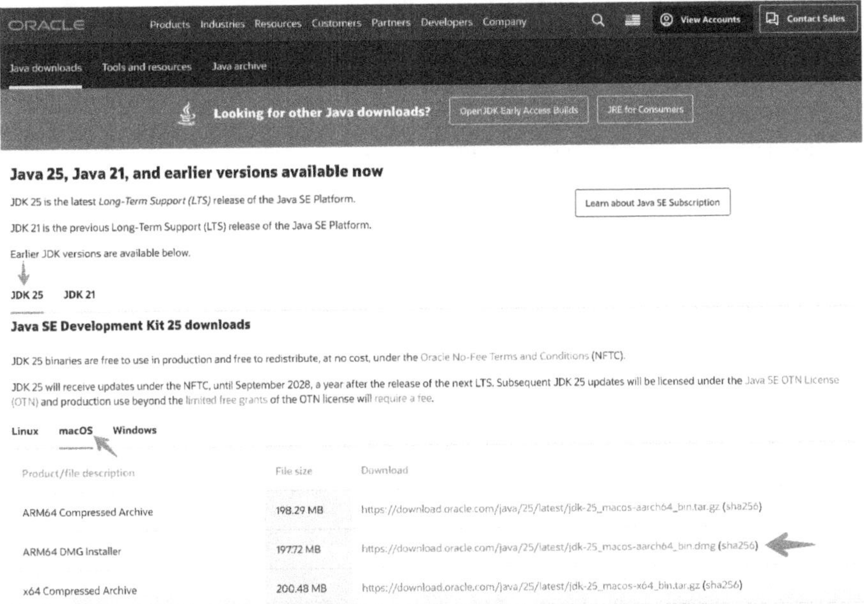

Fig. 1.3 Java download page

> **Note: Alternatives**
> In this book, we use the Oracle JDK as a reference, as it is widely used and
> easy to install. However, Java is also available through other distributions,
> such as OpenJDK, which are fully compatible for the purposes of this book.
> Advanced users may also choose tools like SDKMAN!, which allow installing
> and managing multiple Java versions side by side. This can be useful when
> working with different projects or Java releases, but is not required to follow
> the examples in this book.

1.5.2   Installing the JDK

Windows

Double-click the `.exe` file (e. g., `jdk-25_windows-x64_bin.exe`) to run the
downloaded installation program. This file can be deleted after successful installation. The directory `C:\Program Files\Java\jdk-25` is the default location,
where the directory name depends on the selected Java version. Accept the default
settings and follow the instructions during the installation.

macOS

To start the installation, double-click the `.dmg` file on macOS and follow the
prompts. You may need to enter the administrator password to continue. Once the
installation is complete, you can delete the `.dmg` file to save storage space.

Unix Derivatives

For Unix derivatives, you can find more information here: https://www.java.com/
en/download/help/download_options.html. There, even for Windows and macOS,
additional installation details are available.

1.5.3   Post-Installation Tasks

To ensure that Java works correctly after downloading and installing it, a few post-
installation tasks are necessary. For ease of use, we should add the installation

directories and those of the executables to the environment variable PATH. The following description applies to both Windows and macOS operating systems.

Follow-Up Steps for Windows

If you are using Windows, you can change the environment variable PATH under "Environment Variables." Press the Win key and then type "umgeb" until "Edit system environment variables" appears (see Fig. 1.4).

Pressing the "Enter" key opens the "System variables" dialog (see Fig. 1.5).

Then click the "Edit" button to open an edit dialog. Add an environment variable named JAVA_HOME. This must refer to the installation directory, for example, C:\Program Files\Java\jdk-25, as shown in Fig. 1.6.

Add the entry %JAVA_HOME%\bin to the variable PATH, as shown in Fig. 1.7. In addition, the entry should be as high up as possible so that it reliably specifies the path to the current Java version.

Please note the following: Always confirm all dialog boxes with "OK" so that the variables are set correctly. Any open command prompts must be closed and reopened for the changed variables to take effect.

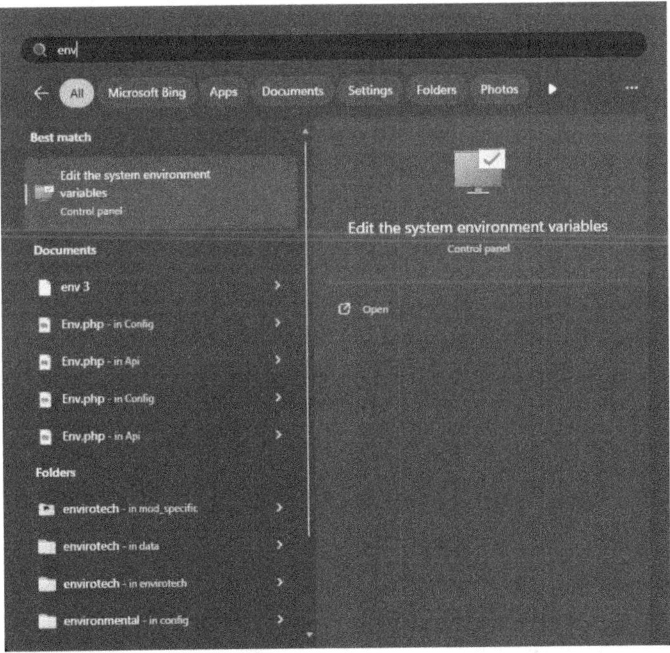

Fig. 1.4 Edit system environment variables

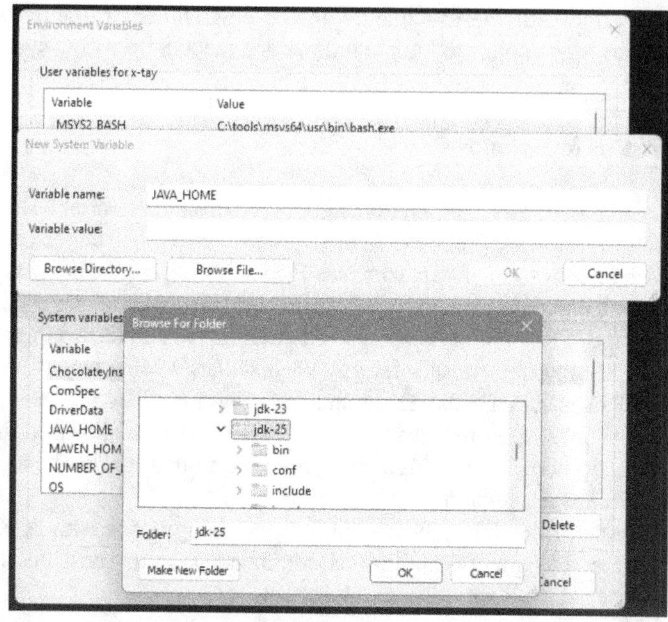

Fig. 1.5 Setting system environment variable `JAVA_HOME`

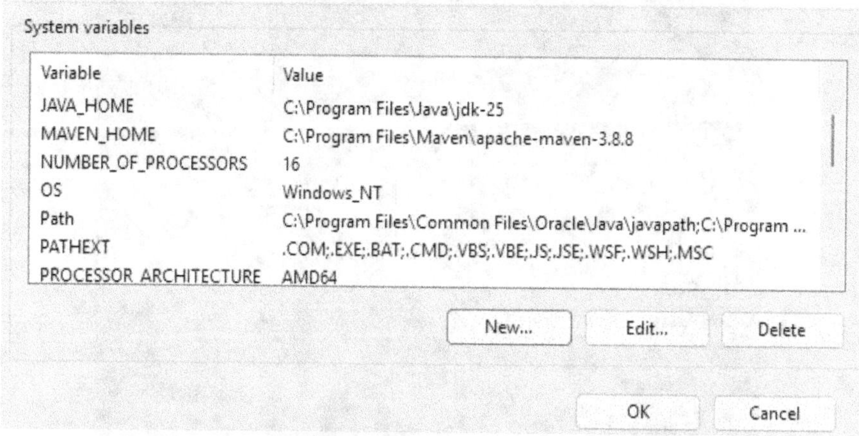

Fig. 1.6 Edit environment variables

The same applies to some IDEs, which also reference and use environment variables. For example, IntelliJ caches the environment. If changes are made, a restart may be required.

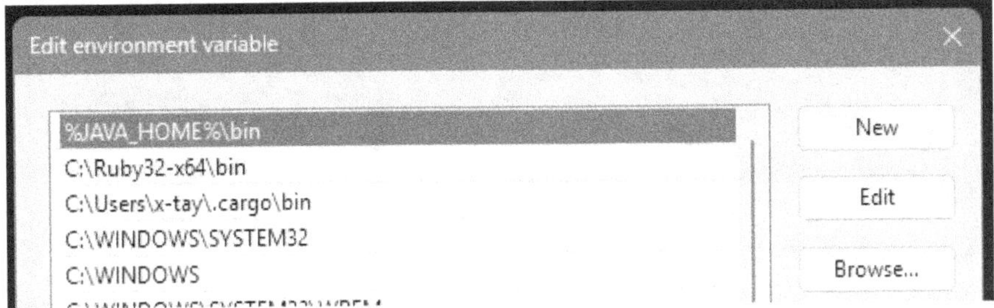

Fig. 1.7 Prioritize environment variables

Follow-Up Work for macOS

On macOS, it is also recommended to set a reference to Java in the path in the respective shell (the terminal) or to enter it in the start script of your shell, for example, ~/.bash_profile or, more recently, ~/.zshrc:

```
export JAVA_HOME=/Library/Java/JavaVirtualMachines/jdk-25.jdk/Contents/Home
export PATH=$JAVA_HOME/bin:$PATH
```

For macOS, this is done by editing a configuration file as follows:

```
$ open ~/.zshrc
```

This opens an editor window displaying the file's contents. It is recommended to define various version change commands there to switch comfortably between Java versions. Java 17 LTS, Java 21 LTS, and Java 25 LTS are relevant for the three parts of the book.

Please add these lines at the end of the configuration file to enable switching:

```
setJdk17()
{
    export JAVA_HOME=/Library/Java/JavaVirtualMachines/jdk-17.jdk/Contents/
        Home
    export PATH=$JAVA_HOME/bin:$PATH
}

setJdk21()
{
    export JAVA_HOME=/Library/Java/JavaVirtualMachines/jdk-21.jdk/Contents/
        Home
    export PATH=$JAVA_HOME/bin:$PATH
}

setJdk25()
{
    export JAVA_HOME=/Library/Java/JavaVirtualMachines/jdk-25.jdk/Contents/
        Home
    export PATH=$JAVA_HOME/bin:$PATH
}
```

Activate Java 25 LTS as follows:

```
$ setJdk25
```

To switch back to Java 21 LTS, for example, use:

```
$ setJdk21
```

> **SDKMAN!**
> The command-line tool SDKMAN! is available for managing (in particular, installing and switching between) different Java versions, as well as other programming languages and tools. It offers a convenient way to switch between installed versions—see https://sdkman.io/usage/.

1.5.4 Verifying Java Installation

After completing the steps above, Java 25 LTS should be installed on your computer and executable from the console, ready for the next steps.

Open a console and enter the command `java --version`—if the output is similar to this, then you have successfully installed Java:

```
$ java --version
java 25.0.1 2025-10-21 LTS
Java(TM) SE Runtime Environment (build 25.0.1+8-LTS-27)
Java HotSpot(TM) 64-Bit Server VM (build 25.0.1+8-LTS-27, mixed mode, sharing)
```

In the following text, I always use $ to indicate textual input on the console, that is, the terminal in macOS or the Windows command prompt.

Verifying JShell

For the sake of completeness, please also check the invocation and termination of the JShell tool, which we will use repeatedly to try out small examples:

```
$ jshell
|  Welcome to JShell -- Version 25.0.1
|  For an introduction type: /help intro

jshell> /exit
|  Goodbye
```

1.6   Configurations for Build Tools and IDEs for Java 25 LTS

Build tools make it easier to compile and bundle Java classes into JARs. I will briefly describe the settings to be considered for Java 25 LTS, focusing on the two prominent representatives: Gradle and Maven. I will also discuss special settings in the configuration of IntelliJ and Eclipse.

1.6.1   Java 25 LTS with Gradle

To experiment with Java 25 LTS, I recommend using Gradle version 9.1 (or newer). In addition, it is essential to no longer configure the Java version as was previously customary via

```
// ATTENTION: this is no longer correct!
sourceCompatibility=25
targetCompatibility=25
```

but instead via the toolchain, as shown in the following listing. To do this, a few entries marked in bold below must be made in the build.gradle file:

```
plugins {
    id 'java'
}

java {
    toolchain {
        languageVersion = JavaLanguageVersion.of(25)
    }
}

// Activation of preview features and incubator module
tasks.withType(JavaCompile).configureEach {
    options.compilerArgs += ["--enable-preview",
                        "--add-modules", "jdk.incubator.vector"]
}
```

After that, we can build a corresponding JAR as usual:

```
$ gradle clean assemble
```

To experiment, start the class Java25RuntimeVersionExample from the package api from the JAR you just created as follows:

```
$ java --enable-preview -cp ./build/libs/Java25Examples.jar \
        api.Java25RuntimeVersionExample
```

If the project was compiled with preview features activated as above, it is also essential to specify the JVM command-line parameter --enable-preview when starting. Then, after the above successful Gradle build, the following output will appear:

```
Runtime required for this: 25
latest: RELEASE_25
valueOf: RELEASE_25
25
RELEASE_25
%
```

If you are not yet using the correct Java version, remember to change the Java version in the path to Java 25 LTS before proceeding, for example, by calling the `setJdk25` command discussed earlier in Sect. 1.5.3.

1.6.2   Java 25 LTS with Maven

Java 25 projects can already be compiled without any problems using the slightly older Maven 3.9.11 (September 2025) or the current Maven 3.9.12 (January 2026) in combination with the Maven compiler plugin version 3.13 (or newer). Overall, Maven continues its proud tradition of supporting newer Java versions more quickly and efficiently than Gradle.

To use Java 25 LTS with Maven and activate preview features and the incubator module for the Vector API, you must enter the following settings, marked in bold, in the `pom.xml` file in the `plugins` section:

```xml
<plugins>
    <plugin>
        <artifactId>maven-compiler-plugin</artifactId>
        <version>3.13.0</version>
        <configuration>
            <release>25</release>
            <!-- Activation of preview features -->
            <compilerArgs>
                <arg>-enable-preview</arg>
                <arg>--add-modules</arg>
                <arg>jdk.incubator.vector</arg>
            </compilerArgs>
        </configuration>
    </plugin>
</plugins>
```

With these modifications, please execute a Maven build like this:

```
$ mvn clean package
```

Accordingly, a corresponding JAR—as usual with Maven—is created in the `target` folder.

Let's take another look at the example of starting the class `Java25Runtime-VersionExample` from the package `api`:

```
$ java --enable-preview -cp target/Java25Examples-1.0.jar \
    api.Java25RuntimeVersionExample
```

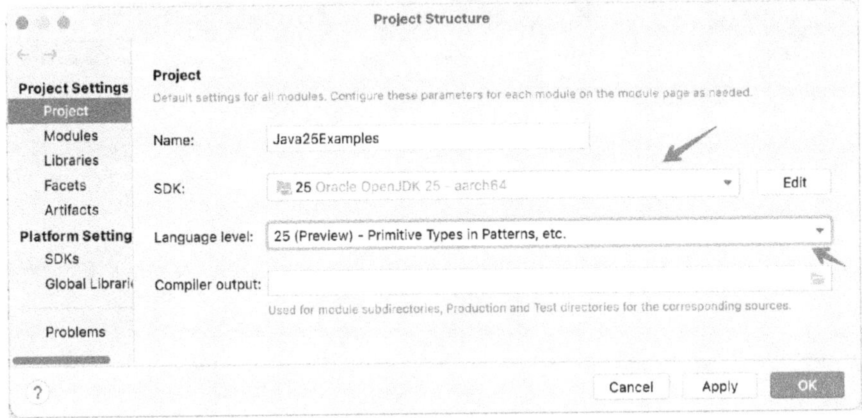

Fig. 1.8 Settings in the Project Structure dialog for Java 25 LTS

The output for Gradle is the same as for the successful Maven build above and is not shown again.

As for Gradle, the same applies to the Maven build: Once the project has been compiled with preview features, as specified in our build file above, it is essential to provide the JVM command-line parameter `--enable-preview` when launching a program from the JAR file, as done in the call above.

1.6.3 Java 25 LTS with IntelliJ

To experiment with Java 25 LTS, please use IntelliJ IDEA 2025.2 or later, released in summer 2025. However, a few settings still need to be made, and the following points need to be mentioned:

- In the "Project Structure" dialog, select the value 25 in the "`Project SDK`" field and, for experimenting with preview features, set the value "`25 (Preview) – Primitive Types in Patterns, etc.`" (Fig. 1.8)
- When using preview features within the project, it is necessary to specify the VM option `--enable-preview` in the respective run configuration of the classes to be started to execute the examples. If you have already selected preview features at the language level as described above, this step is optional (Fig. 1.9).

1.6.4 Java 25 LTS with Eclipse

Starting with version 2025-09, Java 25 LTS is supported by Eclipse, provided that the appropriate plugin has been installed as described below.

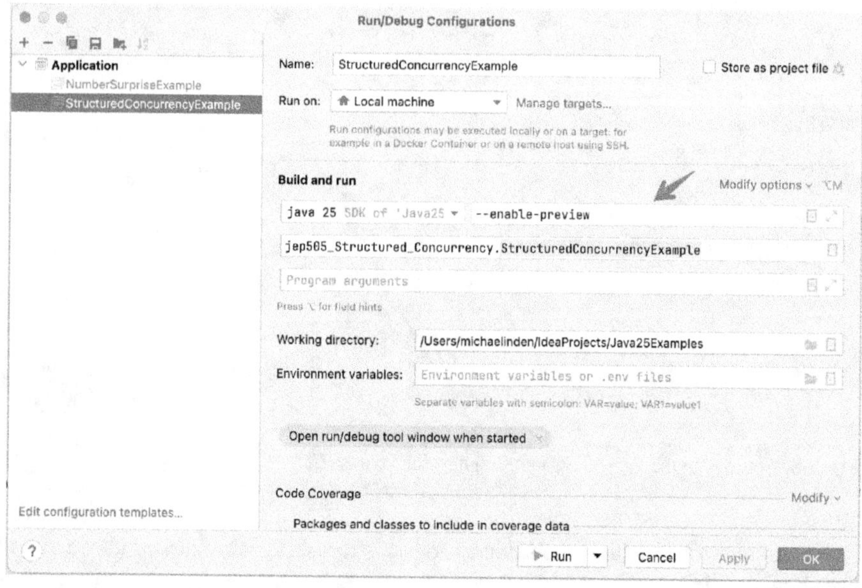

Fig. 1.9 Settings in Run/Debug Configurations

Java 25 Plugin

In Eclipse version 2025-09, support for Java 25 LTS is already prepared and, due to the short time span between the release of Java 25 LTS and Eclipse 2025-09, is initially available as a plugin in the Eclipse Marketplace for subsequent installation, as indicated in Fig. 1.10.

Compiler Settings

Of course, you must set the compiler to Java 25 LTS and activate the preview features to try out all of the examples (Fig. 1.11).

Run Configuration

To run the examples that use preview features, you must specify `--enable-preview` in the run configuration of the class to be started. This is shown for the class `FirstVectorExample`, including activation of the associated incubator module `--add-modules jdk.incubator.vector` in Fig. 1.12.

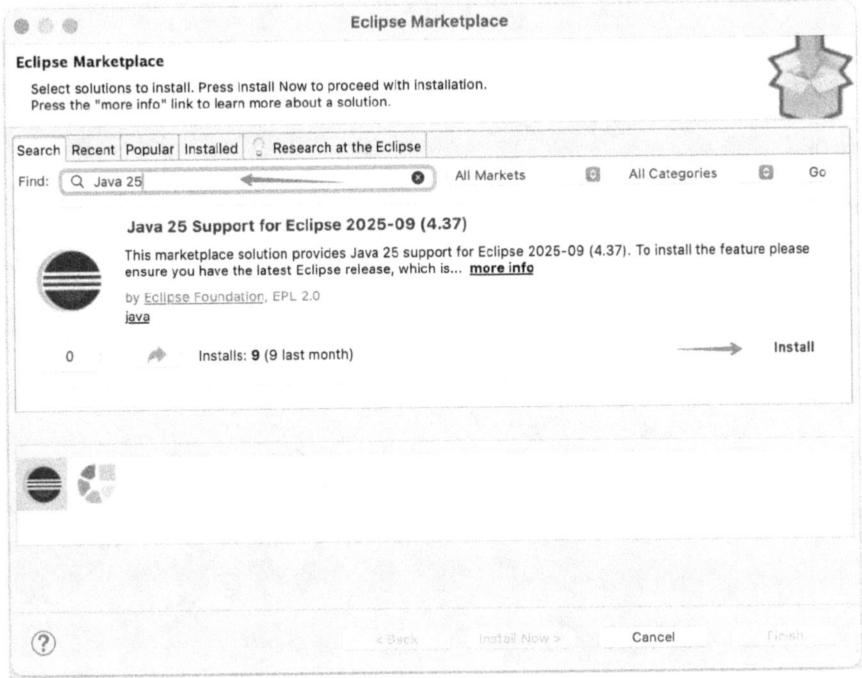

Fig. 1.10 Installing the Java 25 plugin from the Eclipse Marketplace

1.7   Trying Out the Examples and Solutions

In many cases, the source code snippets shown can be integrated into a class with a `main()` method and then executed. Alternatively, there are various ways of executing them on the command line. You will learn more about this shortly. In addition, you can find all relevant source code snippets and programs online at https://github.com/Apress/Java-25-and-Beyond as an accompanying project to this book. IntelliJ allows import as a Gradle or Maven project.

As a rule, I use constructs that are as easy to understand as possible and avoid particularly unusual syntax or API features. Unless explicitly mentioned in the text, you should be able to try out the examples and solutions with the current LTS version of Java 25. From time to time, I use preview features from Java 25 LTS. As shown previously, this requires specific parameterizations in the IDEs and build tools, both during compilation and execution.

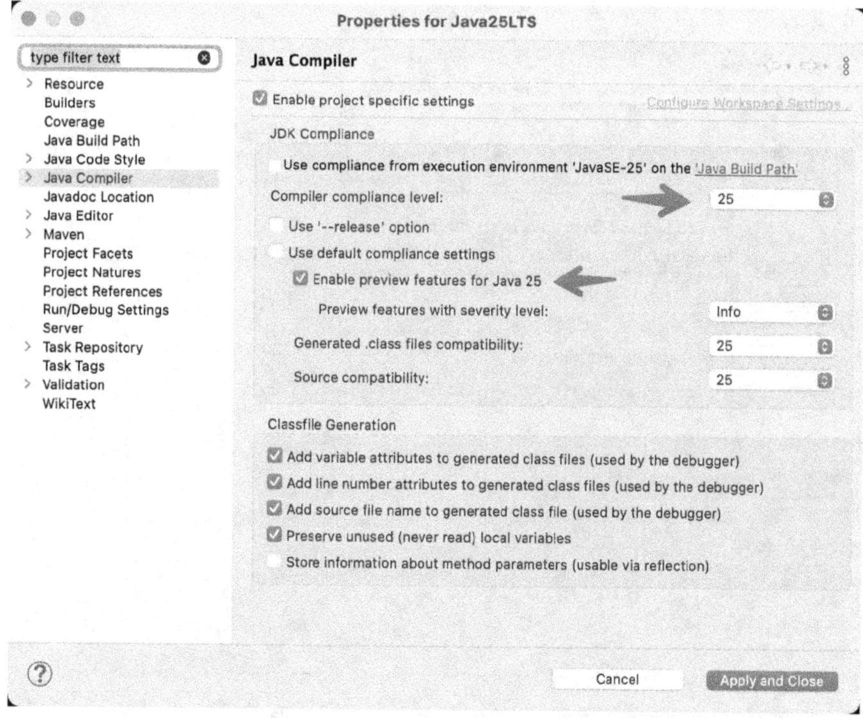

Fig. 1.11 Compiler settings in Eclipse for Java 25 LTS

1.7.1   Trying Out New Java Features with the JShell or the Command Line

Due to the relatively tight six-month release cycles, the tool landscape is not always ready when you want to experiment with pre-release versions. In this case, the following alternatives are available:

1. **JShell:** JShell is a REPL (Read–Eval–Print–Loop) command-line tool and has been part of the JDK since Java 9. It allows you to quickly and easily execute small source code snippets, which is helpful when discovering and trying out new features. Section 15.4 provides a brief introduction.
2. **Command Line Using Direct Compilation:** Since Java 11 LTS, there has been a feature called Direct Compilation, which allows individual Java files to be started directly by calling `java`, that is, without explicit prior compilation (see Sect. 15.5). With Java 22 and JEP 458 (see Sect. 11.2), this restriction has been eliminated, and multiple classes can now be compiled directly.

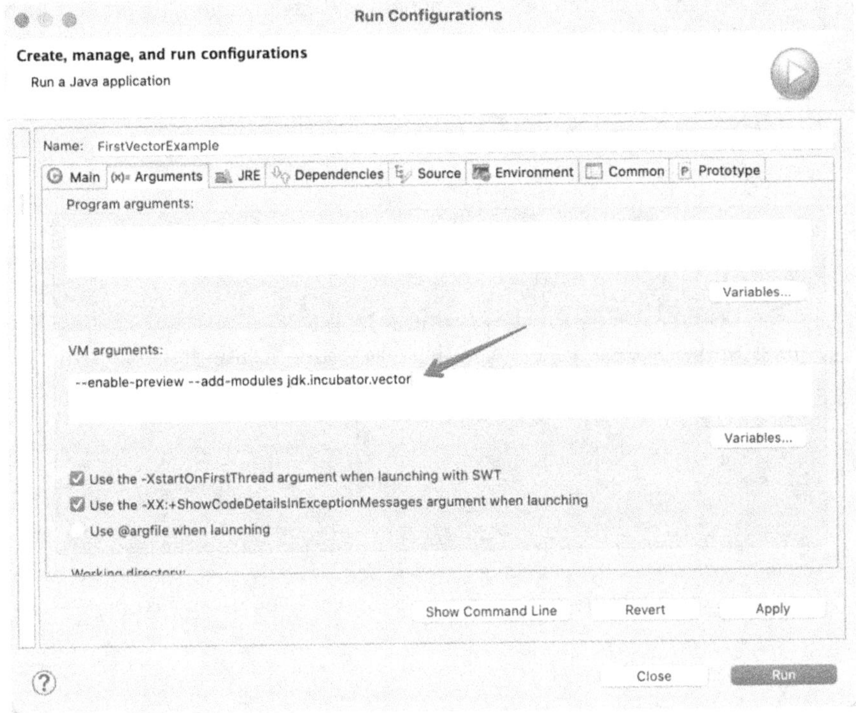

Fig. 1.12 Settings in run configurations

3. **Command Line Using Traditional Compilation and Execution:** Of course, it is still possible to work with `javac` and `java`, although this can sometimes be a bit tedious—which is why I won't go into detail here.

In many cases, you can type the source code snippets shown into the JShell or use a text editor or, better yet, an IDE. Depending on the situation, one or the other may be more appropriate. Let's take a closer look.

Executing with `jshell`

JShell allows you to write Java source code and quickly try things out without having to start the IDE and create a project. You can also use the latest features in JShell.

In the following I present some introductory examples to illustrate how to execute a few commands. I will go into more detail about the possibilities in Sect. 15.4.

Let's start `jshell` and try out a few actions and calculations. A modification of a Hello World example serves as a starting point:

```
$ jshell
|  Welcome to JShell -- Version 25.0.1
|  For an introduction type: /help intro

jshell> System.out.println("Hello JShell")
Hello JShell
```

Special Feature: Using Preview Features in JShell
Similar to the procedure for compiling, the option to use preview features must be activated at startup using the following command:

```
$ jshell --enable-preview
```

You can type any Java statements in the JShell. Usually, this is indicated by the marker `jshell>` and for following lines by `...>` until you're done typing:

```
jshell> int multiply(int a, int b) {
   ...>       return a * b;
   ...> }
|  created method multiply(int,int)

jshell> multiply(7, 2)
$3 ==> 14
```

Thanks to the new features Module Import Declarations and Compact Source Files, including the automatic integration of the `java.base` module, various functions such as file I/O, Stream API, Date and Time API, etc. are already accessible without import.

Other dedicated Java functions can be integrated as usual using `import`, as shown here for HTTP processing:

```
jshell> import java.net.http.*

jshell> var uri = new URI("https://postman-echo.com/get")
uri ==> https://postman-echo.com/get

jshell> var request = HttpRequest.newBuilder()
   ...>                          .uri(uri)
   ...>                          .GET()
   ...>                          .build();
request ==> https://postman-echo.com/get GET

jshell> var response = HttpClient.newHttpClient().send(request,
   ...>                          HttpResponse.BodyHandlers.ofString());
response ==> (GET https://postman-echo.com/get) 200
```

I use this approach for around 10–20 lines. After that, it is advisable to enter the lines using a text editor and execute them using the direct compilation described below. The whole process is even more convenient using an IDE.

Sometimes I want to clarify something conceptually and then dispense with the exact representation shown above in the JShell, because the instructions would become confusing due to the mix of logging with `jshell>` and `...>` and the intermediate results. In such cases, I resort to the following abbreviated representation:

```
int minutesPerHour = 60;
int daysPerYear = 365;

Stream.of("Maria", "Mike", "Jim", "Micha").
       filter(str -> str.length() > 4).
       toList();
```

Such instructions can be entered into the JShell one after the other or embedded in a Java file in a `main()` method.

Executing with the Command Line: Direct Compilation

If the programs increase in length, editing with the JShell becomes tedious. A text editor can help here. Programs are then displayed without `jshell>`. As an example, here is a simple program consisting of one class that checks whether two given time periods of 20 and −12 days are negative:

```
package intro;

import java.time.Duration;
import java.time.temporal.ChronoUnit;

public class DurationIntroExample
{
    public static void main(final String[] args)
    {
        System.out.println(Duration.of(20L, ChronoUnit.DAYS).isNegative());
        System.out.println(Duration.of(-12L, ChronoUnit.DAYS).isNegative());
    }
}
```

These lines must then be saved as a file with the same name as the class, including the extension `.java`, in this case `DurationIntroExample.java`.

Let's take a quick look at the pleasant new features in Java 25 LTS and how they allow the above example to be written in an elegant, short, and concise manner:

```
void main()
{
    IO.println(Duration.of(20L, ChronoUnit.DAYS).isNegative());
    IO.println(Duration.of(-12L, ChronoUnit.DAYS).isNegative());
}
```

Here we use Module Import Declarations (see Sect. 9.4). However, this is not directly visible here, as `import module java.base` is automatically considered an import for this compact notation.

The compact notation is called Compact Source Files and Instance Main Methods (see Sect. 11.4). Furthermore, the class `java.lang.IO` was also introduced, which makes interactions with the console easier than before.

As already mentioned, you can launch (individual) Java files from the console by calling `java`, without explicit prior compilation, assuming they are stored in a folder `src/main/java/intro/`:

```
$ java src/main/java/intro/DurationIntroExample.java
```

Then we get this output:

```
false
true
```

> **Speciality of Preview Features**
>
> For direct compilation, in addition to `--enable-preview`, preview features require the specification of a source version with `--source` as follows—since Java 23, this is no longer necessary:
>
> ```
> $ java --enable-preview --source 21 <YOUR_CLASS_NAME>.java
> ```

1.7.2   Trying Out New Java Features in a Sandbox

Due to frequent release changes and the constant need to install new versions, you may not always be up to date, or you may want to try out a feature before it is officially released. This is precisely what the site https://javaalmanac.io/ offers with its sandbox. There, you can try out the new features (available at that time) in an editor window by creating small programs in the form of a class or just consisting of one `main()` method, as shown here, using the feature Compact Source Files and Instance Main Methods (see Sect. 11.4), as shown in Fig. 1.13. You can use the lines shown as inspiration for your own experiments and execute them from time to time to check the results.

A Journey of Discovery into Modern Java: Wishes to Readers
Enough of the preamble: I hope you will enjoy this book, gain new insights, and have fun experimenting with Java 21 LTS and the brand-new Java 25 LTS. Reading this book may also make it easier for you to switch to the latest Java versions or migrate existing applications.

Sandbox

Instantly compile and run Java 25 snippets without a local Java installation.

```
Java25.java    ▶ Run                                              25-ea+34-3482
1 import module java.base;
2
3 void main() {
4     var v = ClassFileFormatVersion.latest();
5     IO.println("Hello Java bytecode version %s!".formatted(v.major()));
6 }
```

Fig. 1.13 Sandbox for trying out new features

If you first need to refresh your knowledge of key features introduced in Java 8 LTS through Java 11 LTS, take a look at Chap. 15.

Part I provides a concise introduction to important features from Java 12 through Java 17 LTS. Part II then gives a detailed description of the enhancements in Java 18 through Java 21 LTS. Part III concludes with a thorough coverage of the new features in Java 22 through Java 25 LTS.

Finally, an outlook on Java 26 offers a glimpse of upcoming improvements and the future evolution of the platform itself.

Part I
Key Features in Java 12 to 17 LTS

Chapter 2
Key Features in JDK 12 to 17 LTS

This chapter describes the key features included in Java 12 to 17 LTS as a single unit. Java 17 LTS bundles all the relevant additions from its predecessors and thus offers several interesting improvements:

- With **Text Blocks**, multi-line texts can be defined without much effort. In particular, there is no need for escaping line breaks, quotation marks, etc.
- **Switch Expressions** are a great extension that addresses many of the weaknesses of the old syntax, making `switch` more readable and precise.
- **Records** offer an extremely compact notation for defining classes with immutable data,[1] which automatically implement the appropriate API in the form of read-only accessor methods for all implicitly defined attributes as well as other central methods.
- **Pattern Matching** was integrated into the language in the context of `instanceof`. It helps avoid artificial helper variables and unattractive casts, making the source code clearer and easier to understand.

The following sections provide a detailed discussion of the abovementioned new features. Section 2.1 starts with Text Blocks. After that, Sect. 2.2 then highlights the urgently needed improvements to `switch`, which have been successfully implemented with Switch Expressions. Section 2.3 then discusses Records for defining data container classes. Because Records are such a powerful and versatile language feature, I highlight some special features and more advanced use cases in Sect. 2.4. Finally, we examine minor improvements and additions to the syntax, specifically in Sect. 2.5, which involves Pattern Matching for `instanceof` to simplify type queries and reduce casts.

In the section on API innovations, I discuss extensions to the `String` class in Sect. 2.6. Next, in Sect. 2.7, we will look at various new features in the Stream

---

[1] However, immutability is only achievable if only primitive data types are used for the constructor parameters or if only immutable types are specified there.

© The Author(s), under exclusive license to APress Media, LLC,
part of Springer Nature 2026
M. Inden, *Java 25 and Beyond*, https://doi.org/10.1007/979-8-8688-2385-5_2

API, specifically the so-called teeing collector and the methods `toList()` and `mapMulti()`, the latter being a simplification of `flatMap()`.

After that, Sect. 2.8 covers an improvement in the JVM that can significantly facilitate analyzing the root cause of `NullPointerExceptions`.

2.1   Text Blocks

Before Java 17 LTS, the definition of multi-line strings was rather cumbersome. The so-called Text Blocks represent a long-awaited simplification, allowing multi-line strings to be created without tedious concatenation. Better still, you can also dispense with error-prone escaping, which makes it easier to use SQL commands and specify JavaScript and JSON (JavaScript Object Notation) in Java source code. ***By definition, Text Blocks are normal strings internally, which is why you can call all known string methods on them.***

2.1.1   *Basic Syntax*

Text Blocks describe multi-line strings. They are defined by three quotation marks at the beginning and three at the end. No text may follow the opening quotation marks, not even a comment. The textual content must start on a new line and then be specified in subsequent lines, as follows:

```
System.out.println("""
        -I am a-
        -Text Block-
      """);
```

Let's take a look at the output and its indentation:

```
  -I am a-
  -Text Block-
```

We see that there is an indentation of exactly two spaces, even though there are some initial spaces before the two lines of text in the `System.out.println()` call. How does this happen? The answer is that the bottom three quotation marks determine the start of the indentation. Additionally, the last line is followed by a line break, resulting in an extra blank line.

If you do not want or need all lines to be indented, it is better to include the end of the Text Block in the last line as follows:

```
var firstTextBlockNoIndentation = """
        -I am a-
        -Text Block-""";
System.out.println(firstTextBlockNoIndentation);
```

This gives you the somewhat more intuitive result of a two-line string without a blank line after it, but also without indentation at the beginning of the lines:

```
-I am a-
-Text Block-
```

It should be mentioned again briefly: in this case, you can no longer specify a general indentation—of course, indentations can be specified individually, as we will see in a moment with the example of some HTML code.

2.1.2   Special Features and Conveniences

Now that we have a basic understanding of Text Blocks, let's take a look at a few special features and conveniences of the new syntax:

- No string concatenations necessary
- Quotation marks without escaping

No String Concatenations Necessary

Creating multi-line text is tedious without Text Blocks because line breaks must be specified explicitly and various string concatenations are required.

Example HTML Code   For example, if you want to process HTML code in Java, Text Blocks can be helpful.

Let's take a quick look at how tedious this used to be. Previously, you had to write something like the following:

```
var helloWorldHtmlOld = "<html>\n" +
                        "   <body>\n" +
                        "       <p>Hello World</p>\n" +
                        "   </body>\n" +
                        "</html>";
System.out.println(helloWorldHtmlOld);
```

In fact, it is much clearer and more pleasant to specify this as follows:

```
var helloWorldHtml = """
                <html>
                    <body>
                        <p>Hello World</p>
                    </body>
                </html>""";
System.out.println(helloWorldHtml);
```

Both variants lead to an output like the following—as desired, without indentations before the initial character of the content:

```
<html>
    <body>
        <p>Hello World</p>
    </body>
</html>
```

Detailed Information on Indentation The following listing illustrates that alignment is based on the bottom three quotation marks and that you can imagine a line upward, as indicated here by the pipe characters ("|") and in the example below with underscores offset by one character ("_"):[2]

```
jshell> var multiLine = """
   ...>                     | One
   ...>                     |  Two
   ...>                     |    Three
   ...>                     |      Four
   ...>                     """
multiLine ==> "| One\n|  Two\n|    Three\n|      Four\n"

jshell> var multiLine = """
   ...>                     _ One
   ...>                     _  Two
   ...>                     _ _ Three
   ...>                     _ _  Four
   ...>                     """
multiLine ==> "_ One\n _  Two\n_ _ Three\n _ _  Four\n"
```

If you take a closer look, you will see that the definition using Text Blocks results in a regular string, including the integrated line breaks.

Quotation Marks Without Escaping

The following example demonstrates that you can use Text Blocks to specify double quotation marks directly without escaping. Of course, you also benefit from the advantages already mentioned, namely, not having to perform string concatenation explicitly.

JavaScript Example We define JavaScript code with a Text Block as follows:

```
String javaScriptCode = """
        function hello() {
            print("Hello World");
            print("Have a nice day");
        }
        hello();""";
System.out.println(javaScriptCode);
```

---

[2] In fact, the indentation is based on the character specified on the leftmost. However, for a better understanding, it is helpful to use the bottom three quotation marks as the left border.

What an elegant way of programming! In contrast, with Java 11 LTS, you still have to use quite a lot of escaping, integrate line breaks into the string, and concatenate strings to achieve the same result:

```java
String javaScriptCodeOld = "function hello() {\n" +
                "    print(\"Hello World\");\n" +
                "    print(\"Have a nice day\");\n" +
                "}\n" +
                "hello();";
System.out.println(javaScriptCodeOld);
```

Both variants produce the following output:

```
function hello() {
    print("Hello World");
    print("Have a nice day");
}
hello();
```

Example: Defining SQL and Queries in Repositories   Just like JavaScript, SQL queries often contain double quotation marks. If you use a Text Block for the definition, this can be done naturally. This also allows you to create slightly more complex queries in Spring Data repositories in a more readable manner.

```java
String multiLineSQL = """
                SELECT LAST_NAME FROM CUSTOMER
                WHERE CITY = 'ZÜRICH' AND
                    FIRST_NAME LIKE "MI%" """;
```

In the above case, where the SQL string ends with a double quotation mark, a space is required between the double quotation mark in the user text and the three closing double quotation marks for syntactic correctness.

Example: Defining JSON   So far, we have seen that Text Blocks can be helpful in various applications because they reduce typing, help avoid escaping, and improve readability, especially when processing multi-line textual information.

The advantages of Text Blocks are particularly evident for data defined in JSON (JavaScript Object Notation) format. Let's first look at a conventional presentation of some Java 17 LTS information:

```java
String jsonOld = "{\n" +
                "    \"version\": \"Java 17 LTS\",\n" +
                "    \"feature\": \"Text Blocks\",\n" +
                "    \"attention\": \"very cool!\"\n" +
                "}";
```

With the help of the new syntax, this rather daunting structure can be written in a readable and understandable way as follows:

```
String jsonTextBlock = """
                       {
                           "version": "Java 17 LTS",
                           "feature": "Text Blocks",
                           "attention": "very cool!"
                       }""";
```

2.1.3   Escaping

We already know that Text Blocks, in addition to specifying multi-line text, allow the use of double quotation marks without escaping. However, there are exceptional cases, as well as memorable escape sequences. We will now discuss both of these.

Exceptions and Special Features

When escaping, the following must be considered: If the Text Block should contain three quotation marks, these must be masked (escaped). This also applies to the backslash (except at the very end of a line; more on this later). We will look at both using an example in the JShell, including output:

```
jshell> System.out.println("""
   ...>                     First 'line' simple quotes
   ...>                     Second "line" double quotes
   ...>                     Third \"""line\""" three quotes
   ...>                     Fourth line no quotes, just \\ :-)""")
First 'line' simple quotes
Second "line" double quotes
Third """line""" three quotes
Fourth line no quotes, just \ :-)
```

2.1.4   Escape Sequences

For Text Blocks, there are two memorable escape sequences: "\" (followed by a line break) and "\s". These allow fine-grained control over the processing of line breaks and whitespaces. The former helps prevent line breaks from being automatically inserted at the end of a line in a Text Block. The latter helps preserve spaces at the end of a Text Block.

Escape Sequence "\" Sometimes you want to split strings into several smaller components so that the longer string is easier to read in the editor:

```
String literal = "This is a string split " +
                 "into several smaller " +
                 "strings.";
```

If you were to convert this (somewhat naively and without much thought) into a Text Block, a line break would automatically be inserted at the end of each line:

```
jshell> String text = """
   ...>                 This is a string split
   ...>                 into several smaller
   ...>                 strings.
   ...>                 """;
text ==> "This is a string split\ninto several smaller\nstrings.\n"
```

This results in the following output:

```
jshell> System.out.println(text)
This is a string split
into several smaller
strings.
```

Line breaks can be prevented by specifying "\" at the end of lines in a Text Block:

```
String text = """
              This is a string split \
              into several smaller \
              strings.\
              """;
```

This generates the following single-line string:

```
This is a string split into several smaller strings.
```

Escape Sequence "\s" Before I discuss the effect of this escape sequence, I would like to highlight a notable feature. If there are spaces after text in individual lines of a Text Block, these are not included in the result. Let's assume that in the following Text Block, there are spaces after the names in all lines—visible in the listing only for the last entry:

```
jshell> String original = """
   ...>                 Tim
   ...>                 Peter
   ...>                 Mike        """
original ==> "Tim\nPeter\nMike"
```

The output shows that the default behavior is to remove superfluous spaces at the end of a line and add a line break immediately after it.

The escape sequence "\s" is converted to a space and prevents a line break immediately after the text, or more precisely, if there are still spaces before "\s", these are not truncated but retained—however, spaces after "\s" are deleted:

```
jshell> String original = """
   ...>                     Tim  \s
   ...>                     Peter\s
   ...>                     Mike \s    """
original ==> "Tim    \nPeter \nMike   "
```

This produces an output with three lines, each six characters long (without "\s", the lines would be three, five, and four characters long—as illustrated in the example above).

> **Opinion: Escape Sequence "\s"**
>
> In my opinion, it would have been better if the escape sequence "\s" had not been transformed into an artificial space at the end of each entry. The following illustrates the problem, namely, that `Michael\s` is converted into a string of length 8, that is, with a trailing space:
>
> ```
> jshell> """
>    ...> Michael\s""".length()
> $50 ==> 8
> ```
>
> But it's not always that obvious:
>
> ```
> jshell> String names = """
>    ...>                 Pia\s
>    ...>                 Maria\s
>    ...>                 Mike\s"""
> names ==> "Pia \nMaria \nMike "
> ```

If you want to limit the characters to the length of the longest string, you can achieve this by not specifying the escape sequence for the longest string and specifying it at the last position for all others. This changes the output so that all texts have the length of the longest string:

```
jshell> String names = """
   ...>                 Pia    \s
   ...>                 Michael
   ...>                 Mike  \s"""
names ==> "Tim    \nMichael\nMike    "
```

2.1.5   Placeholders

In Text Blocks, placeholders such as %d or %s can be specified and filled with values by calling the `formatted()` method—this method works in the same way as for regular strings (see Sect. 2.6) and corresponds precisely to the static method `String.format()` in its handling:

```java
String placeholders = """
        Michael %s bought %d books
        on "%tF" in '%s'
        """.formatted("Inden", 7, LocalDate.of(2020,1,20), "Bremen");
```

These statements produce the following output:

```
Michael Inden bought 7 books
on "2020-01-20" in 'Bremen'
```

Example: Definition of JSON/XML

The data format JSON has become an integral part of everyday programming, especially in the context of REST services. It is now almost impossible to imagine working without JSON. Although native support for JSON in Java SE would be highly desirable, it is not in sight.[3]

We already know that Text Blocks at least make textual descriptions much easier:

```java
String jsonObj = """
        {
            "name" : "Mike",
            "birthday" : "1971-02-07",
            "comment" : "Text Blocks are nice!"
        }
        """;
```

Better still, you can insert placeholders at specific locations and replace them as needed. Text Blocks can also be defined and filled for simple XML structures using placeholders as follows:

```java
String xmlString = """
        <customer>
            <firstname>%s</firstname>
            <lastname>%s</lastname>
            <birthday>%s</birthday>
        </customer>
        """.formatted("Michael", "Inden", "07.02.1971");
```

For very short snippets, such as input or result data in tests, this feature is often handy. But be aware of this: As a rule, you should generate such outputs for JSON

---

[3] JEP 198 (https://openjdk.org/jeps/198) has been around for many years, but there have been no discernible efforts to really push it forward. However, the integration of JSON into Java SE is being discussed in mailing lists and explained on this YouTube channel: https://www.youtube.com/watch?v=NSzRK8f7EX0. In Jakarta EE (formerly Java EE), for example, there is the type `jakarta.json.JsonObject`.

and XML using, for example, GSON[4] or Jackson[5] as well as JAXB[6] (Jakarta XML Binding) or other libraries. This is especially true as the objects to be mapped become more complex.

> **Introductory Quotation Marks**
>
> Finally, I would like to point out the following fact once again: only spaces (which are ignored) may follow the introductory """, but nothing else—not even a comment in this line!

2.2   Switch Expressions

For a long time, Java remained faithful to the ancient `switch` from the early days of the programming language and the compromises in language design that were intended to make the transition easier for C++ developers. Relics such as `break` and, in its absence, a fall-through[7] were not intuitive and invited careless mistakes.

In addition, `case` was quite limited in terms of the notation of values. Fortunately, all this has changed with the new syntax for `switch`. It allows case distinctions to be expressed much more elegantly than before. Since the old syntax is still permitted, a gradual transition to the new syntax can and should occur.

2.2.1   Introductory Example

The Switch Expressions are covered by JEP 361 (https://openjdk.java.net/jeps/361). Here, I refer to the example from the JEP, which uses a mapping of weekdays to their textual length. But I modified it where appropriate.

To better understand the need for the syntax change, let's first look at how the above mapping would have been formulated using the old syntax. Then we'll look at the advantages of the new `switch` syntax.

---

[4] https://github.com/google/gson.

[5] https://github.com/FasterXML/jackson.

[6] https://javaee.github.io/jaxb-v2/.

[7] If the statements of the `case` branch do not end with a `break`, the statements there are also executed, regardless of whether the value matches the subsequent `case`.

Analysis: What Were Some of the Previous Weaknesses of `switch`?

Let's start with the implementation of mapping weekdays to their textual length using the previous, older syntax of `switch`:

```java
DayOfWeek day = DayOfWeek.WEDNESDAY;
int numOfLetters;
switch (day)
{
    case MONDAY:
    case FRIDAY:
    case SUNDAY:
        numOfLetters = 6;
        break;
    case TUESDAY:
        numOfLetters = 7;
        break;
    case THURSDAY:
    case SATURDAY:
        numOfLetters = 8;
        break;
    case WEDNESDAY:
        numOfLetters = 9;
        break;
    default:
        numOfLetters = -1;
}
```

Let's take a critical look at the source code. First of all, the construct shown does not appear elegant and is also quite long. In particular, specifying multiple values in separate lines requires familiarization. Even worse, a `break` is required to ensure that processing runs without surprises and that no fall-through occurs. In addition, the (artificial) helper variable `numOfLetters` must be correctly assigned in each branch. In particular, despite the complete coverage of the enum values, `default` is necessary, because otherwise the compiler complains that the variable `numOfLetters` may not be initialized   unless it has already been assigned a value. So how can this be improved?

Syntax Extension "Switch Expressions"

The "Switch Expressions" significantly simplifies the definition of case distinctions and even offers an intuitive notation. We can use it to implement our introductory example in a shorter and more understandable way as follows:

```java
DayOfWeek day = DayOfWeek.WEDNESDAY;

int numOfLetters = switch (day)
{
    case MONDAY, FRIDAY, SUNDAY  -> 6;
    case TUESDAY                 -> 7;
    case THURSDAY, SATURDAY      -> 8;
    case WEDNESDAY               -> 9;
};
```

We recognize some syntactic innovations: In addition to the obvious arrow instead of the colon, multiple values can now be specified after `case`. Conveniently, `break` is no longer needed: the statements noted after the arrow are only executed specifically for this `case`. Furthermore, there is no fall-through in this syntax. Conveniently, the `switch` is now able to return a value, which eliminates the need to define helper variables. Instead of simply noting a value after the arrow, expressions such as assignments or method calls can also be specified without any problems and of course without the need for a `break`. What's more, this is no longer permitted in the new syntax after the arrow.

> **Special Feature: `null` as Input**
> The following pitfall lurked in Java: if you pass `null` to a `switch`, this triggers a `NullPointerException`. Conveniently, this vulnerability is addressed with a syntax change in Java 17 LTS in the form of a preview feature and was finalized with Java 21 LTS. The topic is described in more detail in Sect. 4.2.

2.2.2   Completeness Check

In the old version of `switch`, you can omit both the `default` and the specification of a `case` for individual values. The compiler does not complain about either of these omissions in `switch` for the old syntax. Only much later, when the variable is used, the problem is pointed out with a compilation error, indicating in the comment that this variable is not initialized in every case. Let's look at the following example:

```java
DayOfWeek day = DayOfWeek.WEDNESDAY;

int numOfLetters;
switch (day)
{
    case THURSDAY:
    case SATURDAY:
        numOfLetters = 8;
        break;
}

// Compile error:
// The local variable numOfLetters may not have been initialized.
System.out.println(numOfLetters);
```

Improved Completeness Check with "Switch Expressions"

The new Switch Expressions have improved behavior. Since these can return a value, a completeness check has been integrated. Let's assume we convert the above example to the new syntax:

```
DayOfWeek day = DayOfWeek.WEDNESDAY;

// Compile error: A switch expression should cover all possible values.
int numOfLetters = switch (day)
{
    case THURSDAY, SATURDAY -> 8;
};

System.out.println(numOfLetters);
```

With the new syntax, the problem of incomplete coverage is directly flagged by the compiler as follows: "A switch expression should cover all possible values."

Conveniently, in such cases, the IDEs offer the choice of adding either the appropriate `case` or a `default`, but not both. In addition, complete coverage of enum values is automatically detected. This innovation was necessary because the `switch` must now handle all possible cases so that it can return a value in every application case if required.

Completeness Check for Primitive Types Such As `int` While the implementation of the completeness check for enums is quite clear, the question arises as to how to ensure complete coverage for other types, such as `int`s. Due to the extensive value range, the compiler can only determine that not all values are covered and report this as follows: "A switch expression should cover all possible values." As a workaround, it does not make sense for IDEs to suggest specific values as additions, but rather to add a `default`:

```
String numericString = switch (value)
{
    case 1 -> "one";
    case 2 -> "two";
    default -> "N/A";
};
```

2.2.3 Pitfalls of the Old Syntax and Remedies

We have already ascertained that the old syntax of `switch` was not particularly successful. However, it also held some tangible surprises and pitfalls. Let's look at two concrete examples that illustrate why it is often helpful to check the completeness of the values covered in the `case`s.

Pitfall 1: Incomplete Value Specifications

First, let's map a value from the enumeration `java.time.Month` to corresponding month names. This task can be solved conventionally as follows:[8]

```java
Month month = Month.JULY;
String monthAsString;
switch (month)
{
    case JANUARY:
        monthAsString = "January";
        break;
    case FEBRUARY:
        monthAsString = "February";
        break;
    case MARCH:
        monthAsString = "March";
        break;
    //...
    default:
        monthAsString = "N/A";
}
```

Once again, the construct is not particularly elegant. Depending on whether or not a `case` is defined for the value `Month.JULY`, you will get the value "July" or " N/A". Additionally, a `break` is required to ensure that processing runs smoothly without any surprises.

Pitfall 2: `default` Between the breaks

Let's look at something rather clumsy in the context of the old syntax, namely, specifying `default` between `cases` and without a `break`—presumably this is not programmed intentionally from the beginning, but arises over time due to hectic or carelessness during (short-term) extensions:

```java
// ATTENTION: Occasionally a nasty error: default in between the cases
Month month = Month.JULY;
String monthAsString;
switch (month)
{
    case JANUARY:
        monthAsString = "January";
        break;
    default:
        monthAsString = "N/A";   // here also fall through
    case FEBRUARY:
        monthAsString = "February";
        break;
    case MARCH:
        monthAsString = "March";
        break;
}
```

---

[8] The Date and Time API helps in simplifying this complicated construct considerably: `month.getDisplayName(TextStyle.FULL, Locale.UK)`.

The input `Month.FEBRUARY` leads as expected to the value "February". So far, everything seems fine; however, this value is also unexpectedly obtained for the input `Month.JULY` or `Month.APRIL`, for example. How is this possible? First, because the values `Month.JULY` and `Month.APRIL` are not listed in the `cases`, the default branch gets executed, and, because of the missing `break`, a fall-through is also triggered (unexpectedly). This causes the code for `case FEBRUARY` to be executed, which can be pretty confusing.

Remedy by Implementation with "Switch Expressions"

Using the new syntax, the whole thing can be written as follows:

```java
public String monthToName(final Month month)
{
    return switch (month)
    {
        case JANUARY -> "January";
        default -> "N/A";  // here NO fall through
        case FEBRUARY -> "February";
        case MARCH -> "March";
    };
}
```

It is worth mentioning again that you can return the value calculated by the `switch` construct directly. Furthermore, there is no longer a fall-through. As a result, the input `Month.FEBRUARY` returns "February", as expected, and the `default` in the middle of the `cases` is not quite as dramatic, but certainly not very stylish either. Unlike with the old syntax, however, the input `Month.JULY` no longer results in the unexpected output "February", but rather, as specified by `default`, "N/A". Furthermore, if there were a `case JULY`, this would get selected regardless of the position of `default`, that is, analogous to the behavior of the previous `switch` statement.

2.2.4 Return with `yield`

Let's come back to the mapping of weekdays to the length of their names to learn about `yield` as a syntactic feature for returning a value.

I mentioned at the beginning that not only values can follow an arrow, but also method calls or multiple statements. However, if a block of statements follows, how can a value be returned from it? The use of `return` seems obvious, but it does not fit here, as it would exit the method. In addition, there could be a problem if the return type of the method did not match that of the `switch`. This would result in a compilation error. Worse still would be if the types were compatible and potentially unexpected returns occurred. To rule out all eventualities, a `return` in a `switch` is syntactically not allowed and leads to a compilation error.

That is why there is the new keyword `yield`, which terminates the processing of a `case` branch and returns a value:

```java
int numOfLetters = switch (day)
{
    case MONDAY, FRIDAY, SUNDAY ->
    {
        if (day == DayOfWeek.SUNDAY)
            System.out.println("SUNDAY is FUN DAY");

        yield 6;
    }
    case TUESDAY -> 7;
    case THURSDAY, SATURDAY -> 8;
    case WEDNESDAY -> 9;
};
```

2.2.5   Backward-Compatible Specification for `case` with `yield`

When migrating to the new syntax for `switch`, some developers may be hesitant and prefer to approach the changes in syntax gradually. In this case, the specification for `case` can be made quite similar to the old syntax, and instead of a value assignment, `yield` with value can be used.

Inelegant Old Syntax

Let's recap once again the old syntax to map colors from the following enum to their complementary colors—the example here deliberately contains a small careless mistake to demonstrate the fall-through:

```java
enum Color { RED, GREEN, BLUE, ORANGE }

public Color mapToComplementaryColor(Color color)
{
    Color complementaryColor;
    switch (color)
    {
        case RED:
            complementaryColor = Color.GREEN;
            break;
        case GREEN:
            complementaryColor = Color.RED;
            break;
        case BLUE:
            complementaryColor = Color.ORANGE;
            /* break; UPS: FALL THROUGH */
        case ORANGE:
            complementaryColor = Color.BLUE;
            break;
        default:
            throw new IllegalArgumentException("Unknown color: " + color);
    }
    return complementaryColor;
}
```

The initial color `Color.BLUE` results in the (surprising) output of:

```
BLUE
```

The above listing once again shows the disadvantages of the old syntax, which is somewhat cumbersome to use and makes the fall-through hardly noticeable without explicit marking. The need to define an artificial helper variable is more of a cosmetic flaw. In addition, the `default` cannot be omitted because the compiler does not recognize the completeness here. Let's take another look at how it can be done better.

Remedy Through Implementation with the New Syntax

The alternative shown below uses the keyword `yield` in combination with a return value. This variant is quite close to the old syntax but with dedicated improvements and the same effect as the arrow syntax shown before. Overall, this results in the following more readable notation:

```java
public Color mapToComplementaryColorNewSyntax(Color color)
{
    return switch (color)
    {
        case RED: yield Color.GREEN;
        case GREEN: yield Color.RED;
        case BLUE: yield Color.ORANGE;
        case ORANGE: yield Color.BLUE;
    };
}
```

With the new syntax, the input `Color.BLUE` leads to the expected (and correct) mapping to `Color.ORANGE`.

This example once again clearly demonstrates the advantages of the new syntax. First, you no longer need an artificial helper variable. Instead, you can directly return a value with `yield`. This stops processing there, similar to the `return` of a method, but only in the context of `switch`. Second, no `default` is necessary, since all values of the enum are covered by `case` statements.

Curiosity: Changing Type

I want to point out a special characteristic of `switch`, namely, the flexible type. What do I mean by that?

You are probably familiar with the "?" operator! But are you also familiar with its (tricky) special feature? As a rule, the "?" operator works like an `if`. However, there are differences regarding the return type. It is possible to use incompatible types as returns in the two alternatives, here `String` and,

(continued)

according to the numerical value, `int`. Still, after boxing, `Integer`. However, for the assignment to work, the result must be defined as `var` or `Object`:

```
var result = value == 13 ? "Failures, bad luck, and mishaps" : 42;
```

Depending on the value of `value`, you get the type `String` or `Integer`. This fact is also possible for Switch Expressions, although it is just as surprising. Again, the prerequisite is that you use `var` or `Object` for the result:

```
var result = switch (value)
{
    case 13 -> "Failures, bad luck, and mishaps";
    default -> 42;
};
```

2.3 Records

Records are a simplified form of classes for data management, whose API is implicitly derived from the attributes defined as constructor parameters. A record thus represents a simple data container and is therefore a value class that models an immutable state.[9] The necessary implementations of read-only accessor methods and the methods `equals()` and `hashCode()` are generated automatically and, above all, contract-compliant. The same applies to an all-arguments constructor and the method `toString()`. Overall, data container classes can be defined with records in a simple and elegant way.

As an analogy to records, one can refer to the mathematical concept of tuples, that is, a collection of several values of potentially different types.

Records can be utilized profitably in various applications, such as for methods that are supposed to return multiple values, for compound keys for maps, for data transfer objects (DTOs), and for parameter value objects.

2.3.1 Introductory Example

The previous explanations may still sound somewhat abstract and complicated, but everything will become clearer after looking at the following source code. First, we define a point consisting of x and y coordinates, as well as a data container for the three color values red, green, and blue, in the form of separate records:

---

[9] However, immutability is only guaranteed if only primitive data types are used for the constructor parameters or if only immutable types are specified there.

```
record MyPoint(int x, int y) { }

record RgbColor(int red, int green, int blue) {}
```

Accessing Attributes: Implicitly Generated Methods

Now that we have defined the record `MyPoint`, we want to access its attributes. As mentioned in the introduction, an attribute and a corresponding read access method are generated for each constructor parameter, in this case `x()` and `y()`:

```
jshell> record MyPoint(int x, int y) { }
|  Erstellt Datensatz MyPoint

jshell> var myPoint = new MyPoint(47, 11)
myPoint ==> MyPoint[x=47, y=11]

jshell> System.out.println(myPoint)
MyPoint[x=47, y=11]

jshell> System.out.println(myPoint.x() + "/" + myPoint.y())
47/11
```

The example clearly shows that the naming convention for access methods does not follow the JavaBeans standard, and there is no `get` prefix; instead, the method name consists solely of the attribute name.[10]

Records Under the Hood

It is quite interesting to use the `javap` tool integrated into the JDK to examine the generated bytecode in the form of an overview. The command `javap MyPoint` provides this information:

```
Compiled from "MyPoint.java"
final class java17.MyPoint extends java.lang.Record {
  public java17.MyPoint(int, int);
  public int x();
  public int y();
  public java.lang.String toString();
  public int hashCode();
  public boolean equals(java.lang.Object);
}
```

---

[10] This special feature requires newer versions of the libraries in the context of JSON serialization. The same applies to records in the context of JPA (Jakarta Persistence API). They cannot model entities, but they are useful for projections and DTOs.

It is evident that records have the base type `java.lang.Record` and that a suitable access method is provided for each constructor argument.

Conventional Implementation Without Records Let's consider how much source code would be necessary to implement an equivalent[11] functionality with the existing Java language tools for the self-defined point with only two attributes:

```java
public final class MyPoint
{
    private final int x;
    private final int y;

    public MyPoint(int x, int y)
    {
        this.x = x;
        this.y = y;
    }

    @Override
    public boolean equals(Object o)
    {
        if (this == o)
            return true;
        if (o == null || getClass() != o.getClass())
            return false;

        MyPoint point = (MyPoint) o;
        return x == point.x && y == point.y;
    }

    @Override
    public int hashCode()
    {
        return Objects.hash(x, y);
    }

    @Override
    public String toString()
    {
        return "MyPoint[x=" + x + ", y=" + y + "]";
    }

    public int x()
    {
        return x;
    }

    public int y()
    {
        return y;
    }
}
```

---

[11] In fact, the two variants are not 100 % equivalent. For classes, attributes can still be changed later despite `final` using reflection via `setAccessible(true)`. These modifications are not possible with records—they are truly immutable (except with nasty tricks and the `java.misc.Unsafe` class).

> **Note**
> Frameworks and libraries such as Lombok offer annotations that automatically generate much of this boilerplate code (e.g., getters, setters, `equals()`, and `hashCode()`). While such tools are common in real-world projects, this book focuses on standard Java features to ensure a solid understanding of the language itself.

Types in the Definition

So far, we have only used primitive types. In records, various other types can also be used, such as strings and those from the Date and Time API or self-defined enums:

```
jshell> import java.time.*

jshell> enum EyeColor {BLUE, BROWN, GREEN, GRAY}

jshell> record Person(String firstname, String lastname,
   ...>                LocalDate dateOfBirth, EyeColor eyeColor)
   ...> {}
```

It is even possible to use collections such as lists, sets, maps, or arrays:

```
jshell> record CollectionExample(List<String> names,
   ...>                          Long[] favoriteNumbers)
   ...> {}
|  created record CollectionExample

jshell> var surprise = new CollectionExample(List.of("Tim", "Tom", "Mike"),
   ...>                                       new Long[] {2L, 7L, 71L});
surprise ==> CollectionExample[names=[Tim, Tom, Mike], favorit ... Ljava.lang
      .Long;@136432db]
```

Please note, however, that in such cases—as is the case here for `List.of()`—it is often advisable to use immutable classes, because otherwise unforeseen changes could occur to the data set. I will revisit the topic of records and immutability later in Sect. 2.4.4. Below, I show accesses and the (unexpected) change to the array containing the favorite numbers:

```
jshell> Arrays.asList(surprise.favoriteNumbers())
$17 ==> [2, 7, 71]

jshell> surprise.favoriteNumbers()[2] = 13L;
$18 ==> 13

jshell> Arrays.asList(surprise.favoriteNumbers())
$19 ==> [2, 7, 13]
```

This example illustrates the problem of using mutable data types for attributes of records. This should be avoided and is considered an anti-pattern.

2.3.2   Records for DTOs and Return Values

The use of DTOs for exchanging data is a proven approach. DTOs are (often immutable) data container classes that serve to transport data at interfaces or component boundaries. Without records, however, defining them requires a lot of paperwork—worse still, sometimes the implementation of one of the methods, `equals()` and `hashCode()`, is incorrect or missing altogether. In the introduction, we already saw a positive example in the form of the record `MyPoint`. Similar to DTOs, but with a different intention, there are so-called parameter value objects (PVOs), which bundle several method parameters into a single unit, thereby simplifying method signatures.

Let's look at a few examples of records:

```
record Point(int x, int y) { }
record Dimension(int width, int height) { }

record TopLeftAndDimension(Point topLeft, Dimension dim) { }
```

With these records, you could then define a rectangle based on other records using meaningful dimensions in the form of a starting point and a size specification as follows, instead of four `int` values:

```
record PlainRectangle(int x, int y, int width, int height) { }

record Rectangle(Point topLeft, Dimension dim) { }
```

Let's take a look at the application:

```
var oldStyle = new PlainRectangle(10, 10, 70, 20);

var topLeft = new Point(10, 10);
var dimension = new Dimension(70, 20);
var newStyle = new Rectangle(topLeft, dimension);
```

Below, we define colors with names and three RGB values as DTOs, as well as the essential attributes of a person:

```
record NamedRgbColorDTO(String name, int red, int green, int blue) { }

record PersonDTO(String firstname, String lastname, LocalDate birthday) { }
```

Similarly, the top three favorites of a pizza delivery service or calculation results can be modeled using records as follows:

```
record Top3Favorites(String top1, String top2, String top3) {};

record CalcResultTuple(int min, int max, double avg, int count) {};
```

Records for More Complex Return Values

Before Java 17 LTS, it required extra effort and a special class to allow a method to return multiple values, such as providing an error code in combination with a hint or an array of strings. With records, this becomes child's play:

```
record IntStringReturnValue(int code, String info) { }

record IntStringArray(int code, String[] values) { }
record IntStringArray(int code, String... values) { }
```

Please note that the generated string output is not particularly readable when using arrays as attributes of records:

```
jshell> new IntStringArray(5, "Micha", "likes", "Java", "and", "Python")
$8 ==> IntStringArray[code=5, values=[Ljava.lang.String;@5d099f62]
```

To remedy this, records support defining your own methods. Among other things, it is possible to reimplement the standard method `toString()`. Further details are described later in Sect. 2.3.3:

```
jshell> record IntStringArray(int code, String... values) {
   ...>      public String toString()
   ...>      {
   ...>          return "IntStringArray[code=" + code +
   ...>                 ", values=" + Arrays.toString(values) + "]";
   ...>      }
   ...> }
|  created record IntStringArray

jshell> new IntStringArray(5, "Micha", "likes", "Java", "and", "Python")
$9 ==> IntStringArray[code=5, values=[Micha, likes, Java, and, Python]]
```

Records for Compound Keys

Records can act to define so-called compound keys. These are classes that bundle multiple values so that they can be utilized as a unit when accessing a map as a key—be careful to ensure that the types used are ideally immutable to avoid surprises:

```
record CompoundKey(String name, long income) { }
```

Let's make the whole thing more concrete and define a tuple consisting of name and age:

```
jshell> record NameAgeKey(String name, int age) { }
|  created record NameAgeKey
```

With this tuple as the key, we then refer to a list of hobbies:

```
jshell> var mapping = Map.of(new NameAgeKey("Micha", 30),
   ...>                          List.of("Karate", "Inline-Skating"),
   ...>                          new NameAgeKey("Micha", 52),
   ...>                          List.of("Java-Books", "Sophie"))
mapping ==> {NameAgeKey[name=Micha, age=30]=[Karate, Inline-S ... =52]=[Java-
      Books, Sophie]}
```

2.3.3   Extension Options

We will now look at different ways of extending the functionality of records or
adding special operations:

1. Defining your own methods
2. Defining your own constructors
3. Providing a validity check

Extension Option: Defining Your Own Methods

So far, records are very intuitive, and this remains the case—even if we want to add
our own methods, as we have previously done for `toString()`. Let's take the record
`PersonDTO` already presented as an example and assume we want to implement the
concatenation of first and last names in the form of a method `asFullname()`:

```
record PersonDTO(String firstname, String lastname, LocalDate birthday)
{
    public String asFullname()
    {
        return firstname + " " + lastname;
    }
}
```

Let's take a look at this method in action:

```
>> import java.time.*

>> var micha = new PersonDTO("Michael", "Inden", LocalDate.of(1971, 2, 7))
micha ==> PersonDTO[firstname=Michael, lastname=Inden, birthday=1971-02-07]

jshell> micha.asFullname()
$30 ==> "Michael Inden"
```

Similarly, you may want to extend the previously shown record `RgbColor` to
output the three color components as hexadecimal values using a method `asHex()`:

```
record RgbColor(int red, int green, int blue)
{
    public String asHex()
    {
        return String.format("#%02X%02X%02X", red, green, blue);
    }
}
```

Below, we use this record and its method `asHex()` to generate a color combination and its hexadecimal representation:

```
jshell> var darkgray = new RgbColor(21, 11, 23);
darkgray ==> RgbColor[red=21, green=11, blue=23]

jshell> darkgray.asHex()
$38 ==> "#150B17"
```

Extension Option: Defining Your Own Constructors

In records, it is possible to define not only methods, but also constructors. Let's assume we want to enable the record `MyPoint` also to be created based on a textual representation in the format `x,y`. In this case, it makes sense to write the following custom constructor, which relies on the methods `split()` for splitting and `strip()` for removing whitespace:

```
record MyPoint(int x, int y)
{
    public MyPoint(final String values)
    {
        this(Integer.parseInt(values.split(",")[0].strip()),
            Integer.parseInt(values.split(",")[1].strip()));
    }
}
```

This then allows the following constructions:

```
jshell> var point1 = new MyPoint("72,71")
point1 ==> MyPoint[x=72, y=71]

jshell> var point2 = new MyPoint("72, 71")
point2 ==> MyPoint[x=72, y=71]
```

Designing a Simple Constructor
It seems tempting to assign the result of a call to `values.split()` to a local variable as the first action. However, this is not possible because no statements may be performed in a constructor before calling `super()` or `this()`. This behavior was relaxed in Java 22 and continued as a preview feature in Java 23 and 24. Java 25 LTS includes this as a final feature described in JEP 513: Flexible Constructor Bodies (see Sect. 9.5).

Extended Example Now that we have covered the basics, I want to revisit the example from Sect. 2.3.2 and demonstrate how easy it is to define additional constructors based on other records.

Let's start with the two records `Point` and `Dimension` as a basis:

```
record Point(int x, int y) { }
record Dimension(int width, int height) { }
```

With these records, we implement the record `Rectangle`, which can be constructed either on the basis of four `int` values, one `Point`, and two `int` values or on the basis of a `Point` and one `Dimension`:

```
record Rectangle(int x, int y, int width, int height)
{
    Rectangle(Point topLeft, int width, int height)
    {
        this(topLeft.x(), topLeft.y(), width, height);
    }

    Rectangle(Point topLeft, Dimension dim)
    {
        this(topLeft.x(), topLeft.y(), dim.width(), dim.height());
    }
}
```

Special Treatments: Providing a Validity Check

Because records model an immutable data container, it is often essential to verify certain boundary conditions or value ranges for specific parameters when constructing them to avoid inconsistencies. Let's consider the following implementation of a record `ClosedInterval` for defining value ranges of a closed interval, where the lower limit must always be less than or equal to the upper limit. Let's implement the validity check as an example:

```
record ClosedInterval(int lower, int upper)
{
    public ClosedInterval(int lower, int upper)
    {
        if (lower > upper)
        {
            var errorMsg = String.format("invalid: %d (lower) > %d (upper)",
                                          lower, upper);
            throw new IllegalArgumentException(errorMsg);
        }
        this.lower = lower;
        this.upper = upper;
    }
}
```

Short Notation Interestingly, there is a syntactic peculiarity: instead of a constructor, you can use the following construct called Compact Constructor—this performs the same checks. Still, you don't have to write any variable assignments:

```
record ClosedInterval(int lower, int upper)
{
    public ClosedInterval
    {
        if (lower > upper)
        {
            var errorMsg = String.format("invalid: %d (lower) > %d (upper)",
                                    lower, upper);
            throw new IllegalArgumentException(errorMsg);
        }
    }
}
```

Assignment to Attributes in the Compact Constructor

As a speciality, assigning attributes is permitted in the Compact Constructor:

```
public ClosedInterval
{
    if (lower > upper)
    {
        lower = upper;
    }
}
```

Additional Example Let's return to the record RgbColor from the introduction. For this record, it would currently be possible to pass any values for the color components, not just those within the 0–255 range per component. Conveniently, you can define the constructor yourself and integrate a validity check there, relying on the useful utility class java.util.Objects and its method checkIndex(), which checks values in the range from 0 to the specified maximum value (exclusive), in this case 256:

```
record RgbColor(int red, int green, int blue)
{
    public RgbColor
    {
        Objects.checkIndex(red, 256);
        Objects.checkIndex(green, 256);
        Objects.checkIndex(blue, 256);
    }

    public String asHex()
    {
        return String.format("#%02X%02X%02X", red, green, blue);
    }
}
```

This is where the short form of the constructor comes into play, requiring neither the assignment nor the arguments to be specified in the constructor. However, this may be confusing for developers who are still unfamiliar with records.

2.3.4   Special Feature: Generics in Records

Not only for interfaces and classes, but also for records, it is sometimes desirable to be able to offer them generically for different types. Let's consider the following records `Pair<T1,T2>` for value pairs and `MultiTypes<K,V,T>` with a map and another generic parameter:

```
record Pair<T1, T2> (T1 first, T2 second) {}

record MultiTypes<K, V, T> (Map<K, V> mapping, T info) {}
```

Finally, we combine the generics in records with the validation we just learned about and create a record called `ListRestrictions<T>`, which verifies the submitted list against a maximum size that is also passed as a parameter and rejects the construction if it is exceeded. This functionality seems a little artificial and serves primarily to demonstrate the possibilities:

```
record ListRestrictions<T> (List<T> values, int maxSize)
{
    public ListRestrictions
    {
        if (values.size() > maxSize)
            throw new IllegalArgumentException("too many entries! got: "
                    + values.size() + ", but restricted to " + maxSize);
    }
}
```

Hint
Please note the aforementioned problem of using mutable types, such as `List<T>`, for attributes of records. Using this carries the risk of modifications from outside. Therefore, it's favorable to avoid such practices, as they are considered anti-patterns.

Example

Let's now experience the previously defined records in action. To accomplish this, we will implement three methods. In `pairExamples()`, we create pairs, some with different types, output them to the console, and check whether pairs with identical values are actually considered equal with `equals()`:

```
static void pairExamples()
{
    var pair1 = new Pair<>("INFO", 4711);
    var pair2 = new Pair<>("INFO", 4711);

    System.out.println(pair1);
    System.out.println(new Pair<>("FIRST", "SECOND"));
    System.out.println(pair1.equals(pair2));
    System.out.println();
}
```

In `multiTypesExamples()` we create a record with a map and a string as input and determine the respective types:

```
static void multiTypesExamples()
{
    var mapping = Map.of("tim", 42, "tom", 77, "mike", 49);
    var multiGenericTypes = new MultiTypes<>(mapping, "INFO");

    System.out.println(multiGenericTypes);
    System.out.println("mapping type: " +
                    multiGenericTypes.mapping().getClass());
    System.out.println("info type: " + multiGenericTypes.info().getClass());
    System.out.println();
}
```

In addition, we define two lists in the following method `listRestrictions-Examples()` and check whether their length restrictions are adhered to:

```
static void listRestrictionsExamples(final int limit)
{
    var timAndMike = List.of("Tim", "Mike");
    var initialRestricted = new ListRestrictions<>(timAndMike, limit);
    System.out.println("values: " + initialRestricted.values());

    var names = List.of("Tim", "Tom", "Peter", "Franz", "Fritz", "Mike");
    var restrictionViolated = new ListRestrictions<>(names, limit);
}
```

We call these three methods in this `main()` method.

```
public static void main(final String[] args)
{
    // Pairs with partially different types
    pairExamples();

    // Demonstration of generics with different types in records
    multiTypesExamples();

    // Check the restriction to n elements (here 5)
    listRestrictionsExamples(5);
}
```

Listing 2.1 Executable as "RECORDSANDGENERICSEXAMPLE"

Executing the program RECORDSANDGENERICSEXAMPLE, we get the following expected outputs (shortened), including the exception for the length violation:

```
Pair[first=INFO, second=4711]
Pair[first=FIRST, second=SECOND]
true

MultiTypes[mapping={tom=77, mike=49, tim=42}, info=INFO]
mapping type: class java.util.ImmutableCollections$MapN
info type: class java.lang.String

values: [Tim, Mike]
Exception in thread "main" java.lang.IllegalArgumentException: too many
      entries! got: 6, but restricted to 5
```

2.3.5   Special Feature: Records and Interfaces

Up to here, you have already acquired a fair amount of knowledge about records, which you can now put to good use in practice. The following topic, which explores defining interfaces using records, will expand your understanding in this area.

Introductory Example

Let's assume we have defined the following interface:

```
interface RgbAccess
{
    int red();
    int green();
    int blue();
}
```

We let the record `RgbColor` implement this interface—interestingly, we don't have to implement the access methods ourselves, as they were deliberately named after the attributes. This is why the methods are generated automatically:

```
record RgbColor(int red, int green, int blue) implements RgbAccess
{
    public RgbColor
    {
        Objects.checkIndex(red, 256);
        Objects.checkIndex(green, 256);
        Objects.checkIndex(blue, 256);
    }

    public String asHex()
    {
        return String.format("#%02X%02X%02X", red, green, blue);
    }
}
```

The following record constructed solely for demonstration purposes in this example could use a comma-separated string for data storage and then provide the information using parsing as follows:

```
record SpecialRgbColor(String rgb) implements RgbAccess
{
    public int red()
    {
        return Integer.parseInt(rgb.split(",")[0].strip());
    }

    public int green()
    {
        return Integer.parseInt(rgb.split(",")[1].strip());
    }

    public int blue()
    {
        return Integer.parseInt(rgb.split(",")[2].strip());
    }
}
```

The similar calls look awkward. In fact, the record becomes much clearer if you extract and call a helper method as follows:

```
record SpecialRgbColor(String rgb) implements RgbAccess
{
    public int red()
    {
        return parseColorComponent(0);
    }

    public int green()
    {
        return parseColorComponent(1);
    }

    public int blue()
    {
        return parseColorComponent(2);
    }

    private int parseColorComponent(int index)
    {
        return Integer.parseInt(rgb.split(",")[index].strip());
    }
}
```

Let's try this out to sharpen our understanding:

```
jshell> RgbAccess color = new RgbColor(23, 11, 21)
color ==> RgbColor[red=23, green=11, blue=21]

jshell> int red = color.red()
red ==> 23

jshell> RgbAccess color = new SpecialRgbColor("23,11,21")
color ==> SpecialRgbColor[rgb=23,11,21]

jshell> int green = color.green()
green ==> 11

jshell> int blue = new SpecialRgbColor("222, 111, 255").blue()
blue ==> 255
```

Further Example

For some use cases, it is desirable that different records can be treated equally or
fitted into a type hierarchy. To achieve this, records, as seen in the previous example,
can implement a common interface: let's consider a database of books, Blu-ray
discs, and monitors that we want to manage for an online store. To accomplish this,
we define an interface `StockItem` as follows:

```
interface StockItem
{
    String name();
    String description();
    double price();
}
```

We also create the records `Book`, `BluRay`, and `Monitor`, as well as a helper
record `Resolution` as follows:

```
import java.time.Duration;

record Book(String name, String description, double price, int pages)
        implements StockItem {}

record BluRay(String name, String description, double price,
             Duration duration) implements StockItem {}

record Monitor(String name, String description, double price,
             Resolution resolution) implements StockItem {}

record Resolution(int width, int height) {}
```

Let's consider the definition of a stock inventory in the form of a list as an
example. We then access the names of all elements and also determine the prices
and the total. Finally, we output the total value:

```
var items = List.of(new Book("Programming Pearls", "", 27.53, 200),
                new Book("Effective Java", "", 27.53, 354),
                new BluRay("Star Wars", "Long Story", 12.34,
                        Duration.ofMinutes(142)),
                new Monitor("Studio Display", "IPS Retina", 1750.00,
                        new Resolution(5120, 2880)));

double sumOfPrices = 0.0;
for (StockItem item : items)
{
    System.out.println(item.name() + " " + item.price());
    sumOfPrices += item.price();
}
System.out.println("Total price: " + sumOfPrices);
```

The output is as follows:

```
Programming Pearls 27.53
Effective Java 27.53
Star Wars 12.34
Studio Display 1750.0
Total price: 1817.4
```

2.3.6   *Summary*

Because Records are a useful language feature with many special characteristics, I would like to recap or mention a few things:

- Records have the base type `java.lang.Record` and are implicitly `final`, so you cannot derive your own classes from them.
- Records can implement interfaces, which is very useful in the context of inheritance hierarchies and polymorphism.
- The attributes are derived from the constructor parameters. You cannot define any additional attributes yourself, but static attributes are possible.
- Attributes may not have names that are similar to those of parameterless methods from `java.lang.Object`. This means that attributes cannot be named `hashCode` or `toString`, for example; otherwise, compilation errors will occur, such as "`Illegal component name hashCode in record`". Interestingly, `equals` is syntactically allowed as a name, but it does not make much sense.
- Since the attributes are assigned directly during construction, an initializer block is not allowed ("`instance initializers not allowed in records`"). In fact, static initializer blocks can be defined if necessary.
- Unlike final fields in regular classes, the attributes of a record cannot be changed using reflection. However, it is possible with the help of tricks and the class `java.misc.Unsafe`, although this is highly delicate and fragile and not very maintainable.
- The automatically generated access methods deviate from the JavaBeans naming scheme: instead of `getXyz()`, `xyz()` is used. This can be unfavorable in combination with frameworks that expect JavaBeans-compliant getters and setters.
- The methods `equals()`, `hashCode()`, and `toString()` can be implemented for your own records—please exercise caution with the pair `equals()` and `hashCode()` to ensure that they remain contract-compliant and consistent. But beware: calling the base implementation is prohibited (e. g., "`abstract method hashCode() in record cannot be accessed directly`").

Implications for Reflection

To query the properties of records, the Reflection API provides the following new methods in `java.lang.Class<T>`:

```
public boolean isRecord()
public RecordComponent[] getRecordComponents()
```

2.4   Records: Beyond the Basics

The previous introduction to the many possibilities offered by records should have
taught you the basics. Now it's time to learn about a few special features of records,
in particular, the following topics:

- The influence of the data structure in which records are used
- Records in the context of the Builder pattern
- Records and immutability

2.4.1   *The Influence of the Data Structure in Which Records Are Used*

First, we define a simple record to model a person with attributes for name, age, and
place of residence:

```
record SimplePerson(String name, int age, String city) {}
```

Then we manage some data in a HashSet<E>:

```
Set<SimplePerson> speakers = new HashSet<>();
speakers.add(new SimplePerson("Michael", 51, "Zürich"));
speakers.add(new SimplePerson("Michael", 51, "Zürich"));
speakers.add(new SimplePerson("Anton", 42, "Aachen"));
System.out.print(speakers);
```

As expected, when the person Michael is entered multiple times, these duplicates
are recognized as such by the set and get automatically removed. This results in the
following:

```
[SimplePerson[name=Michael, age=51, city=Zürich],
 SimplePerson[name=Anton, age=42, city=Aachen]]
```

Actually, it should make no difference to classes and records in which data
structure they are managed. Let's take a look at what happens when we use a
TreeSet<E> instead of a HashSet<E> for data storage—in this case, the entries
should also be sorted:

```
Set<SimplePerson> sortedSpeakers = new TreeSet<>();
sortedSpeakers.add(new SimplePerson("Michael", 51, "Zürich"));
sortedSpeakers.add(new SimplePerson("Michael", 51, "Zürich"));
sortedSpeakers.add(new SimplePerson("Anton", 42, "Aachen"));
System.out.print(sortedSpeakers);
```

But do expectations match reality? No! In fact, we receive the following error
message (package information that will probably differ for you, depending on where
and how you manage the examples in the file system or the JShell):

```
Exception in thread "main" java.lang.ClassCastException: class b_slides.
    RecordInterfaceExample$1SimplePerson cannot be cast to class java.lang.
    Comparable
```

It becomes apparent that the record does not implement the Comparable<T> interface. Before addressing this issue, a brief overview of the relevant theory is provided.

Recap: Interaction Between `equals()`, `hashCode()`, and `compareTo()`

You may already see the cause of the error. If not, let me remind you of the interaction between the three methods mentioned above. It says the following: If a class overrides `equals()`, it should also consistently implement the `hashCode()` method. In addition, `compareTo()` should be consistent with `equals()`.

Conveniently, we don't have to worry about `equals()` and `hashCode()` for records, as both methods are already provided automatically. What is missing, however, is the contract-compliant implementation of `compareTo()`, the third component of the method trio. The following applies here: if classes are to be managed using a `TreeSet<E>`, they must either fulfill the Comparable<T> interface, or a suitable comparator must be provided when constructing the `TreeSet<E>`. How can we address this requirement?

Remedy: Records That Implement Interfaces

We already know that records can also implement interfaces. Based on this, we correct the original definition of the record as a variant named `SimplePerson2` by specifying the interface Comparable<T> there—initially with a straightforward implementation based purely on a comparison of names:

```java
record SimplePerson2(String name, int age, String city)
        implements Comparable<SimplePerson2>
{
    @Override
    public int compareTo(SimplePerson2 other)
    {
        return name.compareTo(other.name);
    }
}
```

Let's try it out:

```java
Set<SimplePerson2> sortedSpeakers = new TreeSet<>();
sortedSpeakers.add(new SimplePerson2("Michael", 51, "Zürich"));
sortedSpeakers.add(new SimplePerson2("Michael", 51, "Zürich"));
sortedSpeakers.add(new SimplePerson2("Anton", 42, "Aachen"));
System.out.println(sortedSpeakers);
```

This produces the following result, which avoids the initial exception and also filters out duplicates (at least, that's how it appears to work):

```
[SimplePerson2[name=Anton, age=42, city=Aachen],
 SimplePerson2[name=Michael, age=51, city=Zürich]]
```

2.4.2 Detecting Implementation Errors

At the moment, everything seems fine, but we already know from the introductory discussion that the above implementation of `compareTo()` is not contract-compliant and consistent with `equals()`. Why? Let's consider deviations in the other attributes, in this case, age and/or place of residence.

As soon as we modify the data set a little, the inadequacy of the first attempt becomes obvious! To accomplish this, we define several Michaels of different ages and places of residence:

```
Set<SimplePerson2> sortedSpeakers = new TreeSet<>();
sortedSpeakers.add(new SimplePerson2("Michael", 51, "Zürich"));
sortedSpeakers.add(new SimplePerson2("Michael", 51, "Zürich"));
sortedSpeakers.add(new SimplePerson2("Anton", 42, "Aachen"));
sortedSpeakers.add(new SimplePerson2("Michael", 51, "Kiel"));
sortedSpeakers.add(new SimplePerson2("Michael", 41, "Aachen"));
System.out.println(sortedSpeakers);
```

The additional persons with the same name who differ in age or place of residence are not correctly recognized by our inconsistent implementation of `compareTo()` and are incorrectly sorted out as duplicates. This still yields the following result, which, however, does not take into account the differences in age and city for the other Michaels:

```
[SimplePerson2[name=Anton, age=42, city=Aachen], SimplePerson2[name=Michael,
     age=51, city=Zürich]]
```

Remedy: Correction by Defining a Comparator

Conveniently, Java 8 LTS already introduced some beneficial extensions to the `Comparator<T>` interface, namely, various `comparing()` methods that make the definition of comparators elegant (see Sect. 15.3.1). As a developer, you only need to specify the attributes to be used for comparison in the form of access methods, here as method references (see Sect. 15.1.4). With the help of the method `thenComparing()` or `thenComparingXyz()`, more complex comparisons can be easily chained together. This is impressively demonstrated here for the three attributes and the definition of the comparator named `byAllAttributes`, which is then used appropriately in `compareTo()`:

```
record SimplePerson3(String name, int age, String city)
      implements Comparable<SimplePerson3>
{
    static Comparator<SimplePerson3> byAllAttributes = Comparator.
                              comparing(SimplePerson3::name).
                              thenComparingInt(SimplePerson3::age).
                              thenComparing(SimplePerson3::city);

    @Override
    public int compareTo(SimplePerson3 other)
    {
        return byAllAttributes.compare(this, other);
    }
}
```

Let's see what this correction does by redefining the data set as before, but this time using the above record `SimplePerson3`:

```
Set<SimplePerson3> sortedSpeakers = new TreeSet<>();
sortedSpeakers.add(new SimplePerson3("Michael", 51, "Zürich"));
sortedSpeakers.add(new SimplePerson3("Michael", 51, "Zürich"));
sortedSpeakers.add(new SimplePerson3("Anton", 42, "Aachen"));
sortedSpeakers.add(new SimplePerson3("Michael", 51, "Kiel"));
sortedSpeakers.add(new SimplePerson3("Michael", 41, "Aachen"));
System.out.println(sortedSpeakers);
```

After the above correction, `equals()` and `compareTo()` are implemented consistently. Specifically, this means that if `equals()` returns `true`, then `compareTo()` must return the value 0. That was already the case. However, it must also apply the other way around, which it now does. Accordingly, if `compareTo()` returns the value 0, then the `SimplePerson`s are now also equal. This change finally produces the following output, which is as expected—here in a slightly nicer formatting:

```
[SimplePerson3[name=Anton, age=42, city=Aachen],
 SimplePerson3[name=Michael, age=41, city=Aachen],
 SimplePerson3[name=Michael, age=51, city=Kiel],
 SimplePerson3[name=Michael, age=51, city=Zürich]]
```

2.4.3 Records in the Context of the Builder Pattern

The Builder pattern, with its descriptive method names (fluent interface), is widely used for facilitating object creation. It is beneficial when the parameter list of the constructors is long, the class contains various optional components, or both of these apply or the construction is otherwise complex.

Before the introduction of records in Java, Lombok[12] was sometimes used as a workaround. This makes it easy to create `equals()`, `hashCode()`, and, in particular, Builder.

---

[12] https://projectlombok.org/.

Default and User-Defined Constructors and Builder-Like Methods

Let's start with a reasonably simple record that consists of only three attributes and has a default all-arguments constructor derived from the parameters in the definition:

```
record SimplePerson4(String name, int age, String city) {}
```

There is one key difference between records and regular Java classes. The latter have a default constructor (one without parameters), provided there is no user-defined constructor. Interestingly, however, the default constructor is no longer automatically offered for classes as soon as a user-defined constructor is present. With records, things are different: Basically, they do not provide a default constructor, but always automatically possess the all-arguments constructor, which is derived from the parameters in the definition. In addition, further user-defined constructors can be provided.

Let's consider an example of a record that offers one user-defined constructor and two additional methods that are somewhat reminiscent of those from the Builder pattern:

```
record SimplePerson4(String name, int age, String city)
{
    SimplePerson4(String name, int age)
    {
        this(name, age, "");
    }

    SimplePerson4 withAge(int newAge)
    {
        return new SimplePerson4(name, newAge, city);
    }

    SimplePerson4 withCity(String newCity)
    {
        return new SimplePerson4(name, age, newCity);
    }
}
```

The following construction in the JShell shows that the all-arguments constructor still exists despite the two user-defined constructors, especially because we refer to it in the other constructors using `this(...)`. Let's briefly check this:

```
jshell> new SimplePerson4("Michael", 51, "Zürich")
$31 ==> SimplePerson4[name=Michael, age=51, city=Zürich]
```

Both methods serve to enable the call familiar from the Builder pattern to be used with a chaining via "." notation and descriptive names, but at the cost of creating new objects due to their immutability:

```
jshell> new SimplePerson4("Sophie", 5).withAge(2).withCity("Zürich")
$32 ==> SimplePerson4[name=Sophie, age=2, city=Zürich]
```

Option for Reducing Complexity: Define Records for Individual Components

Let us now turn to the definition of a more extensive data set, which requires the specification of many attributes. With more than four or five of these, it quickly becomes unwieldy. The following record `ComplexPerson` illustrates this situation with its eight attributes.

```
record ComplexPerson(String firstname, String lastname,
                     LocalDate birthday,
                     int height, int weight,
                     String street, String houseNumber, String city)
{
    public static void main(final String[] args)
    {
        var mike = new ComplexPerson("Mike", "Peters",
                               LocalDate.of(2021, 1,   21),
                               170, 90,
                               "Fuldastrasse", "16a", "Berlin");
        System.out.println(mike);
    }
}
```

Listing 2.2 Executable as "COMPLEXPERSON"

The program outputs the following:

```
ComplexPerson[firstname=Mike, lastname=Peters, birthday=2021-01-21, height
    =170, weight=90, street=Fuldastrasse, houseNumber=16a, city=Berlin]
```

Field of Application for the Builder Pattern The above implementation shows the typical field of application for the Builder pattern—shown here without address components:

```
var mike = new ComplexPersonBuilder().
           withFirstname("Mike").
           withBirthday(LocalDate.of(2021, 1, 21)).
           withLastname("Peters").build();
System.out.println(mike);
```

The catch is that you have to implement this `ComplexPersonBuilder` yourself. Alternatively, newer versions of Lombok can be used to generate one for records.

However, since Lombok is not always desirable or available, I would like to present a way to simplify this. Upon critical examination of the original parameter list, with some experience, you will notice that the values actually cover three different concerns: personal data, height and weight, and address information.

Defining Records for Individual Components

As an alternative to using a builder, it is possible to break down the content and group the data accordingly. For example, the following three records can be defined as a basis:

```java
record Address(String street, String houseNumber, String city) {}

record BodyInfo(int height, int weight) {}

record Person(String firstname, String lastname, LocalDate birthday) {}
```

These three can be used as parameter objects from which a record is defined as a combination, making the constructor much easier to understand.

```java
record ReducedComplexPerson(Person person, BodyInfo bodyInfo, Address address)
{
    public static void main(final String[] args)
    {
        var john = new Person("John", "Peters", LocalDate.of(2021, 1,  21));
        var bodyInfo = new BodyInfo(170, 90);
        var address = new Address("Fuldastrasse", "16a", "Berlin");

        var johnAndMore = new ReducedComplexPerson(john, bodyInfo, address);
        System.out.println(johnAndMore);
    }
}
```

Listing 2.3 Executable as "**REDUCEDCOMPLEXPERSON**"

The program outputs the following:

```
ReducedComplexPerson[person=Person[firstname=John, lastname=Peters, birthday
    =2021-01-21], bodyInfo=BodyInfo[height=170, weight=90], address=Address
    [street=Fuldastrasse, houseNumber=16a, city=Berlin]]
```

2.4.4   Records and Immutability

At the beginning of the introduction to records, we mentioned that records provide an immutable data container whose values cannot be changed after construction. For this to be true, several key points should be considered. Java's reference semantics, combined with the use of mutable attribute types, give rise to a few pitfalls.

To demonstrate this, let's create a seemingly harmless record for modeling a date range with a start and an end date, where the requirement is that the start date must always be before the end date.

Record for a Date Range

Let's start with a definition of a record for a date range based on the old class
`java.util.Date`:

```
record DateRange(Date start, Date end) {}
```

Obviously, no range check takes place here, which means that any date ranges
can be defined, even those where the end date is before the start date, as happens
with the second range:

```
var range1 = new DateRange(new Date(71, 1, 7), new Date(71, 2, 27));
var range2 = new DateRange(new Date(71, 6, 7), new Date(71, 2, 27));
```

Please note: in the `Date` class, the months are numbered starting with 0, which
is why 1 stands for February, 2 for March, and 6 for July in the example.

2.4.5 Correction 1

We want to add a validity check for the invariant[13] *start < end*. Therefore, we
check this exact condition during construction and introduce a special constructor
(using the shorthand notation already presented):

```
record DateRange(Date start, Date end)
{
    public DateRange
    {
        if (!start.before(end))
            throw new IllegalArgumentException("start >= end");
    }
}
```

To experience the check in action, and in particular when preventing an invalid
value range, we create the two ranges again:

```
jshell> var range1 = new DateRange(new Date(71, 1, 7), new Date(71, 2, 27));
range1 ==> DateRange[start=Sun Feb 07 00:00:00 CET 1971, end=Sat Mar 27
      00:00:00 CET 1971]

jshell> var range2 = new DateRange(new Date(71, 6, 7), new Date(71, 2, 27));
|  Exception java.lang.IllegalArgumentException: start >= end
|        at DateRange.<init> (#15:6)
|        at do_it$Aux (#17:1)
|        at (#17:1)
```

The check ensures validity during construction. Unfortunately, however, there
is a loophole. Why? The class `Date` is mutable, and the individual attributes are
accessible and can be modified (accidentally or even deliberately) afterward:

---

[13] A condition that should generally hold regardless of the execution of certain parts of the program.

```
jshell> var range1 = new DateRange(new Date(71, 1, 7), new Date(71, 2, 27));
range1 ==> DateRange[start=Sun Feb 07 00:00:00 CET 1971, end=Sat Mar 27
     00:00:00 CET 1971]

jshell> range1.start().setTime(new Date(71, 6, 7).getTime());

jshell> System.out.println(range1);
DateRange[start=Wed Jul 07 00:00:00 CET 1971, end=Sat Mar 27 00:00:00 CET
     1971]
```

Therefore, records are only immutable if the types used for all attributes are immutable. Otherwise, the access methods provide a reference to mutable data, allowing for potentially arbitrary modifications. In the case of type List<E>, for example, it would be possible to subsequently, and often unexpectedly, delete or add elements or empty the content. These pitfalls are addressed in the following tip box.

Pitfall: Variable Collections as Attributes of Records

I already mentioned that mutable data containers, such as ArrayList<E>, can lead to unexpected modifications. The following example illustrates this impressively:

```
jshell> record Pitfall(List<String> names) {}
|  created record Pitfall

jshell> var pf = new Pitfall(new ArrayList<>(List.of("Tim", "Tom",
   ...>                                               "Mike")))
pf ==> Pitfall[names=[Tim, Tom, Mike]]

jshell> pf.names().add("UNEXPECTED")
$6 ==> true

jshell> pf
pf ==> Pitfall[names=[Tim, Tom, Mike, UNEXPECTED]]

jshell> pf.names().clear()

jshell> pf
pf ==> Pitfall[names=[]]
```

As a workaround and to prohibit modifications, you can create an immutable copy of the submitted data by calling copyOf() as follows to solve the problem:

```
jshell> record PitfallSolved(List<String> names)
   ...> {
   ...>      public PitfallSolved
   ...>      {
   ...>          names = List.copyOf(names);
   ...>      }
   ...> }
```

Any attempts to modify it will then result in exceptions.

2.4.6 *Correction 2*

Let's briefly consider how we can improve the situation in cases where mutable attributes are involved. Several remedies are conceivable. Suppose you are not allowed to change the API or are limited to the type `Date` for reasons of backward compatibility. In that case, you need to create a copy in the constructor before the assignment and in the corresponding access methods before returning the value, as shown below just for the `start()` method:

```java
record DateRange(Date start, Date end)
{
    public DateRange
    {
        if (!start.before(end))
            throw new IllegalArgumentException("start >= end");

        this.start = new Date(start.getTime());
        this.end = new Date(end.getTime());
    }

    public Date start()
    {
        return new Date(start.getTime());
    }
}
```

However, it is better to use the modern types of the Date and Time API, which is also significantly better in terms of application design. Alongside lambdas and the Stream API, the Date and Time API is an essential component of Java 8 LTS, conveniently offering immutable date classes that help avoid the pitfalls we have become familiar with. Instead of the `Date` class used before, the `java.time.LocalDate` class is favorable and conveniently also provides a `isBefore()` method. Using it helps implement the validity check in a readable way:

```java
record DateRange(LocalDate start, LocalDate end)
{
    public DateRange
    {
        if (!start.isBefore(end))
            throw new IllegalArgumentException("start >= end");
    }
}
```

Let's reconstruct the date ranges we already used before—this time utilizing the `LocalDate` class:

```java
jshell> import java.time.*

jshell> var range1 = new DateRange(LocalDate.of(1971, 1, 7),
   ...>                            LocalDate.of(1971, 2, 27));
range1 ==> DateRange[start=1971-01-07, end=1971-02-27]

jshell> var range2 = new DateRange(LocalDate.of(1971, 6, 7),
   ...>                            LocalDate.of(1971, 2, 27));
```

```
|   Exception java.lang.IllegalArgumentException: start >= end
|         at DateRange.<init> (#21:6)
|         at do_it$Aux (#23:1)
|         at (#23:1)
```

As a result of this modification, it is not possible to modify the value range via attribute access, since the `LocalDate` class only offers methods that do not modify data.

2.5   Pattern Matching for `instanceof`

With pattern matching for `instanceof` as an extension, it is possible to keep the source code clearer and reduce the need for boilerplate. What do I mean by that? Especially in the context of `instanceof`, you often see the definition of a helper variable including a cast after the type check, for example, as follows:

```java
if (obj instanceof Person)
{
    final Person person = (Person) obj;
    // ... Zugriff auf person...
}
```

This common idiom (pattern at the source code level) is used to continue working with the variable in a meaningful and type-specific manner. However, repeated checks and casts can become somewhat confusing, especially when multiple types are involved. Besides, the construct is often not very pleasant to read.

2.5.1   New Syntax and Introductory Example

With modern Java, the whole thing becomes more precise and concise by specifying a so-called binding variable after the type in `instanceof`. This variable can be accessed in the block below:

```java
if (obj instanceof Person person)
{
    // Here you can directly access the variable person.
}
```

In the source code above, `obj` satisfies the type pattern `Person person` if the value of `obj` is an instance of `Person` (or a subtype) at runtime. The variable is then assigned appropriately, and you can continue working without casting.

Let's look at a concrete example for a better understanding:

```java
Object obj = "Hello Java 17 LTS";

if (obj instanceof String str)
{
    // Here you can use str
    System.out.println("Length: " + str.length());
}
else
{
    // No access to str here
    System.out.println(obj.getClass());
}
```

Because the value of `obj` is an instance of `String` at runtime, the type pattern `String str` is satisfied and the variable `str` is assigned. This results in the output of string-specific information:

```
Length: 17
```

Practical Feature

Although what we have just shown is already quite nice, there is room for improvement. You can already access the variable in the `if` expression:

```java
if (obj instanceof String str2 && str2.length() > 5)
{
    System.out.println("Length: " + str2.length());
}
```

This allows the following method to be defined for evaluating different types of messages:

```java
public void handleMsg(final Object obj)
{
    if (obj instanceof String str && str.startsWith("topsecret"))
    {
        processSecretMessage(str);
    }
    else if (obj instanceof String str && str.contains("V2"))
    {
        handleV2(str);
    }
    else
    {
        System.out.println(obj);
    }
}
```

The following construct is even more fascinating, as `str` is available after the `if` block, which checks for "not instance of":

```java
public void handleMsg(final Object obj)
{
    if (!(obj instanceof String str))
        return;

    System.out.println("str = " + str);
}
```

2.5.2   In Practical Use

Especially in the context of frameworks, you sometimes find rather clumsy comparisons and queries with ugly casts like these two:

```java
public void printValueOld(final Object obj)
{
    if (obj instanceof Double)
    {
        final Double d = (Double) obj;
        System.out.println("double with int value = " + d.intValue());
    }
    if (obj instanceof String)
    {
        final String str = (String) obj;
        System.out.println("string with length = " + str.length());
    }
}
```

By using the syntax innovation in `instanceof`, we can now write the whole thing in a more elegant and readable way as follows—in particular, this also eliminates the need for casts:

```java
public static void printValue(final Object obj)
{
    if (obj instanceof Double d)
    {
        System.out.println("double with int value = " + d.intValue());
    }
    if (obj instanceof String str)
    {
        System.out.println("string with length = " + str.length());
    }
}
```

What happens here? In the source code above, `obj` corresponds to the type pattern `Double d` if the value of `obj` is an instance of `Double` at runtime. Similarly, the same applies to `String str` if `obj` is an instance of `String` at runtime.

Further Example

Suppose we need to write a generic method for formatting values. The implementation may get quite confusing and ugly due to the many similar queries. In addition, many casts are required. The following example is based on one from JEP 441 (https://openjdk.org/jeps/441) and illustrates this:

```java
static String formattedOldStyle(Object obj)
{
    String formatted = "unknown";
    if (obj instanceof Integer)
    {
        final Integer i = (Integer) obj;
        formatted = String.format("int %d", i);
    }
    else if (obj instanceof Long)
    {
        final Long l = (Long) obj;
        formatted = String.format("long %d", l);
    }
    else if (obj instanceof Double)
    {
        final Double d = (Double) obj;
        formatted = String.format("double %f", d);
    }
    else if (obj instanceof String)
    {
        final String s = (String) obj;
        formatted = String.format("String %s", s);
    }
    return formatted;
}
```

If we use Java 17 LTS or newer, the construct shown above can be written in a well-readable form using pattern matching and instanceof as follows:

```java
static String formattedNewStyle(Object obj)
{
    String formatted = "unknown";
    if (obj instanceof Integer i)
    {
        formatted = String.format("int %d", i);
    }
    else if (obj instanceof Long l)
    {
        formatted = String.format("long %d", l);
    }
    else if (obj instanceof Double d)
    {
        formatted = String.format("double %f", d);
    }
    else if (obj instanceof String s)
    {
        formatted = String.format("String %s", s);
    }
    return formatted;
}
```

As explained in the introduction, the situation would be significantly worse without pattern matching, as we would have to add a line with a cast and a variable definition for each type per `if` branch.

Although pattern matching with `instanceof` undoubtedly improves readability and reduces the number of lines, you should always keep in mind that similarly structured checks on custom types possibly indicate a violation of the Open–Closed Principle (OCP), one of the SOLID principles. Why? According to OCP, "software entities should be open for extension, but closed for modification." Although extensibility is provided here, the above `if` construct must be adapted for each new type to be supported or handled. Often, compliance with OCP can be achieved by defining and using a common base type and polymorphism. For the above example, an interface `Formatter` and type-specific implementations would be conceivable.

Pitfall

Please note that the defined variable cannot be named the same as the tested variable. Therefore, the following is not permitted:

```java
// ATTENTION: Compile error: Duplicate local variable obj
if (obj instanceof String obj && obj.length() > 5)
{
    System.out.println("Länge: " + obj.length());
}
```

As indicated in the listing, otherwise a compilation error will occur: "`Duplicate local variable obj`".

2.6 Extension in the `String` Class

The `String` class has existed since JDK 1.0 and has undergone only a few API changes since then. It was not until Java 11 LTS and 12 that a few methods were added. Finally, Java 15 introduced the `formatted()` method.

The `formatted()` Method

Since Java 15, strings offer a method `formatted()`. Functionally, it corresponds to the static method `String.format()`.

For demonstration purposes, we could define a minimalistic XML with the two placeholders `%d` and `%s` as follows:

```
jshell> var msg = "<count>%d</count><info>%s</info>"
msg ==> "<count>%d</count><info>%s</info>"
```

With modern Java, you can call `formatted()` directly on the string in a readable way:

```
jshell> msg.formatted(7, "is a nice number")
$44 ==> "<count>7</count><info>is a nice number</info>"
```

Before Java 15, replacing placeholders with numeric and text values was somewhat more cumbersome—this variant still works, but it is not as elegant:

```
jshell> String.format(msg, 7, "is a nice number")
$45 ==> "<count>7</count><info>is a nice number</info>"
```

Text Blocks in Combination with `formatted()`

Especially in combination with the Text Blocks already described in Sect. 2.1, `formatted()` can be used to fill placeholders in texts with appropriate values, as shown in the following example.

```java
public static void main(final String[] args)
{
    var name = "Jim";
    int age = 47;
    var hobbies = List.of("Java", "Movies", "Cycling");

    var textWithPlaceholders = """
                                Name: %s
                                Age: %d
                                Hobbies: %s""".formatted(name, age, hobbies);
    System.out.println(textWithPlaceholders);
}
```

Listing 2.4 Executable as "STRINGFORMATTEDEXAMPLE"

The program produces the following output:

```
Name: Jim
Age: 47
Hobbies: [Java, Movies, Cycling]
```

Performance of `formatted()` and `format()`

The widely respected Java expert Dr. Heinz Kabutz has conducted extensive research into strings and the performance of various operations, particularly concatenation. In his article in *Java Magazine* 5/2022, he shows that with Java 17 LTS, the `String.format()` method and thus also the `String.formatted()` method became three times faster. Interestingly, since Java 9, the simple "+" has generally been the most performant option for concatenating strings—apart from a few special cases in loops. In general, Heinz recommends programming as readable as possible, which is often best achieved with `String.format()` or `String.formatted()`.

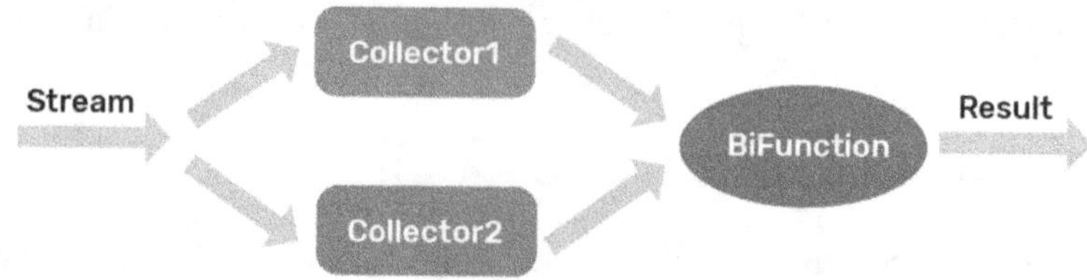

Fig. 2.1 Schematic operation of the teeing collector

2.7   Extensions in the Stream API

The Stream API was one of the most significant innovations in Java 8 LTS and has been extended in subsequent Java versions. For an introduction, please refer to Sect. 15.2.

Next, we will learn about three extensions in the Stream API: `teeing()`, `toList()`, and `mapMulti()`.

2.7.1   The `teeing()` Collector

The comprehensive Stream API features several predefined collectors, including `toCollection()`, `toList()`, `toSet()`, and `toMap()`. All of these convert the elements of a stream into the corresponding collection.

What is missing? To answer this question, let's look at some specific use cases. These include, for example, combining streams and processing values from a stream with multiple collectors. The former is called zipping and is unfortunately not (yet) available in the JDK. The latter is called teeing and has been part of the JDK since Java 12. The name, which may seem strange at first, comes from the English word for T-piece/connector. Figure 2.1 illustrates how it works.

Example 1

Let's assume we want to sum the numerical values of a stream in one go and also determine their total number. This functionality can be implemented relatively easily using the teeing collector and the two collectors `counting()` and `summingLong()`. The method `calcCountAndSum()` contains the realization of the functionality just described—using static imports of the collectors marked in bold increases readability:

```
import static java.util.stream.Collectors.*;

public static LongPair calcCountAndSum(final Stream<Integer> numbers)
{
    return numbers.collect(teeing(
                              counting(),
                              summingLong(n -> n),
                              (count, sum) -> new LongPair(count, sum)));
}
```

To define the result tuple, we use the records already introduced (see Sect. 2.3):

```
record LongPair(long count, long sum) { }
```

For comprehension purposes, two streams of numbers serve as input.

```
public static void main(final String[] args)
{
    System.out.println(calcCountAndSum(Stream.of(1, 2, 3, 4, 5, 6)));

    System.out.println(calcCountAndSum(Stream.of(2, 3, 5, 7, 11, 13, 17)));
}
```

Listing 2.5 Executable as "TEEINGCOLLECTOREXAMPLE"

The program TEEINGCOLLECTOREXAMPLE produces the following output:

```
LongPair[count=6, sum=21]
LongPair[count=7, sum=58]
```

Practical Alternative

Please note that before it was only an introductory example, the results of which could have been determined more easily using the `summarizingInt()`collector—even more elegantly on an `IntStream` by directly calling `summaryStatistics()`:

```
IntSummaryStatistics stats1 =
                Stream.of(1, 2, 3, 4).collect(summarizingInt(n -> n));
IntSummaryStatistics stats2 =
                IntStream.of(2, 3, 5, 7, 11, 13).summaryStatistics();
```

Do not forget the necessary (static) imports:

```
import java.util.*;
import static java.util.stream.Collectors.*;
```

Example 2

Let's make things more challenging: we want to filter out different elements from a stream of strings and then combine the results. The `toList()` collector originating from Java 8 LTS, the `filtering()` collector available since Java 9, and the `teeing()` collector introduced in Java 12 can help us accomplish this.

First, we define a `Stream<String>` with some names and two predicates for filtering. The first ensures that a string starts with "Mi". The second checks whether a string ends with the character "m". Finally, the result lists determined in this way are to be combined, for which we use a `BiFunction` that generates a list of lists and uses the collection factory methods.

```java
public static void main(final String[] args)
{
    var names = Stream.of("Michael", "Tim", "Tom", "Mike", "Bernd");

    final Predicate<String> startsWithMI = text -> text.startsWith("Mi");
    final Predicate<String> endsWithM = text -> text.endsWith("m");

    // Wouldn't var be preferable here? => see text
    final BiFunction<List<String>, List<String>, List<List<String>>>
        combineResults = (list1, list2) -> List.of(list1, list2);

    var result = names.collect(teeing(filtering(startsWithMi, toList()),
                                       filtering(endsWithM, toList()),
                                       combineLists));

    System.out.println(result);
}
```

Listing 2.6 Executable as "TEEINGINTROTWOFILTERS"

Before we look at the result, I would like to point out one detail: The rather extensive definition of the `combineLists` merge function, which is interspersed with various generics, seems to be a prime example of using `var` for syntactic shorthand. Unfortunately, as mentioned in Sect. 15.3.3, this is not possible due to the lack of type inference in lambdas.

Even though it is often helpful to extract a so-called explaining variable, in this particular case, it is advisable to use the lambda expression directly at the point of use to increase comprehensibility:

```java
var result = names.collect(teeing(filtering(startsWithMi, toList()),
                                   filtering(endsWithM, toList()),
                                   (list1, list2) -> List.of(list1, list2)));
```

Let's look at the result. When you run the program TEEINGINTROTWOFILTERS, you get the following output, which nicely shows the respective partial results as lists and then their combination:

```
[[Michael, Mike], [Tim, Tom]]
```

Figure 2.2 facilitates understanding of the process by attaching the partial results to the respective actions.

```
var names = Stream.of("Michael", "Tim", "Tom", "Mike", "Bernd");

final Predicate<String> startsWithMi = text -> text.startsWith("Mi");
final Predicate<String> endsWithM = text -> text.endsWith("m");

var result = names.collect(teeing(filtering(startsWithMi, toList()),
                           [Michael, Mike]
                           filtering(endsWithM, toList()),
                           [Tim, Tom]
                           (list1, list2) -> List.of(list1, list2));

System.out.println(result);   [[Michael, Mike], [Tim, Tom]]
```

Fig. 2.2 The teeing collector in action with partial results

2.7.2   The `toList()` Method as a Shortcut to the Collector

A common use case in practice is to prepare the results of various Stream API
actions as a list. Before Java 16, this required writing the rather cumbersome
`collect(Collectors.toList())`:

```
List<String> namesMi = Stream.of("Tim", "Tom", "Mike", "Michael").
                       filter(str -> str.startsWith("Mi")).
                       collect(Collectors.toList());
```

Conveniently, since Java 16, the method `toList()` provides a shortcut and a
more concise way to create a list from a stream:

```
List<String> namesMi = Stream.of("Tim", "Tom", "Mike", "Michael").
                       filter(str -> str.startsWith("Mi")).
                       toList();
```

This simplification makes it tempting to replace all old calls with the shorter,
more understandable new construct. However, please note that there is a small
but subtle difference: `collect(Collectors.toList())` creates a mutable list,
whereas `toList()` returns an immutable list. If the results are to be processed
further later on, the latter may be unfavorable.

Opinion: Spill the Beans
To this day, I still find it somewhat incomprehensible why the Stream API
offered the rather impractical `toArray()` method right from the start, but
unfortunately did not offer the `toList()` method, which is actually needed
all the time in everyday use—but fortunately, that is now a thing of the past.

2.7.3 The Intermediate Operation `mapMulti()`

Sometimes it can be challenging to use `flatMap()`; however, things become easier to grasp when thinking in terms of individual elements. Java 16 introduces the `mapMulti()` method as an alternative to `flatMap()` for intermediate operations.

Introductory Example

As an introductory example, let's consider a stream that contains a set of values represented as `Optional` (see Sect. 15.3.2). To prepare a consolidated result, all empty `Optional`s should be removed:

```
var searchResults = List.of(Optional.of("0"), Optional.empty(),
                            Optional.of("1"), Optional.of("2"),
                            Optional.empty(), Optional.empty(),
                            Optional.of("3"));
```

The task can be solved using the `flatMap()` method, but requires converting an `Optional` into a stream by calling `stream()`. Calling `flatMap()` flattens the stream of streams and removes the empty `Optional`s that have previously become empty streams:

```
// OLD
searchResults.stream().flatMap(Optional::stream).
                    forEach(System.out::println);
```

The conversion can be written a little more intuitively using the `mapMulti()` method as follows:

```
// NEW
searchResults.stream().mapMulti(Optional::ifPresent).
                    forEach(System.out::println);
```

The new approach is more in line with the idea of an imperative `for` loop:

```
for (Optional optElem : searchResults)
{
    optElem.ifPresent(System.out::println);
}
```

All three variants produce this sequence of numbers as a result:

```
0
1
2
3
```

Further Example: `expandIterables()`

Given a stream containing various elements, which may potentially also contain collections and `null` values:

```
jshell> var nestedValues = Stream.of(List.of(1, 2, 3), "ABC", null,
   ...>                               Set.of("X", "Y", "Z"))
nestedValues ==> java.util.stream.ReferencePipeline$Head@4f47d241
```

To expand our knowledge of `mapMulti()`, the elements from a potentially nested collection should be transferred to a flat stream. The desired result is as follows:[14]

```
[1, 2, 3, ABC, null, Z, Y, X]
```

The question now is: how do we implement this?

Conventional Variant Let us begin with the conventional Stream API. Implementing this approach requires a fairly deep understanding of the underlying helper classes and mechanisms, such as `java.util.stream.StreamSupport` and `spliterator()`. In short, only a small number of developers are likely to implement this quickly—I also found it somewhat challenging:

```
static Stream<Object> expandIterables(final Stream<Object> nestedValues)
{
    return nestedValues.flatMap(elem ->
    {
        if (elem instanceof Iterable<?> iterable)
        {
            // Trick to convert Iterable to Stream
            return StreamSupport.stream(iterable.spliterator(),
                                        nestedValues.isParallel());
        }
        return Stream.of(elem);
    });
}
```

When we execute this source code, we get the desired result:

```
jshell> expandIterables(nestedValues).toList()
$53 ==> [1, 2, 3, ABC, null, X, Y, Z]
```

But let's be honest, who would want to change anything in this particular process or would have been able to do so?

Modern Variant with `mapMulti()` Let's take a look at how we can implement the unpacking of nested collections with `mapMulti()`.

Let's start with the slightly more complex version of `expandIterables2()`, which calls a helper method `expandIterable()` in combination with `map-Multi()`. In the helper method, in the case of an `Iterable<T>`, a `for` loop and a

---

[14] By storing the letters in a set, there is no fixed order. Therefore, in the result, all elements must appear in no special order.

recursive call are used to unpack nested collections. Otherwise, processing is passed
to the `Consumer<Object>`:

```java
static Stream<Object> expandIterables2(Stream<Object> nestedValues)
{
    return nestedValues.mapMulti(MapMultiExample2::expandIterable);
}

static void expandIterable(Object elem, Consumer<Object> consumer)
{
    if (elem instanceof Iterable<?> iterable)
    {
        for (Object iter : iterable)
        {
            expandIterable(iter, consumer);
        }
    }
    else
    {
        consumer.accept(elem);
    }
}
```

Now we define initial data as multiple nested `Iterable<T>`s and use the above
method in the following `main()` method.

```java
public static void main(String[] args)
{
    var nestedValues = Stream.of(List.of(1, 2, 3), "ABC", null,
                                 Set.of("X", "Y", "Z"));
    Stream<Object> expandedStream = expandIterables2(nestedValues);
    System.out.println(expandedStream.toList());

    // freestyle multi nesting of sets
    var multiNestedValues = Stream.of(List.of(1, List.of(2, 3)), "ABC", null,
                                      Set.of("X", Set.of("Y", Set.of("Z"))));
    Stream<Object> expandedStream2 = expandIterables2(multiNestedValues);
    System.out.println(expandedStream2.toList());
}
```

Listing 2.7 Executable as "MAPMULTIEXAMPLE2"

Running the program MAPMULTIEXAMPLE2 produces the following output,
which shows that nested lists and sets are also correctly "flattened"—however, no
order is guaranteed when unpacking sets:

```
[1, 2, 3, ABC, null, X, Y, Z]
[1, 2, 3, ABC, null, Z, Y, X]
```

Multiple Nesting with the Conventional Variant Incidentally, the conventional
implementation shown initially is incapable of resolving multiple nesting—so it
is not only less intuitive, but also more functionally limited than the variant with
`mapMulti()`:

```
jshell> var multiNestedValues = Stream.of(List.of(1, List.of(2, 3)), "ABC",
   ...>                                    null,
   ...>                                    Set.of("X", Set.of("Y", Set.of("Z"))))
multiNestedValues ==> java.util.stream.ReferencePipeline$Head@306a30c7

jshell> expandIterables(multiNestedValues).toList()
$11 ==> [1, [2, 3], ABC, null, X, [Y, [Z]]]
```

Remedy
In fact, the restriction just mentioned can be remedied by a recursive call—as stated before, more detailed knowledge of streams is necessary to formulate the implementation. We skip the details to keep things simple.

2.8 Improvements to `NullPointerExceptions`

Uninitialized references can sometimes lead to a `NullPointerException` at runtime. In your career as a Java developer, you have probably already encountered one or two of these cases. The good news is that Java now offers better support for troubleshooting.

2.8.1 Introductory Examples

Let's look at a few simple examples to get started.

Example 1

The following class with an uninitialized variable in the `main()` method serves as a starting point—the error is obvious here.

```java
public class NPE_Example
{
    class A
    {
        String value;
    }

    public static void main(final String[] args)
    {
        A a = null;
        a.value = "ERROR";
    }
}
```

Listing 2.8 Executable as **"NPE_EXAMPLE"**

If we run this with an older Java version (or without activating this additional functionality), a `NullPointerException` returns the name of the Java file including the line number as context information, as follows:

```
Exception in thread "main" java.lang.NullPointerException
    at jvm.NPE_Example.main(NPE_Example.java:13)
```

This compact type of error logging is beneficial for simple constructs: errors can be roughly localized, but little further information is provided.

Thanks to improvements in `NullPointerExceptions`, we now receive much more detailed information about the cause of the exception:

```
Exception in thread "main" java.lang.NullPointerException: Cannot assign
    field "value" because "a" is null
    at jvm.NPE_Example.main(NPE_Example.java:13)
```

Adjustments at Program Launch To determine these details, this functionality must be activated using the JVM parameter `-XX:+ShowCodeDetailsIn-ExceptionMessages`. Since Java 15, this happens automatically. Otherwise, you should adjust the corresponding run configuration accordingly, as shown in Fig. 2.3 for an IntelliJ IDEA run configuration.

> **Note: Spill the Beans**
> To provide this helpful information, an extension to the JVM was necessary. To generate a dynamic error message with context information, the bytecode is analyzed, and the notes are generated based on this. The whole thing even works with nested method calls.

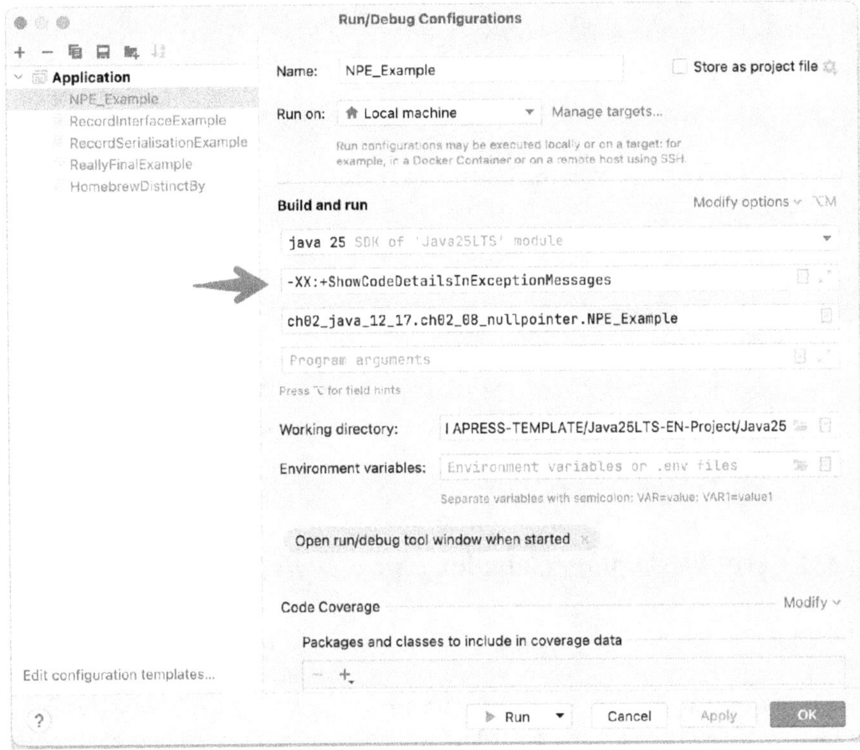

Fig. 2.3 Activating helpful information in the run configuration

Example 2

To supplement the introductory example, let's consider two additional actions that trigger errors. Below, we notice the access to an array deliberately initialized with null values and the unboxing of a null reference.

```java
public static void main(final String[] args)
{
    try
    {
        final String[] stringArray = { null, null, null };
        final int errorPos = stringArray[2].lastIndexOf("ERROR");
    }
    // In practice, please do not catch NullPointerException,
    // here only so that the following statements are executed
    catch (final NullPointerException e)
    {
        e.printStackTrace();
    }

    try
    {
        final Integer value = null;
        final int sum = value + 3;
```

```
    }
    catch (final NullPointerException e)
    {
        e.printStackTrace();
    }
}
```

Listing 2.9   Executable as "NPE_SECOND_EXAMPLE"

When accessing the array and auto-unboxing the `null` reference, helpful hints
are generated in each case:

```
java.lang.NullPointerException: Cannot invoke "String.lastIndexOf(String)"
    because "stringArray[2]" is null
  at jvm.NPE_Second_Example.main(NPE_Second_Example.java:10)
java.lang.NullPointerException: Cannot invoke "java.lang.Integer.intValue()"
    because "value" is null
  at jvm.NPE_Second_Example.main(NPE_Second_Example.java:22)
```

2.8.2   Troubleshooting Complex Expressions

With complex expressions, analyzing the actual cause of the error can be pretty
tricky, as it is often not obvious which part of an expression triggered the
`NullPointerException`. Consider source code such as the following, where it
is unclear without further analysis which variable was `null` or which call returned
`null` in the `NullPointerException`-triggering construct:

```
var red = getPreferences().getFavorites().getBkColor().getRed();
```

Such chains violate good object-oriented design, especially the so-called Law
of Demeter. It states that objects should only interact with objects that they know
directly or that they have created themselves. Nevertheless, those constructs are
(unfortunately) frequently seen in practice.

In such cases, it is desirable to have some additional information provided. The
innovation in Java described here achieves this.

> **Note: "." notation**
> Please do not confuse the concatenations shown above with the "." notation
> with recommended fluent APIs that work on their own or a directly associated
> object:
>
> ```
> new PizzaBuilder().withSalami().small().extraJalapenos().build();
> ```
>
> This facilitates the design process and understanding of systems.

Troubleshooting in Practice

Let's make the discussion a little more realistic and look at an example from everyday programming that uses chains with the "`.`" notation to access referenced objects.

```java
public static void main(final String[] args)
{
    int width = getWindowManager().getWindow(5).size().width();
    System.out.println("Width: " + width);
}
```

Listing 2.10   Executable as "NPE_THIRD_EXAMPLE"

In such chains, in combination with methods returning `null` or uninitialized attributes, `NullPointerExceptions` occur. Without contextual information, determining the causes was difficult in the past. With the new automatically generated informative error texts, troubleshooting is often significantly simplified:

```
Exception in thread "main" java.lang.NullPointerException: Cannot invoke "jvm
    .NPE_Third_Example$Window.size()" because the return value of "jvm.
    NPE_Third_Example$WindowManager.getWindow(int)" is null
    at jvm.NPE_Third_Example.main(NPE_Third_Example.java:7)
```

With this information, we can analyze the error more specifically, and the hints and context information facilitate the correction.

For the sake of completeness, let's take a look at the implementation of `get-Window()`, which deliberately returns the value `null` here to trigger the descriptive error message shown above. In particular, the records and methods used in the call shown above are also listed:

```java
public static class WindowManager
{
    public Window getWindow(final int i)
    {
        return null;
    }
}

public record Window(Size size) {};

public record Size(int width, int height) {};
```

Part II
Key Features in Java 18 to 21 LTS

Chapter 3
Key Features in Java 21 LTS at a Glance

Java 21 LTS (Long-Term Support) was released in September 2023, replacing its predecessor, Java 17 LTS, after approximately two years. In between, there were biannual releases in the form of Java 18, 19, and 20. Logically, one should not expect a multitude of new features from these interim releases. However, overall, a lot has changed since Java 17 LTS. In this chapter, I would like to provide an overview of the new features introduced cumulatively with Java 21 LTS, in the form of so-called JEPs (JDK Enhancement Proposals). The following chapters introduce the significant enhancements from Java 18 to Java 21 LTS in detail.

3.1 JEPs in Java 21 LTS at a Glance

Below, I list the JEPs included in Java 21 LTS to present an outline of the developments. Details on the JEPs can be found on the corresponding websites at https://openjdk.org/jeps/<nr>; you must then replace <nr> with the appropriate value. An overview is provided at https://openjdk.org/jeps/0.

Java 21 LTS contains the following 15 JEPs (8 final, 6 preview, 1 incubator)—preview and incubator features are marked in italics:

- *JEP 430: String Templates (Preview)*
- JEP 431: Sequenced Collections
- JEP 439: Generational ZGC
- JEP 440: Record Patterns
- JEP 441: Pattern Matching for switch
- *JEP 442: Foreign Function and Memory API (Third Preview)*
- *JEP 443: Unnamed Patterns and Variables (Preview)*
- JEP 444: Virtual Threads
- *JEP 445: Unnamed Classes and Instance Main Methods (Preview)*
- *JEP 446: Scoped Values (Preview)*

© The Author(s), under exclusive license to APress Media, LLC,
part of Springer Nature 2026
M. Inden, *Java 25 and Beyond*, https://doi.org/10.1007/979-8-8688-2385-5_3

- *JEP 448: Vector API (Sixth Incubator)*
- JEP 449: Deprecate the Windows 32-bit x86 Port for Removal
- JEP 451: Prepare to Disallow the Dynamic Loading of Agents
- JEP 452: Key Encapsulation Mechanism API
- *JEP 453: Structured Concurrency (Preview)*

In addition, the following final JEPs originate from Java versions 18–20:

- JEP 400: UTF-8 by Default
- JEP 408: Simple Web Server
- JEP 413: Code Snippets in Java API Documentation
- JEP 416: Reimplement Core Reflection with Method Handles
- JEP 418: Internet-Address Resolution SPI
- JEP 421: Deprecate Finalization for Removal
- JEP 422: Linux/RISC-V Port

Recap: Preview and Incubator Features A quick reminder: So-called preview features are fully specified and implemented. However, they are initially integrated into the JDK as a preview to gather experience and feedback. Based on the input received, fine-tuning will be conducted. In exceptional cases, the insights gained may also lead to the discontinuation of further development or a reorientation.

Incubator features are a preliminary stage to preview features and are implemented and provided in the form of corresponding modules. Here, too, the aim is to gather experience and feedback, but based on a preliminary implementation. With incubator features, things may still change fundamentally, or those functionalities may even be discontinued and removed at a later date.

Comments on the JEPs As with many other Java versions, it must be admitted that only some of the JEPs are of particular interest to software developers. Various things, such as JEP 408: Simple Web Server or JEP 422: Linux/RISC-V Port, are of rather marginal importance.

If you take a closer look, you will notice that various features are first released as previews and then appear in subsequent versions as follow-up previews, second, third, and so on, until they are finally incorporated into the JDK.

Sometimes features start as incubator features, then evolve into preview features, and are then finalized. This procedure applies, for example, to the Foreign Function and Memory API, which was a second incubator feature in Java 18, then became a preview feature in Java 19, and reached the final stage with Java 22. The JEPs for Structured Concurrency and Scoped Values are following a similar path.

One special case is the Vector API, which has already undergone various incubators and stayed there for quite some time—its finalization is awaiting the completion of Project Valhalla,[1] which focuses particularly on value objects and improvements in the use of primitive types.

---

[1] https://openjdk.org/projects/valhalla/.

Chapter 4
Syntax Innovations in JDK 18 to 21 LTS

This chapter describes the key new features from Java 18 to 21 LTS as a single unit, as enhancements from previous versions are also included in Java 21 LTS. The release of Java 21 LTS offers these interesting new features cumulatively—preview features are marked in italics:

- **JEP 430: String Templates (Preview)**: String Templates simplify the concatenation of variable and fixed text components into a result string. They were a welcome simplification that was removed from the JDK with Java 23. A revised specification is expected in the future.
- **JEP 440: Record Patterns**: This JEP introduces record patterns. They extend the possibilities of pattern matching for `instanceof` (see Sect. 2.5), which was part of Java 16. The goal of this new feature is to break down records into their components and access them easily.
- **JEP 441: Pattern Matching for `switch`**: Pattern matching was first integrated into the language in the context of `instanceof` (see Sect. 2.5). This feature avoids artificial helper variables and unsightly casts, making the source code clearer and easier to understand. Pattern matching also works in modern Java in `switch`. In particular, it can be combined with record patterns.
- **JEP 443: Unnamed Variables and Patterns (Preview)**: This JEP introduces the ability to replace a variable or multiple elements in an expression with a single underscore ("_") to mark them as unused and unusable.
- *JEP 445: Unnamed Classes and Instance Main Methods (Preview)*: This JEP can be considered both a syntax and a JVM innovation. Since this changes the way applications are executed, this JEP is described in Chap. 6 on the innovations in the JVM.

In the following sections, we examine the abovementioned syntax innovations in closer detail. We start with record patterns in Sect. 4.1 and then examine pattern matching in Sect. 4.2. Finally, in Sect. 4.3, we will look at the interesting extension that allows unused variables and components in record patterns to be marked with an underscore ("_").

© The Author(s), under exclusive license to APress Media, LLC, part of Springer Nature 2026
M. Inden, *Java 25 and Beyond*, https://doi.org/10.1007/979-8-8688-2385-5_4

4.1 JEP 440: Record Patterns

This JEP introduces Record Patterns as a final feature, extending pattern matching for `instanceof` (see Sect. 2.5). The goal of record patterns is to allow records to be broken down into their components in a declarative and easily understandable manner and to provide access to them. Record patterns can even be nested, enabling a powerful and combinable way of data navigation and processing.

4.1.1 Introduction

To demonstrate the innovation of record patterns, let's assume that a record for modeling a 2D point with x and y coordinates is defined as follows:

```
record Point(int x, int y) {}
```

Introductory Example

Let's first recall the pattern matching for `instanceof`—with this new feature, you can write a case distinction without casts as follows:

```
public void printCoordinateInfo(Object obj)
{
    Objects.requireNonNull(obj, "parameter 'obj' must not be null");

    if (obj instanceof Point point)
    {
        int x = point.x();
        int y = point.y();
        System.out.println("x: %d y: %d, sum: %d".formatted(x, y, x + y));
    }
    else
    {
        throw new IllegalArgumentException("Unsupported type: " +
                                    obj.getClass());
    }
}
```

What is the magic behind this? If the type check with `instanceof` is successful and thus evaluates to `true`, the binding variable `point` following the type specification, in this case `Point`, is automatically assigned and can then be used in the corresponding block. If the evaluation with `instanceof` returns the value `false`, the binding variable `point` is not initialized and the block is not executed.

Record Patterns As a Simplification A record pattern is structured similarly to the definition of a record (but without methods and others). It can follow an `instanceof` or a `case` to break down a record into its individual parts. The notation allows direct access to the attributes. In the following example, we utilize this to extract two attributes for the coordinates without having to call methods:

```java
public void printCoordinateInfoRecordPatterns(Object obj)
{
    Objects.requireNonNull(obj, "parameter 'obj' must not be null");

    if (obj instanceof Point(int x, int y))
    {
        System.out.println("x: %d, y: %d, sum: %d".formatted(x, y, x + y));
    }
    else
    {
        throw new IllegalArgumentException("Unsupported type: " +
                                           obj.getClass());
    }
}
```

What is the magic behind this? Suppose the evaluation with `instanceof` returns the value `true`. Then the assignment to a single record variable no longer occurs as before, but instead, the individual pattern components, in this case the variables, are initialized. Their names are independent of the names of the attributes in the definition of the record. However, it is advisable to keep the names quite similar to make it easier to understand. If the evaluation with `instanceof` returns the value `false`, the pattern variables are not initialized and the block is not executed.

Further Example

Let's briefly recap the options we have just learned about and define the following record to manage some information about a person—here deliberately using the wrapper `Boolean` instead of `boolean` so that we can discuss null safety later on:

```java
record Person(String name, int age, Boolean hasDrivingLicense) { }
```

We already know that records save some typing, for example, when used instead of self-written data container classes. This fact is particularly true thanks to the contract-compliant implementation of essential methods such as `equals()` and `hashCode()`. When using records, however, you will eventually need to access their components, such as the name or age in the example, for which records conveniently provide suitable access methods out of the box. The following method uses these and checks whether the person is allowed to drive a car. This verification uses pattern matching with `instanceof` and our record:

```java
public boolean isAllowedToDrive(Object obj)
{
    if (obj instanceof Person person)
    {
        return person.age() >= 18 && person.hasDrivingLicense();
    }
    return false;
}
```

Record Patterns As a Convenience In the example above, we see a type specification including a variable. To access the attributes of a record or subcomponents in the case of nested records, you must call the appropriate access methods and, if necessary, store their returns in local variables. As already mentioned, it is possible to omit these actions by specifying record patterns instead. With this knowledge, you can further simplify the helper method `isAllowedToDrive()`:

```java
public boolean isAllowedToDrive(Object obj)
{
    if (obj instanceof Person(String name, int age, var hasDrivingLicense))
    {
        return age >= 18 && hasDrivingLicense;
    }
    return false;
}
```

The example shows that the record pattern `Person(String name, int age, Boolean hasDrivingLicense)` facilitates access to the variables: in the query, the variable `age` can be used directly instead of calling `person.age()`. We will see later that the benefit is particularly evident with nested record patterns.

> **Note: Clean OO Design**
>
> In the previous example, accessing attributes is used only to illustrate pattern matching in combination with record patterns. A clean OO design would define the method `isAllowedToDrive()` in the record itself:
>
> ```java
> record Person(String name, int age, Boolean hasDrivingLicense)
> {
>     public boolean isAllowedToDrive()
>     {
>         return age >= 18 && hasDrivingLicense;
>     }
> }
> ```

Record Patterns and Null Safety

In practice, null safety is occasionally essential. It is especially true when you are careless with `null`. What should you keep in mind in general?

With `instanceof`, a `null` value never satisfies the check and is always evaluated to `false`. The same applies to record patterns and, also, to our specification `Person(String name, int age, Boolean hasDrivingLicense)`—if `instanceof` returns `false`, the pattern variables are not initialized:

```
jshell> isAllowedToDrive(null)
$3 ==> false
```

Let's now use a valid call:

```
jshell> isAllowedToDrive(new Person("Maria", 25, true))
$5 ==> true
```

But what happens if individual attributes are null? Let's use null for the driving license and once for the name:

```
jshell> isAllowedToDrive(new Person("Maria", 25, null))
|  Exception java.lang.NullPointerException: Cannot invoke "java.lang.Boolean
     .booleanValue()" because "<local3>" is null
|        at isAllowedToDrive (#11:4)
|        at (#12:1)

jshell> isAllowedToDrive(new Person(null, 52, true))
$13 ==> true
```

While the first call (naturally) results in a `NullPointerException` because the value of `hasDrivingLicense` is used in the method, we notice the following difference for the second call: Here, the name parameter is `null`. But the name is not used in the method. Therefore, a `null` value has no negative effect. The bottom line is that attributes with the value `null` do not affect pattern matching itself. Only the use of such an attribute will lead to a `NullPointerException`, as demonstrated above.

4.1.2   Nested Record Patterns

To introduce the topic of nested record patterns, I want to demonstrate that record patterns can be used to deconstruct record values in a nested manner. Specifically, it is permitted to use `var` for the types of variables. In addition, a record pattern is suitable for both `instanceof` and `case`.

Introductory Example

To understand deconstruction in record patterns, we assume that the following types are defined:

```
enum Color { RED, GREEN, BLUE }

record Point(int x, int y) {}
record GradientLine(ColoredPoint startPoint, ColoredPoint endPoint) {}
```

Let's assume we want to read and output different values for the `GradientLine` record. Initially, accessing only the color of the starting point is shown without record patterns:

```java
public void printColorOldStyle(GradientLine line)
{
    var startPoint = line.startPoint();
    if (startPoint != null)
    {
        System.out.println(startPoint.color());
    }
}
```

In practice, you will likely access several components, such as the x coordinate of the starting point and the color of the endpoint. Conventionally, this would look like the following, including various null checks:

```java
public void printXAndColorOldStyle(GradientLine line)
{
    var startPoint = line.startPoint();
    var endPoint = line.endPoint();

    if (startPoint != null && startPoint.point() != null && endPoint != null)
    {
        System.out.println("x: " + startPoint.point().x() +
                          " / color: " + endPoint.color());
    }
}
```

Record Patterns As a Convenience When specifying a record pattern, we can deconstruct other records within the pattern. Conveniently, this eliminates the need to navigate through the data manually. Instead, the record pattern automatically handles navigation, validation (ensuring != null), and assigning the desired variables—remember, the variable names specified there do not have to match the names of the attributes:

```java
public void printXAndColor(GradientLine line)
{
    if (rect instanceof GradientLine(ColoredPoint(Point(int x, int y),
                                                  Color color),
                                     ColoredPoint(Point point2,
                                                  Color color2)))
    {
        System.out.println("x: " + x + " / color: " + color2);
    }
}
```

With this `main()` method, we experience nested record patterns in action.

```java
void main()
{
    var startPoint = new ColoredPoint(new Point(7, 2), Color.RED);
    var endPoint = new ColoredPoint(new Point(23, 11), Color.GREEN);

    printXAndColorOldStyle(new GradientLine(startPoint, endPoint));
    printXAndColor(new GradientLine(startPoint, endPoint));
}
```

Listing 4.1 Executable as "NESTEDRECORDPATTERNSINTROEXAMPLE"

This output occurs twice:

```
x: 7 / color: GREEN
```

Further Example

Because nesting records is a useful feature, I will illustrate this with another example. We are all familiar with deeply nested `if` cascades, which ensure that all relevant subcomponents are not equal to `null` and that the required information is safely accessible.

The following records, which are assembled to form flight booking information, serve as the starting point for this example:

```java
record Person(String firstname, String lastname, LocalDate birthday) {}
record Phone(String areaCode, String number) {}
record City(String name, String country, String languageCode) {}

record FlightReservation(Person person, Phone phoneNumber,
                         City from, City destination) {}
```

Let us further assume that the task is to verify that the passenger's age is 18 or older based on their date of birth and that the language code of the destination is one of the valid values: EN, DE, or FR.

Conventional Implementation Without the use of record patterns, it would first be necessary to ensure that the reservation contains a valid person. Then it must be verified that a destination is specified. This enables the determination of a language code. Finally, the attributes are checked for `null` values to rule out incorrect initializations. However, `null` values in attributes should generally only be allowed in a few exceptional cases.

Let's now look at an exemplary implementation of nested queries of individual subcomponents and access to their attributes, an approach that you are probably familiar with from your own practice:

```java
public boolean checkAgeAndDestinationLanguageCorrectOld(final Object obj)
{
    if (obj instanceof FlightReservation)
    {
        var reservation = (FlightReservation) obj;
        if (reservation.person() != null)
        {
            var person = reservation.person();
            var birthday = person.birthday();

            if (reservation.destination() != null)
            {
                var destination = reservation.destination();
                var languageCode = destination.languageCode();

                if (birthday != null && languageCode != null)
                {
                    long years = ChronoUnit.YEARS.between(birthday,
                                            LocalDate.now());
                    return years >= 18 &&
                            Set.of("EN", "DE", "FR").contains(languageCode);
                }
            }
        }
    }
    return false;
}
```

Let's try this method with a few valid and invalid calls. We'll start with the following definitions of people:

```
jshell> import java.time.*

jshell> import java.time.temporal.*

jshell> var michael = new Person("Michael", "Inden", LocalDate.of(1971, 2, 7))

jshell> var julia = new Person("Julia", "Kern", LocalDate.of(2018, 4, 6))

jshell> var invalidBirthday = new Person("NOT", "AVAILABLE", null)
```

The information for telephone and departure is not relevant, so we could exceptionally assign `null` to them here. However, it is better to define dummy objects, which is why we use this variant:

```
jshell> var dummyPhone = new Phone("0041", "79 1234567")

jshell> var dummyFrom = new City("Zurich", "Switzerland", "DE")

jshell> var toSF = new City("San Francisco", "USA", "US")

jshell> var toParis = new City("Paris", "France", "FR")
```

Now we are ready to define the following flights:

```
jshell> var flight_Paris_Mi = new FlightReservation(michael, dummyPhone,
                                               dummyFrom, toParis)

jshell> var flight_Paris_Ju = new FlightReservation(julia, dummyPhone,
                                               dummyFrom, toParis)

jshell> var flight_SF_Mi = new FlightReservation(michael, dummyPhone,
                                               dummyFrom, toSF)

jshell> var flight_Paris_IV = new FlightReservation(invalidBirthday,
     dummyPhone,                                   dummyFrom, toParis)
```

In the subsequent flight checks, only the first should be valid; in the second, the
passenger is too young; in the third, US is not a valid language code; and in the
fourth, the date of birth is missing:

```
jshell> checkAgeAndDestinationLanguageCorrectOld(flight_Paris_Mi)
$58 ==> true

jshell> checkAgeAndDestinationLanguageCorrectOld(flight_Paris_Ju)
$59 ==> false

jshell> checkAgeAndDestinationLanguageCorrectOld(flight_SF_Mi)
$60 ==> false

jshell> checkAgeAndDestinationLanguageCorrectOld(flight_Paris_IV)
$61 ==> false
```

Interim Solution with Pattern Matching   To avoid all the nested if queries, as
of Java 17 LTS, you could make extensive use of the pattern matching described in
Sect. 2.5 to check all relevant subcomponents for the correct type. In addition, the
check with instanceof automatically fails if such a component is null:

```java
public boolean checkAgeAndDestinationLanguageCorrectOld(final Object obj)
{
    if (obj instanceof FlightReservation reservation &&
            reservation.person() instanceof Person person &&
            person.birthday() instanceof LocalDate birthday &&
            reservation.destination() instanceof City destination &&
            destination.languageCode() instanceof String languageCode)
    {
        long years = ChronoUnit.YEARS.between(birthday, LocalDate.now());
        return years >= 18 && Set.of("EN", "DE", "FR").contains(languageCode)
            ;
    }
    return false;
}
```

Record Patterns As a Simplification   With nested record patterns, we rewrite the
cascade of ifs shown above more compactly and understandably, even if it may
seem a little unfamiliar at first. We use record patterns when we need to access

attributes and pure pattern matching for subcomponents that are not relevant to the query:

```java
public boolean checkAgeAndDestinationLanguageCorrectNew(final Object obj)
{
    if (obj instanceof FlightReservation(
            Person(String firstname, String lastname, LocalDate birthday),
            Phone phoneNumber,
            City from,
            City(String name, String country, String languageCode)))
    {
        if (birthday != null && languageCode != null)
        {
            long years = ChronoUnit.YEARS.between(birthday, LocalDate.now());
            return years >= 18 &&
                    Set.of("EN", "DE", "FR").contains(languageCode);
        }
    }
    return false;
}
```

Note: Possible Extension for Practical Use

In the case of Boolean return values, it can be helpful in practice to provide additional information. For this purpose, various error codes could be defined as enums, for example, and an error text could also be provided. A result record could be described as follows—since we are primarily concerned with record patterns here, we will not pursue this variant further:

```java
record ReservationResult(Errorcode result, String hint) {}
```

Overall, it becomes clear that significantly fewer `if` queries and `null` checks are necessary: in addition, the check with `instanceof` automatically fails if one of the record components is `null`, that is, `Person` or city (`Destination`). Please note that the attributes of the records are not secured in this way and may still need to be checked for `null`. However, if you get into the good habit of avoiding `null` as the value of parameters in calls, you can even dispense with `null` checks.

Let's examine the four calls, all of which yield the same results as the conventional implementation. Ideally, now would be the time to think about writing some unit tests—but due to the scope of this book, I will refrain from doing so here:

```
jshell> checkAgeAndDestinationLanguageCorrectNew(flight_Paris_Mi)
$64 ==> true

jshell> checkAgeAndDestinationLanguageCorrectNew(flight_Paris_Ju)
$65 ==> false

jshell> checkAgeAndDestinationLanguageCorrectNew(flight_SF_Mi)
$66 ==> false

jshell> checkAgeAndDestinationLanguageCorrectNew(flight_Paris_IV)
$67 ==> false
```

> **Note: " Don't care" Parameters**
>
> Another thing you might desire are " don't care" parameters. What do I mean by that? For example, you may not want to access the person's first or last name. The same applies to the phone number and the attributes in the destination. The following example shows a notation form, where _dc stands for " don't care" and is initially only a naming convention:

```java
if (obj instanceof FlightReservation(
        Person(var _dc_firstname, var _dc_lastname,
            LocalDate birthday),
        var _dc_phone, var _dc_from,
        City(var _dc_name, var _dc_country, String languageCode)))
```

Remedies in Modern Java   JEP 443, called " Unnamed Patterns and Variables (Preview)," already allows local variables, variables in record patterns, and even parts of a pattern to be marked as unused in Java 21 LTS by noting an underscore ("_") (see Sect. 4.3). This extension was finalized in Java 22 as JEP 456 called " Unnamed Variables and Patterns" (see Sect. 9.1).

The following example provides a first impression:

```java
if (obj instanceof FlightReservation(
        Person(_, _, LocalDate birthday),
        _, _,
        City(_, _, String languageCode)))
```

4.1.3   Type Inference for Generic Record Patterns

It is possible to use generics in record patterns. However, up to and including Java 19, the diamond operator (<>) could not be used there; instead, explicit type specifications were required. Java 20 introduced a syntax shortcut, and in Java 21 LTS, type inference was further enhanced.

Example

For this quick start, we will use the following type definitions for our examples, specifically one interface and two records:

```java
interface Container<T> {}

record Tuple<T>(T t1, T t2) implements Container<T> {}

record Triple<T>(T t1, T t2, T t3) implements Container<T> {}
```

Let's consider a query for Java 19 that uses generics in record patterns. For nested structures, this notation with type specification in <> is somewhat more difficult to read:

```java
public void nestedOld(Container<Tuple<String>> container)
{
    if (container instanceof Tuple<Tuple<String>>(Tuple(var s1, var s2),
                                                  Tuple(var s3, var s4)))
    {
        System.out.println("Tuple of strings " +
                           String.join("/", List.of(s1, s2, s3, s4)));
    }
    else
    {
        System.out.println("Container " + container);
    }
}
```

Improvements in Java 21 LTS

Since Java 21 LTS, type inference has been so good that in every case, even with nesting, the attributes can be defined as var and specific functionalities of the attributes are still accessible, as shown below for toLowerCase(), toUpper-Case(), length(), and repeat():

```java
if (container instanceof Tuple(Tuple(var s1, var s2),
                              Tuple(var s3, var s4)))
{
    System.out.println("Tuple of strings " +
                       String.join("/", List.of(s1.toLowerCase(),
                                                s2.toUpperCase(),
                                                s3.repeat(s3.length()),
                                                s4)));
}
```

While the old syntax works fine in Java 20 or Java 21 LTS, the new syntax causes the error message "raw deconstruction patterns are not allowed".

Opinion: Strange Syntax

In my opinion, it would have been more consistent to use a syntax similar to that of the diamond operator. However, the following results in a compilation error with the comment " Invalid type start".

```java
if (container instanceof Tuple<>(var s1, var s2))
{
    System.out.println("Tuple: " + s1 + ", " + s2);
}
else if (container instanceof Triple<>(var s1, var s2, var s3))
{
    System.out.println("Triple: " + s1 + ", " + s2 + ", " + s3);
}
```

4.1.4 Summary

Finally, I would like to briefly recap the language features Pattern Matching and, in particular, Record Patterns: Record patterns allow you to access and read the values of attributes of a record without explicitly calling access methods. There were three ways to apply pattern matching to records—in Java 21 LTS, only the first two are supported:

1. Pattern matching—access via variables and accessor methods
2. Record pattern—decomposition of the record into individual components
3. Named record pattern—combination of (1) and (2) (Java 19 only)

The two relevant variants are indicated in the following source code excerpt:

```java
record StringListStringPair(String name, List<String> values) {}

var obj = new StringListStringPair("Michael", List.of("Java", "Python"));

// 1. Pattern Matching
if (obj instanceof StringListStringPair pair)
{
    System.out.println("object is a StringListStringPair, name = " +
                    pair.name() + ", values = " + pair.values());
}

// 2. Record Pattern
if (obj instanceof StringListStringPair(String name, List<String> values))
{
    System.out.println("object is a StringListStringPair, " +
                    "name = " + name + ", values = " + values);
}
```

4.2 JEP 441: Pattern Matching for `switch`

Java 16 introduced pattern matching for `instanceof`. It enables the acceptance of a so-called type pattern and performing pattern matching. This eliminates the need for tedious casts. We have seen this impressively demonstrated in Sect. 2.5. In addition, as part of the introduction of Switch Expressions (see Sect. 2.2), the syntax now allows omitting the specification of `default` if the compiler detects complete coverage for enums or sealed types.

First, let's take a quick look back at Java 17 LTS, for which the first version of pattern matching for `switch` was introduced as a preview feature. Recapitalizing makes it easier to understand and follow the gradual development and refinement in subsequent Java versions. The improvements mainly relate to dominance checking, completeness analysis, and the ability to specify record patterns.

4.2.1 Simple Pattern Matching with Java 17 LTS (Preview)

Let's briefly recap: without activated preview features, Java 17 LTS limited you in a `switch` statement to the types `byte`, `short`, `char`, and `int`, the corresponding wrapper classes, as well as enums and strings.

As a starting point, let's consider several type checks with `instanceof`. These are necessary when you want to perform different actions based on the type of an object, and it is impossible to simplify things using a common base class and polymorphism: a construct consisting of `if`, `else if`, and `else` is often used as a workaround. For demonstration purposes only, the first `if` uses the old style, and the other queries use pattern matching for `instanceof`:

```java
public String typeBasedAction(Object obj)
{
    // It's unfortunate that you can't query specific generics.
    if (obj instanceof List)
    {
        final List<?> things = (List<?>)obj;
        return "A List of things with size: " + things.size();
    }
    else if (obj instanceof Map map)
    {
        return "A Map containing these keys: " + map.keySet();
    }
    else if (obj instanceof int[] ints)
    {
        return "Processing int array: " + Arrays.toString(ints);
    }
    else if (obj instanceof String str)
    {
        return "This is a string with content: " + str;
    }
    else
    {
        return "This is something else.";
    }
}
```

Unfortunately, as shown before, generic specifications such as `List<String>` are not permitted due to type erasure. Instead, they lead to error messages such as `"'Object' cannot be safely cast to 'List<String>'"`.

Java 17 LTS Preview Features: Pattern Matching in `switch`

As already mentioned, before Java 17 LTS, only a few data types, among others `int`, `String`, or `enum`, could be used in the `cases` in a `switch`.

Java 17 LTS offers more possibilities with this preview feature because it allows you to specify a type pattern. This enables elegant, shorter, and more concise case distinctions.

Simple Pattern Matching   The syntax changes in Java 17 LTS allow us to write the above queries in a more readable, shorter, and more straightforward way, as follows:

```java
public String typeBasedActionWithSwitch(Object obj)
{
    return switch (obj)
    {
        // It's unfortunate that you can't query specific generics.
        case List things -> "A List of things with size: " + things.size();
        case Map<?,?> map -> "A Map containing these keys: " + map.keySet();
        case String str -> "This is a string with content: " + str;
        case int[] ints -> "Processing int array: " + Arrays.toString(ints);
        default -> "This is something else.";
    };
}
```

Please note again that it is impossible for type checks to use specific generic types like List<String> and List<Person> and to treat them differently.

For both examples, please note one more detail: In some cases, a declaration similar to this one is used: case List things. However, this results in a raw type, which means that, in theory, modifying actions are also possible on the respective collection. To avoid such problems, use a generic specification, such as the one shown for the map, that is, Map<?,?> map.

Pattern Matching with Conditions   Analogous to `instanceof`, you can specify conditions in the `case`s such as the following:

```java
public void processData(Object obj)
{
    switch (obj)
    {
        case String str && str.startsWith("V1") ->
            System.out.println("Processing V1");
        case String str && str.startsWith("V2") ->
            System.out.println("Processing V2");
        case Integer i && i > 10 && i < 100 ->
            System.out.println("Processing ints");
        default -> throw new IllegalArgumentException("invalid input");
    }
}
```

However, due to these fine-grained case distinctions, it is essential to note that, theoretically and practically, several `case`s may fulfill the condition—namely, whenever the expression specified there evaluates to `true`.

Dominance Check   To avoid problems, the more specific case must be handled before the more general one. Why? Otherwise, the more general case would always override or dominate the more specific one, and the more specific one would never be executed. Therefore, this should be recognized during compilation and result in an error. Let's look at the situation for the previous method, to which we add a `case CharSequence cs` as a more general case at the very top:

```java
// Attention: Java 17 LTS preview example
public void processDataWithDominance(Object obj)
{
    switch (obj)
    {
        case CharSequence cs -> System.out.println("Processing CharSequence")
            ;
        case String str && str.startsWith("V1") ->
            System.out.println("Processing V1");
        case String str && str.startsWith("V2") ->
            System.out.println("Processing V2");
        case Integer i && i > 10 && i < 100 ->
            System.out.println("Processing ints");
        default -> throw new IllegalArgumentException("invalid input");
    }
}
```

In fact, as a result, we get the error "Label is dominated by a preceding case label 'CharSequence cs'" for both lines starting with case String. In newer versions of Java, minor changes have been made to conditions and dominance checking. Details will follow later.

Special Case: Handling of null Before Java 17 LTS, it was not possible to specify the value null in the cases of a switch. For this reason, in practice, special handling was sometimes required in the form of an explicit check using an if beforehand. Leaving unhandled, a NullPointerException in the switch was the result, provided that the value null was passed to the switch:

```java
// Attention: Old-style variant
public void switchSpecialNullSupport(String str)
{
    if (str == null)
    {
        System.out.println("special handling for null");
        return;
    }

    switch (str)
    {
        case "Java", "Python" -> System.out.println("cool language");
        default -> System.out.println("everything else");
    }
}
```

With Java 17 LTS and preview features enabled, we can consistently specify null values in switch and simplify and standardize the entire construct as follows:

```java
// Note: Java 17 LTS preview example and Java 21 LTS variant
public void switchSupportingNull(String str)
{
    var output = switch (str)
    {
        case null -> "null is allowed in preview";
        case "Java", "Python" -> "cool language";
        default -> "everything else";
    };
    System.out.println(output);
}
```

Improvements Since Java 17 LTS

All in all, pattern matching has been further developed since Java 17 LTS in various JEPs covering the following topics, which are described in more detail in the subsequent subsections:

- Adjustments to the specification of conditions (guarded patterns)
- Improvement of the dominance check
- Correction of the completeness analysis
- Specification of record patterns
- Qualified enums

You may not be familiar with terms such as completeness analysis or qualified enums at this point. I will explain these briefly now and illustrate them later with examples in the respective subchapter on the extensions to switch.

Completeness Analysis The completeness analysis checks whether all possible paths are covered by the cases within a switch. This is easily possible for enums, for example. For types such as int, it can at least be determined that a default must be specified.

Qualified Enums Up to and including Java 20, it was syntactically only allowed to write case ABC for a switch over an enum, such as MyEnum with the values ABC and DEF. However, specifying the qualified name, such as case MyEnum.ABC, was not allowed. This becomes possible with Java 21 LTS.

4.2.2   Adjustments to the Specification of Conditions (Guarded Patterns)

When specifying conditions in case in switch, the so-called guarded patterns have undergone some fine-tuning since Java 17 LTS. As shown previously, the regular && operator was initially used to specify conditions:

```
// ATTENTION: Java 17 LTS syntax, not valid any longer
case String str && str.startsWith("INFO") -> System.out.println("an info");
```

With Java 19, the keyword when was introduced for this purpose:

```
case String str when str.startsWith("INFO") -> System.out.println("an info");
```

Please note that this change leads to an inconsistency: the syntax for specifying conditions in switch and instanceof differs slightly—in switch using when and in instanceof using &&.

Note: Special Keyword when

The introduction of new keywords potentially creates problems with backward compatibility. For when, there is a concern that a definition from older program code, such as

```
Object when = "APPOINTMENT-TIME: 16:17:18";
```

would no longer compile. However, conveniently, when is only reserved locally in the context of switch directly after the name in the type declaration and can be used as an identifier otherwise. Thus, there is no breaking change effect.

For fun, you can enter the following definition in the JShell:

```
jshell> Object when = "APPOINTMENT-TIME: 16:17:18";
when ==> "APPOINTMENT-TIME: 16:17:18"
```

Then you write a switch for it:

```
jshell> switch (when)
   ...> {
   ...>       case String when when when.startsWith("APPOINTMENT") ->
   ...>                            System.out.println("Keep it private
         :-)");
   ...>       case Integer val when val > 1000 ->
   ...>                            System.out.println("value > 1000");
   ...>       default -> System.out.println("something else");
   ...> }
Keep it private :-)
```

Linking Multiple Conditions

In practice, it is often necessary to check multiple conditions. Only the first part is introduced with when, and linked conditions are then connected using && or | |.

Below, we check whether a string begins with the abbreviation INFO: and contains more than 40 or 10 characters. Based on this, the abbreviation is then truncated, and in the case of longer texts, a portion of the remainder is also extracted. If neither of these conditions applies, the string is converted to lowercase:

```
public void multipleConditionsExample(String input)
{
    switch (input)
    {
        case String str when str.startsWith("INFO:") && str.length() > 40 ->
            System.out.println("Long Info: " + str.substring(5, 20));
        case String str when str.startsWith("INFO:") && str.length() > 10 ->
            System.out.println(str.substring(5));
        case String str -> System.out.println(str.toLowerCase());
    }
}
```

If we call the above method with inputs specifically selected for each case, we get the following outputs as expected:

```
jshell> multipleConditionsExample("INFO:Java 21 rocks")
Java 21 rocks

jshell> multipleConditionsExample("INFO:Java 21 rocks !!!
    xxxxxxxxxxxxxxxxxxxxx")
Long Info: Java 21 rocks !

jshell> multipleConditionsExample("MICHAEL")
michael
```

Checking Multiple Conditions with || In addition to the AND (&&) operator used here to link the conditions, it is also possible to use an OR (||) operator after when:

```java
public void multipleConditionsWithOrExample(String input)
{
    switch (input)
    {
        case String str when str.startsWith("INFO") ||
                             str.startsWith("WARN") ->
            System.out.println("Info or Warning");
        case String str when str.startsWith("ERROR") ||
                             str.startsWith("FATAL") ->
            System.out.println("Error or Fatal");
        case String str -> System.out.println("Something else");
    }
}
```

Once again, we call the above method with selected inputs. As expected, the following outputs are generated:

```
jshell> multipleConditionsWithOrExample("INFO")
Info or Warning

jshell> multipleConditionsWithOrExample("WARN")
Info or Warning

jshell> multipleConditionsWithOrExample("ERROR")
Error or Fatal

jshell> multipleConditionsWithOrExample("FATAL")
Error or Fatal

jshell> multipleConditionsWithOrExample("Michael")
Something else
```

Special Case: Description of Value Ranges with `switch`

Below, we examine one way to cover values and value ranges using `switch`. As an example, we query various cases for a variable `value` of type `Integer`. First, a few fixed values are checked, then the remaining values from the positive value range, and, finally, the leftover values:

```java
public void specialCasesAndRanges(Integer value)
{
    switch (value)
    {
        case 1, 2, 3 -> System.out.println("Special cases i: 1, 2 or 3");
        case Integer i when i > 3 -> System.out.println("i > 3");
        case Integer i -> System.out.println("all remaining int, i: " + i);
    }
}
```

For this example, we also use selected inputs for each case to verify the functionality. As expected, the following outputs are generated:

```
jshell> specialCasesAndRanges(2)
Special cases i: 1, 2 or 3

jshell> specialCasesAndRanges(71)
i > 3

jshell> specialCasesAndRanges(-13)
all remaining int, i: -13
```

4.2.3   Improvement of the Dominance Check

If several patterns match an input, the one that fits best is referred to as the dominant pattern. The dominance check ensures that this pattern is placed before the more general pattern(s), because otherwise the more specific case would never be evaluated. Let's take a closer look at this below.

Introductory Example

Let's assume that we accidentally ignored dominance when specifying various checks on type `String` and wrote the following variant of the method shown in the introduction, which first checks for `case String str` and then for `case String str when str.length() > 5`:

```java
public void dominanceExample(Object obj)
{
    switch (obj)
    {
        case String str -> System.out.println(str.toLowerCase());
        case String str when str.length() > 5 -> System.out.println(str);
        default -> throw new IllegalArgumentException("Unsupported Type");
    }
}
```

In the example, the shorter pattern `String str` dominates the longer `String str when str.length() > 5` specified after it, because the former is more general. Thus, the latter never comes into play.

In Java 17 LTS, this flaw remained undetected and only became apparent at runtime through unexpected behavior. Java 21 LTS provides a remedy and includes a correction in the dominance check. Therefore, the above source code results in a compilation error:

```
Error:
this case label is dominated by a preceding case label
    case String str when str.length() > 5 -> System.out.println(str);
         ^---------^
```

4.2.4 Special Case: Constants

Although the reasoning behind the cases of dominance is easy to understand, there is another detail to consider. If a constant is used instead of a general type specification, the constant must be checked first.

Let's consider the following method as an example:

```java
public void dominanceExampleWithConstant(Object obj)
{
    switch (obj.toString())
    {
        case String str when str.length() > 5 -> System.out.println(str);
        case "Sophie" -> System.out.println("My lovely daughter");
        default -> System.out.println("FALLBACK");
    }
}
```

Although this construct semantically makes no sense, since the upper case completely covers the middle case, it is syntactically allowed. However, the IDEs indicate that the branch with the constant is unreachable.

Semantically, only the variant shown below with the string literal before the expression makes sense—however, you must take care to adhere to this yourself:

```java
public void dominanceExampleWithConstant(Object obj)
{
    switch (obj.toString())
    {
        case "Sophie" -> System.out.println("My lovely daughter");
        case String str when str.length() > 5 -> System.out.println(str);
        default -> System.out.println("FALLBACK");
    }
}
```

Special Characteristic of Guarded Patterns

Both the specification of conditions with guarded patterns and the dominance check are relatively easy to understand once you get used to them. I want to highlight one notable aspect: the dominance check only applies to the front part, that is, the type, and can only ensure that a type specification and a condition are listed in the correct order. When specifying conditions of varying levels of strictness, developers must be careful to respect the correct ordering. For ease of understanding, the method shown at the beginning of Sect. 4.2.2 is repeated here:

```java
public void multipleConditionsExample(String input)
{
    switch (input)
    {
        case String str when str.startsWith("INFO:") && str.length() > 40 ->
            System.out.println("Long Info: " + str.substring(5, 20));
        case String str when str.startsWith("INFO:") && str.length() > 10 ->
            System.out.println(str.substring(5));
        case String str -> System.out.println(str.toLowerCase());
    }
}
```

If we were to bring the most general case to the top

```java
public void multipleConditionsExampleWrong1(String input)
{
    switch (input)
    {
        case String str -> System.out.println(str.toLowerCase());
        case String str when str.startsWith("INFO:") && str.length() > 40 ->
            System.out.println("Long Info: " + str.substring(5, 20));
        case String str when str.startsWith("INFO:") && str.length() > 10 ->
            System.out.println(str.substring(5));
    }
}
```

the following compilation errors would occur (shown here as an example for the JShell):

```
|  Error:
|    this case label is dominated by a preceding case label
|        case String str when str.startsWith("INFO:") && str.length() > 40 ->
|             ^---------^
|  Error:
|    this case label is dominated by a preceding case label
|        case String str when str.startsWith("INFO:") && str.length() > 10 ->
|             ^---------^
```

However, the situation differs if we swap the two instructions with the conditions:

```java
public void multipleConditionsExample(String input)
{
    switch (input)
    {
        case String str when str.startsWith("INFO:") && str.length() > 10 ->
            System.out.println(str.substring(5));
        case String str when str.startsWith("INFO:") && str.length() > 40 ->
            System.out.println("Long Info: " + str.substring(5, 20));
        case String str -> System.out.println(str.toLowerCase());
    }
}
```

Java accepts this silently, and unfortunately, unexpected actions occur in the second call:

```
jshell> multipleConditionsExample("INFO:Java 21 rocks")
Java 21 rocks

jshell> multipleConditionsExample("INFO:Java 21 rocks !!!
    xxxxxxxxxxxxxxxxxxxx")
Java 21 rocks !!!xxxxxxxxxxxxxxxxxxxx

jshell> multipleConditionsExample("MICHAEL")
michael
```

> **Attention: No Evaluation of Conditions**
> When specifying conditions, always remember that, as a developer, you are responsible for ensuring they are specified correctly. Similar to the above, multiple subcriteria specified with && would not be considered in the dominance check integrated into Java.

4.2.5 Improvement of Completeness Analysis

The completeness analysis, that is, the check whether the cases within a switch cover all possible input values, still contained a bug for sealed types in Java 17 LTS. As a quick reminder: Sealed types allow you to control inheritance (more precisely, subtype relationships) and specify which types can extend a base type. For more detailed information, please refer to the information box below.

> **Note: Sealed Types in a Nutshell**
> The keyword sealed prevents or controls inheritance. The keyword permits allows the permitted direct subtypes to be listed. If classes, records, enums, or interfaces other than the specified types attempt to extend or implement a sealed type (class or interface), this results in a compilation error. As a unique option, the keyword non-sealed allows you to offer an extension option.

Let's return to the actual problem: still with Java 17 LTS, the completeness analysis incorrectly returned the error message "the switch statement does not cover all possible input values", even if all cases were described by a case (Fig. 4.1).

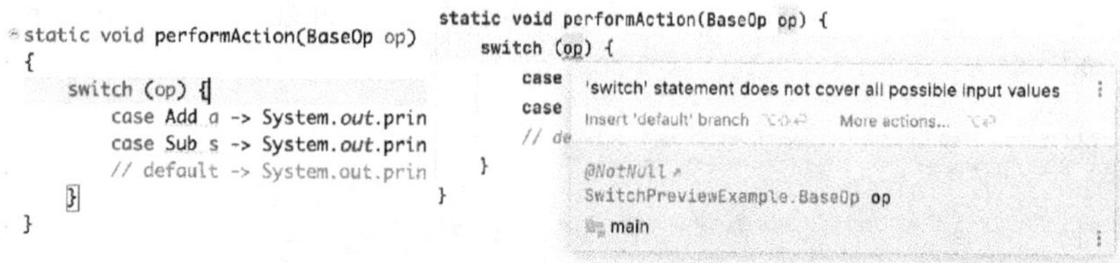

Fig. 4.1 Error message during completeness analysis with Java 17 LTS

With modern Java 21 LTS, it is no longer necessary to specify `default`; instead, you can write the following in a shorter and more precise way:

```java
static void performAction(final BaseOp op)
{
    switch (op)
    {
        case Add add -> System.out.println(add);
        case Sub sub -> System.out.println(sub);
    }
}
```

For a better understanding, let's take a look at the class hierarchy of the two mathematical operators **Add** and **Sub** and their base type `BaseOp`:

```java
static sealed abstract class BaseOp permits Add, Sub {}

static final class Add extends BaseOp {}
static final class Sub extends BaseOp {}
```

4.2.6   Specifying Record Patterns

As is well known, with Java 17 LTS (without activated preview features), the type in a `switch` is limited to primitive values (`byte`, `short`, `int`, and `char`), wrapper classes (`Byte`, `Short`, `Integer`, and `Character`), as well as enums and strings. Java 17 LTS only allows simple pattern matching, but not combined with record patterns, since these were introduced later and got finalized in Java 21 LTS (see Sect. 4.1). As a new feature, Java 21 LTS allows you to use record patterns to break down records into individual components during pattern matching directly.

The following example illustrates this for specifying conditions and breaking down an item into its individual components. Let's first define a record and an enum as types:

```java
record Pos3D(int x, int y, int z) {}

enum RgbColor {RED, GREEN, BLUE}
```

Now we create a method that demonstrates record patterns and pattern matching in `switch`. With the help of record patterns, we have direct access to the values, which is particularly evident in `case Pos3D(int x, int y, int z) when y > 0`. Here, the combination with `when` for querying a condition is used:

```java
public void simpleRecordPattern(final Object obj)
{
   switch (obj)
   {
      case Pos3D(int x, int y, int z) when y > 0 ->
         System.out.println("decomposed: " + x + ", " + y + ", " + z);
      default -> System.out.println("Something else");
   }
}
```

Such queries in `switch` can also be made more comprehensive:

```java
public void recordPatternsAndMatching(final Object obj)
{
   switch (obj)
   {
      // Pattern matching
      case RgbColor color when color == RgbColor.RED ->
         System.out.println("RED WARNING");
      case RgbColor color -> System.out.println("Enum: " + color);
      case Pos3D pos when pos.z() == 0 ->
         System.out.println("Record: " + pos);

      // Record pattern
      case Pos3D(int x, int y, int z) when y > 0 ->
         System.out.println("decomposed: " + x + ", " + y + ", " + z);
      default -> System.out.println("Something else");
   }
}
```

Type Arguments for Generic Patterns and Record Patterns in `switch`

Let's consider the following record as an example of generic patterns, which includes a method that utilizes various record patterns in combination with generics. Java 19 forces us to implement it as follows:

```java
record MyPair<T1, T2>(T1 first, T2 second) {}

public void recordInferenceJdk19(MyPair<String, Integer> pair)
{
   switch (pair)
   {
      case MyPair<String, Integer>(var text, var count)
         when text.contains("Michael") ->
         System.out.println(text + " is " + count + " years old");
      case MyPair<String, Integer>(var text, var count)
         when count > 5 && count < 10 ->
         System.out.println("repeated " + text.repeat(count));
      case MyPair<String, Integer>(var text, var count) ->
         System.out.println(text + count);
      default -> System.out.println("NOT HANDLED");
   }
}
```

As already stated for `instanceof`, the above type specification, including the record pattern, in this case `MyPair<String, Integer>`, was somewhat more challenging to read and somewhat confusing. With Java 20 (specifically, from version 20.0.1 onward), the code is significantly shorter and easier to understand. Using plain `MyPair` results in the following implementation:

```java
public void recordInferenceJdk20(final MyPair<String, Integer> pair)
{
    switch (pair)
    {
        case MyPair(String text, var count)
            when text.contains("Michael") ->
            System.out.println(text + " is " + count + " years old");
        case MyPair(String text, Integer count)
            when count > 5 && count < 10 ->
            System.out.println("repeated " + text.repeat(count));
        case MyPair(var text, var count) ->
            System.out.println(text + count);
        default -> System.out.println("NOT HANDLED");
    }
}
```

For a better understanding, let's take a look at how to call this:

```
jshell> recordInferenceJdk20(new MyPair<>("Mike", 7))
repeated MikeMikeMikeMikeMikeMikeMike
```

Description of All Cases with Subsequent Modification

There is a rare, exceptional case: which can typically only occur due to incomplete compilation (more on this below). Let's assume no `case` from the `switch` applies at runtime, then no complete description of all cases in a `switch` is provided. This triggers a `MatchException` and not, as before, an `IncompatibleClass-ChangeError`. By the way, both originate from the package `java.lang`.

To demonstrate this, let's start with a definition of two graphic figures as records with a base interface Shape defined as sealed types, a new feature in Java 17 LTS:

```java
record Position(int x, int y) {}

public sealed interface Shape permits Rectangle, Circle {}

public record Rectangle(Position topLeft,
                        Position bottomRight) implements Shape {}

public record Circle(Position center, int radius) implements Shape {}
```

The usage could look like this:

```java
static void printInfoFor(Shape shape)
{
    var output = switch (shape)
    {
        case Rectangle(var topLeft, var bottomRight) ->
            "Rect: top left = " + topLeft + "; bottom right = " +
                bottomRight;
        case Circle(var center, var radius) ->
            "Circle: center = " + center + "; radius = " + radius;
    };
    System.out.println(output);
}
```

In the above example, based on `sealed` and the implementations of Shape, the compiler can ensure that this `switch` is exhaustive, meaning that it does not require a `default` branch.

If a new type, such as Square or Ellipse, is added as a variant of Shape, that is, listed after `permits`, the above `switch` is obviously no longer exhaustive, as not all cases are covered. It is penalized with a compilation error: " The switch statement does not cover all possible input values." However, if you only compile individual classes selectively, there may be missing coverage in the `switch`, which then results in a `MatchException` at runtime. The same applies to `switch` over the values of an enum if we later on extend it, but do not recompile the application that uses it.

Special Case: Provoked `MatchException`

It is also possible to construct an example where a `MatchException` is provoked despite clean compilation, but passing a `null` value:

```java
class ForcedMatchExceptionExample
{
    sealed interface Base permits Sub1, Sub2 {}

    final class Sub1 implements Base {}
    final class Sub2 implements Base {}

    record Wrapper(Base value) {}

    public static void main(final String[] args)
    {
        switch (new Wrapper(null))
        {
            case Wrapper(Sub1 a) -> System.out.println("Sub1: " + a);
            case Wrapper(Sub2 b) -> System.out.println("Sub2: " + b);
        }
    }
}
```

Starting in the JShell demonstrates this:

```
jshell> ForcedMatchExceptionExample.main(null)
|   Exception java.lang.MatchException
|        at ForcedMatchExceptionExample.main (#60:12)
|        at (#61:1)
```

4.2.7   Qualified Enums

In combination with the feature Pattern Matching for `switch`, another detail has changed in the syntax for specifying enums.

Let's consider an example application that models cardinal directions using an enum and implements a selection in a classic and easily readable way using a `switch` and appropriate calls to methods as follows:

```java
enum CompassDirection {NORTH, SOUTH, EAST, WEST}

// initial situation
static void handleDirection(CompassDirection dir)
{
    switch (dir)
    {
        case NORTH -> handleUp();
        case SOUTH -> handleDown();
        case EAST -> handleRight();
        case WEST -> handleLeft();
    }
}
```

For many use cases, this is already an adequate option. In addition, thanks to the completeness analysis, we do not need to specify a `default` here.

Simple Form of Syntax Renewal

Since Java 21 LTS, it is permitted to specify the constants of the enum fully qualified:

```java
static void handleDirection(CompassDirection dir)
{
    switch (dir)
    {
        case CompassDirection.NORTH -> handleUp();
        case CompassDirection.SOUTH -> handleDown();
        case CompassDirection.EAST -> handleRight();
        case CompassDirection.WEST -> handleLeft();
    }
}
```

In this simple example, the advantage is not yet apparent. To illustrate it, we first need to take a step back.

Modern Syntax with Pattern Matching

Let's assume we want to use pattern matching to integrate additional checks, such as taking speed into account. Then the whole thing could be rewritten as follows, with pattern matching only shown for NORTH:

```java
static void handleDirection(Direction dir, int speed)
{
    switch (dir)
    {
        // With conditions
        // Not allowed: case CompassDirection.NORTH when speed >= 10 ->
        case CompassDirection d when d == CompassDirection.NORTH &&
            speed >= 10 ->
        {
            handleUp();
            handleUp();
        }
        case CompassDirection d when d == CompassDirection.NORTH ->
            handleUp();
        case SOUTH -> handleDown();
        case EAST -> handleRight();
        case WEST -> handleLeft();
        default -> throw new IllegalStateException("Unhandled value: " +
                                                    dir);
    }
}
```

However, this implementation has the problem that the completeness analysis no longer works and you need a `default` again. Overall, this is worse than better because it is significantly longer and more confusing.

Potentially Better Implementation   If only a check for NORTH were necessary, the entire implementation should be rewritten as follows:

```java
switch (dir)
{
    case NORTH ->
    {
        if (speed >= 10)
            handleUp();
        handleUp();
    }
    case SOUTH -> handleDown();
    case EAST -> handleRight();
    case WEST -> handleLeft();
}
```

Because we want to expand the example piece by piece and also learn about various things, we will now use the source code snippet shown earlier again.

Inheritance Hierarchies of Enums

The need for the syntax renewal of qualified enums only becomes apparent when we enhance the example just shown and extend the modeling of the directions by defining a base interface `Direction` and creating two subtypes:

```java
sealed interface Direction permits CompassDirection, PlayerDirection {}

enum CompassDirection implements Direction {NORTH, SOUTH, EAST, WEST}

enum PlayerDirection implements Direction {UP, DOWN, LEFT, RIGHT}
```

If you want to handle all these directions within a `switch`, then up to and including Java 20, this quickly becomes unreadable:

```java
static void handleDirection(Direction dir, int speed)
{
  switch (dir)
  {
    case CompassDirection d when
         d == CompassDirection.NORTH && speed >= 10 ->
    {
      handleUp();
      handleUp();
    }
    case CompassDirection d when d == CompassDirection.NORTH -> handleUp();
    case CompassDirection d when d == CompassDirection.SOUTH -> handleDown();
    case CompassDirection d when d == CompassDirection.EAST -> handleRight();
    case CompassDirection d when d == CompassDirection.WEST -> handleLeft();
    case PlayerDirection d when d == PlayerDirection.UP -> handleUp();
    case PlayerDirection d when d == PlayerDirection.DOWN -> handleDown();
    case PlayerDirection d when d == PlayerDirection.LEFT -> handleLeft();
    case PlayerDirection d when d == PlayerDirection.RIGHT -> handleRight();
    default -> throw new IllegalArgumentException("Unhandled value: " + dir);
  }
}
```

Improvements with Java 21 LTS

Let's use the new features in Java 21 LTS for a step-by-step improvement.

Step 1: Improvement with Qualified Enum Instead of using pattern matching, queries become more convenient using qualified enums—however, the lines with the cases are still repetitive:

```java
static void handleDirection(Direction dir, int speed)
{
  switch (dir)
  {
    case CompassDirection d when
         d == CompassDirection.NORTH && speed >= 10 ->
    {
      handleUp();
      handleUp();
    }
    case CompassDirection.NORTH -> handleUp();
```

```
    case CompassDirection.SOUTH -> handleDown();
    case CompassDirection.EAST -> handleRight();
    case CompassDirection.WEST -> handleLeft();
    case PlayerDirection.UP -> handleUp();
    case PlayerDirection.DOWN -> handleDown();
    case PlayerDirection.RIGHT -> handleRight();
    case PlayerDirection.LEFT -> handleLeft();
    }
}
```

Step 2: Multiple Constants in a case The above construct can be compressed by listing the respective similar constants in a case. With Java 21 LTS, different subtypes, that is, CompassDirection and PlayerDirection, of a common base type, here Direction, are allowed:

```java
static void handleDirection(Direction dir, int speed)
{
    switch (dir)
    {
        case CompassDirection d when
            d == CompassDirection.NORTH && speed >= 10 ->
        {
            handleUp();
            handleUp();
        }
        case CompassDirection.NORTH, PlayerDirection.UP -> handleUp();
        case CompassDirection.SOUTH, PlayerDirection.DOWN -> handleDown();
        case CompassDirection.EAST, PlayerDirection.RIGHT -> handleRight();
        case CompassDirection.WEST, PlayerDirection.LEFT -> handleLeft();
    }
}
```

Step 3: Static Imports We now use static imports:

```java
import static ch04_syntax_java_18_21.ch04_02_pattern_matching.qualified_enums
    .CompassDirection.*;
import static ch04_syntax_java_18_21.ch04_02_pattern_matching.qualified_enums
    .PlayerDirection.*;
```

This results in the following easy-to-read version, which looks very similar to the original version but permits pattern matching and specifying constants from several different subtypes:

```java
static void handleDirection(Direction dir, int speed)
{
    switch (dir)
    {
        case CompassDirection d when d == NORTH && speed >= 10 ->
        {
            handleUp();
            handleUp();
        }
        case NORTH, UP -> handleUp();
        case SOUTH, DOWN -> handleDown();
        case EAST, RIGHT -> handleRight();
        case WEST, LEFT -> handleLeft();
    }
}
```

4.3   JEP 443: Unnamed Patterns and Variables (Preview)

This JEP introduces the ability to replace various elements in an expression or variable with a single "_" character, thereby marking them as unusable and prohibiting the compiler from further utilizing the variable.

4.3.1   Motivation for Unnamed Variables and Patterns

Let's recap: In recent Java versions, pattern matching was introduced as a syntax innovation, initially in `instanceof` (see Sect. 2.5) and later in `switch` (see Sect. 4.2). This was practical. However, accessing the components of a record, that is, its attributes, still required corresponding method calls. The feature Record Patterns (see Sect. 4.1) avoids this and keeps the source code shorter and clearer. Record patterns help break down the type (record) specified in `instanceof` directly into its individual parts, as shown below for the variables x and y:

```java
if (obj instanceof Point(int x, int y))
{
    System.out.println("x: %d y: %d, sum: %d".formatted(x, y, x + y));
}
```

In the previous listing and for the upcoming examples, we assume that the following records and enums are defined:

```java
record Point(int x, int y) { }

enum Color { RED, GREEN, BLUE }

record ColoredPoint(Point point, Color color) { }
```

Observations from Practical Experience with Record Patterns

When using record patterns, you may find that some components are not needed for evaluation. What does this mean? Let's take the record `ColoredPoint` as an example: For specific actions, as in this case, only one component, specifically the x coordinate, is actually of interest. In particular, you don't even need the y coordinate, let alone the color:

```java
var greenPoint = new ColoredPoint(new Point(3, 4), Color.GREEN);

if (greenPoint instanceof ColoredPoint(Point point, Color color))
{
    System.out.println("x = " + point.x());
}
if (greenPoint instanceof ColoredPoint(Point(int x, int y), Color color))
{
    System.out.println("x = " + x);
}
```

Observations from Practical Experience with Lambdas

Unused components are known from lambdas for parameters, namely, when some of the variables specified on the left side are not used on the right side of the expression. This fact is not always obvious, and in the hectic pace of everyday programming, it can easily be overlooked.

Let's consider, as an example, the repetition of a text using the predefined functional interface `java.util.function.BiFunction`:

```
// "str2" not used
BiFunction<String, String, String> doubleFirst = (str1, str2) -> str1.repeat
    (2);
```

Another example is a custom functional interface `IntTernaryOperator` (see below). It is used here to define an addition of only two of its three parameters:

```
// "z" not used
IntTernaryOperator addFirstTwo = (int x, int y, int z) -> x + y;
```

In both cases, one component of the parameter list, specifically `str2` and `z`, is not used in the lambda for the action.

For the sake of completeness, I will show the implementation of the functional interface `IntTernaryOperator`:

```
@FunctionalInterface
public interface IntTernaryOperator
{
    int applyAsInt(int x, int y, int z);
}
```

Observations from Practical Experience with Exception Handling

Unused components may occur during exception handling—specifically, if the exception variable is sometimes not accessed in the `catch` block. Strictly speaking, this means that it does not need to be explicitly named. However, this is currently required for syntactic reasons, which is why you often find letter abbreviations such as e or `ex` or names such as `ignored`, which indicate even more clearly that they are unused:

```
try
{
    Files.writeString(Path.of("UnnamedVars.txt"), "_");
}
catch (IOException ex)
{
    // just some logging
}
```

4.3.2   Remedy Using Unnamed Variables and Patterns

Before we go into more detail, it should be mentioned that there are the following
three variants, which we will look at in more detail using examples:

1. **Unnamed Variable**: Allows the use of "_" to mark unused variables (in
   `catch` blocks, lambdas, and local variable declarations, but not when declaring
   attributes or method parameters)
2. **Unnamed Pattern Variable**: Allows an identifier that would typically follow the
   type (or `var`) in a record pattern to be omitted
3. **Unnamed Pattern**: Allows the type and name of a component of a record pattern
   to be omitted entirely (and replaced with a simple "_")

Unnamed Variable

Let's look at some examples of unnamed variables. The most obvious example is
the `try-catch` presented earlier, where the exception variable is not accessed and
is therefore marked with "_":

```java
try
{
    Files.writeString(Path.of("UnnamedVars.txt"), "_");
}
catch (IOException _)
{
    // ATTENTION: not permitted
    // _.printStackTrace();
}
```

It is particularly worth noting that a variable marked with "_" cannot be read or
written. Especially, it is impossible to call a method on it. Attempting to do so will
result in a compilation error.

The following example deals with invalid user input. In this case, the focus is not
on the exception itself, but rather on informing the user of the incorrect input and
the expected values. With an underscore as a new feature, this is written as follows:

```java
String userInput = "E605";
try
{
    processInput(Integer.parseInt(userInput));
}
catch (NumberFormatException _)
{
    System.out.println("Expected number, but was: '" + userInput + "'");
}
```

Unnamed Variable in Lambdas Interestingly, multiple unnamed variables can be used in the same scope, since the underscore is not a variable name, but a keyword. This is helpful for lambdas, for example—the following shows that only y is relevant in the calculation:

```
IntTernaryOperator doubleSecond = (int _, int y, int _) -> y * 2;
```

Unnamed Variable in Local Variable Definitions One use case for assignment to "_" is when you call a method, but the return value is (intentionally) not evaluated or used. To clarify this behavior in the source code, you would write something like this:

```
boolean _ = file.delete();
```

For the sake of completeness, I will also show syntactically permitted uses that often do not provide any added value in practice or can be replaced by better constructs:

```
jshell> var _ = "UNUSED"
 ==> "UNUSED"

jshell> int count = 0
count ==> 0

jshell> for (int _ : new int[] { 2, 3, 5, 7})
   ...>       count++

jshell> count
count ==> 4
```

The first variable definition is not necessary because the values cannot be used for further processing. Looking at the for loop for counting elements, there are more suitable alternatives in Java for achieving the same functionality, such as the Stream API and the count() method:

```
jshell> Arrays.stream(new int[] { 2, 3, 5, 7}).count()
$1 ==> 4
```

Unnamed Pattern Variable

An unnamed pattern variable can be used in a record pattern, regardless of whether the record pattern is " normal" or nested:

```
// Unnamed pattern variable
if (pt instanceof Point(int x, int _))
{
    System.out.println("x: " + x);
}
```

```java
if (cp instanceof ColoredPoint(Point point, Color _))
{
    System.out.println(point);
}

// Several times '_' and mixed with and without type
if (cp instanceof ColoredPoint(Point(int x, var _), Color _))
{
    System.out.println(x);
}
```

Special Case   The following construct is permissible, but it takes record patterns to absurd extremes, since the same result can be achieved with a simple `instanceof`:

```java
if (pt instanceof Point _)
{
    System.out.println("it's a Point, but why use record patterns for" +
                       " checking this?");
}
```

Unnamed Pattern

In the previous example, we saw that components not required for later statements could be masked out using "_". However, type information or `var` is still specified there. Of course, this makes little sense if the variable is not used at all. Therefore, it is logical to omit the type specification in such cases. This is precisely what unnamed patterns allow us to do. This makes our example even shorter. In addition, all unused components are clearly marked and recognizable:

```java
if (cp instanceof ColoredPoint(Point(int x, _), _))
{
    System.out.println("unnamed pattern, x: " + x);
}
```

> **Hint: Unsupported Special Cases**
> These constructs are not allowed:
>
> ```java
> instanceof _
> instanceof _(int x, int y)
> ```

Special Feature in case

Finally, let's look at a special case, namely, the enumeration of different patterns in a `case` that you don't want to name.

Until now, if you wanted to treat each case separately, you had to write something like this:

```java
switch (obj)
{
    case Byte b -> "Integer number";
    case Short s -> "Integer number";
    case Integer i -> "Integer number";
    case Long l -> "Integer number";
    case Float f ->"Floating point number";
    case Double d -> "Floating point number";
    default -> "Not a number";
}
```

Now you could mark the unused variables appropriately:

```java
switch (obj)
{
    case Byte _ -> "Integer number";
    case Short _ -> "Integer number";
    case Integer _ -> "Integer number";
    case Long _-> "Integer number";
    case Float _ -> "Floating point number";
    case Double _ -> "Floating point number";
    default -> "Not a number";
}
```

That looks rather bloated and unattractive. One might come up with the idea of writing it down more concisely as follows:

```java
// ATTENTION: SYNTACTICALLY INCORRECT
...
case Byte, Short, Integer, Long _ -> "Input is an integer number";
case Float, Double _ -> "Input is a floating-point number";
...
```

The following, on the other hand, is syntactically correct:

```java
switch (obj)
{
    case Byte _, Short _, Integer _, Long _ -> "Input is an integer number";
    case Float _, Double _ -> "Input is a floating-point number";
    default -> "Not a number";
}
```

Chapter 5
API Extensions in JDK 18 to 21 LTS

This chapter describes various API innovations that are cumulatively found in Java versions 18 to 21 LTS.

In individual sections, we address the topics listed below. The preview and incubator features are marked in italics—since these are all part of Java 25 LTS, they are described separately in the corresponding chapters on Java 22 to Java 25 LTS.

- JEP 416: Reimplement Core Reflection with Method Handles.
- JEP 418: Internet-Address Resolution SPI.
- JEP 431: Sequenced Collections.
- JEP 444: Virtual Threads.
- *JEP 442: Foreign Function and Memory API (Third Preview)*—got finalized with Java 22 as JEP 454 and is covered in Sect. 10.1.
- *JEP 446: Scoped Values (Preview)*—Java 25 LTS brings Scoped Values as a final feature in the form of JEP 506, which is described in Sect. 10.7.
- *JEP 448: Vector API (Sixth Incubator)*—remains in incubator status in Java 25 LTS as JEP 508 and is covered in Sect. 10.8.
- *JEP 453: Structured Concurrency (Preview)*—is included in Java 25 LTS again as a preview in the form of JEP 505 and is described in Sect. 10.6.

In Sect. 5.1, I present JEP 416 as an internal change in the area of reflection using method handles. A detailed change to the resolution of Internet addresses in the form of JEP 418 is covered in Sect. 5.2. For many developers, the Sequenced Collections, which facilitate special tasks with collections, are probably more exciting and relevant. They are the subject of Sect. 5.3. The Virtual Threads, which were finalized as JEP 444 and are described in Sect. 5.4, are a real gem in the context of multithreading and scalability.

Section 5.5 then provides an overview of various minor changes in the form of a potpourri of innovations, some of which found their way into the JDK independently of JEPs, such as those related to UTF-8 or the classes `FileInputStream`, `Math`, `Duration`, and a few others. Finally, in Sect. 5.6 I present some deprecations.

© The Author(s), under exclusive license to APress Media, LLC, part of Springer Nature 2026
M. Inden, *Java 25 and Beyond*, https://doi.org/10.1007/979-8-8688-2385-5_5

5.1   JEP 416: Reimplement Core Reflection with Method Handles

Method handles were introduced in Java 7. They provide a more efficient, low-level mechanism for method lookup and invocation than the traditional Reflection API in `java.lang.reflect`.[1]

As part of JEP 416, the classes `Method`, `Constructor`, `Field` from the package `java.lang.reflect`, as well as several classes residing in the package `java.lang.invoke` were reimplemented using method handles. This reimplementation yields several benefits. In addition to performance improvements, it reduces maintenance and development effort by simplifying future changes to the reflection infrastructure in `java.lang.reflect` and `java.lang.invoke`.

Note: Internal Effects Only

Before we proceed to the content changes, I would like to point out the following: This JEP does not modify the externally visible API or behavior of the components in the `java.lang.reflect` package. It is purely an internal refactoring. However, in the unlikely event that you are deeply involved in the JDK, for example, because you are co-developing a framework, this JEP may have an impact. For example, calling method handles may consume more resources than the old reflection implementation. To mitigate a possible compatibility risk, you can disable the new implementation and enable the old implementation as a workaround by using the following JVM invocation parameter: `-Djdk.reflect.useDirect-MethodHandle=false`.

Example

Let's consider, as an example, accessing the private attribute named `value` in the class `java.lang.String`, which represents a `byte[]`. First, we use the conventional approach to retrieve the value using the `Field` class and its `get()` method. To enable access in the first place, you have to override the visibility protection. This requires calling `setAccessible(true)`:

```java
public void accessFieldOldStyle(final String input)
            throws ReflectiveOperationException
{
    var field = String.class.getDeclaredField("value");
    field.setAccessible(true);

    System.out.println(Arrays.toString((byte[]) field.get(input)));
}
```

---

[1] Method handles are constructs used to locate and invoke methods with minimal overhead.

To demonstrate the new features, we write a call with method handles as follows—the internal changes are not visible in the API:

```
import java.lang.invoke.*

// ...

public void accessFieldNewStyle(final String input)
            throws ReflectiveOperationException
{
    var lookup = MethodHandles.privateLookupIn(String.class,
                                        MethodHandles.lookup());
    var handle = lookup.findVarHandle(String.class, "value", byte[].class);

    System.out.println(Arrays.toString((byte[]) handle.get(input)));
}
```

When the method is called, a `java.lang.reflect.InaccessibleObjectException` occurs:

```
jshell> accessFieldNewStyle("Java 21 LTS Rocks");
|  Exception java.lang.IllegalAccessException: module java.base does not open
       java.lang to unnamed module @57fffcd7
|       at MethodHandles.privateLookupIn (MethodHandles.java:287)
|       at accessFieldNewStyle (#6:3)
|       at (#8:1)
```

This output indicates that access to private attributes is not permitted. In recent Java versions, reflection has been increasingly restricted to prevent misuse and abuse.

Adjustments for Execution

The strong encapsulation of internal APIs makes it necessary for both variants to specify `--add-opens java.base/java.lang=ALL-UNNAMED` when starting the program. It allows access from unnamed modules (i. e., the example code above) to the package `java.lang` in the module `java.base`.

This modification results in the following output:

```
[74, 97, 118, 97, 32, 50, 49, 32, 76, 84, 83, 32, 82, 111, 99, 107, 115]
```

> **Hint: Effects on JShell Experiments**
>
> It is impossible to simply try out these examples in the JShell because the JVM parameter `--add-opens` cannot be set directly there at startup. However, there is a trick—before starting the JShell, you must set the environment variable `JDK_JAVA_OPTIONS`:
>
> ```
> $ export JDK_JAVA_OPTIONS=--add-opens=java.base/java.lang=ALL-UNNAMED
> ```
>
> The example can then also be executed in the JShell:
>
> ```
> jshell> accessFieldNewStyle("Java 21 LTS Rocks");
> [74, 97, 118, 97, 32, 50, 49, 32, 76, 84, 83, 32, 82, 111, 99, 107, 115]
> ```

> **Hint: Effects on Module Encapsulation**
>
> The adjustment for program startup described above is not recommended practice, as it violates the principle of module encapsulation. It reduces the benefits of modularity and can compromise maintainability, security, and performance.

5.2   JEP 418: Internet-Address Resolution SPI

This JEP introduces an SPI (Service Provider Interface) for host and name address resolution. It supports both the translation of host names into IP addresses (IP = Internet protocol) and the reverse mapping from IP addresses to host names. Previously, address resolution was done internally by the `java.net.InetAddress` class, where the operating system's native resolver was used, typically in conjunction with a local host's file and DNS.

Using an SPI provides more flexibility because other resolvers besides the platform standard can also be used in `InetAddress`. Under the hood, a service loader serves to find a suitable resolver provider (or several) in the class path or module path. The previous variant is employed as a fallback if no such provider is found.

Example

To find the IP address(es) for a host name, the class `InetAddress` provides the method `getAllByName()`, which we use below to determine the IP addresses of dpunkt.verlag and Heise-Verlag:

```
jshell> InetAddress.getAllByName("www.dpunkt.de")
$1 ==> InetAddress[1] { www.dpunkt.de/109.71.73.205 }

jshell> InetAddress.getAllByName("www.heise.de")
$2 ==> InetAddress[2] { www.heise.de/193.99.144.85, www.heise.de/2a02:2e0:3fe
    :1001:7777:772e:2:85 }
```

Custom Resolver

The extensions introduced by this JEP allow fine-grained control over address resolution. To make use of this capability, we implement a custom resolver by providing our own implementation of the `lookupByName()` method. Our specialized method checks whether the host name is `www.dpunkt.de` or `www.heise.de`. If so, it returns a reference to `localhost` (`127.0.0.1`). For all other host names, an `UnsupportedOperationException` is thrown, to explicitly signal that reverse address lookup is not supported—as implementing a fallback mechanism would exceed the scope of this introduction:

```java
import java.net.InetAddress;
import java.net.UnknownHostException;
import java.net.spi.InetAddressResolver;
import java.util.stream.Stream;

public class OwnInetAddressResolver implements InetAddressResolver
{
    @Override
    public Stream<InetAddress> lookupByName(String host,
                                LookupPolicy lookupPolicy)
                                throws UnknownHostException
    {
        if (host.equals("www.dpunkt.de") || host.equals("www.heise.de"))
        {
            var localhost = new byte[]{127, 0, 0, 1};
            return Stream.of(InetAddress.getByAddress(localhost));
        }
        throw new UnsupportedOperationException();
    }

    @Override
    public String lookupByAddress(byte[] addr)
    {
        throw new UnsupportedOperationException();
    }
}
```

Own Provider

The above resolver is provided by a suitable provider. We define this provider as follows by implementing the `get()` method appropriately and creating an instance of our own resolver there:

```
import java.net.spi.InetAddressResolver;
import java.net.spi.InetAddressResolverProvider;

public class OwnInetAddressResolverProvider extends
    InetAddressResolverProvider
{
    @Override
    public InetAddressResolver get(final Configuration configuration)
    {
        return new OwnInetAddressResolver();
    }

    @Override
    public String name()
    {
        return "Own Internet Address Resolver Provider";
    }
}
```

Execution

To experiment with the functionality, we write the following `main()` method.

```
public static void main(String[] args) throws UnknownHostException
{
    InetAddress[] addresses = InetAddress.getAllByName("www.dpunkt.de");
    System.out.println("dpunkt = " + Arrays.toString(addresses));

    InetAddress[] addresses2 = InetAddress.getAllByName("www.heise.de");
    System.out.println("heise = " + Arrays.toString(addresses2));
}
```

Listing 5.1 Executable as "INETADDRESSEXAMPLE"

When the program starts, you get the following result:

```
dpunkt = [www.dpunkt.de/109.71.73.205]
heise = [www.heise.de/193.99.144.85, www.heise.de/2a02:2e0:3fe:1001:7777:772e
    :2:85]
```

Activating the Service Lookup

To activate the previously created provider in the service lookup mechanism,
a corresponding UTF-8-encoded file named `java.net.spi.InetAddress-`
`ResolverProvider` must be located in the class path under `META-INF/services`.
The content must be the fully qualified name (adjust the package, here `api.inet`,
if you are using a different one):

```
api.inet.OwnInetAddressResolverProvider
```

In the directory structure, this looks something like Fig. 5.1.

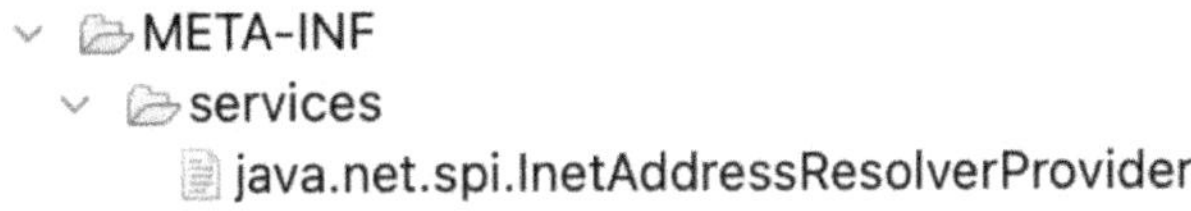

Fig. 5.1 Custom `ResolverProvider` in the package view

Modified Version

If you restart the address retrieval with the appropriately modified file, you will get
the following result, which shows the modification to 127.0.0.1 (`localhost`):

```
dpunkt = [/127.0.0.1]
heise = [/127.0.0.1]
```

5.3   JEP 431: Sequenced Collections

The Java Collections API provides three main types: `List<E>`, `Set<E>`, and
`Map<K,V>`. However, what is missing is a representation of an ordered sequence
of elements in the form of a type. Nevertheless, some collections have a so-called
encounter order/iteration order, that is, the order in which the elements are traversed
is defined, for example:

- `List<E>`: Index-based, from front to back
- `TreeSet<E>`: Indirectly via `Comparable<E>` or a `Comparator<E>`
  passed during construction
- `LinkedHashSet<E>`: According to the insertion order

In contrast, the class `HashSet<E>` possesses such an encounter order—this also
applies to the class `HashMap<K,V>`.

We observe the following: The first and last elements are defined based on the
encounter order. It also allows elements to be added and removed at the front and
back. In addition, the reverse order is also possible. All these functionalities are
offered by Sequenced Collections.

Introductory Examples: Problem Context

Until Java 21 LTS, accessing the first or last element of a collection was tedious.
Worse still, there were several different ways of doing this, depending on the type
of collection.

For the following examples, we assume that the respective collections are not
empty, because otherwise accessing an empty collection triggers a `NoSuch-`
`ElementException` or an `IndexOutOfBoundsException`.

Accessing the last element had to be implemented for different collections, as indicated in the listing:

```
var lastListElement = list.get(list.size() - 1);
var lastSortedElement = sortedSet.last();
var lastDequeElement = deque.getLast();
```

Accessing the first element was almost as cumbersome, especially for sets:

```
var firstListElement = list.get(0);
var firstOrderedSetElement = treeSet.first()
var firstLinkedHashSetElement = linkedHashSet.iterator().next();
```

Remembering all these variants is tedious and prone to error. Even with IDE support, the inelegance remains. As a remedy, let's now examine Sequenced Collections and how they simplify not only this task, but also the addition and deletion of elements at the front and back.

5.3.1 Remedy Sequenced Collections

As already mentioned, Java does not yet offer a type that represents an ordered sequence of elements. Java 21 LTS fills this gap with Sequenced Collections, more specifically the interfaces `SequencedCollection<E>`, `SequencedSet<E>`, and `SequencedMap<K,V>` from the package `java.util`. These interfaces define methods for working with elements at the front or back of the collection or map, as well as for providing them in reverse order.

The `SequencedCollection<E>` Interface

Let's consider the `SequencedCollection<E>` interface:

```
interface SequencedCollection<E> extends Collection<E>
{
    SequencedCollection<E> reversed();
    void addFirst(E);
    void addLast(E);
    E getFirst();
    E getLast();
    E removeFirst();
    E removeLast();
}
```

Obviously, `SequencedCollection<E>` extends the `Collection<E>` interface and offers methods for adding, retrieving, and deleting elements at the front or back. The methods `addXyz()` and `removeXyz()` trigger an `UnsupportedOperationException` for immutable collections. The reversed() method allows the elements to be processed in reverse order. In fact, the return value of reversed() is a view, similar to the subList() method for lists. This means that changes in the view are also reflected in the original collection and vice versa.

The `SequencedSet<E>` Interface

The SequencedSet<E> interface extends Set<E> and is based on Sequenced-Collection<E>, but without defining any new methods. However, there is a slight deviation in the return type of reversed(). Here, covariant overriding allows us to change the type of the return value. However, this is only possible for a more specific type, in this case from SequencedCollection<E> to SequencedSet<E>. The covariant overriding allows you to continue working directly with the SequencedSet<E> without a cast:

```java
interface SequencedSet<E> extends Set<E>, SequencedCollection<E>
{
    SequencedSet<E> reversed();     // covariant override
}
```

The `SequencedMap<K,V>` Interface

Analogous to SequencedCollection<E>, SequencedMap<K,V> provides the following methods:

- Entry<K,V> firstEntry(): Returns the first key–value pair
- Entry<K,V> lastEntry(): Returns the last key–value pair
- Entry<K,V> pollFirstEntry(): Removes and returns the first key–value pair
- Entry<K,V> pollLastEntry(): Removes and returns the last key–value pair
- V putFirst(K,V): Inserts a key–value pair at the front
- V putLast(K,V): Inserts a key–value pair at the back
- SequencedMap<K,V> reversed(): Returns a view in reverse order

There are also three methods: namely, sequencedKeySet() for determining the keys, sequencedValues() for the values, and sequencedEntrySet() for providing key–value pairs.

This results in the following interface definition:

```java
interface SequencedMap<K,V> extends Map<K,V>
{
    SequencedMap<K,V> reversed();
    SequencedSet<K> sequencedKeySet();
    SequencedCollection<V> sequencedValues();
    SequencedSet<Entry<K,V>> sequencedEntrySet();
    V putFirst(K,V);
```

```
    V putLast(K,V);
    Entry<K,V> firstEntry();
    Entry<K,V> lastEntry();
    Entry<K,V> pollFirstEntry();
    Entry<K,V> pollLastEntry();
}
```

Decisions to Avoid API Pollution

The APIs of `SequencedCollection<E>` and `SequencedMap<K,V>` do not match particularly well because the latter was created in analogy to `NavigableMap<K,V>`. Therefore, instead of `getFirstEntry()`, it offers the method `firstEntry()`, and instead of `removeLast-Entry()`, it offers the method `pollLastEntry()`. These names do not correspond to those of `SequencedCollection<E>`. However, attempting to do so would have resulted in `NavigableMap<K,V>` having four new methods that do the same thing as the four other methods it already has. That is the price you pay for changing the interface hierarchy after the fact. Let's take a look at that now.

5.3.2   A Look Behind the Scenes

Before we see the Sequenced Collections in action, I would like to provide some background information to enhance your understanding of the following examples.

Integration of Sequenced Collections into the Interface Hierarchy

Sequenced Collections fit seamlessly into the existing interface hierarchy. Figure 5.2 shows the existing and newly introduced interfaces (the latter are marked with arrows). The figure is taken from the description of JEP 431 and can be found online at https://openjdk.org/jeps/431.

Implementation of Sequenced Collections

A look behind the scenes reveals that default methods can be used to fit the interfaces into the existing interface hierarchy. However, this also has certain (undesirable) side effects: for example, there are now two ways to access the first and last elements for `SortedSet<E>`—these are the methods `first()` and `last()` from before Sequenced Collections, as well as `getFirst()` and `getLast()`, a tribute to

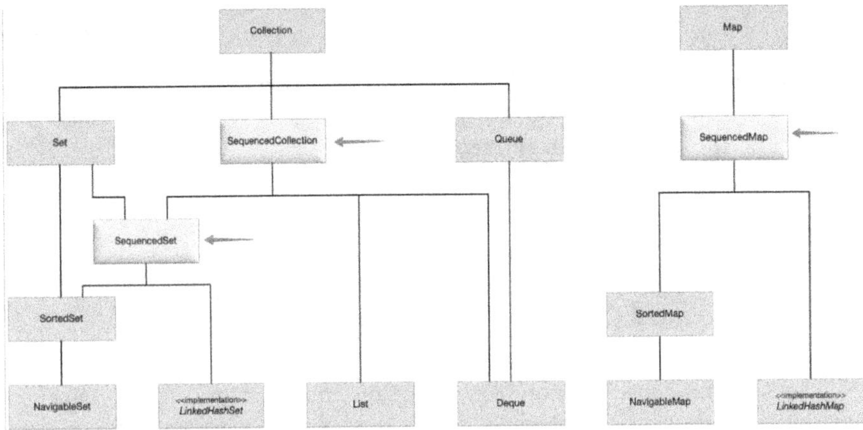

Fig. 5.2 Sequenced Collection in the interface hierarchy

the fact that these functionalities were subsequently introduced into the inheritance hierarchy of `Collection<E>`.

Consistently, accessing the first or last element of an empty collection results in a `NoSuchElementException`:

```java
public interface SequencedCollection<E> extends Collection<E> {
    SequencedCollection<E> reversed();

    default void addFirst(E e) {
        throw new UnsupportedOperationException();
    }

    default void addLast(E e) {
        throw new UnsupportedOperationException();
    }

    default E getFirst() {
        return this.iterator().next();
    }

    default E getLast() {
        return this.reversed().iterator().next();
    }

    default E removeFirst() {
        var it = this.iterator();
        E e = it.next();
        it.remove();
        return e;
    }

    default E removeLast() {
        var it = this.reversed().iterator();
        E e = it.next();
        it.remove();
        return e;
    }
}
```

> **Note: Type-Specific Implementations**
> Interestingly, for specializations such as lists, it is possible to modify the
> implementation specified by the default methods, for example, to achieve
> better performance through indexed access.

5.3.3   Sequenced Collections in Action

Now let's see the capabilities of Sequenced Collections for lists and sets in action.
For this purpose, we will implement two methods, each of which executes different
calls for `SequencedCollection<E>` and `SequencedSet<E>` and presents
the results via console output.

List as `SequencedCollection<E>`

We define a list of letters and then query the first and last elements of the list. Next,
we use `reversed()` to create a Sequenced Collection with the order reversed,
which we iterate through using `forEach()`, and convert to a stream calling
`stream()`. For demonstration purposes, we skip three elements and finally query
the first and last elements of the reversed order:

```java
public void sequenceCollectionExample()
{
    System.out.println("Processing letterSequence with list");
    SequencedCollection<String> letterSequence = List.of("A", "B", "C",
                                                          "D", "E");
    System.out.println(letterSequence.getFirst() + " / " +
                       letterSequence.getLast());

    System.out.println("Processing letterSequence in reverse order");
    SequencedCollection<String> reversed = letterSequence.reversed();
    reversed.forEach(System.out::print);
    System.out.println();
    System.out.println("reverse order stream skip 3");
    reversed.stream().skip(3).forEach(System.out::print);
    System.out.println();
    System.out.println(reversed.getFirst() + " / " +
                       reversed.getLast());
    System.out.println();
}
```

The output is as follows:

```
jshell> sequenceCollectionExample()
Processing letterSequence with list
A / E
Processing letterSequence in reverse order
EDCBA
reverse order stream skip 3
BA
E / A
```

View Property for `reversed()`   The following method `modifyOriginal-AndView()` demonstrates the view property. After creating a list as the original and a view of it using `reversed()`, we add data with method calls. These affect both data structures:

```java
public void modifyOriginalAndView()
{
    var original = new ArrayList<>(List.of("B", "C", "D"));
    SequencedCollection<String> reversedView = original.reversed();

    original.addLast("EEE");
    reversedView.addLast("AAA");
    reversedView.addFirst("FFF");

    System.out.println(original);
    System.out.println(reversedView);
}
```

This results in the following output, which clearly shows that changes are also reflected in the other collection:

```
jshell> modifyOriginalAndView()
[AAA, B, C, D, EEE, FFF]
[FFF, EEE, D, C, B, AAA]
```

One thing that could still be interesting is the double execution of `reversed()`. This is identical in content and even corresponds to the same reference:

```
jshell> var original = List.of(1, 2, 3, 4, 5);
original ==> [1, 2, 3, 4, 5]

jshell> original.reversed().reversed() == original
$6 ==> true
```

Special Case: Single-Element List   For a single-element list, the first and last elements match, as expected, which is why `getFirst()` and `getLast()` refer to the same element:

```
jshell> SequencedCollection<String> oneElement = new ArrayList<>(List.of("A"))
oneElement ==> [A]

jshell> oneElement.getFirst() == oneElement.getLast()
$4 ==> true
```

You can add further elements to such a collection. Afterward, the first and last elements are, of course, no longer identical, but potentially possess the same value:

```
jshell> oneElement.addLast("-")

jshell> oneElement.addLast("Z")

jshell> System.out.println(oneElement)
[A, -, Z]

jshell> oneElement.getFirst() == oneElement.getLast()
$8 ==> false
```

Special Case: Empty List For an empty list, accessing the first and last elements will, as expected, result in a `NoSuchElementException`, shown here as an example for `getFirst()`:

```
jshell> SequencedCollection<String> noElements = List.of()
noElements ==> []

jshell> noElements.getFirst()
|  Exception java.util.NoSuchElementException
|        at List.getFirst (List.java:825)
|        at (#2:1)
```

Sets as `SequencedSet<E>`

Let's now vary the data structure and use sets. First, normal sets:

```
public void plainSetExample()
{
    // "normal" sets possess no order ...
    System.out.println("Processing set of letters A-D");
    Set.of("A", "B", "C", "D").forEach(System.out::print);
    System.out.println("\nProcessing set of letters A-G");
    Set.of("A", "B", "C", "D", "E", "F", "G").forEach(System.out::print);
    System.out.println();
}
```

The output is as follows—with possible deviations in the letter sequences, as these are not fixed for sets and may vary with each execution, sometimes even appearing to be sorted by chance:

```
jshell> plainSetExample()
Processing set of letters A-D
ABCD
Processing set of letters A-G
ABCDEFG
```

As an example of `SequencedSet<E>`, let's consider a few possibilities based on the concrete implementation using a `TreeSet<E>`:

```
public void sequencedSetExample()
{
    // TreeSet possess an order and is a SequencedSet.
    SequencedSet<String> sortedLetters =
                    new TreeSet<>((Set.of("C", "B", "A", "D")));
    System.out.println(sortedLetters.getFirst() + " / " +
                    sortedLetters.getLast());
    sortedLetters.reversed().forEach(System.out::print);
    System.out.println();
}
```

The output is as follows:

```
jshell> sequencedSetExample()
A / D
DCBA
```

Special Case: Single-Element Set For a single-element set, the first and last elements match as expected, which is why `getFirst()` and `getLast()` refer to the same element:

```
jshell> SequencedSet<String> oneElementSet = new TreeSet<>(Set.of("A"))
oneElement ==> [A]

jshell> oneElementSet.getFirst() == oneElementSet.getLast()
$8 ==> true
```

Unlike lists, it is not so easy to add data to a `SequencedSet<E>`. We will look at this separately in a moment.

Special Case: Empty Set As expected, accessing the first and last elements of an empty set results in a `NoSuchElementException`, shown here as an example for `getFirst()`:

```
jshell> SequencedSet<String> noElementSet = new TreeSet<>()
noElementSet ==> []

jshell> noElementSet.getFirst()
|   Exception java.util.NoSuchElementException
|        at TreeMap.key (TreeMap.java:1638)
|        at TreeMap.firstKey (TreeMap.java:303)
|        at TreeSet.first (TreeSet.java:397)
|        at SortedSet.getFirst (SortedSet.java:307)
|        at (#6:1)
```

Special Case: `TreeSet<E>` and Insertion Operations Because the class `TreeSet<E>` is a concrete implementation of `SequencedSet<E>` it provides the methods `addFirst()` and `addLast()`. These would either have to maintain the sequence or raise an exception. The former cannot be achieved universally, so the decision was made in the JDK to raise an exception:

```
jshell> SequencedSet<String> sortedLetters = new TreeSet<>(Set.of("C", "B"))
sortedLetters ==> [B, C]

jshell> sortedLetters.addFirst("A")
|  Exception java.lang.UnsupportedOperationException
|        at TreeSet.addFirst (TreeSet.java:476)
|        at (#8:1)

jshell> sortedLetters.addLast("D")
|  Exception java.lang.UnsupportedOperationException
|        at TreeSet.addLast (TreeSet.java:488)
|        at (#9:1)
```

Special Feature: `LinkedHashSet<E>` and Insertion Operations The class `LinkedHashSet<E>` is also a specialization of `SequencedSet<E>`. Here, the insertion order is preserved, which is why the methods `addFirst()` and `addLast()` can be implemented in a meaningful way. Therefore, you are allowed to insert elements at the front or back:

```
jshell> SequencedSet<String> lhs = new LinkedHashSet<>(Set.of("B"))
lhs ==> [B]

jshell> lhs.addFirst("A")

jshell> lhs.addLast("C")

jshell> lhs
lhs ==> [A, B, C]
```

> ### Note: Insertion Actions for Maps
> The API of `SequencedMap<K,V>` offers two methods for adding at the front or back: `putFirst()` and `putLast()`. Analogous to the argumentation for `SequencedSet<E>`, the same effects apply here for `LinkedHashMap<K,V>` and `TreeMap<K,V>`—a reversed view can be generated in any case with `reversed()`:
>
> ```
> jshell> var lhm = new LinkedHashMap<String, Long>()
> lhm ==> {}
>
> jshell> lhm.putLast("Michael", 53L)
> $52 ==> null
>
> jshell> lhm.putFirst("Sophie", 3L)
> $53 ==> null
>
> jshell> lhm
> lhm ==> {Sophie=3, Michael=53}
>
> jshell> var reversedView = lhm.reversed()
> ```
>
> (continued)

```
reversedView ==> {Michael=53, Sophie=3}

jshell> var sortedMap = new TreeMap<String, Long>()
sortedMap ==> {}

jshell> sortedMap.putAll(Map.of("Mike", 53L, "Peter", 77L))

jshell> sortedMap
sortedMap ==> {Mike=53, Peter=77}

jshell> sortedMap.putFirst("Anne", 42L)
|  Exception java.lang.UnsupportedOperationException
|        at TreeMap.putFirst (TreeMap.java:321)
|        at (#42:1)

jshell> sortedMap.putLast("Sophie", 3L)
|  Exception java.lang.UnsupportedOperationException
|        at TreeMap.putLast (TreeMap.java:333)
|        at (#44:1)

jshell> var reversedSortedView = sortedMap.reversed()
reversedSortedView ==> {Peter=77, Mike=53}
```

5.4   JEP 444: Virtual Threads

This JEP introduces the concept of lightweight virtual threads. As a special
characteristic, these are not directly mapped to the operating system's threads. This
fact enables the use of virtual threads in server programming, with one separate
thread per request, providing lightweight support for multithreading. Better still,
existing code that uses the previous Thread API can be converted to virtual threads
with minimal changes: factory methods allow to select whether virtual threads (e. g.,
via `Executors.newVirtualThreadPerTaskExecutor()`) or platform
threads (e. g., with `Executors.newCachedThreadPool()`) should be used.

5.4.1   Introductory Examples

Virtual threads are a lightweight implementation of `java.lang.Thread` that can
be created in different ways: either individually with `ofVirtual()` or `start-
VirtualThread()` or in the context of multiple actions to be executed using
`Executors.newVirtualThreadPerTaskExecutor()`.

Fundamental Actions: `ofVirtual()` and `isVirtual()`

First, let's examine how to define and start virtual threads manually. The basis for
this is a `Runnable` defined as a lambda, which executes a simple action and

uses `isVirtual()` to check whether a virtual thread executes it. To create the virtual thread, we call `ofVirtual()`, which we define as to be run later using `unstarted()`:

```
jshell> var virtualThread = Thread.ofVirtual().unstarted(() ->
   ...>                              System.out.println("isVirtual? " +
   ...>                              Thread.currentThread().isVirtual()))
virtualThread ==> VirtualThread[#32]/new

jshell> virtualThread.start()
isVirtual? true
```

Let's expand on the example a little and create a `Runnable` that, in addition to `isVirtual()`, also accesses the thread's name via `getName()`:

```
Runnable action = () ->
{
    var currentThread = Thread.currentThread();
    System.out.println("name: '" + currentThread.getName() + "'" +
                       " isVirtual(): " + currentThread.isVirtual());
};
```

This `Runnable` is then used first as input for a platform thread and then as input for a virtual thread. It is worth noting that the previous " normal" threads are now called platform threads for better distinguishability.

For both types of threads, there are factory methods called `ofPlatform()` and `ofVirtual()` as well as the methods `name()` and `unstarted()` for specifying names and actions before starting by calling `start()`. In addition, the last call provides a shortcut for direct execution via `startVirtualThread()`. However, in that case, the name is not set:

```
var platformThread = Thread.ofPlatform().name("myPlatform").
                                    unstarted(action);
platformThread.start();

var virtualThread = Thread.ofVirtual().name("myFirstVirtual").
                                    unstarted(action);
virtualThread.start();
virtualThread.join();
System.out.println("is Thread? " + (virtualThread instanceof Thread));

Thread.startVirtualThread(action);
```

With `join()`, we wait for the end of execution. This gives us the following output, which confirms the statement above that virtual threads possess the base type `Thread`:

```
name: 'myPlatform' isVirtual(): false
name: 'myFirstVirtual' isVirtual(): true
is Thread? true
name: '' isVirtual(): true
```

Virtual Threads for Executing Many Actions

In practice, virtual threads will probably rarely be used in the way shown at the beginning, but rather in the context of an `ExecutorService` for the parallel processing of many different subtasks.

As an example, 100,000 tasks are started below using `submit()`. For each task, a new virtual thread is created, which sleeps for five seconds to simulate a slightly longer action.

```java
public static void main(final String[] args)
{
    System.out.println("Start");

    try (var executor = Executors.newVirtualThreadPerTaskExecutor())
    {
        for (int  i = 0; i < 100_000; i++)
        {
            executor.submit(() ->
            {
                Thread.sleep(Duration.ofSeconds(5));
                return 42; // The return makes it type Callable<E>.
            });
        }
    }
    // executor.close() is called implicitly => waits for tasks to finish
    System.out.println("End");
}
```

Listing 5.2 Executable as "VIRTUALTHREADSEXAMPLE"

Starting the program VIRTUALTHREADSEXAMPLE produces the output `Start` followed by `End` on an Apple M3 Max after approximately five seconds—in principle, this corresponds only to the waiting time for processing one thread and not that for 100,000, a terrific result. Even with slightly older hardware, such as an Intel Core i7-1065G7, the program takes approximately eight seconds to complete execution.

This example illustrates that modern hardware can indeed support 100,000 virtual threads without any problems and, depending on the hardware, even many more. Why? Behind the scenes, the JDK executes these actions in a significantly smaller number of operating system threads—known as carrier threads. More on this in a moment.

5.4.2   Restrictions of Conventional Threads

A classic platform thread is always represented by an operating system thread. When using `Executors.newCachedThreadPool()`, another platform thread and thus a new operating system thread is potentially created for each task, provided that the threads of the thread pool are all busy. This results in a significantly different processing situation.

To understand this, let's switch from virtual threads to platform threads, that is, operating system threads. To do this, we only need to change one line in the above program

```
// try (var executor = Executors.newVirtualThreadPerTaskExecutor())
// =>
try (var executor = Executors.newCachedThreadPool())
```

Listing 5.3 Executable as "PLATFORMTHREADSEXAMPLE"

With this change, the `ExecutorService` would, in extreme cases, even attempt to create up to 100,000 operating system threads during (very) high utilization. Depending on the computer and operating system, this will fail and result in a crash like the following (output truncated)—try it out by running the PLATFORMTHREADSEXAMPLE program:

```
Start
[1.828s] [warning] [os,thread] Failed to start thread "Unknown thread" -
    pthread_create failed (EAGAIN) for attributes: stacksize: 2048k,
    guardsize: 16k, detached.
[1.828s] [warning] [os,thread] Failed to start the native thread for java.lang.
    Thread "pool-1-thread-12254"
Exception in thread "main" java.lang.OutOfMemoryError: unable to create
    native thread: possibly out of memory or process/resource limits
    reached
   at java.base/java.lang.Thread.start0(Native Method)
   at java.base/java.lang.Thread.start(Thread.java:1553)
   at java.base/java.lang.System$2.start(System.java:2577)
   at java.base/jdk.internal.vm.SharedThreadContainer.start(
       SharedThreadContainer.java:152)
   at java.base/java.util.concurrent.ThreadPoolExecutor.addWorker(
       ThreadPoolExecutor.java:953)
...
```

You must specify a wait time of a few seconds, in this case, roughly five. Why? Modern processors often have ten or more processing units and are therefore capable of processing a large number of threads in parallel. With powerful hardware and an unfavorably short wait time, such as one second, it appears as if 100,000 operating system threads could actually be processed—I experienced this very phenomenon during a presentation after switching from my MacBook Pro with M1 Pro to M3 Max. Another effect observed is that the memory consumption for this minimal program exceeds 1 GB and the CPU load rises to over 600%. With Intel processors and, especially, the Windows operating system, the above program can often still be executed—resulting in runtimes of over 30 seconds, 30,000 operating system threads, and exceeding 2 GB of memory consumption.

Explanation and Background Information on Threads In the following, I would like to shed some light on the background: An operating system thread is the smallest unit of execution. Within a process, threads share the same memory space and resources. The threads can be executed simultaneously. As practical as this may seem, threads also incur certain costs, for example, in the form of memory for the respective call stack—this is evident in the previous example, which indicates a memory bottleneck or a limitation in the operating system's threads or other resources. Accordingly, some operating systems can only create and manage a limited number of threads.

Idea: Thread Pooling One strategy for addressing the issue of limited operating system threads is to maintain a pool of threads. For example, assuming 10,000 possible operating system threads, you could use about 5,000 for a thread pool, which you create with `Executors.newFixedThreadPool(5000)`. Then many of the 100,000 tasks would not be executed in parallel, but in batches of 5,000. This procedure only makes sense if the individual tasks require a significant amount of I/O; for CPU-intensive tasks, parallelism is limited by the number of CPU cores. For the server example, which presumably involves a lot of I/O, it would then be possible to process a (very) large number of tasks per second, depending on the individual calculation times. Let's assume a few thousand. That doesn't sound bad at first, but it's clearly not enough for high-traffic websites. If the entire process were executed with virtual threads, the example would result in around 100,000 tasks per second, and the number could be increased significantly without any problems.

5.4.3   Motivation for Virtual Threads in Practice

To address the limitations of operating system threads, virtual threads were introduced as a lightweight alternative. One goal is to achieve the optimal CPU utilization, particularly for workloads with a high I/O load.

Virtual Threads in the JVM and in the Context of Operating System Threads

In practice, hundreds of thousands of virtual threads can be started without any problems. This is possible because they are not mapped 1:1 to operating system threads.

Regarding scheduling and management: The operating system schedules the execution of *platform threads*. The JVM can intervene to control this (e. g., via thread pools). In addition, the JVM decides when a *virtual thread* is executed. For this purpose, a virtual thread is temporarily assigned (*mounted*) to a platform thread; the operating system then schedules this platform thread as it would any other. The platform thread on which a virtual thread is currently running is referred to as a *carrier thread*.

The relationship is dynamic: virtual threads are *demounted* from the carrier during blocking or parking operations and later *remounted* onto (possibly a different) carrier. Thus, there is no separate thread type " carrier thread" and no permanent binding. Carrier thread is therefore a temporary role of a thread, not a separate thread type.

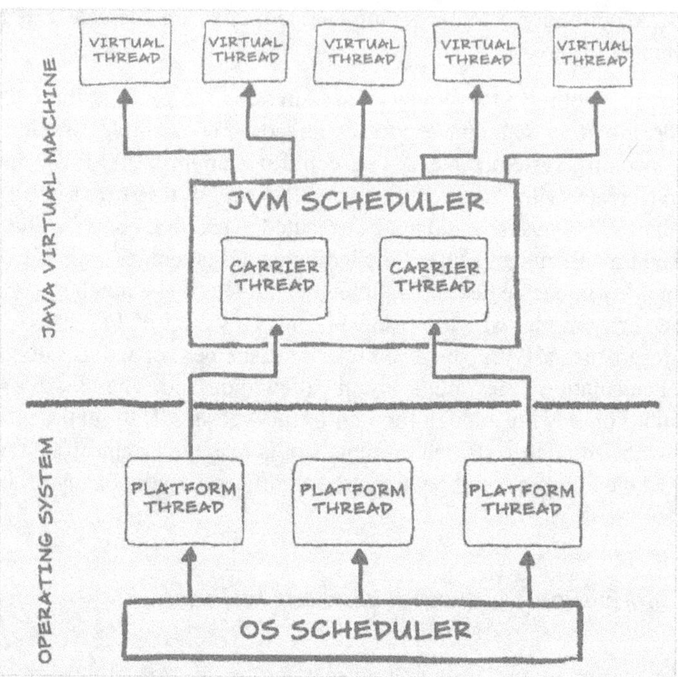

Fig. 5.3 Virtual threads in the JVM and in the context of operating system threads

Figure 5.3 illustrates this relationship.[2] The carrier threads shown separately there are only conceptually separate; in the JVM, they are normal platform threads that temporarily execute virtual threads.

Problems with Conventional Approaches to I/O

Within applications, I/O actions are common, such as accessing REST services or databases, which typically first convert data for the calls into a desired format and then transform the results delivered back into the required formats. We recognize that preparing the data (marshalling and unmarshalling) typically incurs only a low CPU load and, in the best case, can be completed in a few nanoseconds. Sending the data over the network, on the other hand, often takes milliseconds, sometimes even longer. This is illustrated in the Fig. 5.4).

Quite obviously, precisely these pauses caused by waiting for results during transmission lead to increasingly poor CPU utilization when processed by platform threads.

---

[2] Source: https://belief-driven-design.com/looking-at-java-21-virtual-threads-bd181/.

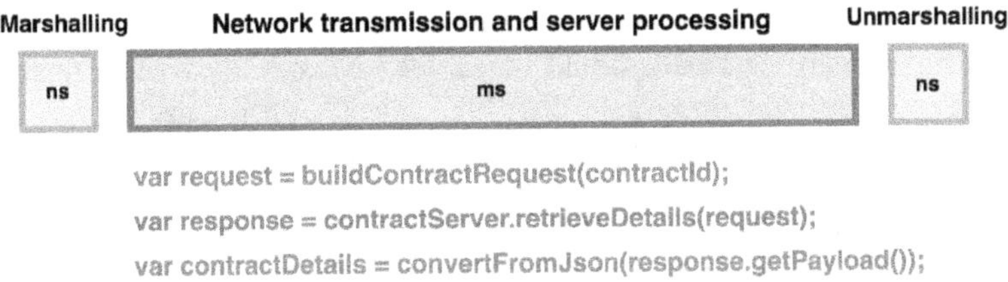

Fig. 5.4 Problematic I/O without virtual threads

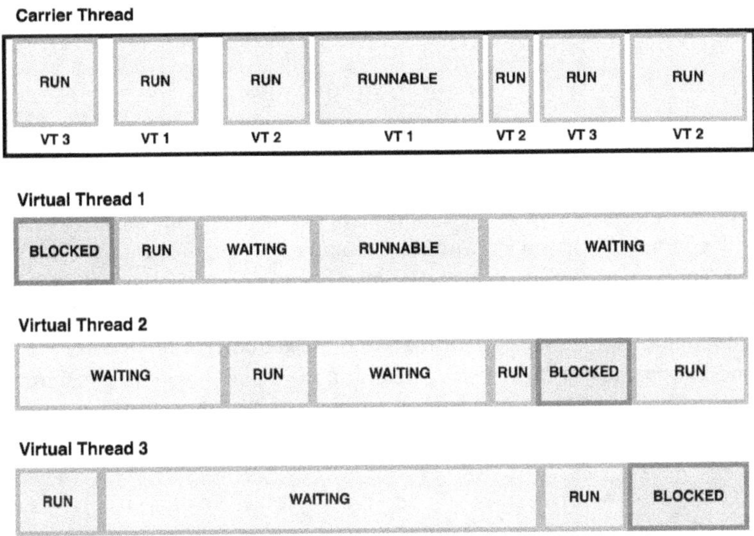

Fig. 5.5 Allocation of virtual threads to carrier threads

However, if the CPU could process other tasks, or, more precisely, threads, during the waiting time, many tasks could be completed in almost the same amount of time instead of just one. This approach of decoupling virtual threads from the carrier thread when they enter the `BLOCKED`, `WAITING`, or `TIMED_WAITING` state is illustrated in Fig. 5.5. Another virtual thread can then start its work and enter the `RUNNABLE` state—sometimes abbreviated as `RUN`.[3] This approach allows many virtual threads to be executed by a few carrier threads.

It should be explicitly mentioned here that virtual threads are only advantageous and useful in situations where a lot of I/O or actions that require waiting are performed—however, not when very computationally intensive tasks need to be

---

[3] In Java, there are different states for threads. The following are relevant here: `RUNNABLE` (ready for execution), with a substate `RUNNING` (currently executing). `BLOCKED` means that the thread is waiting for a monitor lock to (re)enter a `synchronized` block or a synchronized method. In `WAITING`, the thread is waiting for another thread to perform a specific action and fulfill a condition—this may happen with a timeout specified (`TIMED_WAITING`).

executed. In addition, with Java 21 LTS up to and including Java 23, calls to blocking methods in `synchronized` should be avoided because the virtual thread then blocks the carrier thread. In Java 24, JEP 491, called " Synchronize Virtual Threads without Pinning," ensures that the binding of virtual threads to carrier threads can be unmounted and the restriction described above no longer applies.

When calling native methods, virtual threads are currently (with Java 21 LTS) not detached from the carrier thread. This potentially affects parallelism and scalability, as the JVM then cannot execute other virtual threads with that carrier thread. In the case of `synchronized`, an alternative is to ensure a critical section using `java.util.concurrent.locks.ReentrantLock`.[4]

5.4.4   *Performance Comparison for Platform and Virtual Threads*

We will conduct a simple performance comparison to illustrate the number of platform and virtual threads that can be generated in each case and the throughput for simple tasks.

For this purpose, we will perform several measurements for 2k, 4k, ..., 10k, ..., 18k, and 20k threads of each type. In addition to virtual threads, measurements for platform threads are taken based on a fixed and a cached thread pool.

```java
public static void main(final String[] args)
{
    for (int factorInThousands : List.of(2, 4, 6, 8, 10, 12, 14, 16, 18, 20))
    {
        // This creates an executor with virtual threads
        try (var executor = Executors.newVirtualThreadPerTaskExecutor())
        {
            measureExecution(executor, "Virtual", factorInThousands);
        }

        // Creates a pool of platform threads with a fixed size (10,000)
        try (var executor = Executors.newFixedThreadPool(10000))
        {
            measureExecution(executor, "Pooled Platform", factorInThousands);
        }

        // Creates a pool of Platform threads that can potentially grow.
        try (var executor = Executors.newCachedThreadPool())
        {
            measureExecution(executor, "Platform", factorInThousands);
        }
    }
}
```

Listing 5.4   Executable as "**VIRTUALTHREADSPOOLINGEXAMPLE**"

---

[4] For details, see https://docs.oracle.com/en/java/javase/21/core/virtual-threads.html.

We implement the measurement in the method `measureExecution()`. There, we catch exceptions so that we can also cleanly measure the situations already shown with insufficient thread resources. At the end, the total time is determined:

```java
private static void measureExecution(ExecutorService executor,
                                     String info, int factor)
{
    System.out.println("Start Measuring " + info);
    long start = System.nanoTime();

    try
    {
        for (int i = 0; i < factor; i++)
        {
            System.out.println("Start of " + info + " " + (i + 1) * 1000);
            submit1000Threads(executor);
        }
    }
    catch (Throwable th)
    {
        th.printStackTrace();
    }

    // Important, so that you wait until all tasks have been processed
    executor.close();

    System.out.println("End Measuring " + info);
    long end = System.nanoTime();
    System.out.println(info + " took " + (end-start) / 1_000_000 + " ms");
    System.out.println("-------------------------------------");
}
```

The method `submit1000Threads()` then creates 1,000 threads, each of which waits three seconds to simulate access to an external resource:

```java
private static void submit1000Threads(ExecutorService executor)
{
    for (int i = 0; i < 1_000; i++)
    {
        executor.submit(() ->
        {
            Thread.sleep(Duration.ofSeconds(3));
            return 42;
        });
    }
}
```

Execution Results

When we run the program VIRTUALTHREADSPOOLINGEXAMPLE shown above, the execution times are logged on the console. It becomes clear that these are almost constant for virtual threads. For platform threads, the execution time increases steadily, and depending on the CPU and main memory, this ultimately leads to an exception, resulting in termination. In the case of pooled platform threads, linear increases with jumps can be observed.

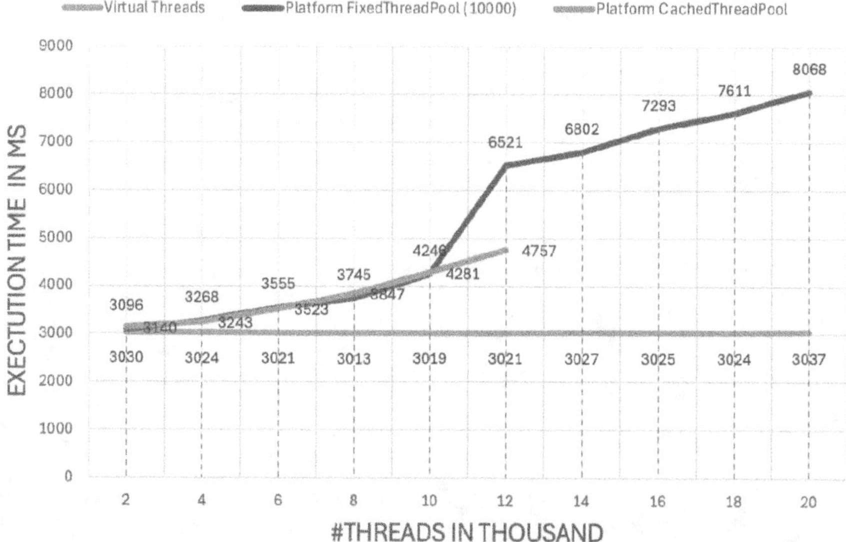

Fig. 5.6 Performance comparison of virtual threads and platform threads

If the figures are evaluated more precisely and plotted on a line graph, the result is a curve similar to the one shown in Fig. 5.6.

We can clearly see the increase and drop-off in platform threads when their number exceeds a threshold value. The pooled platform threads exhibit a linear increase, followed by a jump, and then another linear increase. The jump occurs each time the pool size is reached. This fact is logically inevitable with a fixed-size pool. If you were to continue increasing its size to reduce runtime, you would inevitably encounter a similar limit as before for unpooled platform threads. In fact, it is not that easy to determine the best-fitting sizes. However, the pooled platform threads can process any task load, resulting in a linear increase in runtime, with occasional jumps. Finally, we see the nearly constant execution time with virtual threads, which runs parallel to the x-axis at a constant height. The runtime value is determined here by the duration of the calculations in the threads, specifically the three-second waiting time.

Just as a reminder: The platform threads are created by the `newCached-ThreadPool()`. For the pooled platform threads, we used `newFixedThread-Pool()`. The virtual threads are created by the `newVirtualThreadPerTask-Executor()`.

5.4.5 Conclusion

By introducing virtual threads as a lightweight alternative to platform threads, you can often pursue a one-thread-per-request strategy again without worrying about the actual number of threads. This procedure works well because many blocking I/O operations in one virtual thread cause another virtual thread to take over. In this way, the hardware is utilized almost optimally, resulting in a high degree of concurrency and, consequently, high throughput.

Due to their characteristics, virtual threads should not be reused or pooled; instead, it is recommended that each task be processed by its own virtual thread.

Please note that the scaling effects outlined above are most effective when a task primarily involves I/O, such as database access or REST calls, and involves only a few CPU-intensive calculations. In contrast, virtual threads cannot leverage their advantages for complex calculations and provide throughput that is, for the most part, comparable to that of platform threads.

The following applies: virtual threads can significantly improve the throughput of applications if

- A large number of simpler tasks must be processed in parallel.
- There is a lot of I/O, as waiting times arise due to file system and/or network access. Such load situations can be handled better with virtual threads than with operating system threads.[5]

In other words, if server applications execute a large number of tasks simultaneously and spend a significant amount of time waiting, for example, for resources or the file system, then virtual threads help improve throughput.

However, it is also important to note that if the calculations to be performed are computationally intensive, therefore, CPU-bound, it makes almost no difference whether virtual threads or operating system threads are used.

5.5 Miscellaneous

Beyond the enhancements described above, several features have been incorporated into the JDK, some with and some without JEPs. In this section, I present a potpourri of various functionalities.

---

[5] This applies in particular to TCP sockets, but not to UDP. Various file system operations have also not yet been fully adapted to the requirements of virtual threads.

5.5.1 *JEP 400: UTF-8 by Default*

Charsets (character set encodings) map characters to specific numbers. Well-known examples are ASCII and ISO-8859-1 (Latin-1).

When processing textual information, difficulties arise quickly when special characters, such as umlauts or Cyrillic or Chinese characters, are used—especially when the character set encodings differ between senders/producers of information and recipients/consumers. This can make the exchange of information (input, processing, and output of data) extremely difficult or even prevent it altogether.

The UTF-8 character set encoding provides a solution here, as it enables the representation of a large number of existing characters. Although UTF-8 is often selected as the default in operating systems, this is not the case in all of them. The standard character set, therefore, varies depending on the operating system. In Windows, for example, it even depends on user settings, such as language and region.

JEP 400 addresses the problem of different and potentially incompatible character set encodings, as well as the resulting need for conversions. By using UTF-8 as the standard character set in Java programs, the same results are reproducibly delivered on different operating systems, making Java programs even more reliable and portable. However, existing source code that uses the previous methods without the optional character set specification may behave differently than before. This should definitely be taken into account.

Example

You can check the default character set in JShell as follows:

```
jshell> import java.nio.charset.Charset

jshell> Charset.defaultCharset()
$21 ==> UTF-8
```

Alternatively, you can use the following command-line instruction, which extracts the character set encoding from the system properties and outputs it:[6]

```
$ java -XshowSettings:properties -version 2>&1 | grep file.encoding
    file.encoding = UTF-8
```

Since Java 18, there has been a system property called `native.encoding`. A variant for later use, based on this native encoding, can be written with fallback to the standard character set as follows:

---

[6] For Windows, you can use `findstr` instead of `grep`.

```
jshell> var encoding = System.getProperty("native.encoding")
encoding ==> "UTF-8"

jshell> var charset = (encoding != null) ?
   ...>                  Charset.forName(encoding) : Charset.defaultCharset()
charset ==> UTF-8
```

> **Note: The Problem in Detail**
> To illustrate the difficulties once again, let's look at the results under Windows
> for different calls:
>
> ```
> jshell> import java.nio.charset.Charset;
>
> jshell> Charset.defaultCharset()
> $2 ==> UTF-8
>
> jshell> System.getProperty("native.encoding")
> $3 ==> "Cp1252"
>
> jshell> Charset.forName("Cp1252")
> $4 ==> windows-1252
> ```

5.5.2   JEP 452: Key Encapsulation Mechanism API

The Key Encapsulation Mechanism (KEM) is a modern encryption technology that
enables the exchange of symmetric keys using an asymmetric encryption method.
Very few of us are directly involved in implementing low-level encryption and
decryption. In general, we only use it indirectly, for example, through the use of
SSH (Secure Shell) or access via HTTPS.

5.5.3   New Features in the `Math` Class

The utility class `java.lang.Math` contains various useful methods. Several
practical ones have been added in recent Java versions.

Further Innovations in `xyzExact()`

Java 8 LTS already includes various " exact" methods. These counteract silent
overflow when values exceed the range during calculations, for example, at the
maximum limit of an `int`, by raising an exception.

As an introductory example, let's consider adding the value 10 to a value close to the maximum of `int`:

```
jshell> int nearlyMax = Integer.MAX_VALUE - 7
nearlyMax ==> 2147483640

jshell> nearlyMax + 10
$2 ==> -2147483646

jshell> Math.addExact(nearlyMax, 10)
|   Exception java.lang.ArithmeticException: integer overflow
|         at Math.addExact (Math.java:878)
|         at (#3:1)
```

Java 18 introduces overloaded variants of `divideExact(int, int)` and `floorDivExact(int, int)`.[7]

The process is illustrated below using `divideExact()`. Dividing by -1 produces an incorrect value, whereas using `divideExact()` results in an exception that indicates the error:

```
jshell> int minInteger = Integer.MIN_VALUE
minInteger ==> -2147483648

jshell> minInteger / -1
$16 ==> -2147483648

jshell> Math.divideExact(minInteger, -1)
|   Exception java.lang.ArithmeticException: integer overflow
|         at Math.divideExact (Math.java:1065)
|         at (#17:1)
```

Further Innovations in `ceilXyz()`

Java 18 also adds variants of `ceilDiv(int, int)` and `ceilMod(int, int)`. Let's look at a few calls for `ceilDiv(int,int)`. This method returns the rounded-up value of a division and is thus the counterpart to `floorDiv(int, int)`, which returns the rounded-down value:

```
jshell> Math.ceilDiv(4, 3)
$10 ==> 2

jshell> Math.ceilDiv(-4, 3)
$11 ==> -1

jshell> Math.floorDiv(4, 3)
$12 ==> 1

jshell> Math.floorDiv(-4, 3)
$13 ==> -2
```

---

[7] The same applies to the utility class `java.lang.StrictMath`.

Further Innovations in `clamp()`

The two methods `Math.clamp()` and `StrictMath.clamp()` accept three
arguments: the value, a lower (MIN) limit, and an upper (MAX) limit. If the value
lies between MIN and MAX, it is returned. If the value is less than MIN, then MIN
is returned; if the value is greater than MAX, then the method returns the value
MAX. This functionality is helpful for keeping a number within a range of values
between MIN and MAX, inclusive:

```
jshell> Math.clamp(10, 6, 42)
$1 ==> 10

jshell> Math.clamp(0, 6, 42)
$2 ==> 6

jshell> Math.clamp(100, 6, 42)
$3 ==> 42
```

Before Java 21 LTS, an implementation that was admittedly already slightly
confusing would look something like this:

```java
public int clamp(int value, int min, int max)
{
    return Math.max(min, Math.min(max, value));
}
```

5.5.4 New Features When Creating a `HashMap<>`

When creating instances of the class `java.util.ArrayList<E>`, the desired
initial size can be specified directly in the constructor, thereby defining the initial
capacity, as shown here for 1,000 names:

```java
List<String> names = new ArrayList<>(1_000);
```

For the class `java.util.HashMap<K,V>`, something similar was not possible until now, even though there was a seemingly similar call:

```java
Map<String, String> map = new HashMap<>(1_000);
```

First, we need to take a look at some background information on the implementation of the `HashMap<K,V>` class. When you pass a value to the constructor,
it refers to the number of possible mappings. However, maps should never be
completely filled to ensure good performance. This is achieved using a so-called
load factor, which determines the proportion of memory that can be used; by default,
this value is 0.75. If the `HashMap<K,V>` is then about 75 % full, it is enlarged and
space is made available for more mappings. In the above example, a map with space

for 1,000 mappings would be created, but only 750 key–value mappings could be stored there.

As a new feature, you can now create a map with the desired number of actually possible mappings using a factory method as follows:

```
Map<String, String> mapping = HashMap.newHashMap(1000);
```

By default, the load factor is 0.75; therefore, the above statement creates a map with an initial capacity of approximately 1,330.

5.5.5 Various Changes

As examples of some further changes, I will list a few API innovations here.

New Features in the `SourceVersion` Enumeration

Since Java 21 LTS, there is a new constant `RELEASE_21` in the enumeration `javax.lang.model.SourceVersion`. This can be queried using the method `runtimeVersion()`:

```
jshell> import javax.lang.model.SourceVersion

jshell> SourceVersion.RELEASE_21.runtimeVersion()
$7 ==> 21

jshell> SourceVersion.latest()
$8 ==> RELEASE_21
```

`Duration.isPositive()`

The `java.time.Duration` class now (since Java 18) offers a method `isPositive()` to determine whether a `Duration` is a positive duration. This completes the functionality, as checking for negative duration or the value 0 was already an initial part of the class.

```
jshell> import java.time.*

jshell> import java.time.temporal.*

jshell> Duration.of(20L, ChronoUnit.DAYS).isPositive()
$3 ==> true

jshell> Duration.of(-12L, ChronoUnit.DAYS).isPositive()
$4 ==> false
```

`FileInputStream.transferTo()`

Java 9 introduced a `transferTo()` method in the `InputStream` class for transferring data from a `java.io.InputStream` to a `java.io.OutputStream`. With Java 18, we also find a `transferTo()` method in the `java.io.File-InputStream` class.

`StringBuffer.repeat()` and `StringBuilder.repeat()`

Both methods, like `String.repeat()`, are used to repeat one or more characters and have been part of the JDK since Java 21 LTS. However, their behavior in JShell had not been free of surprises up to and including Java 21.0.8 LTS. The author has reported the malfunction in JShell as a bug https://bugs.openjdk.org/browse/JDK-8324810 to Oracle. This got solved with Java 21.0.9 LTS.

Let's just play around a bit to see the functionality in action:

```
jshell> var buffer = new StringBuffer().repeat("BLA", 3)
buffer ==> BLABLABLA

jshell> new StringBuffer().repeat("BLA", 3)
$32 ==> BLABLABLA

jshell> var buffer = new StringBuffer()
buffer ==>

jshell> buffer = buffer.repeat("HELLO", 2)
buffer ==> HELLOHELLO

jshell> System.out.println(buffer)

jshell> var sb = new StringBuffer()
sb ==>

jshell> sb.repeat('*', 10)
$48 ==> **********
********
```

`HttpClient`

Since Java 21 LTS, the `java.net.http.HttpClient` class implements the interface `AutoCloseable` and can therefore now be used in a try-with-resources block, which simplifies releasing of system resources. To illustrate this, we are sending a REST request to the page https://reqres.in/, which provides sample data:

```
jshell> import java.net.http.*

jshell> try (var client = HttpClient.newHttpClient())
   ...> {
   ...>     var request = HttpRequest.newBuilder()
   ...>         .uri(URI.create("https://reqres.in/api/users/2"))
   ...>         // recently required
```

```
...>             .header("x-api-key", "reqres-free-v1")
...>             .build();
...>
...>      var stringHandler = HttpResponse.BodyHandlers.ofString();
...>      var response = client.send(request, stringHandler);
...>
...>      System.out.println(response.body());
...> }
{"data":{"id":2,"email":"janet.weaver@reqres.in","first\_name":"Janet","last\
   _name":"Weaver","avatar":"https://reqres.in/img/faces/2-image.jpg"},"
   support":{"url":"https://reqres.in/\#support-heading","text":"To keep
   ReqRes free, contributions towards server costs are appreciated!"}}
```

Locale.availableLocales()

The method `availableLocales()` extends the class `java.util.Locale`
and returns the available `Locales` as `Stream<Locale>`. Before Java 21
LTS, only the method `Locale[] getAvailableLocales()` existed, which
returned an array as the result. A stream offers far more possibilities; in particular,
it is not necessary to first determine and provide all locales:

```
jshell> Stream<Locale> localeStream = Locale.availableLocales()
localeStream ==> java.util.stream.ReferencePipeline\textdollarHead@21588809

jshell> var first\_7\_de = localeStream.filter(loc ->
   ...>                              loc.getLanguage().equals("de")).
   ...>                              limit(7).
   ...>                              toList()
first\_7\_de ==> [de\_IT, de\_CH, de\_BE, de\_DE\_\#Latn, de, de\_LU, de\_DE]
```

Collections.shuffle(List,RandomGenerator)

Since Java 21 LTS, this extension allows for the random shuffling of a list
using a `RandomGenerator` from package `java.util.random`. The method
`shuffle()` has been overloaded accordingly. The following calls demonstrate its
use, creating a `RandomGenerator` and using it to shuffle a list of names that is
initially sorted alphabetically:

```
jshell> import java.util.random.*

jshell> var generator =
   ...>     RandomGenerator.JumpableGenerator.of("Xoroshiro128PlusPlus")
generator ==> jdk.random.Xoroshiro128PlusPlus@78ac1102

jshell> var names = new ArrayList<>(List.of("Anton", "Beat", "Cay", "Don"))
names ==> [Anton, Beat, Cay, Don]

jshell> Collections.shuffle(names, generator)

jshell> names
names ==> [Anton, Don, Beat, Cay]
```

**`String.splitWithDelimiters()` and
`Pattern.splitWithDelimiters()`**

Since Java 21 LTS, these methods have been available for splitting a string based on a regular expression. They return both the individual strings and the matching delimiter characters as the result. Therefore, the separator strings : : and : : : are also included in the result below:

```
jshell> String[] splits = "tom:and::jerry".splitWithDelimiters(":+", 3)
splits ==> String[5] { "tom", "::", "and", ":::", "jerry" }
```

**`String.indexOf(String str,int beginIndex,int
endIndex)` and `String.indexOf(int ch,int beginIndex,int
endIndex)`**

These methods, introduced in Java 21 LTS, return the index of the first occurrence of the specified string or character within the specified range of the string. The following example returns the index for the term SECRET depending on the specified range of the message:

```
jshell> var msg = "TOP SECRET: This is a SECRET msg"
msg ==> "TOP SECRET: This is a SECRET msg"

jshell> int pos1 = msg.indexOf("SECRET", 0, 10)
pos1 ==> 4

jshell> int pos2 = msg.indexOf("SECRET", 10, msg.length())
pos2 ==> 22
```

5.6 Deprecations

5.6.1 JEP 421: Deprecate Finalization for Removal

Originally, finalization was planned to serve as a safety net, enabling cleanup or resource release when an object dies. To this end, it is intended that during garbage collection, the respective finalizer is called in the form of a `protected` method named `finalize()` before the object's memory is released. However, there are various hurdles and difficulties associated with finalization. For example, it is not defined when the call occurs exactly or whether it happens at all (possibly some time after the object is no longer referenced or possibly not at all if finalization is disabled). It is also possible that the object is returned to an active state with the help of the finalizer and is revived.

As part of JEP 421, the finalization process is marked as deprecated and for removal (`forRemoval=true`). In addition, all `finalize()` methods are deprecated. Furthermore, finalization remains active by default, but can now also be deactivated to facilitate the transition.

The background to this JEP is explained in detail by Nicolai Parlog online at https://www.youtube.com/watch?v=eDgBnjOid-g.

5.6.2 Further Deprecations

In the `Runtime` Class

In the `Runtime` class, various overloaded `exec()` methods were deprecated in Java 18, as was the `runFinalization()` method.

In the `Thread` Class

Various methods are deprecated in the `java.lang.Thread` class. One example is the `stop()` method, which has not only been deprecated since JDK 21 LTS, but is also marked as `forRemoval=true`.

In the `Locale` Class

In Java 19, the constructors of the `java.util.Locale` class were marked as deprecated. Alternatively, the static factory methods can be used:

- `Locale.of(language)`,
- `Locale.of(language, country)`
- `Locale.of(language, country, variant)`

In addition, there is the `Locale.Builder` class for creating `Locale` instances:

```
var specialLocale = new Locale.Builder().setLanguage("sr").
                              setScript("Latn").
                              setRegion("RS").
                              build();
```

I prefer the factory methods to the builder variant, which I consider to be strangely implemented. In this case, I expect `with()` methods or methods such as `language()` in accordance with the design pattern of the same name, but not `set()` methods.

In the URL Class

The constructors of the `java.net.URL` class are deprecated as of Java 20. Instead, they should be replaced by those of the `java.net.URI` class, as follows:

```java
// old
URL myUrl = new URL("http://example.com");

// new
URI myUri = new URI("http://example.com");
URL myUrl = myUri.toURL();
```

The original URL constructors provided points of attack, which led to security issues. Using URI to create a URL allows for more precise validation and parsing of URL components.

Chapter 6
JVM Innovations in JDK 18 to 21 LTS

In this chapter, we will examine some of the changes, enhancements, and new features in the JVM that have been cumulatively included in Java 18 to 21 LTS.

In the following sections, we will focus specifically on these topics—preview features are marked in italics:

- JEP 408: Simple Web Server
- JEP 413: Code Snippets in Java API Documentation
- *JEP 445: Unnamed Classes and Instance Main Methods (Preview)*

6.1 JEP 408: Simple Web Server

The goal of this JEP was to integrate a minimalist web server into the JDK that can only serve static files and requires little configuration. This web server facilitates prototyping and file sharing and is helpful for simple testing. For example, it can be used to create a rudimentary REST API stub that delivers static content, such as for calls like GET `localhost:8080/items/` delivering all items or GET `localhost:8080/items/<id>` for providing a specific item.

Example

You can easily start the web server from the command line as follows:

```
$ jwebserver
Binding to loopback by default. For all interfaces use "-b 0.0.0.0" or "-b ::
".
Serving /Users/michaelinden and subdirectories on 127.0.0.1 port 8000
URL http://127.0.0.1:8000/
```

As is apparent from the output, the directory in which the web server was started is provided. However, you need to have the appropriate rights to the directory from which the web server was started. Otherwise, you will see a "404 File Not Found"

© The Author(s), under exclusive license to APress Media, LLC,
part of Springer Nature 2026
M. Inden, *Java 25 and Beyond*, https://doi.org/10.1007/979-8-8688-2385-5_6

Fig. 6.1 Directory content
provided with jwebserver

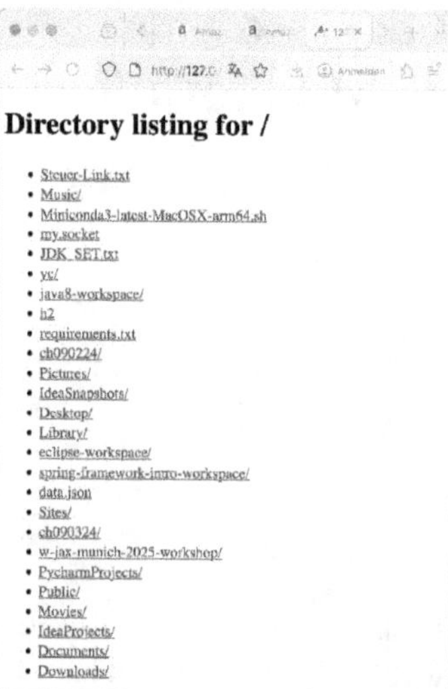

error. Let's try this out by opening the URL `http://127.0.0.1:8000` in our
browser. Your home directory should be displayed, as shown in Fig. 6.1 for my
computer.

When accessing from the browser, we receive the following console output:

```
127.0.0.1 - - [20/Feb./2022:11:20:39 +0100] "GET / HTTP/1.1" 200 -
127.0.0.1 - - [20/Feb./2022:11:20:39 +0100] "GET /favicon.ico HTTP/1.1" 404 -
```

Let's look at an alternative command-line call:

```
$ java -m jdk.httpserver
Binding to loopback by default. For all interfaces use "-b 0.0.0.0" or "-b ::
".
Serving /Users/michaelinden and subdirectories on 127.0.0.1 port 8000
URL http://127.0.0.1:8000/
```

Conveniently, you can change the port by specifying -p:

```
$ java -m jdk.httpserver -p 9000
Binding to loopback by default. For all interfaces use "-b 0.0.0.0" or "-b ::
".
Serving /Users/michaelinden and subdirectories on 127.0.0.1 port 9000
URL http://127.0.0.1:9000/
```

Programmatic Start: What Actually Happens in the Background? If you want to start and use the web server within a Java program, the `com.sun.net.http-server.SimpleFileServer` class offers the method `createFileServer()` to customize the port and path according to your requirements:

```java
public static void main(final String[] args)
{
    var address = new InetSocketAddress(7777);
    var path = Path.of("/Users/michaelinden"); // PLEASE ADJUST
    var server = SimpleFileServer.createFileServer(address, path,
                                        OutputLevel.VERBOSE);
    server.start();
    System.out.println("SimpleWebServerApp is up and running");
}
```

Note: Good to Know

This functionality resides in the package `com.sun.net.httpserver`, which is located in the module `jdk.httpserver`. It is therefore part of the JDK, but not necessarily part of a Java SE distribution. Given its rudimentary range of functions, this is probably not a significant issue.

Additionally, the web server only supports the older HTTP/1.1 and does not offer any security or SSL encryption. Likewise, only a subset of HTTP commands is supported, namely, GET and HEAD. It means that only requests are possible, but no modifying actions are allowed. However, this should be sufficient for the use cases mentioned at the beginning.

6.2   JEP 413: Code Snippets in Java API Documentation

Until now, there has been no standard for including source code fragments in HTML documentation generated with JavaDoc. JEP 413 introduces the inline tag `@snippet`, which enables the specification of source code fragments in JavaDoc comments for inclusion in the generated JavaDoc documentation.

Example

The whole thing can then be used in the source code as follows, for example, whereby in addition to `@snippet`, the possibility of highlighting using `@highlight` is also demonstrated:

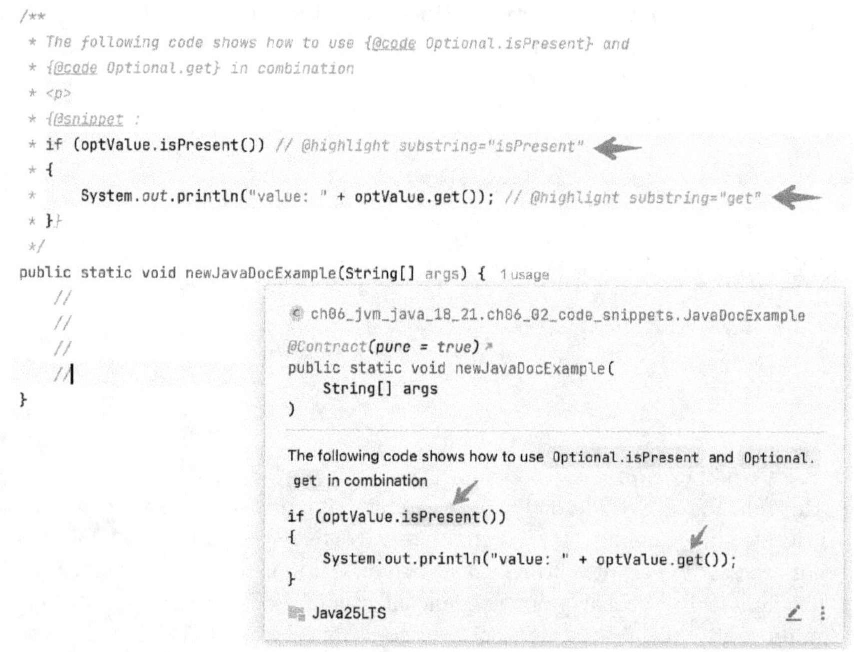

```
/**
 * The following code shows how to use {@code Optional.isPresent} and
 * {@code Optional.get} in combination
 * <p>
 * {@snippet :
 * if (optValue.isPresent()) // @highlight substring="isPresent"
 * {
 *     System.out.println("value: " + optValue.get()); // @highlight substring="get"
 * }}
 */
public static void newJavaDocExample(String[] args) {  1 usage
    //
    //
    //
    //
}
```

Fig. 6.2 Demonstration of the new JavaDoc tags for source code fragments

```
/**
 * The following code shows how to use {@code Optional.isPresent} and
 * {@code Optional.get} in combination
 *
 * {@snippet :
 * if (optValue.isPresent()) // @highlight substring="isPresent"
 * {
 *     System.out.println("value: " +
 *                        optValue.get()); // @highlight substring="get"
 * } }
 */
```

Figure 6.2 illustrates an example of the representation in the IDE for IntelliJ
IDEA; the visualization differs slightly in Eclipse.

Alternatives Available to Date

Although the tags `pre` and `code` have been available to achieve similar results,
both cause different problems: with the former, you have to escape, and with the
latter, line breaks are lost. For more information, see https://reflectoring.io/howto-
format-code-snippets-in-javadoc/ and https://docs.oracle.com/en/java/javase/18/
code-snippet/.

> **Note: Markdown as a Future Alternative**
> With Java 23, and thus also with Java 25 LTS, it will be possible to use Markdown instead of HTML for documentation. It is very pleasing, as Markdown has become increasingly popular for documentation in recent years, replacing the HTML elements that were the obvious choice in the early days of Java, with a more contemporary alternative. Unfortunately, Markdown does not (yet) offer highlighting. For more details, see Sect. 9.2.

6.3   JEP 445: Unnamed Classes and Instance Main Methods (Preview)

Perhaps it has been a while since you learned Java. But you probably still remember how tough it was. Even when teaching Java to programming beginners, you notice how difficult it is to get started and how much there is to explain. From a beginner's perspective, Java has a steep learning curve.

This JEP aims to simplify the process of getting started with and learning Java. To this end, Java should be as easy to use as possible for smaller experiments, especially in combination with direct compilation, the direct invocation of a Java program from the console (see Sect. 15.5).

As already indicated, up to now this has required a considerable amount of preparatory work, and it has always been necessary to explain or roughly introduce various concepts that are initially somewhat confusing, such as classes, arrays, and visibility. However, these topics are actually only important and meaningful in the context of larger programs. Beginners may initially find them overwhelming. With increasing knowledge and a little experience, concepts such as classes, visibility control, and static components become more significant and can be introduced gradually.

6.3.1   Introduction

As an example, let's revisit a simple Hello World program. Previously, this had to be written as a separate class with a static `main()` method as follows:

```java
public class OldStyleHelloWorld
{
    public static void main(String[] args)
    {
        System.out.println("Hello, World!");
    }
}
```

As a trainer, you often said the following to novices: "The terms `public`, `class`, `static`, `void`, etc. are not important; simply look at the line with the method call of `System.out.println()`. Oh, and `System.out` is an instance of a class, but that's not important right now either." If you, as a beginner, weren't lucky enough to have a trainer or experienced developer to assist you, the path to understanding was rather arduous. Several confusing elements are required to output a simple text message to the console. This boilerplate code distracts from the actual task.

In the Python programming language, you only write the following:

```
print("Hello, World!")
```

This is reduced to the essentials—it is hardly surprising that Python is becoming increasingly popular and has often replaced Java as the primary programming language taught in universities.

This JEP aims to make Java more appealing to beginners. It was crucial to Oracle's language architects that no separate Java dialect (or modification of the language) emerge and that no separate toolchain be required.

6.3.2 Simplification I: Instance `main()`

As a first simplification, it is now permissible to define the `main()` method as neither `static` nor `public` and without parameters, which significantly reduces the amount of boilerplate code and improves comprehensibility for beginners, as shown in the following variant:

```
class InstanceMainMethod
{
    void main()
    {
        System.out.println("Hello, World!");
    }
}
```

This class can still be compiled and started like a regular Java program. It is easier to use direct compilation (see Sect. 15.5), which involves a direct call from the console, similar to Python's script-based execution. If you have saved the lines from the listing into a file named `InstanceMainMethod.java`, you may execute the above class as follows:

```
$ java --enable-preview --source 21 InstanceMainMethod.java
Hello, World!
```

Interim Conclusion

Conveniently, this simplification means that you don't need to know about visibility modifiers or static elements to write and execute a small Java program. Furthermore, it is not necessary to deal with the input parameter and its array type. This simplification is already a good first step, but it goes further and becomes better and shorter.

6.3.3   Simplification II: Unnamed Class

You can even omit the class definition by using the Unnamed Classes feature, which leads to a program that is almost as short as the one-liner in Python:

```
void main()
{
    System.out.println("Hello, World!");
}
```

Save these lines as `SimplerHelloWorld.java`. To start them, enter the following command:

```
$ java --enable-preview --source 21 SimplerHelloWorld.java
```

Interestingly, Java generates some messages mentioning the use of preview features on the console that were not output in the previous version. Finally, the program output is displayed:

```
Note: SimplerHelloWorld.java uses preview features of Java SE 21.
Note: Recompile with -Xlint:preview for details.
Hello, World!
```

Interim Conclusion

The resulting unnamed class (obviously) has no (visible) class definition. However, you can still implement a `main()` method there. In addition, the class is automatically assigned to the unnamed package.

6.3.4   Further Possibilities

For practical purposes, variables and methods can also be defined and used in addition to the `main()` method. This allows you to expand the functionality incrementally. As an example, we define a variable `greeting` and a method `enhancer()` for marking text. We use both in the `main()` method:

```
String greeting = "Hello again!";

String enhancer(String input, int times)
{
   return "  ---> " + input.repeat(times) + " <---";
}

void main()
{
    System.out.println("Hello, World!");
    System.out.println(greeting);
    System.out.println(enhancer("Michael", 2));
}
```

If you save these lines as `UnnamedClassesMoreFeatures.java`, use the following command to execute, and you will get the following output:

```
$ java --enable-preview --source 21 UnnamedClassesMoreFeatures.java
Note: UnnamedClassesMoreFeatures.java uses preview features of Java SE 21.
Note: Recompile with -Xlint:preview for details.
Hello, World!
Hello again!
 ---> MichaelMichael <---
```

6.3.5   Multiple `main()`: What Happens in the Background?

The functionality implemented with this JEP significantly simplifies things. However, it is now theoretically possible to have multiple `main()` methods with a mix of visibility modifiers and with and without parameters, as follows:

```
public class MultipleMains
{
    protected static void main()
    {
        System.out.println("protected static void main()");
    }

    public void main(String[] args)
    {
        System.out.println("public void main(String[] args)");
    }
}
```

To determine how to launch the application, a multi-step procedure is used: look in the class for a static or instance method named `main` with any access, that is, `public`, `protected`, or package private except `private`, in this order:

1. `static void main(String[] args)`
2. `static void main()`—without parameter
3. `void main(String[] args)`
4. `void main()`—without parameter

Which `main()` method is executed? To determine this, study the bullet points or start the program with this command:

```
$ java --enable-preview --source 21 src/main/java/preview/MultipleMains.java
```

Don't worry, you don't have to memorize these four steps. The underlying launch protocol has already been simplified in Java 22 as part of JEP 463. Even better: Java 25 LTS includes JEP 512, which introduces a renaming and a few minor changes. For details, see Sect. 11.4.

6.3.6 *Java on the Way to Script-Based Execution?*

These new features make it much easier to get started with Java, and that's not all. If you want to create small tools that should be executed via direct compilation, that is, without prior explicit compilation, the effort involved can be reduced to a minimum. This benefits not only beginners but also experienced users, provided the programs are small and consist of a single Java file. Fortunately, since Java 22 and Java 25 LTS, this restriction has been lifted, allowing direct compilation to execute larger structures consisting of multiple classes and files without prior explicit compilation. Details are available in the description of JEP 458: Launch Multi-File Source Code Program in Sect. 11.2.

Potential Future Simplifications

As a further simplification, you can identify `System.out.println()` or console output and input in general. Python's built-in functions `print()` and `input()` offer some valuable lessons here.

And that is precisely what has been done! Java 23 introduces an IO class as part of JEP 477. This class provides the static methods `print()`, `println()`, and `readln()`, which simplify textual interaction with the console. With Java 25 LTS, this class is finalized as `java.lang.IO`. Section 11.4 provides more details.

6.4 Miscellaneous

In this section, I briefly describe some minor changes that have less practical impact than the innovations presented above.

6.4.1 Linux/RISC-V Port

In view of the increasing availability of RISC-V hardware, a port of the JDK was deemed useful and implemented as part of JEP 422 (https://openjdk.org/jeps/422). RISC-V is an open source RISC instruction set architecture (ISA) developed at the University of California. This feature is now being continued under the responsibility of RISC-V International.

6.4.2 Generational ZGC

The ZGC (Z Garbage Collector) was already introduced experimentally in Java 11 LTS. In Java 15, the ZGC was declared a production-ready feature.

ZGC is expected to achieve pause times of less than one millisecond—which is significantly less than the pause times of the standard garbage collector G1, which can range from several milliseconds to seconds.

So far, ZGC does not distinguish between old and new/young objects. Based on numerous observations, a hypothesis suggests that objects often have a short lifespan. It means that most objects die shortly after they are created, while objects that have survived several GC cycles tend to remain relevant for a longer period of time. A so-called generational garbage collector takes advantage of this fact by dividing the heap into two logical areas: a young generation, where new objects are created, and an old generation, where objects that have reached a certain age are moved.

There is a high probability that the objects in the old generation will continue to be used for longer. Garbage collection can be optimized by cleaning up the young generation more frequently and checking and attempting to clean up the old generation less often. This procedure should also have a positive impact on the application's actual performance.

For more details, see https://openjdk.org/jeps/439.

6.4.3 Deprecate the Windows 32-bit x86 Port for Removal

The 32-bit version of Windows 10 is nearly no longer in use. Windows 11, which has been available since October 2021, did not offer a 32-bit version. Accordingly, there is little to no need for a 32-bit Windows version of the JDK.

To speed up the development of the JDK, Virtual Threads (see Sect. 5.4) have not been implemented for 32-bit Windows. Anyone attempting to start a virtual thread on 32-bit Windows will instead receive a platform thread.

JEP 449 (https://openjdk.org/jeps/449) marks the 32-bit Windows port as deprecated and intends to remove it. A look at Java 25 LTS shows that, as part of JEP 479: Remove the Windows 32-bit x86 Port (see Sect. 11.5), the port will be completely removed.

6.4.4 Prepare to Disallow the Dynamic Loading of Agents

If you have ever used a Java profiler, you have probably started the application to be analyzed with a parameter such as `-agentpath:....` This loads a so-called agent into the application, which modifies it at runtime to perform the necessary measurements and either writes the results to a file or sends them to the profiler's front end.

If the application was started without this parameter, the agent can also be injected into the JVM retrospectively using the so-called Attach API. This dynamic loading is enabled by default, posing a significant security risk.

In a future Java version, dynamic loading will be turned off by default and can be enabled using the VM option `-XX:+EnableDynamicAgentLoading`. In addition, warnings are already displayed when an agent is loaded via the Attach API.

For more details, see https://openjdk.org/jeps/451.

Chapter 7
Exercises on the Features in JDK 18 to 21 LTS

The following exercises are designed to help deepen your understanding of the features in JDK 18 to 21 LTS. The corresponding sample solutions can be found in Sect. 7.2.

7.1 Exercises

✍ Exercise 1: Simplify with Record Patterns ✍

A trip is defined using the following records (contrary to reality, for the sake of simplicity, only numbers without leading zeros are allowed for postal codes):

```
record Person(String firstname, String lastname, LocalDate birthday) {}

record TravelInfo(LocalDate start, Duration maxTravellingTime) {}

record City(Integer zipCode, String name) {}

record Journey(Person person, TravelInfo travelInfo, City from, City to) {}
```

Various consistency checks and tests are performed to verify validity. Nested components such as `Person` or `City` of a `Journey` object are checked for `!= null`, thus ensuring their existence for a subsequent query. To this end, implementations containing deeply nested `ifs` and various `null` checks are sometimes seen, especially in legacy code, for example, as follows:

```
static boolean checkFirstNameTravelTimeAndDestZipCode(final Object obj)
{
    if (obj instanceof Journey journey)
    {
        if (journey.person() != null)
        {
            var person = journey.person();

            if (journey.travelInfo() != null)
```


M. Inden, *Java 25 and Beyond*, https://doi.org/10.1007/979-8-8688-2385-5_7

```java
            {
                var travelInfo = journey.travelInfo();

                if (journey.to() != null)
                {
                    var to = journey.to();

                    var firstname = person.firstname();
                    var travelTime = travelInfo.maxTravellingTime();
                    var zipCode = to.zipCode();

                    if (firstname != null && travelTime != null &&
                        zipCode != null)
                    {
                        return firstname.length() > 2 &&
                               travelTime.toHours() < 7 &&
                               zipCode >= 8000 && zipCode < 8100;
                    }
                }
            }
        }
    return false;
}
```

The task now is to utilize record patterns to simplify and compact the complex
test logic described above.

________ ✍ **Exercise 2: Use Record Patterns for Recursive Calls** ✍________

Let's define figures using the following interface and three records:

```java
public sealed interface Figure permits Line, Point, Triangle {}

record Point(int x, int y) implements Figure {}

record Line(Point start, Point end) implements Figure {}

record Triangle(Point pointA, Point pointB, Point PointC) implements Figure {}
```

In addition, the following method is defined, which multiplies the x and y coordinates of a `Point`. The `switch` should be supplemented with an implementation
of the `cases` for the types `Line` and `Triangle`. This is already indicated for `Line`.
For the calculation, the respective subcomponents should be added in the form of
`Point`s by calling the existing method `process()`:

```java
static int process(final Figure figure)
{
    return switch (figure)
    {
        case Point(int x, int y) -> x * y;
        case Line(Point start, Point end) -> // TODO
        // TODO
        default -> throw new IllegalArgumentException("Unexpected: " + figure);
    };
}
```

_______________ ✍ **Exercise 3: Convert to Virtual Threads** ✍_______________

The starting point for this task is the execution of various tasks using an `Executor-Service` and a pool size of 50 as follows:

```java
static void runThreads(int amount)
{
    try (var executor = Executors.newFixedThreadPool(50))
    {
        IntStream.range(0, amount).forEach(i ->
        {
            executor.submit(() ->
            {
                Thread.sleep(Duration.ofSeconds(1));

                System.out.println("Task " + i + " finished!");
                return i;
            });
        });
    }
}
```

Convert the entire system to utilize virtual threads and verify the results. For this purpose, use a suitable new method from the `Thread` class.

_______ ✍ **Exercise 4: Experimenting with Sequenced Collections** ✍_______

The following method, which contains several TODO comments, is intended to generate the first prime numbers and store them in a list. Therefore, elements should be inserted at the front and back. In addition, an output in reverse order should be prepared:

```java
static void primeNumbers()
{
    List<Integer> primeNumbers = new ArrayList<>();
    primeNumbers.add(3); // [3]
    // TODO: add 2
    primeNumbers.addAll(List.of(5, 7, 11));
    // TODO: add 13

    System.out.println(primeNumbers); // [2, 3, 5, 7, 11, 13]
    // TODO print first and last element
    // TODO print reverse order

    // TODO: add 17 as last
    System.out.println(primeNumbers); // [2, 3, 5, 7, 11, 13, 17]
    // TODO print reverse order
}
```

Bonus Experiment with the `SequencedSet<E>` interface and use the appropriate methods to create a sorted set containing the letters A, B, and C:

```java
static void createABCSet()
{
    Set<String> numbers = new LinkedHashSet<>();

    // TODO populate set, print first and last element and reverse order
}
```

___✍ **Exercise 5: Preview Feature Unnamed Patterns and Variables** ✍___
Simplify the following method, already using advanced record patterns but
still appears somewhat confusing, as not all components are employed in
the `if` block. Using unnamed patterns and variables increases readability and
comprehensibility—take advantage of the fact that IDEs mark unused variables:

```java
static boolean checkFirstNameAndCountryCodeAgainImproved(final Object obj)
{
    if (obj instanceof Journey(
                        Person(var firstname, var lastname, var birthday),
                        TravelInfo(var start, var maxTravellingTime),
                        var from, City(var zipCode, var name)))
    {
        if (firstname != null && maxTravellingTime != null
                        && zipCode != null)
        {
            return firstname.length() > 2 &&
                maxTravellingTime.toHours() < 7 &&
                zipCode >= 8000 && zipCode < 8100;
        }
    }
    return false;
}
```

7.2   Solutions

___________✍ **Solution 1: Simplify Using Record Patterns** ✍___________
The objective was to use record patterns to make complex test logic more understandable and compact.

The original implementation contains various nested `null` checks, which make
the source code difficult to read and understand. Such checks can be entirely
dispensed with for the individual subcomponents. Why? When deconstructing subcomponents for record patterns, they only match successfully if the subcomponents
are not `null`.

However, deconstructing does not affect attribute validity. If an attribute may
contain `null` as a value, an additional hand-made check is necessary. Always
remember, attributes are not automatically checked for `null` during deconstruction:

```java
static boolean checkFirstNameAndCountryCodeAgain(Object obj)
{
    if (obj instanceof Journey(
                        Person(String firstname, String lastname,
                            LocalDate birthday),
                        TravelInfo(LocalDate start,
                                Duration maxTravellingTime),
                        City from, City(Integer zipCode, String name)))
    {
        if (firstname != null && maxTravellingTime != null && zipCode != null)
```

```
        {
            return firstname.length() > 2 &&
                    maxTravellingTime.toHours() < 7 &&
                    zipCode >= 8000 && zipCode < 8100;
        }
    }
    return false;
}
```

Influence of Good Programming Style With a good programming style, avoiding null values for attributes, the whole thing could be shortened further:

```
static boolean checkFirstNameAndCountryCodeAgain(final Object obj)
{
    if (obj instanceof Journey(
                    Person(String firstname, String lastname,
                        LocalDate birthday),
                    TravelInfo(LocalDate start,
                            Duration maxTravellingTime),
                    City from, City(Integer zipCode, String name)))
    {
        return firstname.length() > 2 &&
                maxTravellingTime.toHours() < 7 &&
                zipCode >= 8000 && zipCode < 8100;
    }
    return false;
}
```

________ ✍ **Solution 2: Use Record Patterns for Recursive Calls** ✍________

Given were the definitions of figures and a rudimentary switch. To solve the problem, cases must be added for the types Line and Triangle. The default that was previously necessary can now be omitted, as all cases for the sealed type Figure are covered. With the help of record patterns, you can access the respective components of Line and Triangle in the form of Points. This means that process() needs to be called only for these:

```
static int process(final Figure figure)
{
    return switch (figure)
    {
        case Point(int x, int y) -> x * y;
        case Line(Point start, Point end) -> process(start) + process(end);
        case Triangle(Point a, Point b, Point c) -> process(a) + process(b) +
                                                    process(c);
    };
}
```

_______________🖎 **Solution 3: Convert to Virtual Threads** 🖎_______________

The task was to execute various tasks using an `ExecutorService` and a pool size of 50. To switch to virtual threads, change from `newFixedThreadPool()` to `newVirtualThreadPerTaskExecutor()`, which creates an `ExecutorService` for virtual threads. The `isVirtual()` method can be used to check that the threads created in this way are indeed virtual threads. The rest of the source code remains the same:

```java
static void runThreads(int amount)
{
    try (var executor = Executors.newVirtualThreadPerTaskExecutor())
    {
        IntStream.range(0, amount).forEach(i ->
        {
            executor.submit(() ->
            {
                Thread.sleep(Duration.ofSeconds(5));

                var isVirtual = Thread.currentThread().isVirtual();
                System.out.println("Task " + i + " finished! " +
                                        "virtual = " + isVirtual);
                return i;
            });
        });
    }
}
```

When we run the program, concurrency results in approximately the following output (reduced to the essentials):

```
Task 9996 finished! isVirtual = true
Task 9999 finished! isVirtual = true
FINISHED
```

_______🖎 **Solution 4: Experimenting with Sequenced Collections** 🖎_______

Given was a method with some TODO comments. The task was to fill an `ArrayList<Integer>` with the first prime numbers. This is achieved by inserting the appropriate prime numbers at the front and back of the list using the methods `addFirst()` and `addLast()` and then retrieving them with `getFirst()` and `getLast()`. Additionally, the reverse order can be retrieved by calling the `reversed()` method:

```java
static void primeNumbers()
{
    SequencedCollection<Integer> primeNumbers = new ArrayList<>();
    primeNumbers.add(3); // [3]
    primeNumbers.addFirst(2); // [2, 3]
    primeNumbers.addAll(List.of(5, 7, 11)); // [2, 3, 5, 7, 11]
    primeNumbers.addLast(13); // [2, 3, 5, 7, 11, 13]

    System.out.println(primeNumbers); // [2, 3, 5, 7, 11, 13]
    System.out.println(primeNumbers.getFirst()); // 2
    System.out.println(primeNumbers.getLast()); // 13
    System.out.println(primeNumbers.reversed()); // [13, 11, 7, 5, 3, 2]

    primeNumbers.addLast(17);
    System.out.println(primeNumbers); // [2, 3, 5, 7, 11, 13, 17]
    System.out.println(primeNumbers.reversed()); // [17, 13, 11, 7, 5, 3, 2]
}
```

Bonus If you experiment a little with SequencedSet<E>, you can create the set containing the letters A, B, and C as follows and then access the first and last elements as well as the reverse order:

```java
static void createABCSet()
{
    SequencedSet<String> numbers = new LinkedHashSet<>();
    numbers.addFirst("B"); // [B]
    numbers.addFirst("A"); // [A, B]
    numbers.addLast("C"); // [A, B, C]
    System.out.println(numbers);

    System.out.println(numbers.getFirst()); // A
    System.out.println(numbers.getLast()); // C
    System.out.println(numbers.reversed()); // [C, B, A]
}
```

___✍ **Solution 5: Preview Feature Unnamed Patterns and Variables** ✍___

In the method given in the task, some parameters within the nested record patterns are unused. A visually more apparent variant can be achieved by using unnamed pattern variables. If you use a modern IDE such as IntelliJ or Eclipse, these unused variables are recognized and marked accordingly. In IntelliJ, they are colored gray. Variable names marked in this way can be replaced by an "_", which results in the following construct:

```java
static boolean checkFirstNameAndCountryCodeAgainImproved(Object obj)
{
    if (obj instanceof Journey(
                    Person(var firstname, var _, var _),
                    TravelInfo(var _, var maxTravellingTime),
                    var _, City(var zipCode, var _)))
    {
        if (firstname != null && maxTravellingTime != null && zipCode != null)
        {
            return firstname.length() > 2
                    && maxTravellingTime.toHours() < 7
                    && zipCode >= 8000 && zipCode < 8100;
        }
    }
    return false;
}
```

Further Optimization In a further step, you benefit not only from unnamed pattern variables but especially from unnamed patterns. This allows you to dispense with var _ and write the shorter "_":

```
static boolean checkFirstNameAndCountryCodeAgainImproved_UNNAMED_2(Object obj)
{
    if (obj instanceof Journey(
                        Person(var firstname, _, _),
                        TravelInfo(_, var maxTravellingTime),
                        _, City(var zipCode, _)))
    {
        if (firstname != null && maxTravellingTime != null && zipCode != null)
        {
            return firstname.length() > 2
                    && maxTravellingTime.toHours() < 7
                    && zipCode >= 8000 && zipCode < 8100;
        }
    }
    return false;
}
```

Part III

New Features in Java 22 to 25 LTS

Chapter 8
New Features in Java 25 LTS at a Glance

Java 25 LTS (Long-Term Support) was released in September 2025, replacing its predecessor, Java 21 LTS, after approximately two years. In the meantime, minor releases in the form of Java 22, 23, and 24 were published every six months. While you should not expect many new features in these interim releases, a lot has happened overall since the release of Java 21 LTS. In this chapter, I would like to deliver an overview of the new features introduced cumulatively with Java 25 LTS in the form of so-called JEPs (JDK Enhancement Proposals). The following chapters cover the significant enhancements from Java 22 to Java 25 LTS in detail.

8.1   JEPs in Java 25 LTS at a Glance

Below, I list the JEPs included in Java 25 LTS to provide a rough guide and overview of the developments. In that case, you are interested in details about the JEPs; further information is available on the respective websites at https://openjdk.org/jeps/<nr>. You have to replace <nr> appropriately; for example, for JEP 400, use https://openjdk.org/jeps/400.

Java 25 LTS contains the following 18 JEPs (12 final, 4 preview, 1 incubator, and 1 experimental)—preview, incubator, and experimental features are marked in italics:

- *JEP 470: PEM Encodings of Cryptographic Objects (Preview)*
- *JEP 502: Stable Values (Preview)*
- JEP 503: Remove the 32-bit x86 Port
- *JEP 505: Structured Concurrency (Fifth Preview)*
- JEP 506: Scoped Values
- *JEP 507: Primitive Types in Patterns, instanceof, and switch (Third Preview)*
- *JEP 508: Vector API (Tenth Incubator)*
- *JEP 509: JFR CPU-Time Profiling (Experimental)*

© The Author(s), under exclusive license to APress Media, LLC, part of Springer Nature 2026
M. Inden, *Java 25 and Beyond*, https://doi.org/10.1007/979-8-8688-2385-5_8

- JEP 510: Key Derivation Function API
- JEP 511: Module Import Declarations
- JEP 512: Compact Source Files and Instance Main Methods
- JEP 513: Flexible Constructor Bodies
- JEP 514: Ahead-of-Time Command-Line Ergonomics
- JEP 515: Ahead-of-Time Method Profiling
- JEP 518: JFR Cooperative Sampling
- JEP 519: Compact Object Headers
- JEP 520: JFR Method Timing and Tracing
- JEP 521: Generational Shenandoah

In addition, the following 19 final JEPs originate from Java versions 22–24, some of which represent preparations for the above JEPs, such as the work surrounding the removal of the 32-bit x86 ports:

- JEP 423: Region Pinning for G1
- JEP 454: Foreign Function and Memory API
- JEP 456: Unnamed Variables and Patterns
- JEP 458: Launch Multi-File Source Code Programs
- JEP 467: Markdown Documentation Comments
- JEP 471: Deprecate the Memory-Access Methods in sun.misc.Unsafe for Removal
- JEP 472: Prepare to Restrict the Use of JNI
- JEP 474: ZGC: Generational Mode by Default
- JEP 475: Late Barrier Expansion for G1
- JEP 479: Remove the Windows 32-bit x86 Port
- JEP 483: Ahead-of-Time Class Loading and Linking
- JEP 484: Class-File API
- JEP 485: Stream Gatherers
- JEP 486: Permanently Disable the Security Manager
- JEP 490: ZGC: Remove the Non-Generational Mode
- JEP 491: Synchronize Virtual Threads without Pinning
- JEP 493: Linking Run-Time Images without JMODs
- JEP 498: Warn upon Use of Memory-Access Methods in sun.misc.Unsafe
- JEP 501: Deprecate the 32-bit x86 Port for Removal

Comments on the JEPs

When describing the JEPs included in Java 21 LTS, I already pointed out the following fact, and I would like to repeat it here: Only some of the JEPs are actually of increased interest to Java developers. Various things are of marginal importance or serve to clean up and cut off old habits.

If you take a closer look, you will notice that features are often first released as a preview and then, in subsequent versions, as a follow-up preview, until they are finally incorporated into the JDK.

Sometimes features start as incubators, then develop into previews, and are finally finalized. The work then proceeds in separate JEPs, each with a unique number. This path is taken by scoped values, for example. These were first introduced in Java 20 as an incubator. In Java 21 LTS, they became a preview feature, which was further refined in subsequent versions and ultimately finalized in Java 25 LTS as JEP 506. The JEPs for Structured Concurrency are following a similar path. It all started in Java 19 as an incubator. With Java 21 LTS, it became a preview feature, which then underwent several iterations until Java 24. With Java 25 LTS, the whole thing was revised again and presented once more as a fifth preview.

One special feature is the Vector API, which has already gone through various incubators and is expected to stay an incubator for some time—its transition to preview status and then finalization is awaiting the completion of Project Valhalla,[1] which focuses in particular on value objects and improvements in the use of primitive types.

Note on Preview, Incubator, and Experimental Features
Before we begin, I would like to briefly remind you of the special features of preview and incubator features, as well as the experimental features introduced in Java 24.

Preview Features Preview features are already entirely specified and fundamentally implemented (although not yet finalized). The aim is to gather feedback from the Java community for fine-tuning and thus increase their practical usefulness. In exceptional cases, however, the findings may also lead to a discontinuation of further development or a reorientation. The best example of this is the feature named String Templates, whose further development was halted with Java 23, despite having already been introduced as a second preview in Java 22.

To activate preview features, you must specify the flag `--enable-preview` when compiling and executing your source code. When compiling, also remember to use the flag `--source` including the desired version number:

```
$ javac --enable-preview --source 25 <YOUR_CLASS_NAME>.java
```

Alternatively, instead of specifying `--source`, you can also use `--release`:

```
$ javac --enable-preview --release 25 <YOUR_CLASS_NAME>.java
```

For short examples consisting of only one class (or a few classes), a direct call using Launch Single-File Source Code Programs (Direct Compilation) (see Sect. 15.5) is recommended. Since Java 22, JEP 458: Launch Multi-File Source-Code Programs (see Sect. 11.2) has been helpful. Here, only `--source` is allowed:

```
$ java --enable-preview --source 25 <YOUR_CLASS_NAME>.java
```

---

[1] https://openjdk.org/projects/valhalla/

Conveniently, since Java 25 LTS, specifying `--source` is optional for direct compilation—but not for the `javac` command:

```
$ java --enable-preview <YOUR_CLASS_NAME>.java
```

Incubator Features Incubator features are somewhat experimental. There is no guarantee that such a feature will eventually be integrated into the JDK. Instead, the aim is to gather feedback from developers at an early stage and further improve the functionality. Incubator features are implemented as modules. To use them, the command-line parameters `--add-modules <module-name>` must be specified appropriately when compiling and executing.

Experimental Features In addition to the preview and incubator features, experimental features have been added in Java 24. These are experimental and must therefore be explicitly activated with **-XX:+UnlockExperimentalVMOptions**.

Chapter 9
Syntax Innovations in JDK 22 to 25 LTS

This chapter describes the key new features from Java 22 to 25 LTS in one comprehensive overview, as enhancements from previous versions are also included in Java 25 LTS. The release of Java 25 LTS offers the following interesting features cumulatively—preview features are marked in italics:

- JEP 456: Unnamed Variables and Patterns
- JEP 467: Markdown Documentation Comments
- *JEP 507: Primitive Types in Patterns, instanceof, and switch (Third Preview)*
- JEP 511: Module Import Declarations
- JEP 512: Compact Source Files and Instance Main Methods[1]
- JEP 513: Flexible Constructor Bodies

In the following sections, we will examine various syntax innovations in closer detail. Starting with Unnamed Variables and Patterns in Sect. 9.1, allowing us to mark unused variables and record pattern components. Then I discuss the documentation options with Markdown Documentation Comments in Sect. 9.2. The support of primitive types in pattern matching, titled " Primitive Types in Patterns, instanceof, and switch," is covered in Sect. 9.3. After that, I will introduce simplifications for imports through Module Import Declarations in Sect. 9.4. JEP 512, titled " Compact Source Files and Instance Main Methods," can be classified as either a syntax or a JVM innovation. It will be discussed in more detail later in the context of JVM innovations in Sect. 11.4. Finally, in Sect. 9.5, we look at the interesting extension that allows specific actions to be performed before calling `super()`, which makes parameter checks and other actions more elegant and natural to perform.

---

[1] Can also be considered a JVM innovation.

M. Inden, *Java 25 and Beyond*, https://doi.org/10.1007/979-8-8688-2385-5_9

9.1   JEP 456: Unnamed Variables and Patterns

This JEP finalizes its predecessor, JEP 443 (see Sect. 4.3), and allows variables or parts within record patterns to be marked as unused and unusable with an underscore ("_"). This practical syntax innovation provides greater clarity.

As a reminder and for clarification, I will show the following three variants:

1. **Unnamed Variable**: Allows the use of "_" for naming or marking variables as unused:

```java
static void unnamedVariable(String userInput)
{
    try
    {
        System.out.println(Integer.parseInt(userInput));
    }
    catch (NumberFormatException _) // UNNAMED VARIABLE
    {
        System.out.println("Expected number, but was: '" + userInput + "'");
    }
}
```

2. **Unnamed Pattern Variable**: Allows the identifier that would generally follow the type (or `var`) to be omitted in a record pattern. The corresponding example follows in the third point.

3. **Unnamed Pattern**: Allows the type and name of a component of a record pattern to be omitted entirely and replaced with "_":

```java
static void unnamedPatternVariableAndPattern()
{
    enum Color { RED, GREEN, BLUE, BLACK, WHITE }
    record Point(int x, int y) { }
    record ColoredPoint(Point point, Color color) { }

    var cp = new ColoredPoint(new Point(1234, 567), Color.BLUE);

    if (cp instanceof ColoredPoint(Point(int x,
                              var _), // UNNAMED PATTERN VARIABLE
                         _)) // UNNAMED PATTERN
    {
        System.out.println("x: " + x);
    }
}
```

A quick reminder: Pattern matching checks if the variable `cp` represents the type `ColoredPoint` and, if so, deconstructs it into its individual components. Deconstruction breaks down `ColoredPoint` into `Point` and `Color`—and `Point` is in turn broken down into its two coordinates. Since only the x coordinate is relevant here, the y coordinate is marked by an unnamed pattern variable (`var _`). The same applies to the color component, which is marked as unused by the unnamed pattern ("_").

9.2   JEP 467: Markdown Documentation Comments

When Java became popular in the late 1990s, the choice of HTML elements as the JavaDoc comment specification was entirely logical. In recent years, however, Markdown has gained significant popularity as a documentation tool. This JEP enables comments to be created using Markdown instead of HTML elements.

9.2.1   Introductory Example

To get started with this topic, let's look at the definition of the max() method from the java.lang.Math class in the JDK, including the associated JavaDoc comment, to recap the documentation options available to date:

```
/**
 * Returns the greater of two {@code int} values. That is, the
 * result is the argument closer to the value of
 * {@link Integer#MAX_VALUE}. If the arguments have the same value,
 * the result is that same value.
 *
 * @param   a   an argument.
 * @param   b   another argument.
 * @return  the larger of {@code a} and {@code b}.
 */
```

The following listing shows how the comment can be rewritten using Markdown, which is introduced by the character string of three slashes (///):

```
/// Returns the greater of two `int` values. That is, the
/// result is the argument closer to the value of
/// [Integer#MAX_VALUE]. If the arguments have the same value,
/// the result is that same value.
///
/// @param   a   an argument.
/// @param   b   another argument.
/// @return  the larger of `a` and `b`.
```

Even this short example shows that comments can be written more concisely with Markdown and are somewhat easier to read—the real advantages become clearer in the following examples.

The improvements with Markdown are based on the following, among other things:

- If class names or source code in general is to be displayed, backticks (`...`) are used instead of {@code ...}—where the three dots represent the text to be formatted.
- Links are described with [...] instead of {@link ...}.
- JavaDoc-specific items, such as @param and @return, remain unchanged.

The resulting documentation is shown in Fig. 9.1.

max

```
public static int max(int a,
                      int b)
```

Returns the greater of two int values. That is, the result is the argument closer to the value of Integer.MAX_VALUE. If the arguments have the same value, the result is that same value.

Parameter:

 a - an argument.

 b - another argument.

Gibt zurück:

 the larger of a and b.

Fig. 9.1 JavaDoc comment on the method Math.max() generated from Markdown

9.2.2   Brief Overview of Markdown Features

Below, we will examine some of the features offered by Markdown, including text formatting, table descriptions, and embedding links.

Formatting Text

From time to time, you may want to highlight passages of text and display them in *italics* or **bold**. Italics is achieved by using *...* or _...._. Switching to bold type is done with **...**. Additionally, the font can be changed to typewriter font (Courier) by using backticks ('...') and emphasized in bold and/or italics. Furthermore, it is possible to integrate multi-line source code snippets into a comment using ('''...'''). The following listing contains examples of the commands mentioned. For information on the purpose of backslashes, please refer to the information box below:

```
/// **BOLD**   \
/// *italic*   \
/// _italic_   \
/// _**BOLD and ITALIC**_\
/// `code-font`  \
/// _**`code-font BOLD and ITALIC`**_ \
///
/// Multi-line source code:
/// ```
/// public static int max(int a, int b) {
///     return (a >= b) ? a : b;
/// }
/// ```
```

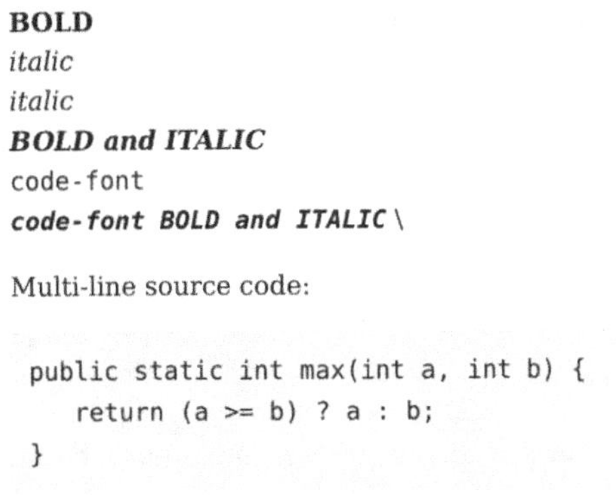

Fig. 9.2 Different fonts with
Markdown

> **BOLD**
> *italic*
> *italic*
> ***BOLD and ITALIC***
> `code-font`
> **`code-font BOLD and ITALIC`** \
>
> Multi-line source code:
>
> ```
> public static int max(int a, int b) {
>     return (a >= b) ? a : b;
> }
> ```

Figure 9.2 shows the different fonts and formatting based on the Markdown format specifications.

Info: Special Feature of Forced Line Breaks

In the above listing, we often see a backslash ("\") at the end of a line. It is a trick to ensure that each text appears on a new line. Backslashes ("\") can be used to force line breaks.

However, this does not apply if the following line is a blank line for a paragraph break (///). If you then add a backslash ("\"), as shown above for the bold italic typewriter font, this results in the backslash character ("\").

Enumerations/Lists

Sometimes, you need to use enumerations or numbered lists in comments. Both can be created very easily with Markdown. Enumerations starting with bullet points are defined by the characters "-" or "*" before the entry. You can also mix these characters, but it is best to avoid doing so for consistency.

For a numbered list, use " 1.", "2.", "3.", etc. as placeholders. It is also possible to use "1." multiple times. During generation, the numerical value is assigned appropriately in any case, as indicated below by the texts for the respective entry:

```
/// - item A
/// * item B
/// - item C
///
/// 1st entry 1
/// 1st entry 2 -- **is automatically numbered, i.e. 2.**
/// 1st entry 3
/// 2nd entry 4 -- **is automatically changed to 4. changed**
```

The above Markdown elements result in lists as shown in Fig. 9.3.

Fig. 9.3 List with bullet points and numbering created using Markdown

- item A

- item B

- item C

1. entry 1
2. entry 2 -- **is automatically numbered, i.e. 1. => 2.**
3. entry 3
4. entry 4 -- **is automatically changed to 4.**

Although Markdown automatically generates the resulting numerical value, it is recommended in practice to always count correctly and specify the value, as the unformatted documentation should also be readable and understandable to other developers.

Tables

With Markdown, simple tables can be created using dashes (pipe characters ("|") and minus signs ("-")). However, a table must not begin with a delimiter line; otherwise, the Markdown content will not be correctly recognized as a table. Apart from that, you are free to specify additional delimiter lines.

With this knowledge, we can map a few letters to their Greek equivalents in the form of a table:

```
/// | Latin | Greek |
/// |-------|-------|
/// | a     | &alpha; (alpha) |
/// | b     | &beta; (beta)  |
/// | c     | &gamma; (gamma) // &Gamma; |
/// | ...   |  ...   |
/// | z     | &omega; (omega) |
```

It is also possible to define multiple columns, as shown in the following example, and format the text in bold or italics or use special Unicode characters. For correct alignment in the generated documentation, the horizontal lines separating the columns don't need to be aligned with each other—the Markdown conversion process takes care of this automatically:

```
/// | Column A | Column B | Column C | Column D |
/// |-------|-------|-------------|-------|
/// | one   | two   | three       | _last_ |
/// | one   | two   | three       | **last** |
/// |-------|-------|-------------|-------|
/// | one   | two   | three       | _**last**_ |
/// |-------|-------|-------------|`----`|
/// | Euro  | &euro; | &#8364; | &#x1F44D; |
```

The Markdown shown generates tables similar to those in Fig. 9.4.

Latin	**Greek**	**Column A**	**Column B**	**Column C**	**Column D**
a	α (alpha)	one	two	three	*last*
b	β (beta)	one	two	three	**last**
c	γ (gamma) // Γ	-------	-------	--------------	-------
		one	two	three	***last***
...	...	-------	-------	--------------	- - - -
z	ω (omega)	Euro	€	€	

Fig. 9.4 Two tables with Markdown

When looking at the generated JavaDoc comment, that is, the tables in this case, the following becomes apparent:

- The column headings are derived from the first row and are displayed in bold with a small horizontal gap to the next column.
- The width of the table columns is automatically adjusted to the content.

9.2.3   References

In Markdown documentation, references to any type of program element (modules, classes, methods, etc.) can be specified using [<ref>] as we saw in the introduction for [String#MAX_VALUE]. In particular, for types from java.lang, it is possible to omit the package specification—all other types must be listed fully qualified (or imported beforehand). For methods, the signature must be correct, that is, the types of the parameters must match.

Sometimes, the text displayed for the link needs to be other than the link itself. In this case, you can specify a label using the syntax [<description>][<link>], as shown in the last line:

```
/// [java.base/] - refers to a module \
/// [java.util] - refers to a package
///
/// Note: _**`java.lang`**_ can be omitted from the reference: \
/// [java.lang.String] - refers to a class \
/// [String] - refers to a class \
/// [Integer] - refers to a class
///
/// [String#chars()] - refers to a method \
/// [Integer#valueOf(String, int)] - refers to a method
///
/// [String#CASE_INSENSITIVE_ORDER] - refers to an attribute \
/// [SPECIAL_ORDER][String#CASE_INSENSITIVE_ORDER] - reference with label
```

Based on the previous Markdown specifications, the JavaDoc comment shown in Fig. 9.5 gets generated.

`java.base`☒ - refers to a module
`java.util`☒ - refers to a package

Note: ***java.lang*** can be omitted from the reference:
`String`☒ - refers to a class
`String`☒ - refers to a class
`Integer`☒ - refers to a class

`String.chars()`☒ - refers to a method
`Integer.valueOf(String, int)`☒ - refers to a method

`String.CASE_INSENSITIVE_ORDER`☒ - refers to an attribute
`SPECIAL_ORDER`☒ - reference with label

Fig. 9.5 Examples of references generated using Markdown

9.2.4 Summary

Let's summarize the main differences between HTML-based JavaDoc and Markdown:

- **Markup**: The use of Markdown is enabled by a new form of documentation comments, where each line begins with /// instead of the traditional /** ... */ syntax.
- **Paragraphs**: The HTML element <p> is required to mark paragraphs. With Markdown, a blank line is sufficient for a new paragraph.
- **Bullet Points**: The HTML elements <ul> and <li> are used to define bullet points and enumerated lists. In Markdown, the character "-" marks the beginning of each element in a bullet point or list. Similar to <ol> in HTML, numbering is possible in Markdown. By repeatedly specifying the placeholder " 1.", the number is automatically incremented in the generated documentation. A more comprehensible approach is to use the desired number directly.
- **Emphasis**: The HTML element <em> delivers emphasis. In Markdown, the underscore ("_") is used for this purpose. With <b>...</b>, you can switch to bold in HTML. In Markdown, this is achieved with **...**.
- **Source Code Blocks**: To mark certain text blocks as source code, JavaDoc offers the tag {@code ...}. In Markdown, source code is enclosed in backticks ('...').
- **Links**: {@link ...} is used to reference other program elements in JavaDoc. In Markdown, square brackets ([...]) are used for this purpose.

> **Note: Markdown Dialects**
> In the context of spoken language, there are no Markdown dialects; however, there are two standards, CommonMark and GFM (GitHub Flavored Markdown), which aim to standardize or extend different implementations of Markdown. It means they can be considered a (kind of) dialect.

9.3   JEP 507: Primitive Types in Patterns, `instanceof`, and `switch` (Third Preview)

Type and value checks can be performed using the `instanceof` and `switch` keywords. Conveniently, modern Java already allows record patterns to be specified there (see Sects. 4.1 and 4.2).

The goal of this JEP was to improve pattern matching further and make it more universally applicable by supporting so-called primitive type patterns for `instanceof` and `switch` wherever " normal" patterns are already allowed. This extension removes the previously existing restrictions on primitive types, thereby increasing Java's consistency and ease of use.

Preliminary Considerations

Before we get started, let's briefly recall the syntax peculiarities of `instanceof` and `switch`.

The following examples illustrate checks for the types `String` and `Double` using value checks:

```java
// Pattern matching with instanceof
if (obj instanceof String str && str.length() > 7)
{
    System.out.println("string " + str + " is longer than 7 characters");
}
else if (obj instanceof Double d && d > 100)
{
    System.out.println("double " + d + " is larger than 100");
}
else
{
    System.out.println("arbitrary obj: " + obj);
}
```

With `instanceof`, the construct seems clumsy, especially when performing just two checks. Let's examine an implementation using `switch`, which is shorter and more elegant. However, conditions start with `when` instead of `&&` for `instanceof`:

```java
// Pattern Matching mit switch
switch (obj)
{
    case String str when str.length() > 7 ->
        System.out.println("string " + str + " is longer than 7 characters");
    case Double d when d > 100 ->
        System.out.println("double " + d + " is larger than 100");
    default ->
        System.out.println("arbitrary obj: " + obj);
}
```

That looks good so far. So why is this JEP needed? The answer is simple: Until now, you could only perform pattern matching on reference types, that is, with the base type `Object` or subtypes such as `String` or `Double`, but not with primitive types. As a workaround, you had to convert them to the corresponding wrapper types explicitly. In the past, there existed the following exception: If checks were only required for fixed values, it was possible in `switch` to check for constant values, such as "EXPWECTED" or 10, 20, 30, etc. However, in addition to strings and enums, only integer values and single letters (specifically the types `byte`, `short`, `char`, and `int`) could be used here.

9.3.1 Introductory Example

To get started with this topic, we use a program fragment including `switch`, which outputs various information on the console based on a log level and the numerical value of the severity:

```java
record LogLevel(int severity) {}

LogLevel logLevel = new LogLevel(2);

String msg = switch (logLevel.severity())
{
    case 0 -> "info";
    case 1 -> "warning";
    case 2 -> "error";
    default -> "unknown severity: " + logLevel.severity();
};
System.out.println(msg);
```

As you can easily see, you have to call the `severity()` method again in the `default` case to provide an informative message. While the duplication is more of a cosmetic issue here, the advantage becomes apparent when considering a complex, lengthy calculation or a side effect that occurs when the method is called.

The innovation introduced with JEP 507 allows the `default` to be replaced by a `case` with a primitive type pattern. This also simplifies access to the value, here with the syntax `case int <varname>` for `int` values:

```
String msg = switch (logLevel.severity())
{
    case 0 -> "info";
    case 1 -> "warning";
    case 2 -> "error";
    // JEP 507
    case int severity -> "unknown severity: " + severity;
};
System.out.println(msg);
```

Another Example

Let's make the example a little less abstract and more tangible by mapping some HTTP status codes using a `switch` and, in particular, processing all codes not explicitly listed using a primitive type pattern:

```
jshell> void mapStatus(int statusCode)
   ...> {
   ...>       switch (statusCode)
   ...>       {
   ...>           case 200, 201 -> IO.println("OK or CREATED");
   ...>           case 404 -> IO.println("Resource Not Found");
   ...>           case 500 -> IO.println("Internal Server Error");
   ...>           case int code -> IO.println("Unknown status: " + code);
   ...>       }
   ...> }
|  Erstellt Methode mapStatus(int)
```

Let's try this out using two status code values as examples:

```
jshell> mapStatus(201)
OK or CREATED

jshell> mapStatus(417)
Unknown status: 417
```

Just a reminder: This example already uses the `java.lang.IO` class, which is new to Java 25 LTS, making interactions with the console easier and more pleasant than before.

Example with Guarded Patterns

As with other patterns, primitive type patterns allow for checking conditions, which are referred to as guards. The following demonstrates the evaluation of a score. For classification, multiple `int` values and various conditions are used in the `case` statements, which map specific value ranges to a rating and also detect cheating for scores > 100:

```
jshell> void evaluate(int score)
   ...> {
   ...>       var result = switch (score)
   ...>       {
   ...>           case int value when value > 100 -> "DISQUALIFIED (CHEATING)";
   ...>           case int value when value >= 80 -> "excellent";
   ...>           case int value when value >= 50 -> "okaish";
   ...>           case int value when value >= 0 -> "to low";
   ...>           default -> throw new IllegalStateException("Invalid score:" +
   ...>                                                      " " + score);
   ...>       };
   ...>       System.out.println("Your score: " + result);
   ...> }
|  created method evaluate(int)
```

Let's try this out again using a few values as examples:

```
jshell> evaluate(85)
Your score: excellent

jshell> evaluate(50)
Your score: okaish

jshell> evaluate(150)
Your score: DISQUALIFIED (CHEATING)

jshell> evaluate(-2)
|  Exception java.lang.IllegalStateException: Invalid score: -2
|        at evaluate (#1:9)
|        at (#3:1)
```

9.3.2   Special Features

Special Features due to Value Ranges of Types

Since Java 23, literals of all primitive types can be used in `switch`. However, there are a few special aspects to be aware of, particularly with floating-point numbers.

To illustrate this, let's consider a check for the two `float` values `1.0f` and `0.999999999f` using the following `switch`. Without looking too closely, one would assume that the check is for (albeit minimally) different values:

```
jshell> float val = 1.0f;
   ...> switch (val)
   ...> {
   ...>     case 1.0f -> System.out.println("1.0");
   ...>     case 0.999999999f -> System.out.println("0.9999..");
   ...>     default -> System.out.println("something else");
   ...> }
val ==> 1.0
|  Error:
|  duplicate case label
|        case 0.999999999f -> System.out.println("0.9999..");
|        ^-----------------------------------------------------^
```

Conveniently, the compiler provides support for detecting this problem: the above construct leads to a compilation error " duplicate label". Why is this? The reason is that floating-point numbers have only limited precision. For type float, values are generally only distinguishable up to about seven decimal places; thus, for float, the literals 1.0f and 0.999999999f represent the same value.

When using double, this restriction does not apply to these two values due to the higher precision and thus the number of supported decimal places (of course). The following construct is therefore valid, although not recommended due to recurring rounding inaccuracies with floating-point numbers—the problem is actually only shifted and would then occur for numbers with more decimal places as well:

```
jshell> double val = 1.0;
   ...> switch (val)
   ...> {
   ...>     case 1.0 -> System.out.println("1.0");
   ...>     case 0.999999999d -> System.out.println("0.9999..");
   ...>     default -> System.out.println("something else");
   ...> }
val ==> 1.0
1.0
```

Calculations with Rounding Inaccuracies Even when using the more accurate type double, rounding errors often occur, meaning that additions or general calculations within case, although syntactically possible, are not recommended. *As a general rule, you should avoid comparing values with floating-point numbers, as the following example clearly illustrates*. Although both cases represent the value 0.3, these branches are not executed:

```
jshell> double val = 0.1 * 3
val ==> 0.30000000000000004

jshell> switch (val)
   ...> {
   ...>     case 0.6 - 0.2 - 0.1 -> System.out.println("0.3a");
   ...>     case 0.3 -> System.out.println("0.3b");
   ...>     case double other -> System.out.println("other: " + other);
   ...> }
other: 0.30000000000000004
```

The restrictions described above are relatively easy to understand. However, there are a few special features that are not immediately obvious.

Special Feature: Value Checks Before Casts

In older Java versions, before the introduction of this JEP, if you wanted to cast from a type with a larger value range, such as long, to a smaller data type, such as byte or **short**, you had to ensure the current value was suitable and therefore use a value range check similar to this one:

```
if (value >= -128 && value <= 127)
{
    byte byteValue = (byte) value;
    // ...
}
if (value >= -32768 && value <= 32767)
{
    short shortValue = (short) value;
    // ...
}
```

Let's look at an example in the form of the following method, which focuses on checking type **byte** instead of the two checks above. The block is only executed if the original value is within the value range of a **byte**. In this case, a conversion takes place, and the actions are performed, namely, the console output:

```
public void checkByteAndPrint(int value)
{
    if (value >= -128 && value <= 127)
    {
        byte byteValue = (byte) value;
        System.out.println("byte: " + byteValue);
    }
}
```

To grasp this conventional implementation, we call it for two values, once with 53 within the value range of a **byte** and with the value 255 outside it:

```
jshell> checkByteAndPrint(53)
byte: 53

jshell> checkByteAndPrint(255)
```

With Java 25 LTS and the preview feature of Primitive Types in Patterns, it is feasible to write a check with **instanceof** and type specification as follows, making it shorter, clearer, and less prone to errors:

```
if (value instanceof byte byteValue)
```

We therefore redefine the above method as follows:

```
jshell> public void checkByteAndPrint(int value)
   ...> {
   ...>     if (value instanceof byte byteValue)
   ...>     {
   ...>         System.out.println("byte: " + byteValue);
   ...>     }
   ...> }
|  created method checkByteAndPrint(int)
```

Then we call the modified method for two values, again, once with the value 53 within the value range of a byte and once with the value 255 outside it:

```
jshell> checkByteAndPrint(53)
byte: 53

jshell> checkByteAndPrint(255)
```

The instructions of the `if` block are only executed if the value originates from the value range of the specified type. Consider that a mistake had been made in the value range specifications in the above case of conventional implementation. For example, if the upper limit had been checked for 128 or 255, the cast would then potentially return unexpected values:

```
jshell> byte byteValue = (byte) 234;
byteValue ==> -22
```

9.3.3   Special Feature: Possibilities of Type Checking

To improve our understanding of the just demonstrated type checking possibilities, we will supplement the previous check for `byte` with additional checks for `short`, `int`, etc.:

```
public void checkType(long value)
{
    if (value instanceof byte b) System.out.println("byte " + b);
    if (value instanceof short s) System.out.println("short " + s);
    if (value instanceof int i) System.out.println("int " + i);
    if (value instanceof long l) System.out.println("long " + l);
    if (value instanceof char c) System.out.println("char '" + c + "' " +
                                              "(" + value + ")");
}
```

This method can be called as follows, with values selected explicitly for the respective value ranges of the types. Although they each have the compilation type `int`, they can be assigned to different types based on their value:

```
jshell> int byteValue = 53;
byteValue ==> 53

jshell> checkType(byteValue);
byte 53
short 53
int 53
long 53
char '5' (53)

jshell> int shortValue = 32_767;
shortValue ==> 32767
```

```
jshell> checkType(shortValue);
short 32767
int 32767
long 32767
char '?' (32767)

jshell> int charValue = 'M';
charValue ==> 77

jshell> checkType(charValue);
byte 77
short 77
int 77
long 77
char 'M' (77)
```

The output illustrates the above and shows, among other things, that for the value 32767, the evaluation for type byte fails. For the value 123456789, only int and long are suitable, as the following call demonstrates:

```
jshell> int intValue = 123_456_789;
intValue ==> 123456789

jshell> checkType(intValue);
int 123456789
long 123456789
```

Special Feature: Numbers That Cannot Be Represented Exactly

Surprisingly, there are some int values in the value range of a float that cannot be represented exactly and are mapped to the next larger or smaller number:

```
jshell> float val = 16_777_217
val ==> 1.6777216E7

jshell> float val = 16_777_216
val ==> 1.6777216E7
```

This is confusing because it is generally assumed that float provides more values than int. However, as just shown, there are perfectly normal int values that cannot be represented precisely by a float number. This applies, for example, to the int value 16_777_217, which is instead surprisingly mapped to the smaller float number 16_777_216f. In contrast, the int value 16_777_216 can be mapped correctly. This behavior is surprising at first. Worse still, this oddity applies to over 95 % of int values. If you want to experiment, consult the following practical tip.

Note: For Experimentation ...
Do you feel the same way? Intuitively, one assumes that a `float` can represent all numbers of an `int`. As the previous example has shown, this assumption is incorrect. In fact, only a fraction of the `int` values can be accurately mapped to `float`—and it can be observed that the deviations become more frequent as the value increases. As long as the values are within the range of $+/-$ 10,000,000, everything seems fine. However, try expanding the value range ...only about 3 % of all `int` values can be correctly mapped to a `float`. To understand this, you can adjust the limit values to the value range of an `int`.

Feel free to try it out, but don't be too alarmed. The following program serves as a basis:

```
record Count(int matchingCount, int nonMatchingCount) {}

void main()
{
    final int MIN = -10_000_000;
    final int MAX = 50_000_000;

    var result = calcMatchingStatistics(MIN, MAX);

    printStatistics(result.matchingCount,
                    result.nonMatchingCount,
                    MAX, MIN);
}
void printStatistics(int matchingCount,
                     int nonMatchingCount,
                     int MIN, int MAX)
{
    int total = matchingCount + nonMatchingCount;

    IO.println("float/int values");
    IO.println("non matching: " + nonMatchingCount);
    IO.println("    matching: " + matchingCount);
    IO.println("       total: " + total);
    IO.println();
    IO.println("in %");
    double factor = Math.abs(100.00d / (MAX - MIN));
    IO.println("non matching %: " + (Math.round(factor *
                                     nonMatchingCount)));
    IO.println("    matching %: " + (Math.round(factor *
                                     matchingCount)));
}
```

You will then receive the following output:

```
float/int values
non matching: 20722784
    matching: 39277216
       total: 60000000

in %
non matching %: 35
    matching %: 65
```

9.4 JEP 511: Module Import Declarations

JEP 511 makes it possible to import all the public types of a module into your own classes with just one line—more precisely, all public types from the packages exported by a module. This is useful in that it reduces the number of import statements required and written by the developer; however, it also has some peculiarities when conflicts arise due to multiple types with the same name. Let's take a closer look at this new feature.

Review

Ever since Java's early days, a conscious decision was taken to simplify programming by making all types from the `java.lang` package automatically available in every class without having to be explicitly imported. The reason for this is convenience and ease of use. This mechanism allows you to employ the common types `String`, `Integer`, or `Exception` directly in any program.

However, as programs become larger, you will need types from other packages, such as the collection classes `ArrayList<E>`, `HashSet<E>`, and `HashMap<K,V>` or the corresponding interfaces `List<E>`, `Set<E>`, and `Map<K,V>`. This requires separate imports such as these:

```
import java.util.ArrayList;
import java.util.HashMap;
import java.util.HashSet;
import java.util.List;
import java.util.Map;
import java.util.Set;
```

There are controversial opinions and debates in the Java community as to whether a general import, such as the following, is better or worse than the previous explicit import statements:

```
import java.util.*;
```

In any case, importing each type separately can significantly bloat the import statements. The added value is highly debatable.

Modules in Java

With Java 9, the JDK was subdivided into individual, smaller building blocks, known as modules. Modules bundle functionalities that belong together thematically. There is a module called `java.base`, which serves as the basis for all other modules and bundles all essential and commonly used packages. There is something similar for classes: basic functionalities are provided by the class `Object` as the basis for all classes.

Fig. 9.6 Transitive
dependencies of the module
java.sql

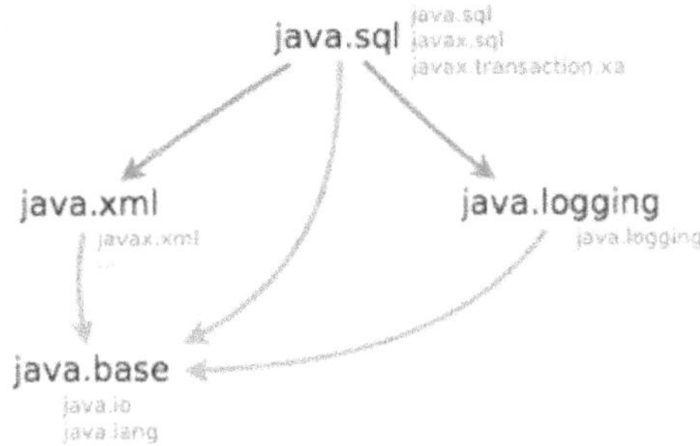

9.4.1   New Feature: Module Import Declarations

Module imports allow you to import all public types of a module at once. This is often convenient and reduces the amount of typing, but it also makes it slightly more challenging to trace the exact origin of types.

Syntax

A module import declaration has the following syntax:

```
import module <modulename>;
```

This results in the provision of all public types, that is, classes, interfaces, enums, annotations, and records from all packages that are exported by the module without any further imports. This avoids similar and sometimes tedious import statements, which can be very repetitive. This behavior is also pleasing when creating small standalone programs (see Sect. 11.4).

Transitive Import

The JDK is subdivided into individual modules, some of which are interdependent or build on each other. The basis for all modules is the java.base module.

Let's assume that you want to execute a database query and therefore need to include the java.sql module. However, this module also uses functionalities from the java.xml module and the java.logging module, which both in turn ultimately use the java.base module. The relationships are shown in Fig. 9.6.[2]

It would be time-consuming and error-prone to need to know all the dependencies of included modules, such as those for the java.xml module, and to specify them in your own programs.

---

[2] The graphic is taken from a blog article by Mark Reinhold, available online at https://openjdk.org/projects/jigsaw/spec/sotms/.

Conveniently, module imports work transitively. If you specify

```
import module java.sql;
```

all types that otherwise have to included with `import java.sql.*` and `import javax.sql.*` are provided. In addition, the types from the `java.xml` module and the `java.logging` module are also available. This helps to keep the imports at the beginning of Java source files clear.

You are familiar with something similar from the build tools Gradle and Maven. There, you specify the desired external library. Based on this, the build tools transitively integrate all transitive dependencies required by a dependency. This is a significant strength, as it dramatically simplifies the creation of build scripts.

Advantages

As mentioned at the beginning, individual imports can result in many lines. Imagine you wanted to provide all types analogous to those from this module import:

```
import module java.base;
```

This would require over 50 individual imports, because you would have to specify many types that are included via `import java.io.*` and `import java.util.*`. In particular, the above shortcut provides direct access to central classes and interfaces, such as `List<E>`, `HashMap<K,V>`, `Stream<E>`, and many others.

Introductory Example

As an introduction, let's examine an example that utilizes the `List<E>` interface, which resides in the `java.util` package and also needs the Stream API supplied by the `java.util.stream` package, and therefore requires two imports. By the way, the program already uses the simplified syntax for `main()`, described in more detail in Sect. 11.4:

```java
import java.util.List;
import java.util.stream.Stream;

public class InitialModuleImportExample
{
    void main()
    {
        var result = Stream.of("AB", "BC", "CD", "DE").
                         filter(str -> str.contains("C")).toList();
        System.out.println(result);
    }
}
```

It is easy to imagine how quickly the list of imports would grow if additional classes and interfaces are needed.

Simplification with Module Import If we perform a module import, this results in the following simplification and shorter variant:

```java
import module java.base;
// Provides all types as if the individual imports
// import java.util.*;
// import java.util.stream.*;
// and others had been made

public class InitialModuleImportExample_V2
{
    void main()
    {
        var result = Stream.of("AB", "BC", "CD", "DE").
                          filter(str -> str.contains("C")).toList();
        System.out.println(result);
    }
}
```

Integrating Graphical Output

Let's go one step further and integrate a simple message box into the program. This brings us to three lines of imports, one of which is even a "*" import:

```java
import javax.swing.*;
import java.util.List;
import java.util.stream.Stream;

public class InitialModuleImportExample3
{
    void main()
    {
        List<String> result = Stream.of("AB", "BC", "CD", "DE").
                          filter(str -> str.contains("C")).
                          toList();
        System.out.println(result);

        IO.print("New Style IO");

        JOptionPane.showMessageDialog(null, "Info");
    }
}
```

Simplification with Module Import Until now, thanks to the use of a module import, the simplification step shown in the examples has been relatively unproblematic. Moreover, it seemed to be a practical abbreviation.

```java
import module java.base;
import module java.desktop;

public class InitialModuleImportExample3_V2
{
    public static void main(final String[] args)
    {
        List<String> result = Stream.of( ...values: "AB", "BC", "CD", "DE").
```

> Reference to 'List' is ambiguous, both 'java.util.List' and 'java.awt.List' match
>
> Import class ⌥⇧↵   More actions... ⌥↵

```java
        IO.print("New Style IO");

        JOptionPane.showMessageDialog( parentComponent: null,  message: "Info");
    }
}
```

Fig. 9.7 Error message for conflicts caused by module imports

Let's try the same thing for these imports:

```java
import javax.swing.*;
import java.util.List;
import java.util.stream.Stream;
```

Keeping in mind that the Swing library comes from the module `java.desktop`, we end up with the following two lines with module imports:

```java
import module java.base; // import java.util.*, java.util.stream.*, ...
import module java.desktop; // import javax.swing.*; usw.
```

The following aspect is worth considering: Because a module import provides all public types from all packages exported by the module, types with the same name may exist in different packages. A simple name without a package specification can therefore sometimes be ambiguous, as we will see in a moment.

After changing the individual import to two module imports, we encounter the problem that the type `List` is no longer unique, as illustrated by Fig. 9.7 showing an error message from an IDE.

As can be easily seen from the error message, the type `List` resides in two packages: `java.awt` and `java.util`.

9.4.2   *Special Cases: Ambiguous Imports*

We have just seen that there are a few details to consider when importing modules and especially that the type List, for example, is no longer unique. Let's now take a look at how we can avoid the compilation error caused by the type List being defined in both the package java.awt and the package java.util.

Solution

The problem can be solved by adding an explicit import, like this:

```
jshell> import java.util.List
```

Thereafter, we can use the desired version of type List, namely, the one out of package java.util:

```
jshell> List names = List.of("Tim", "Tom", "Mike")
names ==> [Tim, Tom, Mike]
```

Further Ambiguity from the JDK

For the type Date, it is also quite likely that problems will arise when importing a module, because the class Date exists in the packages java.util and java.sql:

```
jshell> import module java.base;

jshell> import module java.sql;

jshell> Date today = new Date()
|  Error:
|  reference to Date is ambiguous
|    both class java.sql.Date in java.sql and class java.util.Date in java.
|     util match
|  Date today = new Date();
|  ^--^
|  Error:
|  reference to Date is ambiguous
|    both class java.sql.Date in java.sql and class java.util.Date in java.
|     util match
|  Date today = new Date();
|                 ^--^
```

Once again, an explicit import solves the problem:

```
jshell> import java.util.Date

jshell> Date today = new Date()
today ==> Sat Jul 06 18:12:30 CEST 2024
```

9.4.3 Correction of the Sample Program

When replacing multiple individual imports with module imports, we encountered
the problem of ambiguity, for which we previously discussed the solution.

　　With this knowledge, we correct the program as follows with an explicit import:

```java
import module java.base;
import module java.desktop;

import java.util.List; // This explicit import solves the problem.

public class InitialModuleImportExample3_V2
{
    void main()
    {
        List<String> result = Stream.of("AB", "BC", "CD", "DE").
                                  filter(str -> str.contains("C")).
                                  toList();
        System.out.println(result);

        IO.print("New Style IO");

        JOptionPane.showMessageDialog(null, "Info");
    }
}
```

9.4.4 Module Imports and the JShell

The JShell provides some imports automatically. Remember: By default, the JShell
already imports some packages, making it easy to get started without needing to
import any additional packages. You can determine which types or packages are
provided by imports by calling the /imports command immediately after starting
the JShell.

　　Since Java 25 LTS, there is an automatic module import of java.base:

```
$ jshell
|  Welcome to JShell -- Version 25
|  For an introduction type: /help intro

/imports
|     import java.base
```

This means that the following common imports are directly available:

```java
import java.io.*
import java.net.*
import java.nio.file.*
import java.util.*
import java.util.stream.*
```

Due to the many imports, the Stream API and File IO, among others, can be used
without further ado, that is, without explicit import.

This is demonstrated below by using types from different packages to first perform some actions on a stream with fixed values, such as filtering and mapping. The result is then written to a file named `authors.txt` using the interface `Path` and the utility class `Files` by invoking `writeString()` and then reading the content using the `readString()` method:

```
jshell> var authors = Stream.of("Tim", "Tom", "Mike")
authors ==> java.util.stream.ReferencePipeline$Head@2d928643

jshell> var result = authors.filter(str -> str.contains("i")).
   ...>                        map(String::toUpperCase).
   ...>                        toList();
result ==> [TIM, MIKE]

jshell> Path destFile = Path.of("authors.txt")
destFile ==> authors.txt

jshell> Files.writeString(destFile, result.toString())
$4 ==> authors.txt

jshell> Files.readString(destFile)
$5 ==> "[TIM, MIKE]"
```

Before Java 25 LTS, the handy Date and Time API was unfortunately not available without importing it. This inconvenience is resolved due to the automatic module import of `java.base`. Therefore, nothing stands in the way of directly using the class `java.time.LocalDate`:

```
jshell> LocalDate.parse("2025-07-31")
$2 ==> 2025-07-31
```

9.5   JEP 513: Flexible Constructor Bodies

One goal of this JEP is to allow more flexibility in the implementation of constructors, permitting specific actions, for example, checking constructor arguments, before calling `super()` (and even `this()`). Until now, this verification has only been possible using tricks such as static helper methods or additional helper constructors. In Java 22, JEP 447: Statements before super(...) (Preview) was introduced as a remedy, then continued in Java 23 and 24 under the name " Flexible Constructor Bodies," and finalized in Java 25 LTS.

With this extension, it should still be guaranteed that constructors are executed from top to bottom in the inheritance hierarchy during class instantiation. This processing order ensures that the statements in a subclass constructor do not interfere with the instantiation of the base class and that all necessary actions have been completed. Furthermore, the whole thing should not require any changes to the JVM.

9.5.1   Validation of Arguments for the Base Class Constructor

For a better understanding, let's consider the following requirement: sometimes it makes sense to validate the constructor parameters before passing them to the base class constructor, rather than leaving them unchecked. Let's look at a simplified base class named `BaseBigInteger`, which only encapsulates a `long` value:

```java
public class BaseBigInteger
{
    private final long value;

    public BaseBigInteger(long value)
    {
        this.value = value;
    }

    // ...
}
```

Standard Case (Without This Innovation): Check After Initialization

As an extension of the class `BaseBigInteger`, the class `PositiveBigInteger` should, as its name suggests, represent neither negative numbers nor the digit 0. If such values are passed during construction, it should fail. This requirement sounds logical and easy to implement. However, there is a detail in Java that makes the whole thing a bit cumbersome: Without JEP 513, the first statement in the constructor must always be a call to `super()` (or `this()`). It executes the constructors of the base class(es) or the class itself. Without tricks, it was previously only possible to validate the parameter(s) passed after initialization, as shown in the listing:

```java
public class PositiveBigInteger extends BaseBigInteger
{
    public PositiveBigInteger(long value)
    {
        super(value); // Potentially unnecessary work

        if (value <= 0)
            throw new IllegalArgumentException("non-positive value");
    }
}
```

Upon examining the source code, it doesn't appear particularly elegant. But what is the actual problem? Calls to `super()` like this potentially result in unnecessary calls and object constructions. Worse yet, older legacy code, in particular, is unfortunately characterized by (too) many actions already taking place in the constructor.

Practical Concerns Worth Considering

In practice, there are other factors to consider, including static initializer blocks and constructors that consume resources. This will not be discussed further here, as it distracts from the actual feature.

Note: Background Information

When a class inherits from another class, the subclass can provide additional functionality in the form of attributes and methods. The initial values of the attributes may depend on those of the base class. Therefore, the superclass must always be initialized first. Up to now, this restriction requires that the constructor must always first call `super()` or `this()`.[3] Thus, the constructors are processed in the order of the class hierarchy, starting with the top base class and ending with the actual class itself. This procedure ensures that the state of the object is always initialized correctly.

Implementation Trick: Static Helper Method(s)

We have previously recognized that it is desirable to be able to perform checks before or during the call to `super()` to react to potential problems such as invalid arguments in the constructor call as quickly as possible. In fact, even before Java 25 LTS, there is a way to achieve this: the introduction of a static helper method. Because it is static, it can be invoked during construction to verify the validity of the passed parameter. If successful, the parameter's value is returned. If the check fails, an exception is thrown, and the constructor call of the base class does not even occur:

```java
public class PositiveBigInteger extends BaseBigInteger
{
    public PositiveBigInteger(long value)
    {
        super(verifyPositive(value)); // Verifikation als Ummantelung
    }

    private static long verifyPositive(long value)
    {
        if (value <= 0)
            throw new IllegalArgumentException("non-positive value");

        return value;
    }
}
```

---

[3] This can be done either explicitly or implicitly. If there is no explicit call, `super()` is called implicitly without parameters.

With this trick, you can validate the arguments in a constructor before the superclass constructor is called. Problem solved? Yes and no! Let's take the more practical case of a constructor with two to four arguments. The more there are, the less precise and more challenging it becomes to understand the constructor call, including all verification method calls. And the more unwieldy things are, the less likely they are to be applied consistently. This tendency increases the risk of inconsistencies. In addition, the trick shown is not widely known.

New Feature in Java 25 LTS

The parameter check would be much easier to read and understand if the validation logic could be performed in the constructor before calling `super()`. It is now possible to validate the arguments in a constructor before calling the superclass constructor, as shown below by the `if`:

```java
public class PositiveBigInteger extends BaseBigInteger
{
    public PositiveBigInteger(long value)
    {
        if (value <= 0)
            throw new IllegalArgumentException("non-positive value");

        super(value);
    }
}
```

It is even possible to define local variables and execute actions, such as static method calls or loops, before calling `super()`, as long as they do not access instance attributes.

Additional Access to Static Variables   Sometimes, in addition to validity checks, other things need to be ensured: for example, the correct value assignment of a static attribute.

As in older Java versions, static attributes can be read and checked in constructors and helper methods. This is possible since they are already available when the class is initialized, that is, well before the constructor calls. Unlike in earlier Java versions, since Java 22, checks can also be performed before calling a base class constructor.

Let's look at an example of an inspection of the static variable `STATIC_VAR`, whose value is verified in the constructor using `equals()`. In addition, the lower limit has been moved to a helper variable to show access in the `if` condition:

```java
public class PositiveBigIntegerStaticVar extends BaseBigInteger
{
    public static final String STATIC_VAR = "STATIC_CONTENT";

    public static final int LOWER_BOUND = 0;

    public PositiveBigIntegerStaticVar(long value)
    {
        if (!STATIC_VAR.equals("STATIC_CONTENT"))
            throw new IllegalArgumentException("STATIC INIT Exception");
```

```
            if (value <= LOWER_BOUND)
                throw new IllegalArgumentException("non-positive value");

            super(value);
        }
}
```

9.5.2   *Preparing Arguments for the Base Class Constructor*

Sometimes, instead of a simple validity check, you need to perform a more complex conversion of data to pass it to the base class constructor.

Let's look at two classes as an example, starting with the base class `PlainByte-Message` with a constructor parameter of type `byte[]` as follows:

```java
public class PlainByteMessage
{
    private final byte[] payload;

    public PlainByteMessage(byte[] payload)
    {
        this.payload = payload;
    }

    // ...
}
```

Conventional Implementation

Let us now consider the subclass `StringMessage` and its constructor, which processes a string parameter. To call the base class constructor, the string must first be converted into a byte array:

```java
public class StringMessage extends PlainByteMessage
{
    public StringMessage(String payload)
    {
        super(convertToByteArray(payload));
    }

    // ...
}
```

This is done using the static method `convertToByteArray()`, which is invoked in the subclass constructor to prepare the data for the base class constructor. This method is implemented as follows:

```java
private static byte[] convertToByteArray(String payload)
{
    if (payload == null)
        throw new IllegalArgumentException("payload should not be null");

    return switch (payload)
    {
        case "TYPE_A" -> new byte[] { 1, 2, 3, 4 };
        case "TYPE_B" -> new byte[] { 7, 2, 7, 1 };
        default -> payload.getBytes();
    };
}
```

This example is similar to the static helper method trick, but is more practical because it performs data conversion rather than just a simple validity check. How can the constructor be implemented more effectively and clearly?

> **Integration of the null Check into the switch**
>
> In the example above, it is possible to integrate the null check into the switch instead of performing it separately. When does this make sense, and when is it better to avoid it? The answer is relatively simple: if null is a valid value that should be treated in the same way as the other values, it belongs in the switch. However, it is often desirable to handle invalid values or errors beforehand. In this case, the check should be performed before the switch. The latter is the case above, and according to the previous argument, the implementation is exactly as shown.

New Feature in Java 25 LTS

The whole thing becomes more readable if the argument preparation is performed before calling the base class constructor. This is especially true if you have to perform several such argument conversions and checks.

```java
public StringMessage(String payload)
{
    byte[] convertedPayload = convertToByteArray(payload);

    super(convertedPayload);
}
```

I like to point out one thing: Since this is merely an example to demonstrate the new feature in Java 25 LTS, we will refrain from using sophisticated processing with different CharSets. In practice, dealing with multiple CharSets is common.

9.5.3   *Improvements in Inheritance*

The options described so far already help to make constructors easier to understand, for example, by allowing validity checks to be performed before values are assigned or before a constructor call is made to the base class.

In the context of inheritance, surprises can sometimes occur when methods that are overridden in subclasses are called in constructors.

Preliminary Considerations and Conventional Behavior

For a better understanding, let's take a look at an inheritance hierarchy and, in particular, the method `logValues()` and its invocation in the base class constructor and the overridden variant in the subclass:

```java
public class BaseClass
{
    private final int baseValue;

    public BaseClass(int baseValue)
    {
        this.baseValue = baseValue;

        logValues();
    }

    protected void logValues()
    {
        System.out.println("baseValue: " + baseValue);
    }
}
```

The subclass is defined as follows and supplements the base class with an attribute and overwrites the method `logValues()`:

```java
public class SubClass extends BaseClass
{
    private final String subClassInfo;

    public SubClass(int baseValue, String subClassInfo)
    {
        super(baseValue);
        this.subClassInfo = subClassInfo;
    }

    @Override
    protected void logValues()
    {
        super.logValues();
        System.out.println("subClassInfo: " + subClassInfo);
    }
}
```

When a constructor call is made like this

```java
new SubClass(42, "SURPRISE");
```

you would expect the two values passed to the constructor to be logged, but instead you get this output:

```
baseValue: 42
subClassInfo: null
```

The reason is as follows: while the base class constructor is being processed, the attribute `subClassInfo` remains unassigned, since the call to `super()` occurs before the variable is assigned. This results in the above output.

Joshua Bloch's classic *Effective Java* [1] also describes calling an overridden method in the constructor as bad style. Why? Because a constructor in a base class potentially sees uninitialized attributes in the subclass.

New Feature in Java 25 LTS

Since Java 23 and thus Java 25 LTS, it has been possible to assign values to the attributes of the current instance before calling the constructor of the base class. The subclass constructor can be changed as follows:

```java
public class SubClassNew extends BaseClass
{
    private final String subClassInfo;

    public SubClassNew(int baseValue, String subClassInfo)
    {
        // Assignment to attribute of this class before calling super()
        this.subClassInfo = subClassInfo;
        super(baseValue);
    }

    // ...
}
```

With this small but significant change, which also feels natural, you can often avoid the problem described above. Let's check it out and repeat the previous call:

```java
new SubClassNew(42, "SURPRISE");
```

This time, the two values passed to the constructor are logged correctly:

```
baseValue: 42
subClassInfo: SURPRISE
```

9.5.4 Special Feature: Actions Before Calling `this()`

In Sect. 2.3.3 on records, we modeled a 2D coordinate as a record and created a special constructor that parses the x and y values from a string as follows:

```java
record MyPoint(int x, int y)
{
    public MyPoint(String values)
    {
        this(Integer.parseInt(values.split(",")[0].strip()),
            Integer.parseInt(values.split(",")[1].strip()));
    }
}
```

Obviously, repeatedly calling `split(",")[<index>].strip()` is not particularly elegant. In a 3D system with a z coordinate, this would be quite a lot of work and would get even more difficult to read.

New Feature in Java 25 LTS

Using the new syntax, the actions can be extracted from the call to `this()` and, in particular, it is only necessary to call `split()` once. In addition, we can define local variables in advance:

```java
record MyPoint(int x, int y)
{
    public MyPoint(String values)
    {
        var separatedValues = values.split(",");
        int x = Integer.parseInt(separatedValues[0].strip());
        int y = Integer.parseInt(separatedValues[1].strip());

        this(x, y);
    }
}
```

However, it is advisable to write an additional helper method `parseInt()` and utilize it as follows to make the stripping, which is irrelevant for the logic, more elegant and the constructor easier to read:

```java
record MyPoint(int x, int y)
{
    public MyPoint(String values)
    {
        var separatedValues = values.split(",");
        int x = parseInt(separatedValues[0]);
        int y = parseInt(separatedValues[1]);

        this(x, y);
    }

    private static int parseInt(String strValue)
    {
        return Integer.parseInt(strValue.strip());
    }
}
```

Chapter 10
API Extensions in JDK 22 to 25 LTS

This chapter describes various API innovations that are cumulatively found in Java versions 22 to 25 LTS. We will address the topics listed below in individual sections—the preview and incubator features are marked in italics:

- JEP 454: Foreign Function and Memory API
- JEP 471: Deprecate the Memory-Access Methods in `sun.misc.Unsafe` for Removal
- JEP 484: Class-File API
- JEP 485: Stream Gatherers
- *JEP 502: Stable Values (Preview)*
- *JEP 505: Structured Concurrency (Fifth Preview)*
- JEP 506: Scoped Values
- *JEP 508: Vector API (Tenth Incubator)*

In Sect. 10.1, I introduce the possibilities for accessing native memory and functionality provided by external libraries. Section 10.2 covers a minor change for greater stability and reliability but involves marking various methods in the class `sun.misc.Unsafe` for removal. Additionally, the Class-File API offers a low-level API for generating and transforming bytecode from inside Java programs. This API is discussed in Sect. 10.3.

For many developers, the feature named Stream Gatherers is more exciting and relevant, as it allows creating your own intermediate operations or choosing from a set of predefined ones in the JDK. Stream gatherers are covered in Sect. 10.4.

One convenience feature in the preview status is Stable Values. These model constant-like values, which are discussed in Sect. 10.5. Two other JEPs simplify multithreading and the transfer of values to different parts of the application. Structured concurrency enables the effortless splitting up and combining of various tasks concurrently. This feature is a real gem that, unfortunately, has not yet been finalized in Java 25 LTS, but whose latest preview version is described in Sect. 10.6. Finally, the feature Scoped Values facilitates passing values through an application. This topic is the subject of Sect. 10.7.

M. Inden, *Java 25 and Beyond*, https://doi.org/10.1007/979-8-8688-2385-5_10

Still in incubator status, the Vector API (see Sect. 10.8) represents an exciting innovation that benefits from optimizations in modern processors.

Finally, Sect. 10.9 provides an overview of various minor changes in the form of a potpourri of innovations that have found their way into the JDK.

10.1 JEP 454: Foreign Function and Memory API

JEP 454 named " Foreign Function and Memory (FFM) API" develops an API for accessing functionalities and memory areas that are located outside the JVM. Why is this necessary?

Sometimes, you need to access functions written in other programming languages, such as C or C++, in Java programs. This applies to special drivers or native libraries from operating systems. It may also be necessary to address memory areas outside the JVM. Although the JNI (Java Native Interface) has been available for such tasks since the early days of Java, supporting calls to native code, it has various shortcomings: the calls are pretty tedious. Additionally, specific conventions must be followed, and the type systems of Java and C are not well aligned. But that's not all! There can also be problems with garbage collection if you reserve memory in C with `malloc` and then want to return it to the Java call.

As an alternative to JNI, class `sun.misc.Unsafe` exists, but as the name suggests, this is potentially unsafe: if used incorrectly, it is even possible to crash other programs or the JVM itself. Consequently, you should employ `Unsafe` with extreme caution or, better yet, refrain from using it altogether and operate with the newly created FFM API,[1] which addresses the shortcomings of JNI and `Unsafe` by providing specific classes such as `MethodHandle`, `MemoryAddress`, and `VarHandle`. It defines classes and interfaces for the following tasks:

- Managing memory (`Arena`, `MemoryAddress`, and `MemorySegment`)
- Manipulating and accessing memory (`MemoryLayout` and `VarHandle`)
- Managing the lifecycle of external resources (`ResourceScope`)
- Calling native functions (`SymbolLookup`, `Linker`, and `NativeSymbol`)

Introductory Example: `strlen`

As an introductory example, we like to invoke the `strlen` function from the C standard library. In doing so, we will learn about the determination (`SymbolLookup` and `Linker`) and the call (`MethodHandle` and `FunctionDescriptor`) of such an external function, as well as memory management (`Arena` and `MemorySegment`). What is unusual or deviates from the previous standard with `MethodHandle` and its `invoke()` method is the procurement of the

---

[1] This note should be considered particularly as Java 23 contains JEP 471 entitled " Deprecate the Memory-Access Methods in sun.misc.Unsafe for Removal," which enforces the removal of memory access methods in the class `Unsafe`.

functionality and memory management. The comments in the listing give an idea of the additional steps required.

```java
import static java.lang.foreign.ValueLayout.ADDRESS;
import static java.lang.foreign.ValueLayout.JAVA_LONG;

void main() throws Throwable
{
    // 1. Determine SymbolLookup for common libraries
    var linker = Linker.nativeLinker();
    SymbolLookup stdlib = linker.defaultLookup();

    // 2. Determine MethodHandle for ?strlen? in the C standard library
    var strlenMethodHandle = linker.downcallHandle(
                    stdlib.find("strlen").orElseThrow(),
                    FunctionDescriptor.of(JAVA_LONG, ADDRESS));

    // 3. Convert Java string to C string and allocate it in C memory
    Arena auto = Arena.ofAuto();
    var text = "direct c call of strlen";
    var strMemorySegment = auto.allocateFrom(text);

    // 4. Call the "foreign function"
    long len = (long) strlenMethodHandle.invoke(strMemorySegment);

    System.out.println("len('" + text + "') = " + len);
    // 5. Memory is automatically cleaned up by "Arena.ofAuto()"
}
```

Listing 10.1 Executable as "CALLSTRLENWITHFFMEXAMPLE"

Upon examining the example, it is evident that the actual call consists of only one line, specifically the one in step 4. However, various preparations must be made in advance, as outlined in steps 1–3. The additional effort increases significantly, even if the functionality to be called is only slightly more complex—this will be apparent later, when making a call to Quicksort, where data must be converted both when invoking the functionality and receiving the result.

The program CALLSTRLENWITHFFMEXAMPLE outputs a few warning messages (not shown here), then determines the length of the text "direct c call of strlen", and logs the value of the length on the console:

```
len('direct c call of strlen') = 23
```

Further Example: `qsort`

As an additional example, let's call Quicksort with the name `qsort` from the C standard library. This functionality is slightly more complex than the previous one because we need to transfer data from Java to the C functionality and then convert the result to a Java list. Additionally, the sorting criterion is defined as a Java method, which we pass to the C functionality. The source data is defined as an array in Java and is then sorted in native memory using the C function `qsort`. Finally, the sorted values are transferred to a Java list for storing the results.

To keep the example understandable, we extract some of the steps previously simplified in the `main()` method into separate methods. This step is beneficial because various other details are involved here, such as memory transfer, the provision of a comparison function in Java, and the conversion of the results from native memory to a results list.

```java
import static java.lang.foreign.Linker.nativeLinker;
import static java.lang.foreign.ValueLayout.*;

void main() throws Throwable
{
    // Step 1: Determine SymbolLookUp + MethodHandle
    var qsortMethodHandle = getQSortMethodHandle();

    // Step 2:
    var arena = Arena.ofAuto();
    var callbackPtr = createCompareCallBack(arena);

    // Step 3: Input data
    int[] values = {9, 4, 8, 6, 11, 13, 17, 19, 7, 5, 3, 2};
    var valuesMemorySegment = arena.allocateFrom(JAVA_INT, values);

    // Step 4: Call "qsort" from the C library
    qsortMethodHandle.invokeWithArguments(valuesMemorySegment,
                                values.length,
                                (int) JAVA_INT.byteSize(),
                                callbackPtr);

    // Step 5: Reconversion: sorted C memory -> Java list
    List<Integer> sortedValues = convertToIntList(valuesMemorySegment);
    System.out.println("sortedValues: " + sortedValues);
}

private static MethodHandle getQSortMethodHandle() throws Exception
{
    var cStdLib = nativeLinker().defaultLookup();
    var qsortSymbol = cStdLib.find("qsort").orElseThrow();

    // qsort receives an address to the data, two int values, and an
    // address to a comparison function for the elements
    var qsortFunc = FunctionDescriptor.ofVoid(ADDRESS, JAVA_INT,
                                JAVA_INT, ADDRESS);

    return nativeLinker().downcallHandle(qsortSymbol, qsortFunc);
}
```

Listing 10.2 Executable as "CALLQSORTWITHFFMEXAMPLE"

To pass the comparison functionality to the C function, we must first define a class with a suitable method and then describe its signature using `MethodType`:

```java
private static MemorySegment createCompareCallBack(final Arena arena)
            throws NoSuchMethodException, IllegalAccessException
{
    var callbackJavaSig = MethodType.methodType(int.class, MemorySegment.class,
                                MemorySegment.class);
    var callbackJava = MethodHandles.lookup().bind(new MyDescComparator(),
                                "compare", callbackJavaSig);
```

```
    // Method signature of the comparison function in C
    var callbackCSig = FunctionDescriptor.of(ValueLayout.JAVA_INT,
                                             ValueLayout.ADDRESS,
                                             ValueLayout.ADDRESS);

    // Provide Java method as callback stub
    return nativeLinker().upcallStub(callbackJava, callbackCSig, arena);
}
```

We define the descending sorting functionality in a class `MyDescComparator` in its `compare()` method as follows:

```
private static class MyDescComparator
{
    private int compare(final MemorySegment left, final MemorySegment right)
    {
        var leftValue = extractValue(left);
        var rightValue = extractValue(right);

        return Integer.compare(rightValue, leftValue);
    }

    private static int extractValue(final MemorySegment memorySegment)
    {
        return MemorySegment.ofAddress(memorySegment.address()).
                        reinterpret(JAVA_INT.byteSize()).
                        get(JAVA_INT, 0);
    }
}
```

Then, we implement the following method for reconversion from the values stored in native memory:

```
private static List<Integer> convertToIntList(MemorySegment
        valuesMemorySegment)
{
    return valuesMemorySegment.elements(JAVA_INT)
                        .map(element -> element.get(JAVA_INT, 0))
                        .toList();
}
```

The program CALLQSORTWITHFFMEXAMPLE outputs a few warning messages (not shown here) and then returns the sorted numbers in descending order:

```
sortedValues: [19, 17, 13, 11, 9, 8, 7, 6, 5, 4, 3, 2]
```

Conclusion

The Foreign Function and Memory API certainly represents an improvement in terms of accessing native functionalities. However, it still requires a fair amount of tinkering and trial and error to get a handle on it. In particular, if you change the data types for Quicksort, for example, you will quickly get an incomprehensible error message and repeatedly encounter obstacles that can only be solved with tricks. To make matters worse, the documentation is sparse, and help on the Internet is often hard to find.

The previous explanations only offer a brief introduction to the topic. This limitation seems justified because accessing native memory and calling native functionality are highly specialized areas that very few programmers will encounter directly.

10.2   JEP 471: Deprecate the Memory-Access Methods in `sun.misc.Unsafe` for Removal

The class `sun.misc.Unsafe` contains various methods that make it possible, for example, to create object instances without calling a constructor, to read and manipulate pointers, and to use memory that the garbage collector does not manage.

As the name of the class suggests, the actions executed with it are potentially unsafe, and you should be very experienced to use them. Typical areas of application are libraries or frameworks. However, there are now good and secure alternatives available in the JDK, namely, the `java.lang.invoke.VarHandle` API and the Foreign Function and Memory API introduced with Java 22 and described in Sect. 10.1—primarily in the form of the `java.lang.foreign.Memory-segment` interface. Bypassing the use of the `Unsafe` class makes programs and libraries future-proof, thereby avoiding incompatibilities or other difficulties when upgrading to newer Java versions.

Since this topic is probably only relevant to a reasonably small percentage of the developer community, I would like to refer you to the JEP and its description: https://openjdk.org/jeps/471.

However, it should be noted that many applications are indirectly dependent on the `Unsafe` class. This applies when libraries integrated into your application perform calls to `Unsafe`. To allow tracking this, Java 23 introduced the option of logging unintended access by specifying this command-line parameter `--sun-misc-unsafememory-access=<option>`. For `<option>`, the following values are permitted: `allow`, `warn`, `debug`, and `deny`.[2] This allows you to specify how memory accesses from `Unsafe` are handled:

- `allow`: Allows the use of memory access methods without warnings at runtime.
- `warn`: Allows the use of memory access methods, but produces warnings at runtime.
- `debug`: Allows the use of memory access methods. In addition to warnings, stacktraces are output at runtime.
- `deny`: Prohibits the use of memory access methods. If an access is attempted nonetheless, it fails and results in a `java.lang.UnsupportedOperation-Exception`.

---

[2] Some developers may remember the command-line option `-illegal-access` introduced in Java 9 as part of modularization.

10.3   JEP 484: Class-File API

This JEP provides a low-level API for generating and transforming bytecode from within a Java class. This is particularly relevant for tool and library developers who need to process bytecode.

Unless you are particularly concerned with the latest Java language innovations, you can use the ASM library[3] to inspect and modify bytecode. However, this library was invented around 20 years ago, and for historical reasons, it is not straightforward to use. Additionally, it is challenging for ASM developers to keep pace with Java's six-month release cycle. As a result, the latest Java class file formats are not always supported. As a remedy, the Class-File API was included in the JDK. This integration not only creates a standard API for class files that is automatically always up to date and evolves along with the format of compiled Java classes, but also a modern alternative to previous libraries such as ASM, Byte Buddy, etc.

Introductory Example

To get started, let's create a simple HelloWorld program using the Class-File API, for example, one whose behavior is like this:

```java
public class HelloWorld
{
    public static void main(String[] args)
    {
        System.out.println("Hello World From Class-File API")
    }
}
```

Using the Class-File API, you can implement the generation of bytecode that corresponds to the instructions of the above class, as follows.

```java
import static java.lang.classfile.ClassFile.ACC_PUBLIC;
import static java.lang.classfile.ClassFile.ACC_STATIC;

void main() throws IOException
{
    ClassFile.of().buildTo(Path.of("HelloWorld.class"),
                    ClassDesc.of("HelloWorld"),
                    classBuilder -> createMain(classBuilder));
}

private static void createMain(ClassBuilder classBuilder)
{
    classBuilder.withMethodBody("main",
                    MethodTypeDesc.ofDescriptor(
                    "([Ljava/lang/String;)V"),
                    ACC_PUBLIC | ACC_STATIC,
                    codeBuilder -> createMainBodyCode(codeBuilder));
}
```

Listing 10.3 Executable as "HELLOWORLDCLASSFILEBUILDER"

---

[3] https://asm.ow2.io/

The method `buildTo()` receives a path specification and information about the class as `java.lang.constant.ClassDesc` and supplies a `ClassBuilder` from the package `java.lang.classfile`, which provides a call to `withMethodBody()` for adding a method. It possesses parameters for the name, a descriptor in the form of a `java.lang.constant.MethodTypeDesc` instance; the access flags, here for `public` and `static`; this procedure is encapsulated in the `createMain()` method. Additionally, you get a `CodeBuilder` that defines the method call for the output of "`Hello World From Class-File API`". We use the `CodeBuilder` to generate the call in the `main()` method in the form of the following method:

```
private static void createMainBodyCode(CodeBuilder codeBuilder)
{
    codeBuilder.getstatic(ClassDesc.of("java.lang.System"), "out",
                          ClassDesc.of("java.io.PrintStream"))
              .ldc("Hello World From Class-File API")
              .invokevirtual(ClassDesc.of("java.io.PrintStream"),
                             "println",
                             MethodTypeDesc.ofDescriptor(
                             "(Ljava/lang/Object;)V"))
              .return_();
}
```

The source code shown above may seem rather cumbersome and complicated to developers who are not yet familiar with the Class-File API. However, it is much easier to employ compared with older libraries such as ASM. Why? Instead of the Visitor pattern, as in ASM, the Class-File API uses the Builder pattern and various newer Java functionalities. Therefore, generating the bytecode of a class that outputs a greeting requires only a handful of lines. Conveniently, the Class-File API also handles blocks, so we don't have to create them explicitly. Similarly, the appropriate jump commands are generated for branches, for example, when using `ifThenElse()`.

When running the above program HELLOWORLDCLASSFILEBUILDER, a file `HelloWorld.class` is created at the root level of the project. Thereafter, you can use

```
$ java HelloWorld
```

for execution of the previously created program. Then you get this output:

```
Hello World From Class-File API
```

A Look Behind the Scenes

Now let's take a look at what actually happens and use the `javap` tool integrated into the JDK to inspect the generated bytecode. The tool can create a readable representation from the bytecode of a Java class. This allows us to verify that the bytecode corresponds to that of a typical HelloWorld class, as expected:

```
$ javap HelloWorld.class
public class HelloWorld {
  public static void main(java.lang.String[]);
}
```

Let's go one level deeper and look at the generated bytecode itself. It becomes clear upon closer inspection that it is analogous to the methods used previously, such as `getstatic` and `invokevirtual`, as well as references to, for example, `System.out` or `java/io/PrintStream`:

```
$ javap -c HelloWorld.class
public class HelloWorld {
  public static void main(java.lang.String[]);
    Code:
       0: getstatic      #10  // Field java/lang/System.out:Ljava/io/
          PrintStream;
       3: ldc            #12  // String Hello World From Class-File API
       5: invokevirtual #18  // Method java/io/PrintStream.println:(Ljava/
          lang/Object;)V
       8: return
}
```

When looking at the bytecode above, you notice references with "#", which refer to constants, such as attributes or texts. If you want to delve deeper into the secrets, the command

```
$ javap -v HelloWorld.class
```

provides a more detailed representation, including a list of constants and further things.

10.4   JEP 485: Stream Gatherers

The Stream API, introduced in Java 8 LTS, was quite powerful right from the start. In subsequent Java versions, various enhancements were added in the area of terminal operations. As a reminder, terminal operations initiate the processing and terminate the calculations of a stream, for example, converting the stream into a collection or a result value.

This JEP introduces an extension to the Stream API that supports user-defined intermediate operations. These are processing steps such as filtering and transforming, which can be combined to accomplish more complex actions. Until now, there have been various predefined intermediate operations, including the methods `filter()` and `map()`. However, there was no provision for extending these. Such an extension is desirable to enable tasks that were previously impossible, difficult, or only possible with tricks and somewhat cumbersome to implement.

For an introduction to the Stream API and some of its operations, please consult Sect. 15.2 in Chap. 15.

10.4.1   Introduction and Motivation

Let's assume, based on a specific criterion, that we want to remove all duplicates and retain only one instance of each type. To achieve this, you need some state info about previously encountered elements. To keep the task easy to understand, let's consider a stream of strings and use their length as the criterion, keeping only one name of each specific length and sorting out the others with the same length.

Hypothetically, the action could be implemented as follows, with an intermediate operation in the form of a fictitious method `distinctBy()` with respect to length, by defining `String::length` as the criterion:

```
var result = Stream.of("Tim", "Lea", "Mike", "Maria", "Peter", "Sophie").
                distinctBy(String::length).       // Hypothetically
                toList();

// result ==> [Tim, Mike, Maria, Sophie]
```

> **Note: Examples Based on Those from JEP 485**
> Please note that for some examples, such as the one just shown, I drew inspiration from those in the JEP (https://openjdk.org/jeps/485) and adapted or expanded them as necessary.

Workaround Using Existing Options

Let's examine how we can eliminate duplicates based on string length using the tools currently available in the Stream API—I will introduce the record `DistinctBy-Length` required for this later:

```
var result = Stream.of("Tim", "Lea", "Jim", "Mike", "Maria", "John", "James",
                "Peter", "Sophie", "Joelle", "Clemens", "Sebastian").
                map(DistinctByLength::new). // #1
                distinct().                 // #2
                map(DistinctByLength::str). // #3
                toList();

// result ==> [Tim, Mike, Maria, Sophie, Clemens, Sebastian]
```

First (#1), `map(DistinctByLength::new)` is used to create a mapping from the strings to instances of `DistinctByLength`. Their `equals()` method is tailored to the length of strings. Using the standard `distinct()` functionality, it removes all duplicates based on string length in a second step (#2). Then, in step three (#3), `map(DistinctByLength::str)` maps back to the original string. To avoid information loss while mapping, the following record is used:

```java
record DistinctByLength(String str)
{
    @Override
    public boolean equals(Object obj)
    {
        return obj instanceof DistinctByLength(String other) &&
                str.length() == other.length();
    }

    @Override
    public int hashCode()
    {
        return str == null ? -1 : str.length();
    }
}
```

This record is merely a wrapper around a string and possesses an attribute `str` as well as the automatically generated corresponding access method named `str()`. To utilize the record for our intended purpose, we must override the `equals()` and `hashCode()` methods to align with the string length. In the implementation of `equals()`, we use pattern matching with `instanceof`. In combination with record patterns (see Sects. 2.5 and 4.1), this keeps the source code very compact. The pattern matching eliminates the need for an explicit `null` check that would otherwise be necessary in `equals()`, as this does not match the pattern.

Another Example of a Desirable Intermediate Operation

Another example of the need for a self-defined intermediate operation is the grouping of data from a stream into sections of fixed size.

For demonstration purposes, two names are to be combined into a single unit, that is, grouped. For our example, only the first three groups are to be included in the result. Once again, I will show the source code tailored based on the JEP with a fictitious method `windowFixed()`:

```java
var result = Stream.of("Maria", "Micha", "Sabine", "Jim", "Angela",
                "Paul", "Jessica", "Pete", "Joelle", "Mike").
            windowFixed(2).                           // Hypothetically
            limit(3).
            toList();

// result ==> [[Maria, Micha], [Sabine, Jim], [Angela, Paul]]
```

This functionality could be achieved in a conventional manner using a few tricks, but only through a terminal operation. Because this requires a significant amount of source code and there has been suitable predefined functionality available since Java 24, and thus also in Java 25 LTS, I have decided not to include a conventional implementation in the book. In the accompanying source code, you will find an example implementation in the class `WindowedExample`.

New Feature: The `Gatherer` Interface and the `gather()` Method

Over the years, the Java community has proposed several suggestions and requests for intermediate operations to supplement the Stream API. These are often useful in specific contexts. However, including all of these potentially useful methods in the JDK would have bloated the API and made it (even more) difficult to get started with the (already extensive) Stream API.

To maintain the flexibility of user-defined intermediate operations, an approach similar to that used for terminal operations and its extension point built by the method `collect(Collector)` and the interface `java.util.stream.Collector` is adopted. As a reminder, this combination enables the extension of predefined terminal operations in the JDK on an individual basis as needed.

The Stream API now offers a method `gather(Gatherer)` in combination with the interface `java.util.stream.Gatherer` as its extension point for flexibly providing new intermediate operations. If we want to implement the `distinctBy()` functionality discussed above ourselves, we could implement our own `Gatherer`. However, this is more complex and would go beyond the scope of this introduction. You can try your hand at this in an exercise in Chap. 12, where you will also find a sample solution.

Instead of getting involved with our own implementations at this stage, let's take a look at some predefined `Gatherers` residing in the JDK.

10.4.2 Overview of Selected Predefined `Gatherer` Methods

Conveniently, a few `Gatherer` methods have already been included in the JDK to fulfill some requests from the Java community for specific intermediate operations. These are defined in the utility class `java.util.stream.Gatherers`.

Preliminary Considerations Regarding Stream Gatherers

Stream gatherers can be characterized as follows:

1. **Transformation**: Stream gatherers define and execute processing steps. The elements involved are converted into output elements in various ways: 1:1, 1:n, n:1, or n:m. Accordingly, a stream gatherer is capable of generating one or more

output elements from a single input element, as well as transforming multiple input elements into one or more output elements.

2. **State Information**: Sometimes, processing data requires information about previously processed elements. Until now, it has only been possible to process state information in streams using dirty tricks, such as referencing and modifying surrounding data structures. Conveniently, stream gatherers allow state information to be used. This allows for collecting information about the amount, content, and other details of the previous elements, influencing the transformation of subsequent elements, for example, depending on the position or when a condition is met.

Window Fixed: n:m

The `windowFixed()` method from the JDK subdivides a stream into smaller components of fixed size without overlap. It is an n:m gatherer and groups n elements into lists of fixed size m.

Let's take the second example from the introduction (grouping names into units of fixed length) and see how easily it can be implemented using basic JDK functionality. First, using factory method `of()` generating a fixed-size stream based on some names, which is then subdivided into sub-ranges of size 2 by calling `gather(Gatherer.windowFixed(2))`. `limit(3)` limits the number of sub-ranges to three, and these are provided as a result in the form of a list by calling `toList()`:

```
jshell> var result = Stream.of("Maria", "Micha", "Sabine", "Jim", "Angela",
   ...>                        "Paul", "Jessica", "Pete", "Joelle", "Mike").
   ...>                 gather(Gatherers.windowFixed(2)).
   ...>                 limit(3).
   ...>                 toList();
result ==> [[Maria, Micha], [Sabine, Jim], [Angela, Paul]]
```

Special Case   When dividing into sub-ranges of fixed size, there is a special case to consider: if a data set does not contain enough elements to fill the desired sub-range size, this will result in the last sub-range containing fewer elements.

An example of this is a stream with a fixed data set of values from 0 to 6 inclusive, generated by calling `of()`. This stream is divided into sub-ranges of size 3 using `windowFixed(3)`, which means that the last sub-range contains only one element. This corresponds to a list with the number 6:

```
jshell> var result = Stream.of(0, 1, 2, 3, 4, 5, 6).
   ...>                 gather(Gatherers.windowFixed(3)).
   ...>                 toList()
result ==> [[0, 1, 2], [3, 4, 5], [6]]
```

Window Sliding: n:m

In addition to dividing into independent sub-ranges, we can also subdivide with overlaps. To split a stream into smaller components of fixed size with overlap, use the `windowSliding()` method from the JDK. It is also an n:m gatherer and works like a sliding window over the input stream. The window is shifted one element to the right, resulting in a value overlap. A potentially desirable shift of more than one element is currently not supported out of the box. To achieve this functionality, you would need to implement your own stream gatherer—Sect. 10.4.7 covers this advanced topic. Please keep in mind that it often makes sense not to reinvent the wheel when well-tested, ready-made libraries are available, as with stream gatherers. Later, a practical note briefly discusses this topic, including relevant URLs.

To demonstrate a subdivision with overlaps, we again use an infinite stream of numbers calling `iterate()`. Invoking `windowSliding(4)` subdivides the data into sub-ranges of size 4, but with an overlap or shift of one element. `limit(3)` limits the number of sub-ranges to three. As before, calling `toList()` prepares the result in the form of a list:

```
jshell> var result = Stream.iterate(0, i -> i + 1).
   ...>                      gather(Gatherers.windowSliding(4)).
   ...>                      limit(3).
   ...>                      toList()
result ==> [[0, 1, 2, 3], [1, 2, 3, 4], [2, 3, 4, 5]]
```

For `windowSliding()`, the special case of an incomplete last sub-range that occurs with `windowFixed()` is impossible; instead, five sub-ranges with three elements each are generated:

```
jshell> var result = Stream.of(0, 1, 2, 3, 4, 5, 6).
   ...>                      gather(Gatherers.windowSliding(3)).
   ...>                      toList()
result ==> [[0, 1, 2], [1, 2, 3], [2, 3, 4], [3, 4, 5], [4, 5, 6]]
```

Special Case For `windowSliding()`, the special case of a data set with an incomplete window, which was discussed earlier, usually does not occur. It is only possible if the total number of input data is smaller than the specified window size. In this case, the result consists of the entire input, as shown below for a data set of three values and a window size of five. The result is a list that in turn contains a list with three elements:

```
jshell> var result = Stream.of(1, 2, 3).
   ...>                      gather(Gatherers.windowSliding(5)).
   ...>                      toList()
result ==> [[1, 2, 3]]
```

Fold: n:1

The `fold()` method combines the values of a stream. It represents an n:1 gatherer and creates an aggregation based on the current element and the result of previous actions. The way it works is similar to the terminal operation `reduce()`, which generates a result from a sequence of elements by repeatedly applying a combination operation, such as "+" or "*" for numbers, to the elements. For this purpose, a start value and a calculation rule are specified. This rule determines how the previous result is combined with the current element.

With this knowledge, we create an example for `fold()` to calculate the sum of values with 0 as the start value and addition as the operation, as follows:

```
jshell> var sum = Stream.of(1, 2, 3, 4, 5, 6, 7).
   ...>                 gather(Gatherers.fold(() -> 0,
   ...>                     (result, number) -> result + number)).
   ...>                 findFirst()
sum ==> Optional[28]
```

Note that `gather()` returns a stream as its result. In this case, it is a single-element stream. Therefore, to extract a value from it, invoke `findFirst()`, which returns an `Optional<T>` (see Sect. 15.3.2) because, theoretically, the stream could also be empty.

Alternatively, multiplication can be employed as a calculation, in this case with a starting value of 1. This calculates the factorial of 7 for the specifically selected sequence of values from 1 to 7, that is, $1 \cdot 2 \cdot 3 \cdot 4 \cdot 5 \cdot 6 \cdot 7$:

```
jshell> var multi = Stream.of(1, 2, 3, 4, 5, 6, 7).
   ...>                 gather(Gatherers.fold(() -> 1,
   ...>                     (result, number) -> result * number)).
   ...>                 findFirst()
multi ==> Optional[5040]
```

In general, it involves multiplying the given numbers:

```
jshell> var multi = Stream.of(10, 20, 30, 40, 50).
   ...>                 gather(Gatherers.fold(() -> 1,
   ...>                     (result, number) -> result * number)).
   ...>                 findFirst()
multi ==> Optional[12000000]
```

Actions for Different Types What happens if we want to combine values using actions that are not defined for the types of the values, in this case `int`? As an example, a numerical value is converted to a string, and this is repeated according to the numerical value by calling the method `repeat()` of the `String` class:

```
jshell> var repeatedNumbers = Stream.of(1, 2, 3, 4, 5, 6, 7).
   ...>                     gather(Gatherers.fold(() -> "",
   ...>                         (result, number) -> result +
   ...>                         ("" + number).repeat(number))).
   ...>                     toList()
repeatedNumbers ==> [12233344445555566666677777777]
```

Variants with `reduce()`   For the sake of completeness, the previous calculations are shown here as variants with `reduce()`. Because `reduce()` is a terminal operation, it does not allow any further processing in the stream:

```
jshell> var sum = Stream.of(1, 2, 3, 4, 5, 6, 7).
   ...>                        reduce(0, (result, number) -> result + number)
sum ==> 28

jshell> var multi = Stream.of(1, 2, 3, 4, 5, 6, 7).
   ...>                        reduce(1, (result, number) -> result * number)
multi ==> 5040

jshell> var multi = Stream.of(10, 20, 30, 40, 50).
   ...>                        reduce(1, (result, number) -> result * number)
multi ==> 12000000

jshell> var repeatedNumbers = Stream.of(1, 2, 3, 4, 5, 6, 7).
   ...>                            reduce("", (result, number) ->
   ...>                            result + ("" + number).repeat(number),
   ...>                            (str1, str2) -> str1 + str2);
repeatedNumbers ==> "1223334444555556666667777777"
```

Just like with `fold()`, a start value and a calculation rule are specified for `reduce()`. It then produces a result value.

Differentiation: Comparison of `fold()` and `reduce()`

The two methods `fold()` and `reduce()` appear to be relatively similar. The differences in calculation are particularly noticeable in parallel processing. While `fold()` works correctly in both sequential and parallel cases, this is not true for `reduce()`. Let's look at an example of different outputs that are deducted from an initial cash balance:

```
void main()
{
    int currentCash = 250;
    var expenses = List.of(25, 42, 32, 18);

    var foldResult = expenses.stream()
                  .parallel()
                  .gather(Gatherers.fold(() -> currentCash,
                                         (a, b) -> a - b))
                  .findAny()
                  .orElseThrow();
    System.out.println("fold: " + foldResult); // 133

    var reduceResult = expenses.stream()
                  .reduce(currentCash, (a, b) -> a - b);
    System.out.println("reduce: " + reduceResult); // 133

    var reduceResult2 = expenses.stream()
                  .parallel()
                  .reduce(currentCash, (a, b) -> a - b);
    System.out.println("reduce parallel: " + reduceResult2); // 31
}
```

(continued)

The following outputs occur:

```
fold: 133
reduce: 133
reduce parallel: 31
```

You can find a detailed discussion online at https://stackoverflow.com/questions/79759286/when-to-use-gatherers-fold-over-stream-reduce.

Scan: 1:1

If all elements of a stream are to be merged into new combinations so that each input element always produces exactly one output element, then this is the task of `scan()`. This is a 1:1 gatherer and generates a new element based on the current status and the input element.

The method works similarly to `fold()`. However, the values are not combined into a single result; instead, `scan()` produces a new result for each element.

First, we use `scan()` to calculate sums:

```
jshell> var sums = Stream.of(1, 2, 3, 4, 5, 6, 7).
   ...>                       gather(Gatherers.scan(() -> 0,
   ...>                           (result, number) -> result + number)).
   ...>                       toList()
sums ==> [1, 3, 6, 10, 15, 21, 28]
```

As a variation, we combine texts instead of numbers, only by changing the start value, for which we use an empty string here, turning "+" into a string concatenation:

```
jshell> var numberStrings = Stream.of(1, 2, 3, 4, 5, 6, 7).
   ...>                       gather(Gatherers.scan(() -> "",
   ...>                           (result, number) -> result + number)).
   ...>                       toList()
numberStrings ==> [1, 12, 123, 1234, 12345, 123456, 1234567]
```

You could also implement an n-time repetition—here the difference to `fold()` becomes particularly clear:

```
jshell> var repeatedNumbers = Stream.of(1, 2, 3, 4, 5, 6, 7).
   ...>                       gather(Gatherers.scan(() -> "",
   ...>                           (result, number) -> result +
   ...>                           ("" + number).repeat(number))).
   ...>                       toList()
repeatedNumbers ==> [1, 122, 122333, 1223334444, 122333444455555, 122 ...
    3334444555556666667777777]
```

10.4.3   Practical Examples

The examples presented so far were primarily intended to provide an initial understanding and were somewhat artificial. But what about their relevance and possible areas of application in practice?

While `fold()` and `scan()` can be helpful for mathematical calculations (more precisely: `fold()` for calculating a final result and `scan()` for providing all intermediate results), `windowFixed()` can be used, for example, for time series to subdivide them into intervals of fixed size. The gatherer `windowSliding()` is useful for analyses where data series overlap, such as detecting significant temperature fluctuations in a stream of temperature values or jumps in the stock market.

Practical Example: Cumulative Daily Expenses for Two Weeks

Let's assume we want to process daily expenses by adding them continuously. `scan()` is suitable for this purpose.

The following source code calculates the cumulative expenses based on a stream of `int` values modeling expenses per day:

```
jshell> var sum = Stream.of(15, 15, 30, 25, 15, 50, 20,
   ...>                      10, 20, 30, 40, 50, 60, 70).
   ...>                 gather(Gatherers.scan(() -> 0L,
   ...>                       (result, number) -> result + number)).
   ...>                 toList();
sum ==> [15, 30, 60, 85, 100, 150, 170, 180, 200, 230, 270, 320, 380, 450]
```

That seems to be easy. However, you need to be cleverer if you want to group these expenses by week and accumulate them within each week. More on that in a moment. But first, let's look at simple links between `Gatherers`.

10.4.4   Combining `Gatherers`

Interestingly, `Gatherers` are combinable. For this purpose, you can either call `gather()` several times in sequence or use the `andThen()` method.

Multiple Calls to `gather()`   As an example, we will use a chain of two calls to `windowFixed()`, here to first collect the data stream into blocks of size 3 and thereafter collect these in turn as two blocks in one list each—due to the data constellation, the last block only contains one list with two values:

```
jshell> var result = Stream.of(1, 2, 3, 4, 5, 6, 7, 8, 9, 10, 11, 12, 13, 14)
   .
   ...>                         gather(Gatherers.windowFixed(3)).
   ...>                         gather(Gatherers.windowFixed(2)).
   ...>                         toList();
result ==> [[[1, 2, 3], [4, 5, 6]], [[7, 8, 9], [10, 11, 12]], [[13, 14]]]
```

Combination with `andThen()` A combination or consecutive execution can also
be conveniently implemented using the default method `andThen()` predefined in
the `Gatherer` interface:

```
jshell> var result = Stream.of(1, 2, 3, 4, 5, 6, 7, 8, 9, 10, 11, 12, 13, 14)
   .
   ...>                         gather(Gatherers.windowFixed(3).
   ...>                              andThen(Gatherers.windowFixed(2))).
   ...>                         toList();
result ==> [[[1, 2, 3], [4, 5, 6]], [[7, 8, 9], [10, 11, 12]], [[13, 14]]]
```

It would also be possible to call different `Gatherers` one after the other. Feel
free to experiment after you have developed a basic understanding of `Gatherers`
by reading this chapter.

**Practical Example: Daily Expenses for Two Weeks, Grouped by Week and
Therein Cumulated**

Let's continue with the first example using this knowledge. The stream of 14
individual expenses is first divided into two sections of seven values each by calling
`windowFixed(7)`:

```
jshell> Stream.of(15, 15, 30, 25, 15, 50, 20,
   ...>              10, 20, 30, 40, 50, 60, 70).
   ...>          gather(Gatherers.windowFixed(7)).
   ...>          toList()
$7 ==> [[15, 15, 30, 25, 15, 50, 20], [10, 20, 30, 40, 50, 60, 70]]
```

This step was still relatively simple. To solve the problem, we need access to the
data from the respective windows to then prepare it as a cumulative sum. We saw
the necessary call to `scan()` at the beginning.

Now the challenge is to append this next step to the previous one. Let's try it with
the tools we just learned about:

```
jshell> Stream.of(15, 15, 30, 25, 15, 50, 20,
   ...>              10, 20, 30, 40, 50, 60, 70).
   ...>          gather(Gatherers.windowFixed(7)).
   ...>          gather(Gatherers.scan(() -> 0,
   ...>                  (result, number) -> result + number)).
   ...>          toList()
|  Error:
|  bad operand types for binary operator '+'
|    first type:  java.lang.Integer
|    second type: java.util.List<java.lang.Integer>
|               (result, number) -> result + number)).
|                    ^--------------^
```

After reading the error message and thinking about it for a moment, it becomes clear that we want to add numerical values to a list of values (the window). But how do we get the data from the window, and how do we convert it to obtain two lists, each with seven cumulative values?

This requires an intermediate step using `map()`. We have to turn the window back into a stream. We can then execute the `scan()` action on this stream of values and convert the result into a list using `toList()`. This yields the following implementation:

```
jshell> Stream.of(15, 15, 30, 25, 15, 50, 20,
   ...>             10, 20, 30, 40, 50, 60, 70).
   ...>         gather(Gatherers.windowFixed(7)).
   ...>             map(window ->
   ...>                 window.stream().gather(Gatherers.scan(() -> 0,
   ...>                 (result, number) -> result + number)).toList())).
   ...>         toList();
$9 ==> [[15, 30, 60, 85, 100, 150, 170], [10, 30, 60, 100, 150, 210, 280]]
```

For your own programs with similar complexity, it makes sense to extract certain components into methods or variables:

```
jshell> List<Integer> asPrefixSum(List<Integer> window) {
   ...>         return window.stream().gather(Gatherers.scan(() -> 0,
   ...>                 (result, number) -> result + number)).toList();
   ...> }
|  created method asPrefixSum(List<Integer>)

jshell> var result = Stream.of(15, 15, 30, 25, 15, 50, 20,
   ...>                 10, 20, 30, 40, 50, 60, 70).
   ...>             gather(Gatherers.windowFixed(7)).
   ...>             map(window -> asPrefixSum(window)).
   ...>             toList();
result ==> [[15, 30, 60, 85, 100, 150, 170], [10, 30, 60, 100, 150, 210, 280]]
```

10.4.5 A Look at `mapConcurrent()`

So far, we have learned about several predefined gatherers that are suitable for various use cases. In addition, there is the method `mapConcurrent(int maxConcurrency, Function<T,R> mapper)`. It behaves functionally like the classic `map()` operation, but converts input elements in parallel using virtual threads according to the specified action—with a maximum upper limit of virtual threads set by `maxConcurrency`.

Introduction to the Topic " Executing Actions in Parallel"

Let's look at a simple example to illustrate this. Since the data set is small, we will limit the parallelism to five virtual threads. The action consists of squaring numbers, for which we specify a lambda:

```
Stream.of(1, 2, 3, 4, 5, 6, 7, 8, 9, 10).
       gather(Gatherers.mapConcurrent(5, x -> x * x)).
       toList();
// [1, 4, 9, 16, 25, 36, 49, 64, 81, 100]
```

The goal of parallel processing is to achieve a shorter overall running time. However, for small amounts of data—as in the example—mapConcurrent() is rarely useful. Notable advantages can only be determined for larger data sets (often only for many thousands or even millions of elements) and/or blocking actions.

Comparison: Parallel Streams A conventional implementation with parallel streams does the job using the ForkJoinPool. This means that the actions in the above example are also distributed across various threads by calling parallel() as follows:

```
Stream.of(1, 2, 3, 4, 5, 6, 7, 8, 9, 10).
       parallel().
       map(x -> x * x).
       toList();
// [1, 4, 9, 16, 25, 36, 49, 64, 81, 100]
```

For small data sets, there is virtually no difference in processing speed.

10.4.6   Potential Limitations

To highlight potential pitfalls, we modify the action so that it blocks—as an example, we use a call to a basic LookupService, which waits one second per invocation of lookup() for demonstration purposes:

```
class LookupService
{
    static int lookup(final int key)
    {
        try
        {
            Thread.sleep(1000);
            return key * key;
        }
        catch (InterruptedException e)
        {
            throw new RuntimeException(e);
        }
    }
}
```

Using a parallel stream with 500 values, you could expect a running time of around one second with ideal parallelism:

```
var result3 = IntStream.rangeClosed(0, 499).
                        boxed().
                        parallel().
                        map(LookupService::lookup).
                        toList();
```

In practice, the running time is significantly higher: on a current laptop, processing 500 elements takes about 30 seconds; with 5,000 elements, it increases almost linearly to several minutes. This behavior illustrates the scaling limitations of parallel streams in blocking operations. The throughput is limited by the degree of parallelism of the shared `ForkJoinPool` (by default, this is equal to the number of logical cores minus one)—for an Apple M3 Max with 16 cores, this results in the following value:

```
jshell> int commonPoolParallelism = ForkJoinPool.getCommonPoolParallelism();
commonPoolParallelism ==> 15
```

The above variant is therefore not recommended and clearly shows the limitations of parallel streams.

Solution: `mapConcurrent()` with Virtual Threads As a remedy, invoking `mapConcurrent()` performs processing with virtual threads—here with 250 of them:

```
var result4 = IntStream.rangeClosed(0, 499).
                        boxed().
                        gather(Gatherers.mapConcurrent(250,
                                        LookupService::lookup)).
                        toList();
```

This version reduces the execution time to around two seconds.

Scaling If we increase the scope to 5,000 values, the time initially increases almost linearly to approximately 20 seconds. But now comes the crucial point—the throughput can be easily increased again by raising `maxConcurrency`, to around 2,500, for example:

```
var result5 = IntStream.rangeClosed(0, 4999).
                        boxed().
                        gather(Gatherers.mapConcurrent(2500,
                                        LookupService::lookup)).
                        toList();
```

This reduces the execution time back to around two seconds. With 5,000 virtual threads, it would even be possible to achieve a time of around one second, depending on system resources:

```
var result6 = IntStream.rangeClosed(0, 4999).
                    boxed().
                    gather(Gatherers.mapConcurrent(5000,
                                    LookupService::lookup)).
                    toList();
```

The positive effects of `mapConcurrent()` compared with `parallel()` increase dramatically as the number of elements to be processed increases.

If this works so well, one might consider further increasing the number of virtual threads. However, an increase would not result in any improvement in running time, as the processing steps themselves always take one second to complete. If, however, the data set to be processed were to become larger, the number of virtual threads could be increased without any problems, thus controlling the maximum running time.

Limitations and Notes

Please note that `mapConcurrent()` cannot perform miracles. Accordingly, parallel processing will never be faster than the latency of the actual calculation or action. Increasing `maxConcurrency` beyond this point will not yield any further benefits, but may hurt system resources. It is important to note that although virtual threads are lightweight, they still require system resources, which is why `maxConcurrency` should be chosen with care.

As with all parallelization strategies, positive effects often only become apparent for (extremely) large data sets. For such data sets in particular, `mapConcurrent()` provides a straightforward method to accelerate blocking or slower mapping tasks with virtual threads, allowing for precise control over the running time by adjusting `maxConcurrency` as demonstrated in the example.

The fact that `mapConcurrent()` excels especially with blocking- and I/O-heavy tasks will be discussed below.

Advantages for I/O

Parallel streams created with `parallel()` are based on the `ForkJoinPool`, and they carry the burden of a fixed parallelism limit—it can be queried by `ForkJoinPool.getCommonPoolParallelism()`. For actions that can be processed quickly and require little or no blocking I/O operations, the effects are often not immediately apparent. With blocking I/O, threads remain idle, and parallelism is exhausted soon, which slows down the common pool.

In contrast, `mapConcurrent()` scales much better for this because each action runs in a virtual thread. Blocking calls (e. g., JDBC/HTTP) park the virtual thread and release the carrier thread (unmounting), allowing other tasks to continue running.

Before Java 24, you had to be extra careful not to call blocking operations inside of `synchronized` blocks or methods, as no unmounting could take place and the carrier threads were therefore blocked. This issue is addressed with JEP 491: Synchronize Virtual Threads without Pinning (see Sect. 11.5).

When working with the Stream API, it is therefore recommended to use simple, CPU-intensive calculations. For complex I/O tasks, structured concurrency is a good choice (see Sect. 10.6). A simple rule of thumb is as follows:

- **CPU-Bound**: Use parallel streams or even the " simple" `map()`.
- **I/O-Bound and Blocking**: `mapConcurrent()` is preferable.

Whether a task is more CPU-bound or I/O-bound can be determined as follows: CPU-bound tasks require almost exclusively computing time, and the CPU cores are heavily utilized. I/O-bound tasks, on the other hand, spend most of their time waiting—typically for database queries, network access, or file access.

10.4.7   Custom Stream Gatherers

Now that we have gained some initial insight into how the built-in stream gatherers work, let's start developing our own stream gatherers.

Basics: The `Gatherer` Interface

Custom stream gatherers must implement the `Gatherer` interface. There are four basic control options, which are defined as methods of the same name in the `Gatherer` interface and allow the behavior to be customized as needed:

1. **Integrator**: This is where the actual processing takes place. An integrator defines the specific processing steps that are to be performed for each input element. If necessary, the status can be updated, and elements can be transferred to the output stream.

2. **Initializer**: Sometimes, certain status information is required during processing. The initializer allows you to create an object for status management.

3. **Combiner**: The combiner is only needed in the case of parallel processing to merge the (interim) results from different calculations.

4. **Finisher**: If some further actions are required after all elements have been processed, the finisher can execute additional actions and even publish additional elements to the output stream.

Of these four methods, you only need to implement the `integrator()` method; the other three central methods have default implementations predefined:

```java
public interface Gatherer<T, A, R>
{
    Integrator<A, T, R> integrator();

    default Supplier<A> initializer()
    {
        return defaultInitializer();
    };

    default BinaryOperator<A> combiner()
    {
        return defaultCombiner();
    }

    default BiConsumer<A, Downstream<? super R>> finisher()
    {
        return defaultFinisher();
    }

    // ...
}
```

In the listing, we notice three types:

- **Type** T: Type of elements to be processed from the input stream.
- **Type** A: Type represents (optional) state information.
- **Type** R: Values of this type are passed on to the output stream.

The three dots shown in the listing above indicate additional methods, such as the already familiar helper method `andThen()` for combining `Gatherers`. Furthermore, the interface contains some previously unmentioned construction methods called `of()` and `ofXyz()`, which make it easier to create your own implementations of stream gatherers. You will learn more about these construction methods later.

Let's look at the four central methods `integrator()`, `initializer()`, `finisher()`, and `combiner()`:

- **`integrator()`**: Represents the centerpiece and defines the actions to be performed for processing elements. The developer needs to implement this method to describe how each element of a stream is to be processed. This procedure may require storing data or other contextual information.
- **`initializer()`**: If state information is required, this method allows providing an initial state as a base before the actual processing starts. In this way, you could initialize a list for already processed elements or a counter, for example.
- **`combiner()`**: If stream gatherers are used in parallel streams, it is the task of the implementation of the method `combiner()` to determine how the individual results of parallel calculation steps are to be linked with each other. This advanced topic is not described further in this book.
- **`finisher()`**: Sometimes, additional calculations or evaluations are required at the end of the actions; for example, you may want to create a summary. It may be necessary to write additional values to the output stream. In such cases, this method can be implemented appropriately.

Custom Triple Gatherer: 1:n

Examples for 1:1, n:1, and n:m have been discussed so far in relation to categories.
The special case where one input element results in n output elements is presented
in this subsection in the form of a self-written triple gatherer that triples values.
Accordingly, it belongs to the 1:n category.

With the knowledge gathered so far, we need to take a closer look at the interface
`Integrator<A, T, R>` to implement the tripling of the elements:

```
interface Integrator<A, T, R>
{
    boolean integrate(A state, T element,
                      Downstream<? super R> downstream);
}
```

The method `integrate()` serves as a callback and is invoked for each element
of a stream. It receives state information of type A, the current element of type T, and
a reference to a downstream of type R as parameters to pass on processed elements
to it. The Boolean return value signals whether further elements are to be processed
after the current element.

In the following listing, the method `triple()` creates the actual triple gatherer.
There, a specific `integrator` is provided that does not require state information
and for which the types T and R match. In particular, in the method `integrate()`,
the current element is passed to the downstream three times by calling `push()`:

```
<T> Gatherer<T, Void, T> triple()
{
    return new Gatherer<T, Void, T>()
    {
        @Override
        public Integrator<Void, T, T> integrator()
        {
            return new Integrator<Void, T, T>()
            {
                @Override
                public boolean integrate(Void unusedState, T element,
                                         Downstream<? super T> downstream)
                {
                    downstream.push(element);
                    downstream.push(element);
                    downstream.push(element);
                    return true;
                }
            };
        }
    };
}
```

In the following, the custom triple gatherer defined above is called for strings and
also for numbers to demonstrate support for different types:

```
void main()
{
    var result = Stream.of("This", "is", "a", "test").
                          gather(triple()).
                          toList();
    System.out.println(result);

    var result2 = Stream.iterate(1, i -> i < 1_000, i -> i + 1).
                          gather(triple()).
                          limit(5).
                          toList();
    System.out.println(result2);
}
```

This example illustrates the elegance of modern Java, for example, with the concise notation called Instance Main Method. It allows you to implement a `main()` method without parameters. For details, please refer to Sect. 11.4—it is precisely these kinds of things that make Java more attractive as a language again.

Executing the above program produces the following output, which in particular also shows the restriction imposed by `limit()`:

```
[This, This, This, is, is, is, a, a, a, test, test, test]
[1, 1, 1, 2, 2]
```

Response to Termination Requests from the Downstream I want to point out one more thing: you should actually evaluate the result of a call to `push()` and only execute further actions if the result is `true`. It ensures that, when limited by `limit()`, termination occurs immediately after the current element and thus in the middle of the tripling process, that is, while `integrate()` is still being processed. Accordingly, a more elaborate processing looks like this:

```
@Override
public boolean integrate(Void unusedState, T element,
                         Downstream<? super T> downstream)
{
    boolean pushed = downstream.push(element);
    if (pushed)
        pushed = downstream.push(element);
    if (pushed)
        pushed = downstream.push(element);

    return pushed;
}
```

Although the query is stylistically more elegant and cleaner, it often does not have such a dramatic effect. Why? When you call `limit()`, a flag is set in the stream processing, and no more actions are executed in the pipeline—the upstream is globally aborted. So whether the `integrator` returns `true` or `false` doesn't change anything.

Note: The Problem in Detail

The difference can be observed within the same `integrate()` call: if the return value of `push()` is ignored, complex calculations may still be performed and further `push()` calls may be made, which immediately return `false`—useless, but the upstream remains stopped nonetheless. Let's look at a possible implementation:

```java
@Override
public boolean integrate(Void unusedState, T element,
                         Downstream<? super T> downstream)
{
    downstream.push(element);
    heavyProcessing();
    downstream.push(element);
    heavyProcessing();
    downstream.push(element);
    heavyProcessing();
    return true;
}
```

Such complex calculations within an `integrate()` method are relatively rare. Nevertheless, you should choose the clean implementation variant shown above—especially if the actions may still modify some state. After a termination, you should avoid state changes or long-running heavy actions.

10.4.8   State Management

As complexity and specific requirements for stream gatherers increase, state management is necessary to implement more ambitious functionality. To continue with the example, the requirement could be to repeat only those elements three times whose index is even. This functionality requires a counter. It seems obvious to use an `Integer` for this. This idea does not work here since `Integer` is immutable. To enable modification and visibility across multiple method calls, the `AtomicInteger` class is suitable—the characteristics of atomic changes are less relevant for this example than their mutability. Furthermore, the input and output types are the same. They are specified as of type T.

Let's consider the implementation of a triple gatherer with state management:

```java
<T> Gatherer<T, AtomicInteger, T> every2ndTriple()
{
    return new Gatherer<T, AtomicInteger, T>()
    {
        @Override
        public Supplier<AtomicInteger> initializer()
        {
            return () -> new AtomicInteger(0);
        }
```

```java
        @Override
        public Integrator<AtomicInteger, T, T> integrator()
        {
            return new Integrator<AtomicInteger, T, T>()
            {
                @Override
                public boolean integrate(AtomicInteger state, T element,
                                         Downstream<? super T> downstream)
                {
                    boolean pushed = true;
                    if (state.getAndIncrement() % 2 == 0)
                    {
                        pushed = downstream.push(element);
                        if (pushed)
                            pushed = downstream.push(element);
                        if (pushed)
                            pushed = downstream.push(element);
                    }
                    return pushed;
                }
            };
        }
    };
}
```

In the following `main()` method, based on the one before, only the invocations
of `triple()` are replaced with `every2ndtriple()` in the two `gather()`
calls:

```java
void main()
{
    IO.println(Stream.of("This", "is", "a", "test").
                      gather(every2ndTriple()).
                      toList());

    IO.println(Stream.of(1, 2, 3, 4, 5).
                      gather(every2ndTriple()).
                      toList());
}
```

This version produces the following outputs, as expected:

```
[This, This, This, a, a, a]
[1, 1, 1, 3, 3, 3, 5, 5, 5]
```

Forms and Evaluation of State Management   We have just seen a straightforward
state management. It can become almost arbitrarily complex. The evaluation may
also get much more sophisticated if necessary. For example, elements could initially
be processed normally as long as no special identifier is found in the stream of
elements. After detecting the identifier, all subsequent elements would be modified
or enriched with information, for example. Alternatively, numbers could be summed
up until they reach a limit and then start again from 0. There are virtually no limits to
creativity: if you prefer something more complex, you could add up three elements
of the input and then transfer these sums to a result stream as an exercise.

Own DistinctBy-Gatherer   Utilizing state handling, you can implement the convenient DistinctBy gatherer mentioned in the introduction yourself. For this purpose,
we need to implement the `Gatherer` interface. This task is a little more complex,

as shown in the exercises and sample solutions for exercise 4. Some achievable simplifications will be discussed in the following section. These simplifications help improve the readability and comprehensibility of your code while solving the exercises. For everyday programming, please remember not to reinvent the wheel— this is the subject of the following practical tip.

> **Note: External Libraries with Predefined Stream Gatherers**
> Although it makes sense to implement specific functionalities yourself (as prototypes) to gain deeper insights, for your applications, you should use ready-made, well-tested libraries if they exist—for stream gatherers, for example, the following:
>
> - https://github.com/pivovarit/more-gatherers
> - https://github.com/tginsberg/gatherers4j

10.4.9   Construction Methods in the `Gatherer` Interface

When examining the construction of the gatherer `every2ndTriple()`, it becomes quickly evident that it appears rather complex and inelegant due to the definition of the anonymous inner class and the implementations of `Supplier` and `Integrator`. Conveniently, as already briefly mentioned, the `Gatherer` interface offers various overloaded factory methods called `of()` and `ofSequential()`. These receive multiple combinations of initializer, integrator, combiner, and finisher as parameters. The variants of `ofSequential()` do not include a combiner, as this is only important for parallel execution, but not for sequential processing.

The use of factory methods helps to simplify the design. Instead of specifying the respective functionalities with anonymous inner classes as before, suitable lambdas or method references allow for a concise and shorter implementation. This results in the following variant:

```
<T> Gatherer<T, AtomicInteger, T> every2ndTriple()
{
    return Gatherer.ofSequential(
                            AtomicInteger::new,
                            (state, element, downstream) ->
                            {
                                if (state.getAndIncrement() % 2 != 0)
                                    return true;

                                return downstream.push(element)
                                        && downstream.push(element)
                                        && downstream.push(element);
                            });
}
```

Although the construction methods are convenient, they cannot be used if you require a configuration option or parameterization for the construction. That is why we have already employed the trick of encapsulating the construction in a method—you will understand the reasons for this in a moment.

10.4.10 *Generalization Through Parameterization*

Ultimately, we aim to develop a parameterizable stream gatherer. The familiar triple repetition of elements should be made more flexible, namely, with a configurable repetition. In addition, we want to skip some elements and then repeat all others n times. Based on the ideas presented earlier, the implementation is relatively simple.

In particular, it now becomes clear why it makes sense to embed the call to the construction methods in another method. The parameters passed there can then be used for configuration when constructing the `Gatherer`—this also generally improves the clarity of the implementation. In the listing, the parameterization option permits the number of elements to be skipped and the frequency of repetition to be specified:

```java
<T> Gatherer<T, AtomicInteger, T> skipAndRepeat(int skip, int times)
{
    return Gatherer.ofSequential(
            AtomicInteger::new,
            (state, element, downstream) ->
            {
                int idx = state.getAndIncrement();
                if (idx >= skip)
                {
                    boolean accepting = true;
                    for (int i = 0; i < times && accepting; i++)
                    {
                        accepting = downstream.push(element);
                    }
                    return accepting; // false => immediate termination
                }
                return true; // skip phase: do not emit,
                             // just continue reading
            }
    );
}
```

We slightly modify the already familiar `main()` method using `gather()` calls and expand the input values a little bit to get a better understanding of how the above stream gatherer works:

```java
void main()
{
    println(Stream.of("This", "is", "a", "test", "A", "B", "C").
                    gather(skipAndRepeat(0, 2)).
                    toList());

    println(Stream.of(1, 2, 3, 4, 5, 6, 7).
                    gather(skipAndRepeat(4, 3)).
                    toList());
}
```

The following outputs show skipping and repeating:

```
[This, This, is, is, a, a, test, test, A, A, B, B, C, C]
[5, 5, 5, 6, 6, 6, 7, 7, 7]
```

10.4.11   Conclusion

Stream gatherers may not be part of every developer's daily toolkit. Still, they are nevertheless an essential extension of the Stream API, closing a long-standing gap in the ability to provide custom implementations of intermediate operations, especially those based on already processed elements or state data.

One limitation of stream gatherers should be noted: like collectors, they are only defined for reference types, not for primitive values, and the corresponding `IntStream`, `LongStream`, and `DoubleStream` are not supported.

10.5   JEP 502: Stable Values (Preview)

Java 25 introduces Stable Values as a preview feature. They provide an API for initializing values *once* (at the latest when needed) and then keeping them immutable. The JVM may treat such stable values as constants and apply appropriate optimizations—with more flexibility than with `final` attributes, which must be assigned at last in the constructor or during static initialization.[4]

Introduction: Typical Use Case

Let's start by examining a typical application that defines some attributes statically because they are relevant throughout the entire application. Such globally used components are often expensive to construct, and it is not really optimal to create them directly as follows:

```java
public class Application
{
    static final OrderController ORDERS = new OrderController();
    static final ProductRepository PRODUCTS = new ProductRepository();
    static final UserService USERS = new UserService();

    // ...
}
```

---

[4] See JEP 502 (https://openjdk.org/jeps/502). The JVM can eliminate future read accesses, especially if the reference to the stable value itself is constant (e. g., `static final` attribute).

As mentioned, some components are heavyweight and tend to be time-consuming to initialize. As a workaround, the idiom of lazy initialization exists, which initializes optional components only when they are actually needed. This requires some effort, and you must perform various checks. Without going into details, I want to point out the consequences: the disadvantages of implementing lazy initialization yourself are that the attributes can no longer be defined as `final` and therefore cannot be optimized by the JVM. To make matters worse, you can only prevent further assignments by taking great care. Additionally, thread-safe initialization in multithreaded environments is a challenging task. The Stable Values API conveniently reduces these hurdles.

Introduction: Stable Values API

Stable values are a form of lazy initialization integrated into the JVM via a suitable API. Stable values enable thread-safe, one-time lazy initialization with constant optimizations of the JVM:

```java
import java.lang.StableValue;

public class Application
{
    // Create unassigned StableValue instances
    static final StableValue<OrderController> ORDERS = StableValue.of();
    static final StableValue<ProductRepository> PRODUCTS = StableValue.of();
    static final StableValue<UserService> USERS = StableValue.of();

    static OrderController orders()
    {
        return ORDERS.orElseSet(OrderController::new);
    }

    static ProductRepository products()
    {
        return PRODUCTS.orElseSet(ProductRepository::new);
    }

    static UserService users()
    {
        return USERS.orElseSet(UserService::new);
    }

    // ...
}
```

By using the wrapper `StableValue<E>`, it is possible to define the attributes `final` and allow only a single initialization. This permits the JVM to treat the stable values as constants and perform optimizations (constant folding). Initialization then takes place at the appropriate point, often a corresponding access method.

The indirect access to these stable values, in addition to the access methods shown above, can (and should) be avoided. Why? You can still access the attributes directly, that is, without using the access methods. In this case, the desired values would potentially not have been initialized. Therefore, it makes sense to restrict the visibility of the attributes as much as possible so that users are forced to call the access methods.

Variant Using `Supplier<T>`, initialization can be ensured as follows:

```java
static final StableValue<OrderController> ORDERS =
            StableValue.supplier(OrderController::new);

static final StableValue<ProductRepository> PRODUCTS =
            StableValue.supplier(ProductRepository::new);

static final StableValue<UserService> USERS =
            StableValue.supplier(UserService::new);
```

Outlook and Conclusion

Stable values simplify lazy initialization by computing a value only when it is first required and then preserving its immutability. This approach can reduce application startup time and enables the JVM to optimize subsequent accesses more effectively.

Stable values provide methods `of()` and `orElseSet()` in combination with `Supplier<T>`. This allows, for example, an expensive JSON parser to be instantiated on first access and then safely reused for all subsequent calls:

```java
import com.fasterxml.jackson.databind.ObjectMapper;

public final class JsonMapper
{
    private static final StableValue<ObjectMapper> MAPPER = StableValue.of();

    public static ObjectMapper mapper()
    {
        return MAPPER.orElseSet(ObjectMapper::new);
    }
}
```

To preallocate a stable value with a list of values, it is possible to call the method `list()`. A suitable example would be a fixed collection of 360 precalculated sine values, which are calculated when first accessed and remain fixed thereafter:

```java
public final class PrecalculatedSinusExample
{
    // 0..359 degrees -- sin(degrees) (lazy per index, then stable)
    public static final List<Double> SIN_LOOK_UP =
                StableValue.list(360, i -> Math.sin(Math.toRadians(i)));

    // Auxiliary access with normalization in [0,360)
    public static double sin(int degree)
    {
        return SIN_LOOK_UP.get(degree % 360);
    }

    void main()
    {
        List.of(0, 45, 90, 180, 270, 360, 450).forEach( degree ->
            System.out.println(sin(degree)));
    }
}
```

> **Differentiation: Use Cases**
>
> Please note the following: if content changes frequently or the value range is not clearly defined, stable values are the wrong choice. Let's take a closer look: One might ask whether stable values should also contain references to resources such as DB connections or (web) sockets. The answer is no! Stable values are intended for values that are set once and then remain unchanged, similar to lazy initialization.
>
> Stable values are very well suited for configurations, parsers, caches, lookup tables, expensive factory objects, etc.—but not for resources with a lifecycle.

10.6   JEP 505: Structured Concurrency (Fifth Preview)

Threads and other low-level concepts have existed since the early days of Java to support multithreading and parallel task execution. If you take a closer look, it becomes clear that a certain amount of expert knowledge (e.g., about `synchronized` and the Java Memory Model) is required to use multithreading as error-free as possible. As a remedy, various extensions and abstractions have been integrated into the JDK, such as the interface `java.util.concurrent.ExecutorService` in Java 5 and the useful class `java.util.concurrent.CompletableFuture<T>` in Java 8 LTS (albeit providing a quite challenging API with over 80 methods).

JEP 505 introduces structured concurrency as an understandable mechanism for concurrent processing in a fifth preview. Instead of dividing tasks using classic multithreading, subtasks can be started in parallel, their results merged in a structured manner, and ongoing calculations interrupted if necessary. The following applies: an interruption means that the affected tasks are interrupted and must respond appropriately by checking `Thread.currentThread().isInterrupted()`.

Structured concurrency facilitates the comprehension of parallelism in the source code, as the start and end are clearly visible through block structures. When exiting a block, all subtasks are either successfully completed or terminated.

You benefit the most from structured concurrency in conjunction with virtual threads, which is why these are used by default—even though the concept is also applicable with platform threads.

Predefined joiners (`StructuredTaskScope.Joiner`) allow for specifying how errors should be handled. Keep in mind each joiner may only be used once and must be recreated for each use case:

- `allSuccessfulOrThrow()` and `awaitAllSuccessfulOrThrow()` are intended for cases where the results of all subtasks are required (" invoke all"). If one subtask fails, the results of the other subtasks are no longer relevant, and their calculation can be terminated.
- `anySuccessfulResultOrThrow()` uses the first successful result that arrives and automatically interrupts all still running subtasks. This behavior is helpful if the result of any subtask is sufficient (" invoke any") and it is not necessary to wait for the results of other, unfinished tasks, which can therefore be canceled.

All these fundamental properties of structured concurrency improve reliability, reduce the risk of errors, and simplify their handling.

10.6.1   Introduction

To get started, let's examine the handling of a request as an example of business functionality with subtasks. Based on a user ID, a suitable user is to be determined by invoking `findUser()`, and the corresponding order is to be retrieved using `fetchOrder()` on the other hand.

Let's first consider a conventional implementation using an `ExecutorService`. For simplicity, the data is represented as a string and `Integer`, and a record models the response:

```java
record Response(String user, Integer order) { }

static Response handleExecutorService(final Long userId)
      throws ExecutionException, InterruptedException
{
    try (var executorService = Executors.newCachedThreadPool())
    {
        Future<String> userFuture =
                    executorService.submit(() -> findUser(userId));
        Future<Integer> orderFuture =
                    executorService.submit(() -> fetchOrder(userId));

        var user = userFuture.get(); // wait for completion of findUser()
        var order = orderFuture.get(); // wait for completion of fetchOrder()

        return new Response(user, order);
    }
}
```

As usual, the happy path is implemented quickly. However, we should consider a few additional points! Because the subtasks are executed in parallel, they may succeed or fail independently of each other. In the latter case, multithreading tends to complicate the correct handling of error situations. For example, you often don't want another action, as in the above example, the second `get()` to be called if an exception has already occurred during the execution of the `findUser()` method. Or more generally, often, the surrounding action, in this case the processing of the method `handleOldStyle()`, should be aborted if one of its subtasks fails. Moreover, `get()` is blocking. So, if the first `get()` does not terminate, we never reach the second one.

These problems are already evident in this simple example, making it clear that a few details need to be taken into account when using multithreading, especially if exceptions can occur during the processing of subtasks. All this raises the following questions, among others:

1. How do we deal with an error that occurs in a subtask?
2. How can we then cancel the other subtasks?
3. After finding the first match in a search, how can we abort other subtasks if their results are no longer needed?

All of this is possible when using an `ExecutorService`, but it requires complex source code that is difficult to maintain and update.

Before moving on to structured concurrency as a remedy, let's look at rudimentary implementations of the two methods for determining a user or an order. Both symbolically wait a certain amount of time (two or three seconds) to simulate a more complex calculation of the result. For the sake of simplicity, they return a fixed value:

```java
static String findUser(final Long userId) throws InterruptedException
{
    Thread.sleep(2_000);

    return "Michael";
}

static Integer fetchOrder(final Long userId) throws InterruptedException
{
    Thread.sleep(3_000);

    return 42;
}
```

10.6.2   *Implementation with Structured Concurrency*

To use structured concurrency instead of an `ExecutorService`, we could proceed mechanically. Therefore, we replace the `ExecutorService` with a `StructuredTaskScope` from package `java.util.concurrent`. Various joiners are available for this; by default, `awaitAllSuccessfulOrThrow()` is used to terminate other subtasks when an error occurs. A comment in the listing below illustrates this behavior.

Instead of using `submit()`, competing subtasks are split off with `fork()`, whereby the respective subtask is processed in its own virtual thread (see Sect. 5.4). The result is not of type `java.util.concurrent.Future<V>`, but rather `java.util.concurrent.StructuredTaskScope.Subtask<T>`. Apart from these details, the implementation is similar to the previous implementation:

```java
static Response handleStructuredTaskScope(final Long userId)
    throws InterruptedException
{
    // var joiner = StructuredTaskScope.Joiner.awaitAllSuccessfulOrThrow();
    try (var scope = StructuredTaskScope.open())
    {
        Subtask<String> userSubtask  = scope.fork(() -> findUser(userId));
        Subtask<Integer> orderSubtask = scope.fork(() -> fetchOrder(userId));

        scope.join(); // combine both actions

        // both branches were successful here; combine results
        return new Response(userSubtask.get(), orderSubtask.get());
    }
}
```

What exactly happens here? After starting the individual subtasks, the results are collected with a blocking call to `join()`. It waits until all subtasks have been processed or until (at least) one of them has encountered an error in the form of an exception. If the latter is the case, the other subtasks are automatically terminated and the exception is propagated, thus skipping the processing of the results. If successful, `join()` returns either `null`, a stream of results, or a single result, depending on the selected joiner. In our case, the results of the subtasks can be retrieved by calling `get()` and then being combined as appropriate.

Advantages of Structured Concurrency

Unlike multithreading code that uses an `ExecutorService`, structured concurrency facilitates understanding the lifecycle of the subtasks involved and how they are merged. The key to this is the `join()` method: After that, it is guaranteed that no subtasks of the surrounding `StructuredTaskScope` will be executed anymore. It is therefore possible to stick to a way of thinking that is analogous to purely sequential processing, such as the following:

```java
static Response handleSynchronously(final Long userId)
    throws InterruptedException
{
    var user = findUser(userId);
    var order = fetchOrder(userId);

    return new Response(user, order);
}
```

The method `fetchOrder()` is only executed during sequential processing if the method `findUser()` has been successfully completed, that is, without exception. In the event of an error, specifically an exception, the entire processing is stopped. If several further actions were to follow, they would never be executed. With structured concurrency, you can maintain this semantics almost entirely, but benefit from parallel execution of the substeps.

Try It Out

To see the examples in action, use the following `main()` method.

```java
void main() throws Exception
{
    IO.println(measureExecution(
            () -> "sync: " + handleSynchronously(123L)) + " ms");
    IO.println(measureExecution(
            () -> "old style: " + handleExecutorService(123L)) + " ms");
    IO.println(measureExecution(
            () -> "new style: " + handleStructuredTaskScope(123L)) +
                " ms");
}
```

Listing 10.4 Executable as **“STRUCTUREDCONCURRENCYEXAMPLE”**

For the measurements, we implement the following method:

```java
static long measureExecution(final Callable<String> action) throws Exception
{
    final long startTime = System.nanoTime();
    final String result = action.call();
    final long endTime = System.nanoTime();
    System.out.println(result);

    return TimeUnit.MILLISECONDS.convert(endTime - startTime, NANOSECONDS);
}
```

When executed, all three variants produce the same calculation result, as expected. But we observe different running times because parallel processing is performed when using structured concurrency and the `ExecutorService`. In the synchronous case, the running times of the individual subtasks add up. In parallel processing, the longest running time of a subtask determines the total duration. Thus, the more subtasks that may execute in parallel, the more you will benefit from using an `ExecutorService` or structured concurrency, as the outputs already illustrate. Instead of waiting around five seconds, you only wait about three seconds for parallel processing:

```
sync: Response[userName=Michael, orderNo=42]
5039 ms
old style: Response[userName=Michael, orderNo=42]
3007 ms
new style: Response[userName=Michael, orderNo=42]
3017 ms
```

Interim Conclusion

So far, structured concurrency has been characterized primarily by better performance compared with sequential execution while maintaining a fairly understandable execution—an advantage that `ExecutorService` does not offer to the same extent, mainly when errors occur in the execution of individual subtasks.

Executions with an `Executorservice` usually deliver performance comparable to that of structured concurrency, but they do not offer the advantage of traceable processing.

Specification of Timeouts

The implementation shown so far still has one weakness: if one or more subtasks take a very long time to deliver a result or do not terminate at all, the entire processing is either severely delayed or blocked completely. This applies equally to sequential processing, the use of an `ExecutorService`, and the use of structured concurrency when calling `join()`.

Structured concurrency is the only one of the three variants that offers an elegant way to deal with this situation using timeouts. Conveniently, it is possible to pass a timeout in a configuration when opening the `StructuredTaskScope` using the `withTimeout()` method. Once this time has elapsed, all calculations still running in the `StructuredTaskScope` are interrupted. It requires special handling (more on this later). If the tasks respond correctly, that is, if there is no endless loop running in a subtask (which would prevent the scope from ever ending), the error situation is communicated to the caller in the form of a `Structured-TaskScope.TimeoutException`. The rest of the implementation remains the same:

```java
static Response handleWithTimeout(final Long userId,
                                  final Duration timeOut) throws
                                        InterruptedException
{
    var joiner = StructuredTaskScope.Joiner.awaitAllSuccessfulOrThrow();
    try (var scope = StructuredTaskScope.open(joiner,
        config -> config.withTimeout(timeout)))
    {
        var userSubtask = scope.fork(() -> findUser(userId));
        var orderSubtask = scope.fork(() -> fetchOrder(userId));

        scope.join();

        // both branches were successful here; combine results
        return new Response(userSubtask.get(), orderSubtask.get());
    }
}
```

Examples of Tasks That Respond Correctly to Abort Requests

So far, I have mentioned several times that subtasks must respond correctly to interrupt requests for structured concurrency to work correctly. What needs to be considered here?

Subtasks must respond cooperatively to interrupt requests so that structured concurrency remains predictable and subtasks can be terminated promptly. Subtasks typically run in virtual threads, but may also be executed by platform threads. However, regardless of the type of threads, the actual executing thread is not known in advance. During processing, however, this can be determined by calling `Thread.currentThread()`. In Java, threads must respond to their interrupted status by checking `Thread.currentThread().isInterrupted()` and stop further processing when an interrupt request is signaled. If they do not follow this procedure, `StructuredTaskScopes` cannot close promptly; in some circumstances, if an infinite loop is running in a subtask, the scope may never end.

There are two classic patterns:

1. Repeated check in a loop

```java
// (1) Loop-based: Blocking calls are interruptible
try
{
    while (!Thread.currentThread().isInterrupted())
    {
        // Simulate work (e.g., I/O, CPU, polling)
        Thread.sleep(200); // throws InterruptedException when interrupted
        System.out.println("[task] working ?");
    }
    // Graceful exit
}
catch (InterruptedException e)
{
    System.out.println("[task] interrupted -> cleanup & exit");
    // Optional: restore flag for caller
    // Thread.currentThread().interrupt();
}
```

2. Checking between clearly defined processing steps

   If task work is done in separate phases or steps, checks for termination (interrupt) between the steps are required:

```java
// (2) Stepwise: Cancel points before/after each step
try
{
    checkCancelled();
    performStep1();

    checkCancelled();
    performStep2();

    checkCancelled();
    performStep3();
}
catch (InterruptedException e)
{
    System.out.println("[task] interrupted -> cleanup & exit");
}
```

```
// Common cancellation check
private static void checkCancelled() throws InterruptedException
{
    if (Thread.currentThread().isInterrupted())
        throw new InterruptedException("cancelled");
}
```

With low-level multithreading and processing using an `ExecutorService`, you must cancel the other threads and higher-level tasks yourself. However, with structured concurrency, things are easier. Here, it is not a single subtask that is canceled, but the scope; the subtasks that are still running receive an interrupt. Therefore, subtasks must behave cooperatively and regularly (and within appropriate intervals between work steps) check `Thread.currentThread().isInterrupted()` or use interruptible APIs such as `Thread.sleep()`.

10.6.3   *Joiner* `anySuccessfulResultOrThrow()`

So far, we have used the practical joiner `awaitAllSuccessfulOrThrow()`, which stops all other subtasks within the scope or their calculations in the event of an error. With `anySuccessfulResultOrThrow()`, an additional helpful predefined joiner is available to start multiple subtasks and, after one has delivered a result, stop all other subtasks. How can this be useful?

Let's imagine various search queries where the fastest one wins. For example, we could model the connection request to the mobile network in variants 5G, 4G, 3G, and WiFi. To achieve this, we implement the connection information as a `NetworkConnection` record and simplify the connection setup with a few methods, such as `tryToGetXyz()`, as well as structured concurrency and the joiner `anySuccessfulResultOrThrow()`. The rule is: as soon as one connection is established (hopefully the fastest and most stable one), the remaining connection attempts to other networks should be stopped. This procedure can be implemented as follows.

```
void main() throws ExecutionException, InterruptedException
{
    var joiner = StructuredTaskScope.Joiner.<NetworkConnection>
                                    anySuccessfulResultOrThrow();
    try (var scope = StructuredTaskScope.open(joiner))
    {
        var result1 = scope.fork(() -> tryToGetWifi());
        var result2 = scope.fork(() -> tryToGet5g());
        var result3 = scope.fork(() -> tryToGet4g());
        var result4 = scope.fork(() -> tryToGet3g());

        NetworkConnection result = scope.join();

        System.out.println("Wifi " + result1.state() +
                        "/5G " + result2.state() +
                        "/4G " + result3.state() +
                        "/3G " + result4.state());

        System.out.println("found connection: " + result);
    }
}
```

```
private static NetworkConnection tryToGet3g() throws InterruptedException
{
    sleepRandomlyUpToOneSec();
    return new NetworkConnection("3G");
}

private static NetworkConnection tryToGet4g() throws InterruptedException
{
    sleepRandomlyUpToOneSec();
    return new NetworkConnection("4G");
}

private static NetworkConnection tryToGet5g() throws InterruptedException
{
    sleepRandomlyUpToOneSec();
    return new NetworkConnection("5G");
}

private static NetworkConnection tryToGetWifi() throws InterruptedException
{
    sleepRandomlyUpToOneSec();
    return new NetworkConnection("Wifi");
}

private static void sleepRandomlyUpToOneSec() throws InterruptedException
{
    Thread.sleep((long) (1000 * Math.random()));
}
```

To ensure that one or the other network wins randomly in this example, each
connection attempt is delayed using `Thread.sleep()` in combination with
`Math.random()`. After calling `join()`, only one result is available. The respective status of the individual `Subtasks` can be determined by calling `state()`.
It is only safe to use `get()` if `state()` has returned the value SUCCESS.
Otherwise, an error message like " `IllegalStateException: Result is
unavailable or subtask did not complete successfully`"
will occur. However, if a calculation was not successful or was interrupted in
the meantime, this results in a status with the value FAILED or UNAVAILABLE.
The latter may also indicate that the calculation of a subtask was not completed
within the time required for the fastest execution. Generally, the result of the first
successful `Subtask` is returned by `join()`.

Executing the program STRUCTUREDCONCURRENCYONSUCCESSEXAMPLE
produces the following output if the calculation for 4G is the fastest:

```
Wifi UNAVAILABLE/5G UNAVAILABLE/4G SUCCESS/3G UNAVAILABLE
found connection: NetworkConnection[type=4G]
```

10.6.4 Details on Predefined and Custom Joiners

We have just learned about `anySuccessfulResultOrThrow()`, a useful predefined joiner that works according to the *Invoke-Any* principle: all subtasks are started, the first successful one delivers the result, and the rest get canceled.[5]

It is already known that there are two *Invoke-All* variants that complement this: `allSuccessfulOrThrow()` and `awaitAllSuccessfulOrThrow()`. Here, all subtasks must be successful; if one fails, the `StructuredTaskScope` is considered as failed, and the currently running subtasks are interrupted. The following examples clarify the difference between `allSuccessfulOrThrow()` and `awaitAllSuccessfulOrThrow()`. A look at the return value of `join()` provides the decisive clue: for `allSuccessfulOrThrow()`, `join()` has the return type `Stream<Subtask<T>>`, whereas for `awaitAllSuccessfulOr-Throw()`, it has `Void`.

How `awaitAllSuccessfulOrThrow()` Works

The default behavior of `StructuredTaskScope.open()` corresponds to the already used `awaitAllSuccessfulOrThrow()`. A call to `join()` waits until all subtasks have been completed successfully; if an error occurs, the scope is aborted. Then `join()` triggers a `FailedException`. Because `join()` has no return type (or more precisely: `Void`), you must access the individual results of the `Subtask` objects via `get()` using the previously held `Subtask` references to determine the result:

```java
// Different result types => Joiner.awaitAllSuccessfulOrThrow() (default)
try (var scope = StructuredTaskScope.open())
{
    String taskProposal = scope.fork(() -> fetchProposal1());
    List<Integer> taskPrices = scope.fork(() -> fetchPrices());
    List<String> taskOrders = scope.fork(() -> fetchOrders());

    scope.join(); // throws an exception if a subtask fails

    String proposal = taskProposal.get();
    var prices = taskPrices.get();
    var orders = taskOrders.get();

    IO.println("result: " + Result.of(proposal, prices, orders));
}
```

---

[5] Strictly speaking, they are interrupted. These subtasks must respond to the interrupt and terminate themselves; otherwise, they will continue to run.

How `allSuccessfulOrThrow()` Works

This joiner is suitable when all subtasks have the same result type: `join()` then returns a `Stream<Subtask<T>>`. This allows you to convert the individual results into a list by calling `map(Subtask::get).toList()`. If an error occurs, the process is terminated and `join()` throws an exception:

```java
// Similar result types => allSuccessfulOrThrow()
var allSuccessful = Joiner.<String>allSuccessfulOrThrow();
try (var scope = StructuredTaskScope.open(allSuccessful))
{
    scope.fork(() -> fetchProposal1());  // String
    scope.fork(() -> fetchProposal2());  // String

    Stream<Subtask<String>> results = scope.join().
                                  map(Subtask::get).
                                  toList();
    IO.println("results: " + results);
}
```

Other Useful Joiners in the JDK

In addition to those joiners presented so far, there are the following useful joiners in the JDK:

- **`awaitAll()`**: This joiner waits for all subtasks to complete or abort, regardless of whether they are successful or failed. The `StructuredTaskScope` is not terminated prematurely. The method `join()` always returns the value `null` because the return type is `Void`.
- **`allUntil(Predicate)`**: This joiner generates a `Stream<Subtask<T>>`. The predicate passed is checked for each completed subtask to see if it returns `true`. This allows flexible rules to be modeled (e. g., " stop after two failures" or " as soon as three successes are achieved"—for the latter, we glimpse an alternative implementation of our own below).

    The JDK documentation provides an example of a combination of a special predicate `CancelAfterTwoFailures` and a factory method, but this contains a compilation error and is not generally applicable enough. I have corrected both of these issues and reported them as bugs to Oracle. Here, you find the improved version:

```java
class CancelAfterTwoFailures<T> implements Predicate<Subtask<? extends T>>
{
    private final AtomicInteger failedCount = new AtomicInteger();

    @Override
    public boolean test(Subtask<? extends T> subtask)
    {
        return subtask.state() == Subtask.State.FAILED
            && failedCount.incrementAndGet() >= 2;
    }
}

var joiner = Joiner.allUntil(new CancelAfterTwoFailures<String>());
```

Custom Joiner

In addition to the built-in strategies, structured concurrency allows you to define your own joiners, for example, for situations where more flexibility is required:

- You want to collect all successful results; the failed ones are ignored.
- You want to collect the first n successful results, for example.
- You want to apply a filter or selection after collecting the results.

Conveniently, you can easily satisfy your own requirements by creating an implementation that realizes the interface `StructuredTaskScope.Joiner<T,R>`. Typically, you override the `onComplete(Subtask)` method to collect the individual results and the `result()` method to generate the join/total result.

Based on the following interface, you can implement your own ideas:

```java
interface Joiner<T, R>
{
    // ...

    default boolean onComplete(Subtask<? extends T> subtask)
    {
        if (subtask.state() == Subtask.State.UNAVAILABLE)
        {
            throw new IllegalArgumentException("Subtask has not completed");
        }
        return false;
    }


    R result() throws Throwable;
}
```

Example of a Custom Joiner: `JustSuccessful` Let's assume we only want to collect the successful tasks, which is quite similar to the standard behavior. We use a `Queue<T>` to store the results of the successful tasks. Because the results may arrive in parallel and competitively, to avoid inconsistencies in concurrent accesses, it is advisable to use a `ConcurrentLinkedQueue<E>` or a `CopyOnWriteArrayList<E>` (or `Collections.synchronizedList()`). In contrast to the standard behavior of `awaitAllSuccessfulOrThrow()`, for our joiner, failing tasks should not lead to termination. The aforementioned requirements lead to the following implementation of the joiner:

```java
class JustSuccessful<T> implements StructuredTaskScope.Joiner<T, List<T>>
{
    private final Queue<T> allSuccessfulResults =
                        new ConcurrentLinkedQueue<>();

    @Override
    public boolean onComplete(StructuredTaskScope.Subtask<? extends T>
            subtask)
    {
        if (subtask.state() == StructuredTaskScope.Subtask.State.SUCCESS)
        {
            allSuccessfulResults.add(subtask.get());
        }
```

```
        return false; // never cancel early
    }

    @Override
    public List<T> result()
    {
        return new ArrayList<>(allSuccessfulResults);
    }
}
```

The choice of collection affects performance: for a small number of results, a `CopyOnWriteArrayList<E>` would also be acceptable; for large amounts of data and high parallelism, `ConcurrentLinkedQueue<E>` is preferable. Further details are provided in a practical tip below.

When querying the results, a copy of the data is returned to prevent unintended modifications within the joiner.

Example of a Custom Joiner: `FirstNSuccessful` It is more interesting in practice to collect only the results of successful tasks, but limit the number of hits to a certain amount, for example, to determine the top three or top ten. Based on the previous implementation, it is possible to add another attribute to specify the maximum number. If the results list reaches this size, returning `true` for `onComplete()` ensures that no further processing occurs:

```
class FirstNSuccessful<T> implements StructuredTaskScope.Joiner<T, Stream<T>>
{
    private final int maxResults;
    private final List<T> firstSuccesfulResults = new CopyOnWriteArrayList
        <>();

    public FirstNSuccessful(int maxResults)
    {
        this.maxResults = maxResults;
    }

    @Override
    public boolean onComplete(StructuredTaskScope.Subtask<? extends T>
        subtask)
    {
        if (subtask.state() == StructuredTaskScope.Subtask.State.SUCCESS)
        {
            firstSuccessfulResults.add(subtask.get());
        }

        // When limit is reached, cancel scope
        boolean cancelProcessing = firstSuccessfulResults.size() >=
            maxResults;
        return cancelProcessing;
    }

    @Override
    public List<T> result()
    {
        // Defensive limiting (overshoot is possible and okay)
        return firstSuccessfulResults.stream().limit(maxResults).toList();
    }
}
```

The following points are worth noting. Results may arrive simultaneously, so processing in `onComplete()` must be thread-safe. Here, we use `CopyOn-WriteArrayList<>` to prevent problems when inserting. We choose this class because we only expect a few results; for large amounts of results and high parallelism, `ConcurrentLinkedQueue<E>` is a better choice.

Before inserting, you should check the size of the results list. Even if you adhere to this, it can still lead to inconsistencies in multithreading when combined with the subsequent insertion action. As a trick, we always insert without checking the size and determine the end of the scope based on the number of results. Because results may still be added to the list, the final limitation of the results is achieved in method `result()` using `limit()` as a safety net.

As already mentioned, this restriction could also be expressed using the pre-defined joiner `allUntil()`. However, this requires more work and results in source code that is more difficult to understand, which is why I prefer the above implementation.

> **Note: Which Thread-Safe Collection to Use?**
> In situations where the results of many parallel actions are collected in a thread-safe manner, the choice of collection can be crucial. Often, the `ConcurrentLinkedQueue<E>` is recommended (in the above example, with just a few data entries, this is not a significant factor). If reading is predominantly parallel, then `CopyOnWriteArrayList<E>` is applicable.
>
> - **`CopyOnWriteArrayList<E>`**: Ideal for many parallel read accesses and few write accesses. Why? Each write access copies the entire data (O(n)), which can be (too) costly for " one result per task."
> - **`ConcurrentLinkedQueue<E>`**: Particularly suitable for many write accesses due to its lock-free, efficient implementation. However, random index access is not possible.
>
> **Distinction:** When using parallel streams, you generally do not need a thread-safe result collection because the stream framework handles the merging. With structured concurrency and custom joiners, you do need this because the collection of potentially parallel results typically takes place in `onComplete()`.

Example of a Custom Joiner: `MeetsCondition` To conclude the introduction to custom joiners, let's examine how to collect only the results of successful tasks that meet specific conditions. For this purpose, we create a joiner named

`MeetsCondition<T>` that uses a `Predicate<T>` that is checked before adding elements to the list of results:

```java
class MeetsCondition<T> implements StructuredTaskScope.Joiner<T, Stream<T>>
{
    private final Predicate<? super T> predicate;

    private final Queue<T> matchingSuccessfulResults =
                        new ConcurrentLinkedQueue<>();

    public MeetsCondition(Predicate<? super T> predicate)
    {
        this.predicate = Objects.requireNonNull(predicate, "predicate");
    }

    @Override
    public boolean onComplete(StructuredTaskScope.Subtask<? extends T>
        subtask)
    {
        if (subtask.state() == StructuredTaskScope.Subtask.State.SUCCESS)
        {
            T result = subtask.get();
            if (predicate.test(result))
            {
                matchingSuccessfulResults.add(result);
            }
        }
        return false; // nie vorzeitig abbrechen
    }

    @Override
    public Stream<T> result()
    {
        return matchingSuccessfulResults.stream();
    }
}
```

10.6.5 *Nested Structured Concurrency*

The possibilities presented so far already impressively demonstrate that multithreading is significantly simplified with structured concurrency compared with traditional approaches.

In practice, however, the requirements are often more complex. Let's imagine, for example, that we want to plan a trip, find offers from various car rental companies and accommodation options, and use this information to prepare a proposal. All of these actions can be performed in parallel, but should be combined in a suitable manner. It is also clear that we need to be successful in finding both a car and a hotel, as the trip cannot take place without either of the two. Errors in querying individual providers, on the other hand, are tolerable as long as there are enough successful results overall.

We would rather not imagine implementing this using conventional tools. The beauty of structured concurrency is that you can nest scopes by having a subtask

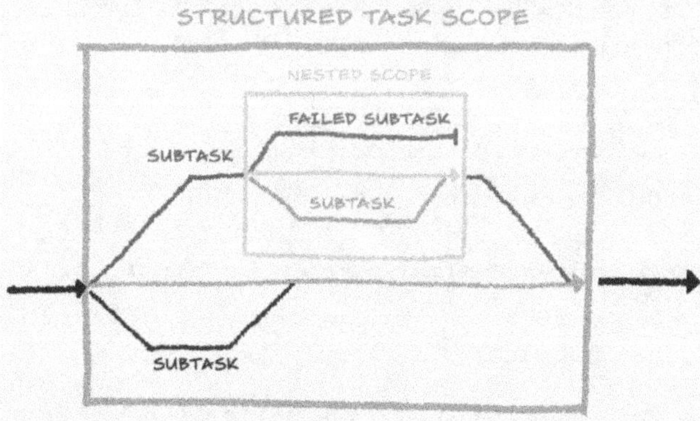

Fig. 10.1 Nesting in structured concurrency

open its own `StructuredTaskScope` and start further tasks in parallel inside of it. This results in clearly defined hierarchies of scopes, as shown in Fig. 10.1.[6]

Each scope manages its own subtasks, allows its own joiners, and also maintains its own error handling. The following applies to the joiner `awaitAll-SuccessfulOrThrow()`: if an inner subtask fails, the inner scope is terminated correctly, and this is propagated to the outer scope. This means that even complex nested concurrency remains clear and deterministic. What does this mean specifically for our application example?

Implementation of the Example

As an outer scope, it makes sense to use the standard joiner `awaitAllSuccess-fulOrThrow()`. In this scope, we divide the tasks into two independent substeps, each of which uses its own `StructuredTaskScope` with its own joiner:

```java
static Proposal performCityTripProposals(String city,
                                         LocalDate startDate)
                                    throws InterruptedException
{
    try (var scope = StructuredTaskScope.open())
    {
        var hotelSubtask = scope.fork(() -> findHotels(city, startDate));
        var carRentalSubtask = scope.fork(() -> fetchCarRentals(city,
                                                        startDate));
                                                        scope.join();

        return new Proposal(hotelSubtask.get(), carRentalSubtask.get());
    }
}
```

---

[6] https://belief-driven-design.com/looking-at-java-21-structured-concurrency-39a81/

The result is provided as a record:

```java
record Proposal(String hotel, List<String> carRentals) {}
```

Nesting for Hotel Search   According to the task, we need exactly one suggestion
for a hotel—ideal for the joiner `anySuccessfulResultOrThrow()`:

```java
static String findHotels(String city,
                         LocalDate startDate) throws InterruptedException
{
    var anySuccessful =
        StructuredTaskScope.Joiner.<String>anySuccessfulResultOrThrow();
    try (var scope = StructuredTaskScope.open(anySuccessful))
    {
        var proposal1 = scope.fork(() -> findProposalTrivago(city, startDate));
        var proposal2 = scope.fork(() -> findProposalBooking(city, startDate));
        var proposal3 = scope.fork(() -> findProposalCheck24(city, startDate));

        // Here, you might want to use FirstNSuccessful
        // if you want multiple suggestions
        return scope.join();
    }
}

private static String findProposalBooking(String city, LocalDate startDate)
{
    randomlyWaitUpToOneSecond();
    return "Booking Hotel";
}

// ...
```

Nesting to Find Car Rental Companies   When selecting car rental companies, we
want to collect the first two successful suggestions. Therefore, we can conveniently
use the already implemented joiner `FirstNSuccessful`. If we had not yet
implemented this, the need for it would arise at this point at the latest:

```java
static List<String> fetchCarRentals(String city,
                                    LocalDate startDate)
    throws InterruptedException
{
    var twoSuccessful = new OwnJoinersExample.FirstNSuccessful<String>(2);
    try (var scope = StructuredTaskScope.open(twoSuccessful))
    {
        var proposal1 = scope.fork(() -> findProposalEuropcar(city,
                                                              startDate));
        var proposal2 = scope.fork(() -> findProposalAvis(city, startDate));
        var proposal3 = scope.fork(() -> findProposalHertz(city, startDate));

        return scope.join();
    }
}
```

10.6.6 Conclusion

In this section, we have examined structured concurrency as a means of simplifying multithreading, using various practical examples to illustrate the concept. Before the introduction of structured concurrency, the parallel execution of tasks, for example, using the `ExecutorService` and `Future` or the JDK veterans `Runnable` and `Thread`, was laborious and error-prone. This was particularly true for the clean merging of partial results. Despite some subsequent additions to the JDK, until the introduction of structured concurrency, there was no intuitive, comprehensible, or even smoothly extensible way to execute subtasks in parallel and merge their results in a structured manner.

Thanks to structured concurrency, this is now much easier to achieve, resulting in an intuitive, extensible structure. Subtasks run in clearly defined scopes, and joiners such as `anySuccessfulResultOrThrow()`, `allSuccessfulOrThrow()`, or custom variants determine how the results are merged. Nested scopes enable the mastery of complex scenarios with multiple levels, as the respective lifetimes of secondary subtasks are embedded within those of the parent subtasks. This nesting also simplifies error handling. In addition, the program flow is easier to follow. Overall, this results in a clearer, more secure concurrency model that noticeably improves readability, comprehensibility, and maintainability.

Further Ideas for Custom Joiners

We have previously seen a few examples of useful custom variants of joiners. If you are interested, you can try implementing the following joiners, for example:

- `MaxNFailures`: After more than n failures, the scope should be aborted.
- `PercentageSuccessful`: If n % or more of the subtasks are successful, the scope should be successfully completed.

Distinction from Structured Concurrency

Is structured concurrency the new silver bullet in the field of multithreading? For many use cases, especially those involving the splitting of tasks into subtasks and the orderly merging of results, the answer is yes. For specific actions, such as recursive decomposition of subtasks, other forms of concurrency may be more suitable. Let's take a closer look at the most critical concurrency methods to gain a deeper understanding.

Structured Concurrency Structured concurrency is characterized by the fact that it allows us to encapsulate concurrency in clearly defined blocks in the source code. This results in the following advantages and disadvantages:

- **Advantage**: Simpler error handling, clean resource management, good readability.
- **Advantage**: Automatic propagation of errors and abortions to all subtasks.
- **Advantage**: Tasks can be logically viewed and managed as " units."
- **Disadvantage**: The additional abstraction may make it somewhat unfamiliar to use at first.
- **Disadvantage**: Not suitable for a large number of small tasks or special requirements such as long-running background services and periodic executions.

Overall, structured concurrency is particularly suitable for situations in which several logically related tasks are to deliver a typical result.

However, structured concurrency is not yet a finalized feature, but a promising candidate to significantly enhance the possibilities of multithreading in Java.

Parallel Streams Parallel streams enable a declarative description for data-parallel operations on collections. This results in the following advantages and disadvantages:

- **Advantage**: Very compact, easy to switch from `stream()` to parallel processing by calling `parallelStream()` or `parallel()`.
- **Advantage**: Automatically optimized use of the shared `ForkJoinPool`.
- **Disadvantage**: Less flexible in terms of error handling, termination, and timeouts.
- **Disadvantage**: Control of parallelism is only possible to a limited extent.

Parallel streams are particularly suitable for simple, independent data processing.

ExecutorService The various specializations of `ExecutorService` provide abstractions over thread pools and allow the asynchronous execution of arbitrary tasks. This results in the following advantages and disadvantages:

- **Advantage**: Flexible, thanks to various pool strategies (fixed, cached, scheduled).
- **Advantage**: Suitable for long-running or regularly recurring background tasks.
- **Disadvantage**: Lifecycle must be managed manually (don't forget to call `shutdown()`).
- **Disadvantage**: Error handling, termination, and timeouts are more complex than with structured concurrency.
- **Disadvantage**: Can quickly become confusing with nested or dependent tasks.

Periodic jobs or permanent services are typical areas of application for `ExecutorService` because explicit control over pools and tasks is required here.

ForkJoinPool The `ForkJoinPool` is optimized for recursive divide-and-conquer algorithms. This results in the following advantages and disadvantages:

- **Advantage**: Uses work-stealing for efficient load distribution.

- **Advantage**: Compelling for highly decomposable computations.
- **Disadvantage**: More complex and difficult to use correctly.
- **Disadvantage**: Debugging and troubleshooting can be rather difficult.

The `ForkJoinPool` has a narrowly defined area of application, namely, in the form of computationally intensive tasks that can be easily decomposed into subproblems (e. g., sorting).

10.7   JEP 506: Scoped Values

If different parts of an application need to access shared data, such as information from a request (e. g., user or timestamp), this usually needs information forwarding. This propagation often requires passing the values as parameters to methods. If the values belong to a specific thread, using `java.lang ThreadLocal<T>` variables is an alternative to avoid the effort of passing parameters, the associated bloating of the parameter list, and the resulting "pollution" of signatures.

Current Java versions introduce the feature Scoped Values as a supplement. They allow values to be made accessible for reading across a clearly defined *execution area (also called scope)* without having to pass them as method parameters through the entire application. Compared with `ThreadLocal<T>`, scoped values are considered the better choice because they

- Are only valid within a clearly defined scope and a specific execution (including the child threads created therein) and are therefore only valid for a certain period of time.
- Are immutable during execution—however, they can be bound with a new value in a nested subscope.
- Cause less overhead and do not require explicit releasing.
- Occupy less main memory than `ThreadLocal<T>` variables.
- Conveniently propagate their allocation automatically to child threads started in the scope (e. g., in the context of `StructuredTaskScopes` (see Sect. 10.6))—but without copy semantics as with `ThreadLocal<T>`. Accordingly, no additional main memory is allocated for scoped values during value propagation to all child threads. In contrast, passing values to all child threads for `ThreadLocal<T>` firstly requires the type `java.lang.InheritableThreadLocal<T>` and secondly needs copies of the values. This procedure consumes additional memory and has an increasingly negative effect as the number of child threads grows.

The limitation to a dynamic scope and the immutability lead to more predictable behavior and thus to source code that is easier to maintain. There is less hidden global state, a clearer lifetime, and a lower risk of memory leaks. Scoped values are therefore particularly suitable for context-specific information (e. g., audit information, trace IDs, `Locales`, etc.), but not as global, mutable storage or cache.

Background: `ThreadLocal<T>` Variables and Scoped Values

Properties of `ThreadLocal<T>` Variables `ThreadLocal<T>` variables are always bound to a specific thread: they are used to store thread-specific values and later read them back or modify them within this thread. For this purpose, each thread internally maintains an assignment " ThreadLocal → Value". This assignment requires memory.

In the context of platform threads, this is rarely critical in practice because the number of threads is limited (typically a few thousand to a few tens of thousands). With virtual threads, the situation changes: their number can run into the hundreds of thousands or millions. If at least one `ThreadLocal<T>` entry is maintained for each virtual thread, the memory requirement grows according to the following formula: $\#threads \times \#threadLocals$. Worse still, this applies regardless of whether multiple threads reference the same object value. The key point is that each thread requires its own mapping entry, which must be managed (and, if necessary, inherited copies in the case of `InheritableThreadLocal<T>`). This fact can result in noticeable overhead when there is a large number of virtual threads.

Scoped Values As an Alternative Scoped values, on the other hand, can propagate a single, immutable object value within a scope to many (virtual) child threads. `ThreadLocal<T>`, on the other hand, requires separate memory for the value (including inherited copies) for each thread. This leads to noticeable memory overhead when many virtual threads are used in combination with `ThreadLocal<T>`.

Scoped values come into play here: A value is bound once *for a dynamic execution area (scope)* and is automatically available to all child threads (including virtual threads) started in the scope. The binding is *immutable* during execution. However, it can be rebounded in subscopes. In terms of memory, bindings are therefore proportional to the number of scopes and bindings, not to the number of threads—in other words, *one binding per scope* instead of *one mapping entry per thread*.

Practical Recommendation Context information (e. g., audit information, trace ID, etc.) should preferably be propagated via scoped values in modern applications, especially in the case of highly parallelized applications. For `ThreadLocal<T>`, it is still the case that it should only be used in a targeted manner and, if necessary, cleaned up properly with `try/finally` or `remove()`.

10.7.1   Fundamentals

Scoped values are modeled by the class `java.lang.ScopedValue<T>`. Applications provide them as public static attributes, allowing them to be accessed directly and easily from anywhere without needing to pass them as parameters to methods. Even better: This procedure avoids having to pass them through the (entire) application to the required location.

Introduction

The factory method `ScopedValue.newInstance()` is used to create scoped values as data containers of the specified type. Below, it is shown for an instance for global information of type `String`:

```
public static final ScopedValue<String> GLOBAL_INFO =
                                ScopedValue.newInstance();
```

The data containers created in this way initially contain no value. Later on, a value is assigned using `ScopedValue.where()`.

Finally, calling the `run()` method on the `ScopedValue<t>` instance executes the action specified in the form of a `Runnable`, that is, without a return value:

```
ScopedValue.where(GLOBAL_INFO, "SECRET-VALUE").run(() -> executeAction());
```

If a more complex calculation is required, the `call()` method also exists. Here, the actions may be specified as `ScopedValue.CallableOp<T,X extends Throwable>`, which simplifies exception handling. For both variants, the value assignment specified by `where()` is only valid for the duration of the call. After starting with `run()` or `call()`, the value of the scoped value for this call is readonly and fixed in the scope. Regardless of this, for other executions with `run()` or `call()` later in the program, different value assignments are possible using `where()`. Based on the modified values, corresponding actions can be executed. In addition, subscopes with modified value assignments can be created.

10.7.2   Value Assignment

For the following example, we assume these records for data transfer:

```
record Request(String payload) {}
record User(String name, char[] pwd) {}
```

We now want to explore how to exchange data. As a starting point, the `Login-Util` class shown below defines a scoped value named `LOGGED_IN_USER`. When the `performLogin()` method is executed, the user data is extracted from the request parameter and stored in the scoped value using `where()`. Invoking the `run()` method and passing an action in the form of a `Runnable`, processing is started in the scope implicitly possessing the associated scoped value. Here, the action consists of calling the `performAction()` method of a service that does not receive any parameters:

```java
public class LoginUtil
{
    public static final ScopedValue<User> LOGGED_IN_USER =
                                    ScopedValue.newInstance();

    // ...

    public void performLogin(final Request request)
    {
        User loggedInUser = extractUserFrom(request);
        ScopedValue.where(LOGGED_IN_USER, loggedInUser).
                run(() -> service.performAction());
    }

    // ...
}
```

Please note that in the called method, in the example, the method `perform-Action()`, the login information for the user is accessible through scoped values, even though it was not explicitly passed as a parameter.

Reading Values

To determine the value of a scoped value during execution, simply call the `get()` method (ideally after checking for existence). Let's look at reading values for the previous example and a service, in this case `XyzService`.

Access via `get()`   The method called in the service can be implemented as shown below. We notice a reference to the static variable `LoginUtil.LOGGED_IN_USER` representing the scoped value, which is accessed with `get()` to retrieve the stored value:

```java
public class XyzService
{
    public void performAction()
    {
        // ATTENTION: Potentially unsafe access if no data
        var loggedInUser = LoginUtil.LOGGED_IN_USER.get();

        IOprintln("performing action with: " + loggedInUser);
        IOprintln("collected data: "  + retrieveDataFor(loggedInUser));
    }

    // ...
}
```

Please note the following pitfall: If no value is stored in the scoped value, calling `get()` will throw a `NoSuchElementException`.

Existence Check Using `isBound()` You can check whether a value has actually been assigned by calling the method `isBound()`. If this returns `true`, then it is safe to access the value using `get()`. This procedure should already be familiar to you in a similar form from usage of the class `Optional<T>` (see Sect. 15.3.2)—however, as a special feature, the stored value in the scoped value can also be `null`, even if `isBound()` returns `true`. This fact must be taken into account separately if necessary:

```java
if (LoginUtil.LOGGED_IN_USER.isBound())
{
    var loggedInUser = LoginUtil.LOGGED_IN_USER.get();

    System.out.println("performing action with: " + loggedInUser);
}
else
{
    // perform fallback actions
}
```

Special Features As an alternative to calling `get()`, analogous to the class `Optional<T>` (see Sect. 15.3.2), the methods `orElse()` and `orElse-Throw()` exist to provide a default value or throw an exception if no value is available in the scoped value.

With `orElse()`, you can provide a fallback as follows:

```java
var loggedInUser = LoginUtil.LOGGED_IN_USER.orElse(new User("FALLBACK",
                                        "PWD".toCharArray()));
```

To throw a descriptive exception, choose `orElseThrow()`:

```java
var loggedInUser = LOGGED_IN_USER.orElseThrow(() ->
                            new IllegalStateException("invalid user"));
```

10.7.3   Further Example

We have previously looked at some of the basics of scoped values. The following example illustrates how this works in a more practical context, simulating a multi-layered call hierarchy with simplified controller and service classes.

Starting Point: The `ScopedValuesExample` Class

The main application consists of the class `ScopedValuesExample`. This defines two scoped values to provide information about the logged-in user and the time of a request, application-wide, without passing the information through different layers.
The following simple record models the user information:

```
record User(String name, String nickName) {}
```

Actions in the application fill the scoped values with appropriate values. Various calls may be made from the application class `ScopedValuesExample` via the classes `Controller` and `Service`. Since scoped values are used, no corresponding parameters are passed around. On the contrary, reading the necessary values happens by accessing the scoped values at appropriate places:

```
public class ScopedValuesExample
{
    public static final ScopedValue<User> LOGGED_IN_USER =
                                    ScopedValue.newInstance();
    public static final ScopedValue<ZonedDateTime> REQUEST_TIME =
                                       ScopedValue.newInstance();

    public static final Controller controller =
                            createController(createService());

    // represent a more complex design in practice
    private static Controller createController(final Service service)
    {
        return new Controller(service);
    }

    private static Service createService()
    {
        return new Service();
    }

    // ...
}
```

Time Logging: The `Controller` Class

The `Controller` class uses the `Service` class. Before method calls are forwarded to it, information about the request time is read and logged. This functionality is extracted into the `logRequestTime()` method. There, a call to `isBound()` on the scoped value REQUEST_TIME ensures that the desired information exists and can be read using `get()`. If no request time is available as information, no logging takes place; instead, the request is delegated to the corresponding method from the `Service` class:

```java
public class Controller
{
    private final Service service;

    public Controller(final Service service)
    {
        this.service = service;
    }

    public void consumingMethod()
    {
        logRequestTime("consumingMethod()");
        service.consumingMethod();
    }

    public String process()
    {
        logRequestTime("process()");
        return service.process();
    }

    private static void logRequestTime(String methodName)
    {
        if (ScopedValuesExample.REQUEST_TIME.isBound())
            System.out.println(methodName + " -- request time: " +
                                ScopedValuesExample.REQUEST_TIME.get());
    }
}
```

Processing: The `Service` Class

The `Service` class accesses user information. In the method `consuming-Method()`, the provision of a fallback via `orElse()` is indicated. The method `process()` performs a more sophisticated processing. First, `isBound()` is used to check whether the scoped value is bound, that is, whether it has been assigned a value. In doing so, it clarifies that it is possible to assign the value `null` and that this should be handled appropriately if necessary. Once we have ensured that we can access the value, we check whether it is really the ADMIN user who wants access or whether access should be denied in all other cases:

```java
public class Service
{
    public void consumingMethod()
    {
        var user =
            ScopedValuesExample.LOGGED_IN_USER.orElse(new User("n/a", ""));

        System.out.println("Consumer: " + user);
    }

    public String process()
    {
        if (!ScopedValuesExample.LOGGED_IN_USER.isBound())
            throw new IllegalStateException("expected user to be bound");
```

```
        // ATTENTION: if bound to null, then isBound() also returns true
        if (ScopedValuesExample.LOGGED_IN_USER.get() == null)
            throw new IllegalStateException("expected to contain a value");

        var user = ScopedValuesExample.LOGGED_IN_USER.get();
        if (user.name().startsWith("ADMIN"))
            return "ACCESS GRANTED!";
        else
            return "Top Secret ... no access to Scoped Value granted";
    }
}
```

Try It Out

To experience scoped values in action, use the following `main()` method. Here,
we simulate various calls in the form of requests with users named ATTACKER and
ADMIN. The former is not allowed to access certain services. The latter is granted
full access.

```
void main() throws Exception
{
    // Simulate Requests
    for (String name : List.of("ATTACKER", "ADMIN"))
    {
        var user = new User(name, name.toLowerCase());
        ScopedValue.where(LOGGED_IN_USER, user).
                  where(REQUEST_TIME, ZonedDateTime.now()).
                  run(controller::consumingMethod);

        ScopedValue.where(LOGGED_IN_USER, user).
                  run(controller::consumingMethod);

        String answer = ScopedValue.where(LOGGED_IN_USER, user).
                                  call(() -> controller.process());
        System.out.println(answer);
    }

    // Outside the scope, the variable is ?unbound?
    System.out.print("Outside bounded scope ");
    System.out.println("isBound(): " + LOGGED_IN_USER.isBound());
}
```

Listing 10.5 Executable as "SCOPEDVALUESEXAMPLE"

The program SCOPEDVALUESEXAMPLE produces output similar to the following, which first logs the request time, then the user, and finally the action or warning
message:

```
consumingMethod() -- request Time: 2024-03-02T14:46:22.889745+01:00[Europe/
    Zurich]
Consumer: User[name=ATTACKER, nickName=attacker]
Consumer: User[name=ATTACKER, nickName=attacker]
Top Secret Processing ... no access to ScopesValue granted
consumingMethod() -- request Time: 2024-03-02T14:46:22.906626+01:00[Europe/
    Zurich]
Consumer: User[name=ADMIN, nickName=admin]
Consumer: User[name=ADMIN, nickName=admin]
ACCESS GRANTED!
Outside bounded scope isBound(): false
```

You will notice that only one value is set for the second invocation with a single `where()`, whereas both values are set with two invocations of `where()`. Therefore, the request time is always logged.

Outside the scope, the variables are unbound, which results in exceptions such as the following when accessing them with `get()`:

```
Exception in thread "main" java.util.NoSuchElementException
    at java.base/java.lang.ScopedValue.slowGet(ScopedValue.java:700)
    at java.base/java.lang.ScopedValue.get(ScopedValue.java:693)
    at jep464_Scoped_Values.ScopedValuesExample.main(ScopedValuesExample.java:42)
```

Interim Conclusion

This example illustrates, in particular, that the information on request time and the user is not passed as method parameters, but is instead included in the respective scope or appended to the respective thread and therefore becomes available for reading in a scope- or thread-specific manner by simply calling `get()`.

Accordingly, information can be passed easily between different components of an application using scoped values. However, some people may consider this to be somewhat reminiscent of global variables, whose system-wide visibility and, above all, modifiability are generally undesirable. Unlike global variables, scoped values enable actions to be performed with a fixed, unchangeable value assignment in a virtual thread, since scoped values are unchangeable after execution is started with `run()` or `call()` and have a clear and precisely defined lifetime.

Finally, as a comparison, without scoped values, the values would have had to be passed as parameters as follows:

```
public void processRequestOldStyle(final User loggedInUser)
{
    System.out.println("processRequestOldStyle: " + loggedInUser);
}
```

As a consequence, all affected methods of all participating classes would then contain a large number of parameters in their signatures. Just imagine three to seven pieces of information that the application needs to pass on. A maintenance nightmare begins ...unless you bundle the parameters into records that carry specific context information, if this is reasonably possible. However, you must still ensure that information is passed correctly through the application to the relevant places.

10.7.4 *Exception Handling*

The methods shown so far, which are called in `run()` or `call()`, for the scoped values have not thrown any exceptions. In practice, however, error propagation via exceptions is quite normal. Therefore, we will now examine how to address this.

For demonstration purposes, let's consider two simple methods that utilize a scoped value `LOGGED_IN_USER` and potentially throw exceptions based on their signature. One is a `java.io.IOException`, which is a checked exception, and the other is a `java.lang.IllegalStateException`, which is an unchecked exception. For simplicity's sake, the exceptions are not thrown, but only listed in the signature:

```java
static String performCalculation() throws IOException
{
    if (ExceptionHandlingExample.LOGGED_IN_USER.isBound())
        return ExceptionHandlingExample.LOGGED_IN_USER.get().name();

    return "FALLBACK FIRST";
}

static String performCalculationUnchecked() throws IllegalStateException
{
    if (ExceptionHandlingExample.LOGGED_IN_USER.isBound())
        return ExceptionHandlingExample.LOGGED_IN_USER.get().nickName();

    return "FALLBACK SECOND";
}
```

In both methods, data about a user is managed in the form of a simple record:

```java
record User(String name, String nickName) {}
```

Example of Easily Readable Exception Handling

Let's assume we want to call the method `performCalculation()` that could potentially throw exceptions in the context of a scoped value.

When calling `call()`, the type `ScopedValue.CallableOp` is used for the action to be executed. This allows a specific exception to be thrown during processing. As a result, exception handling can be made readable and specific:

```java
try
{
    var result = ScopedValue.where(ExceptionHandlingExample.LOGGED_IN_USER, user).
                      call(() -> ExceptionHandlingExample.
                            performCalculation());
    System.out.println("Calculated result: " + result);
}
catch (IOException ioe)
{
    handleIoException(ioe);
}
```

Without Exception Handling If a method, such as `performCalculation-Unchecked()`, only throws a `RuntimeException`, then the whole thing can be written in a more readable way, since no `try-catch` is necessary around the call:

```
var result = ScopedValue.where(ExceptionHandlingExample.LOGGED_IN_USER, user).
                    call(() -> ExceptionHandlingExample.
                             performCalculationUnchecked());
```

10.7.5   Technical Background and Conclusion

Scoped values can act as a lightweight alternative to `ThreadLocal<T>`. Since the introduction of virtual threads, it is possible to start hundreds of thousands or more virtual threads—a scenario in which `ThreadLocal<T>` variables quickly lead to significant problems due to the per-thread overhead.[7]

The most significant scaling advantage arises when many virtual threads are started within an active binding and inherit the value from the parent thread, for example, in the context of structured concurrency. But even without this nesting relationship, scoped values are usually more efficient because they require less memory per thread and do not need to be removed manually. For a large number of short-lived virtual threads, they are therefore the better choice over `ThreadLocal<T>`.

In addition, scoped values offer a simpler programming model and easier traceability due to their immutability.

10.8   JEP 508: Vector API (Tenth Incubator)

The Vector API has nothing to do with the class `java.util.Vector`. Rather, it provides platform-independent support for so-called vector calculations. Modern processors are capable of performing addition or multiplication not only for two values but also for a large number of values in one go (i. e., as a single action). This is also referred to as Single Instruction Multiple Data (SIMD). Provided that the appropriate hardware support is available, calculations can be executed with high performance, since significantly fewer than n actions are required, depending on the number of values m that can be processed simultaneously, that is, n/m.

---

[7] `ThreadLocal<T>` stores entries in a map on the thread. With millions of (virtual) threads, this can quickly lead to significant memory problems in terms of memory consumption. Scoped values avoid this issue because they only keep active bindings on a stack and automatically clean up after the end of the scope.

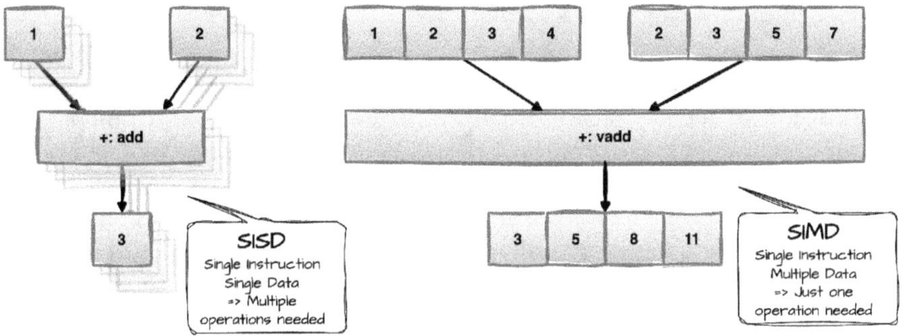

Fig. 10.2 Normal SISD operation (left) vs. SIMD vector operation (right))

Figure 10.2 illustrates the basic principle using the addition of numbers and is inspired by an interesting article published here: https://medium.com/@Styp/auto-vectorization-how-to-get-beaten-by-compiler-optimization-java-jit-vector-api-92c72b97fba3.

10.8.1   Introductory Example

A vector calculation consists of a sequence of operations with vectors. A vector can be thought of as an array of primitive values. The calculation, for example, an addition, is performed for all values. With SIMD, however, this is done in chunks rather than the conventional value-by-value approach.

Conventional Implementation

If you want to combine two vectors or arrays using a mathematical operation, you traditionally loop through all values. A corresponding scalar calculation is implemented as follows:

```java
private static int[] performScalarAddition(int[] a, int[] b)
{
    int[] result = new int[a.length];

    for (int i = 0; i < a.length; i++)
    {
        result[i] = a[i] + b[i];
    }

    return result;
}
```

In our implementation, we start with two arrays, a and b, of equal size as the initial data. To combine these values one by one, in this case by adding them together, we use the i-th element of the first vector and combine it with the i-th element of the second vector.

Implementation Using the Vector API

The Vector API utilizes optimizations in modern processors. For this purpose, an `IntVector` is initially created from each of the arrays a and b with input data of type `int` using `fromArray()`.[8] These can then be used to perform operations such as addition with `add()` (as well as subtraction, multiplication, or division with the corresponding methods `sub()`, `mul()`, and `div()`). The vector is then transferred to a result array by calling `intoArray()`—we notice the value 0 for both transformation methods. It allows you to specify an offset if necessary when referencing other positions in the array.

Additionally, the size of the vector plays a crucial role in processing. In this example, it is set to 256 bits by the argument `IntVector.SPECIES_256`—you will learn more about this in a moment:

```java
private static int[] performVectorAddition(final int[] a, final int[] b)
{
    int[] result = new int[a.length];

    IntVector vectorA = IntVector.fromArray(IntVector.SPECIES_256, a, 0);
    IntVector vectorB = IntVector.fromArray(IntVector.SPECIES_256, b, 0);
    IntVector vectorResult = vectorA.add(vectorB); // vectorA.mul(vectorB)

    vectorResult.intoArray(result, 0);

    return result;
}
```

Execution

To try out both variants, we first define two `int[]` as a data set in a `main()` method. Afterward, we call the respective methods, that is, once `performScalarAddition()` to demonstrate a conventional calculation and once `performVectorAddition()` to illustrate SIMD.

```java
void main()
{
    int[] a = {1, 2, 3, 4, 5, 6, 7, 8};
    int[] b = {1, 2, 3, 4, 5, 6, 7, 8};

    var result1 = performScalarAddition(a, b);
    IO.println("result using scalar calculation: " + Arrays.toString(result1)
        );

    var result2 = performVectorAddition(a, b);
    IO.println("result using Vector API: " + Arrays.toString(result2));
}
```

Listing 10.6 Executable as **"FirstVectorExample"**

---

[8] In addition to `IntVector` for int values, there are the types `ByteVector`, `ShortVector`, `LongVector`, `FloatVector`, and `DoubleVector`, as well as other specializations.

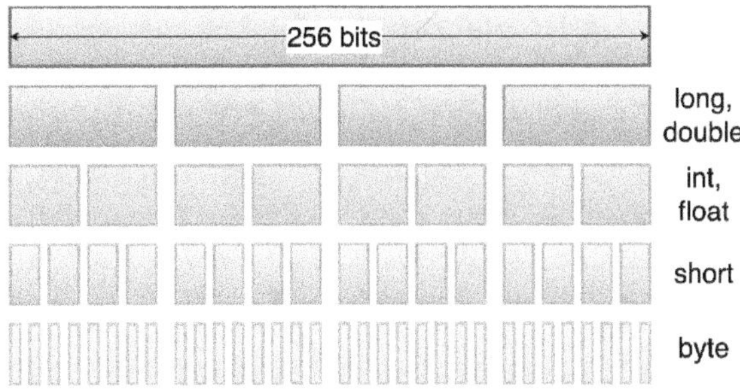

Fig. 10.3 Vector size influences the amount of data that can be processed in parallel

When executing the program FIRSTVECTOREXAMPLE, you will get this output (provided you have specified the incubator module correctly at startup):

```
WARNING: Using incubator modules: jdk.incubator.vector
result using scalar calculation: [2, 4, 6, 8, 10, 12, 14, 16]
result using Vector API: [2, 4, 6, 8, 10, 12, 14, 16]
```

What Effect Does the Vector Size Have?   In Java, `int` values are four bytes in size. Since the input data here consists of eight `int`s, this results in a memory size of 32 bytes or 256 bits. This allows the vector to accommodate and process the entire array. Figure 10.3 provides a clear illustration of the amount of information to be processed.

To achieve maximum platform independence in vector calculations, you should prefer the flexible `IntVector.SPECIES_PREFERRED` instead of fixed specifications such as the previously used `IntVector.SPECIES_256`, as the platform's optimal may be 128 bits or even 512 bits, depending on the computer architecture.

Note: Good to Know
If you choose a smaller species size than the CPU actually supports, the entire process will still work because fewer lanes per vector register are utilized. However, this results in a loss of potential performance, but the behavior is still correct. If you select a larger species size than the platform offers, the JVM will switch to a smaller, suitable size. No error occurs, but the maximum possible hardware vector is used (e.g., 256-bit instead of 512-bit).

Thus, the passed species size represents a preference or an aid—an incorrect choice costs performance, but not correctness. Therefore, when in doubt, `IntVector.SPECIES_PREFERRED` is the best choice.

Especially with larger data sets, the actions must be divided appropriately. This requires processing vector operations within loops, which we will examine now.

10.8.2   Further Example

Let's consider the following formula, $-(a_i^2 + b_i^2)$, from JEP 508 as a starting point. The calculation is less about the specific formula and more about embedding the basic building blocks presented above into a more practical process and learning about special features, especially concerning loops over values.

Please note the following: for the sake of simplicity, we assume that the two input data sets are the same size for both the conventional implementation and the one using the Vector API.

Conventional Implementation

The implementation of the calculation of the above formula is implemented for `float[]` as input data. The calculation is easily understood and comprehensible with the help of a regular `for` loop:

```java
static float[] scalarComputation(float[] a, float[] b)
{
    float[] result = new float[a.length];

    for (int i = 0; i < a.length; i++)
    {
        result[i] = (a[i] * a[i] + b[i] * b[i]) * -1.0f;
    }

    return result;
}
```

10.8.3   Implementation Using the Vector API

To calculate the formula $-(a_i^2 + b_i^2)$ using the Vector API, the already familiar methods `fromArray()` and `intoArray()` are used to convert from and to arrays, as well as various calculations such as `mul()`, `add()`, and `neg()`.

The first special feature is how the number of necessary loop iterations is determined. The method `loopBound()` helps here. Based on the size of the input data array and the vector size, here `SPECIES_PREFERRED`, it determines the number of loop iterations required depending on the step size `SPECIES.length()`. Block-wise processing is based on this:

```
static float[] vectorComputation(float[] a, float[] b)
{
    final VectorSpecies<Float> SPECIES = FloatVector.SPECIES_PREFERRED;
    final float[] result = new float[a.length];

    int i = 0;
    for (; i < SPECIES.loopBound(a.length); i += SPECIES.length())
    {
        var vectorA = FloatVector.fromArray(SPECIES, a, i);
        var vectorB = FloatVector.fromArray(SPECIES, b, i);
        var vectorResult = vectorA.mul(vectorA).add(
                                    vectorB.mul(vectorB)).neg();

        vectorResult.intoArray(result, i);
    }

    for (; i < a.length; i++)
    {
        result[i] = (a[i] * a[i] + b[i] * b[i]) * -1.0f;
    }

    return result;
}
```

The second special feature is the need for a final loop, which works almost exactly like the one from the scalar calculation, but be careful: here it starts with the current value of i, that is, with the value after the upper limit calculated with loopBound(). Additionally, you run through the index one by one and process the data element by element, rather than in blocks.

Nevertheless, one might initially wonder why the lines of the standard algorithm, that is, the scalar calculation, have to be listed again at the bottom. This is simply because the data is only processed up to the upper limit calculated with loopBound() in the first loop, and depending on the vector size and the number of input data, a small amount of offcuts may potentially remain due to the division into blocks of fixed size. This fact is illustrated in the Fig. 10.4.

To ensure that all data, including the remaining elements, is processed correctly, the actions must be performed manually and without the use of the Vector API, as described above in the second loop.

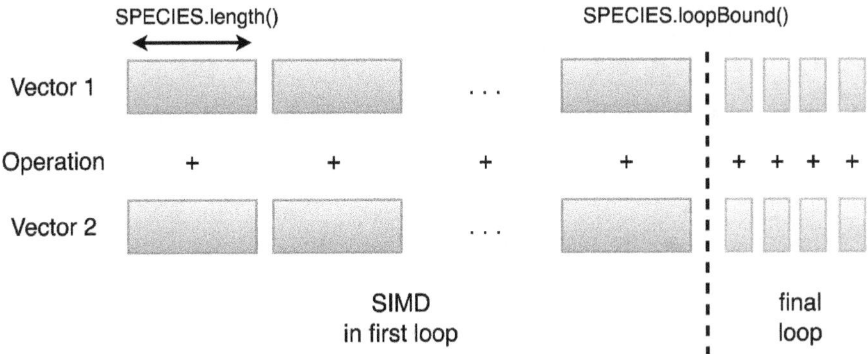

Fig. 10.4 Influence of vector size and final actions

Mask As an Alternative to Loop Alternatively, masks are handy—however, this requires some expert knowledge and is initially more challenging to understand:

```
if (i < n)
{
    var m = SPECIES.indexInRange(i, n);       // Mask for remaining lanes
    var vectorA = FloatVector.fromArray(SPECIES, a, i, m);
    var vectorB = FloatVector.fromArray(SPECIES, b, i, m);
    var vectorResult = vectorA.mul(vectorA).add(vectorB.mul(vectorB)).neg();

    vectorResult.intoArray(result, i, m);    // Write only valid lanes
}
```

Execution

To try out both the scalar and vector calculations, we define the following `main()` method, which provides two `float[]` as a data basis and then calls the respective methods and logs their calculation results on the console.

```
void main()
{
    float[] a = {1, 2, 3, 4, 5, 6, 7, 8, 9, 10};
    float[] b = {1, 2, 3, 4, 5, 6, 7, 8, 9, 10};

    float[] result1 = scalarComputation(a, b);
    IO.println("result using scalar calculation: " + Arrays.toString(result1)
        );

    float[] result2 = vectorComputation(a, b);
    IO.println("result using Vector API: " + Arrays.toString(result2));
}
```

Listing 10.7 Executable as "SECONDVECTOREXAMPLE"

When executing the program SECONDVECTOREXAMPLE, the following calculation results are output:

```
WARNING: Using incubator modules: jdk.incubator.vector
result using scalar calculation: [-2.0, -8.0, -18.0, -32.0, -50.0, -72.0,
    -98.0, -128.0, -162.0, -200.0]
result using Vector API: [-2.0, -8.0, -18.0, -32.0, -50.0, -72.0, -98.0,
    -128.0, -162.0, -200.0]
```

Influence of the Final Loop If the final loop were commented out as suggested above

```
//    for (; i < a.length; i++)
//    {
//        // c[i] = (a[i] * a[i] + b[i] * b[i]) * -1.0f;
//    }
```

depending on the computer architecture, the following outputs would result:

```
WARNING: Using incubator modules: jdk.incubator.vector
result using scalar calculation: [-2.0, -8.0, -18.0, -32.0, -50.0, -72.0,
     -98.0, -128.0, -162.0, -200.0]
result using Vector API: [-2.0, -8.0, -18.0, -32.0, -50.0, -72.0, -98.0,
     -128.0, 0.0,0.0]
```

We observe that some values would not be calculated (e.g., the last two for an
Apple M3 Max) and therefore have a value of 0.0.

The impact of the final loop on performance is negligible because only a minimal
fraction of the values are calculated with it for huge vectors. However, it is necessary
to ensure correct calculation for arbitrary vector lengths.

> **Note: Providing Extensive Test Data**
> The Vector API excels in handling large data sets and more complex
> operations. If, for example, you want to experiment with a million or more
> input data items, the following implementation trick with the Stream API can
> be helpful—shown here for the type `long`. Unfortunately, this only works
> for the types `int`, `long`, and `double`, as there are only suitable primitive
> streams for these:
>
> ```
> long[] values = LongStream.iterate(1, i -> i + 1).
>                          limit(size).toArray();
> ```
>
> Alternatively, this can be written as follows:
>
> ```
> var values = LongStream.range(1, size).toArray();
> ```

10.8.4   Auto-vectorization

The JVM already includes excellent optimizations, such as auto-vectorization,
which can automatically execute similar operations like the explicit actions and calls
of the Vector API described above, resulting in good performance at runtime while
keeping the source code understandable and clear.

This might raise the following question: Why all the effort? Why should I use the
Vector API, or why not? The answer to this question is quite simple: unless you are
a proven expert in the field, do not need to perform particularly unusual calculations,
and do not have extreme requirements for the optimizations possible with the Vector
API, you should probably only use the Vector API once to familiarize yourself with
it. For the remaining less than 1 % of users, the Vector API can sometimes deliver
improvements of a factor of 5–20.

Finally, it is worth noting that the Vector API is primarily intended for framework and library developers.

10.9   Miscellaneous

JEP 472: Prepare to Restrict the Use of JNI

This JEP 472 continues JEP 471, which was finalized in Java 23 and is titled "Deprecate the Memory-Access Methods in sun.misc.Unsafe for Removal," and also indirectly affects the Foreign Function and Memory (FFM) API, which is used for memory access or calls to native code. Both APIs now behave similarly and produce warnings when accessed.

The command-line parameter `--illegal-native-access` allows control of the behavior for both the class `sun.misc.Unsafe` and the FFM API in a uniform manner. The following values are allowed as options: `allow`, `warn`, and `deny`.[9] This allows you to specify how memory accesses or calls to native code from `Unsafe` and the FFM API are handled:

- `allow`: Allows usage without runtime warnings.
- `warn`: Allows usage, but produces runtime warnings.
- `deny`: Prohibits usage. If an access is nonetheless attempted, it fails and results in a `java.lang.IllegalCallerException`.

In the future, there will be a tightening of the rules, and instead of the current `warn`, `deny` will become the default. There are also plans to remove `allow`.

JEP 486: Permanently Disable the Security Manager

In the early days of Java, security managers were designed to secure applets, limiting the scope of action or capabilities of programs executed from them, such as preventing file access. Applets have long since ceased to be relevant, and the same applies to the security manager. Consequently, both were marked as " deprecated for removal" in Java 17 LTS.

With this JEP, activation of the security manager is no longer supported, resulting in an error message. For one of the future Java versions, it is planned to completely remove the remaining functionality from the JDK classes.

JEP 498: Warn upon Use of Memory-Access Methods in `sun.misc.Unsafe`

This JEP 498 is the successor to JEP 471, finalized in Java 23, entitled " Deprecate the Memory-Access Methods in sun.misc.Unsafe for Removal."

Java 23 introduced the command-line parameter `--sun-misc-unsafe-memory-access=<option>`. It allows the following values: `allow`, `warn`,

---

[9] Some developers may remember the `--illegal-access` command-line option introduced as part of the modularization in Java 9.

debug, and deny. Thereby, you may specify how memory accesses from Unsafe are handled.

In Java 23, warnings were issued during compilation, but allow was the default at runtime. With Java 25 LTS, warnings are issued by default during runtime access, as warn is now the default setting—unless otherwise specified.

JEP 510: Key Derivation Function API

JEP 510 introduces an API for key derivation functions, which are cryptographic algorithms that can be used to derive additional keys from a secret key and other data.

In Java 25 LTS, the API has become final, having previously been a preview feature in Java 24. This JEP focuses specifically on low-level details of key derivation. For the vast majority of developers, this topic will not be relevant. Therefore, I refer interested readers to the original JEP: https://openjdk.org/jeps/510.

Chapter 11
JVM Innovations in JDK 22 to 25 LTS

In this chapter, we will look at some of the changes, enhancements, and new features in the JVM that are cumulatively included in Java 22 to 25 LTS.

In the following sections, we will focus specifically on these topics:

- JEP 423: Region Pinning for G1
- JEP 458: Launch Multi-File Source Code Programs
- JEP 474: ZGC: Generational Mode by Default
- JEP 512: Compact Source Files and Instance Main Methods

Section 11.1 introduces a new feature in the G1 garbage collector. I will then discuss the direct execution of Java programs without explicit prior compilation. This feature has been extended with JEP 458, allowing more complex programs consisting of multiple classes and Java files to be processed as well. Section 11.2 covers this. As a result of a minor change in the area of garbage collection, the generation-oriented mode of the ZGC is now the default. This change is discussed in Sect. 11.3. For many developers, the innovations in the context of JEP 512, entitled "Compact Source Files and Instance Main Methods," are probably more relevant. This JEP helps get started with Java, and Java programs can now be defined more concisely, which has advantages in conjunction with JEP 458. Section 11.4 discusses this topic in more detail. Finally, Sect. 11.5 provides an overview of various little changes brought as a potpourri of innovations that have been incorporated into the JDK.

11.1 JEP 423: Region Pinning for G1

To grasp this JEP, it is worth taking a brief look at the garbage collector G1 (short for Garbage First)—in particular, its origins and how it works.

M. Inden, *Java 25 and Beyond*, https://doi.org/10.1007/979-8-8688-2385-5_11

The G1 was introduced with Java 7 and became the default GC in Java 9. G1 aims to strike a balance between pause times and throughput and works both *concurrently* and *in parallel*.

Concurrently refers to simultaneous with the application. Parallel means that multiple threads are used simultaneously for cleanup work. However, there is one more detail to consider: STW (Stop-the-World). This means that all application threads are stopped; then only VM/GC threads work. This is sometimes necessary to obtain a consistent memory image.

After this excursion, let's return to G1. G1 divides the memory into regions of equal size and works with generations: younger objects that have only existed for a short time and older objects with a longer lifespan. When cleaning up, G1 moves objects from one subset of regions to another.

A problem can arise when Java interacts with native programs via the Java Native Interface (JNI). If memory areas are shared, garbage collection could cause native pointers to become invalid when Java objects are moved. Such objects are called critical objects. If entire regions must not be transferred, they are referred to as critical regions.

Previously, G1 disabled garbage collection for critical regions, which could increase latency. Region pinning solves this problem: critical regions are moved directly to the old generation. This allows G1 to clean up the young generation undisturbed—without being influenced by critical regions or JNI—and without having to turn off garbage collection.

11.2   JEP 458: Launch Multi-File Source Code Programs

The feature named Direct Compilation has been available since Java 11 LTS. It allows individual Java files to be compiled and executed with a single command, that is, without explicit prior compilation. This is useful for smaller experiments and simple command-line tools. You can find out more about this feature in Sect. 15.5.

Up to and including Java 21 LTS, there was a restriction regarding direct compilation: only a single Java file could be executed. As programs become larger, the desire to provide more structure and subdivide functionalities into separate classes increases, resulting in distinct Java files. However, handling multiple files is not supported by direct compilation before Java 22. The workaround was to put all Java classes in the same file. To achieve this, direct compilation even allowed multiple `public` classes to be saved as a single unit, which differs from the standard. Even worse, this approach quickly becomes confusing, and there is also a risk of source code duplication. Furthermore, as indicated, this approach contradicts the rule "a Java file contains one public class." In all other contexts, a violation of this rule results in a compilation error.

This JEP addresses precisely these weaknesses and introduces an improvement in the Java program startup. This allows the transition from small programs to larger programs to occur gradually, without the need to introduce a build tool such as Maven or Gradle. This is particularly helpful for novice programmers.

Introductory Example

First, we consider an application that has been divided into two Java files. Let's start with the main class `MainApp`, already using the simplified syntax for `main()` methods, which will be presented in more detail later in Sect. 11.4:

```
package jep458_launch_multifile_sourcecode_programs;

public class MainApp
{
    void main()
    {
        var result = Helper.performCalculation();
        System.out.println(result);
    }
}
```

We implement the helper class `Helper` as follows:

```
package jep458_launch_multifile_sourcecode_programs;

public class Helper
{
    public static String performCalculation()
    {
        return "Heavy, long running calculation!";
    }
}
```

To launch class `MainApp`, enter the following command:

```
$ java MainApp.java
```

This loads the `MainApp` class and compiles it automatically. The same happens for the `Helper` class. Then the `main()` method is executed, resulting in this output:

```
Heavy, long running calculation!
```

> **Note: Including libraries**
>
> It is possible to integrate any `jar` files and, in particular, existing libraries such as Google Guava.[a] For this purpose, the required JAR must be explicitly included in the class path at startup:
>
> ```
> $ java --class-path '*' MyProg.java
> ```
>
> ---
>
> [a]This library offers practical additional functions and is available for free download at https://github.com/google/guava.

Multiple Executable Programs

Let's assume we want to deploy another application called `MainAppV2` in that directory:

```java
package directcompilation;

public class MainAppV2
{
    void main()
    {
        var result = Helper.performCalculation();
        var resultMarked = StringHelper.mark(result);

        System.out.println(resultMarked);
    }
}
```

For demonstration purposes, this not only accesses the helper class `Helper` already presented, but also the following helper class `StringHelper`, which was created solely for demonstration purposes:

```java
package directcompilation;

public class StringHelper
{
    public static String mark(final String input)
    {
        return ">>" + input + "<<";
    }
}
```

To launch the program, enter the following command in the directory where you saved these Java files:

```
$ java MainAppV2.java
```

The output illustrates the execution of the two helper methods by highlighting the original text:

```
>>Heavy, long running calculation!<<
```

Conclusion

Even when using direct compilation, an application can now be split into multiple Java files, and the Java compiler automatically resolves dependencies. This means that classes that are needed are recognized and compiled.

In combination with JEP 512, entitled "Compact Source Files and Instance Main Methods," getting started with Java programming is made even easier. This extension is discussed in Sect. 11.4. Based on the innovations described, smaller programs can be created and executed quickly. If necessary, additional functionality may be added later in the form of other Java classes.

11.3   JEP 474: ZGC: Generational Mode by Default

There are different approaches to garbage collection. One approach that often makes sense is to subdivide objects into so-called generations. This means that objects differ in their lifetime and, in particular, in their usage profile. Typically, Java generates a large number of temporary or at least short-lived objects, that is, objects that are created, are used for a short time, and then become irrelevant. In contrast, relatively few objects are long-lived. Suppose this circumstance is taken into account in garbage collection. In that case, the cleanup process becomes more efficient by prioritizing the cleaning of young objects and less frequently cleaning up older ones, as these tend to still be in use and cannot be disposed of.

The Z Garbage Collector (ZGC) was initially not implemented as a generational garbage collector. But such a generation-oriented mode has been introduced and tested for the ZGC for several Java versions. This JEP aims to establish the generation-oriented mode as the default and to focus future work primarily on it. Therefore, the other mode of the ZGC, which does not work with generations, is marked as obsolete and intended to be removed in future Java versions.

Effects at the Command-Line Level

The flag `-XX:+UseZGC` activates the ZGC. Since Java 23, the following variations have been available:

- `-XX:+UseZGC`: Activates the ZGC in generation-oriented mode.
- `-XX:+UseZGC -XX:+ZGenerational`: Activates ZGC in generation-oriented mode. Since the `ZGenerational` option is obsolete, the following warning message appears:

```
OpenJDK 64-Bit Server VM warning: Option ZGenerational was deprecated in
       version 23.0 and will likely be removed in a future release.
```

- `-XX:+UseZGC -XX:-ZGenerational`: ZGC is activated, but not in gene-ration-oriented mode. Since the `ZGenerational` option is obsolete and the mode without generations is intended to be removed, warning messages similar to the following will appear:

```
OpenJDK 64-Bit Server VM warning: Option ZGenerational was deprecated in
         version 23.0 and will likely be removed in a future release.
OpenJDK 64-Bit Server VM warning: Non-generational ZGC is deprecated.
```

11.4   JEP 512: Compact Source Files and Instance Main Methods

JEP 445 introduced Unnamed Classes and Instance Main Methods as a preview feature in Java 21 LTS. I already discussed this feature and the motivation behind it in detail in Sect. 6.3. Here, I provide a brief recap to help you better understand the enhancements from Java 22 to 25 LTS. The functionality has been continuously improved and refined. Java 25 LTS finalizes the whole thing and once again changes the name of the JEP title.

Preliminary Considerations

The goal of this JEP and its predecessors was to address the tedious introduction to Java and simplify the learning process. To this end, Java should be as easy to use as possible for small experiments. It applies in particular in combination with Launch Single-File Source Code Programs, also known as Direct Compilation, the direct invocation of a Java program from the console (see Sect. 15.5), and its continuation as JEP 458 for processing more complex programs consisting of multiple source files (see Sect. 11.2).

Let's put ourselves in the shoes of a beginner and consider implementing a simple console output as an example. We'll start with the conventional variant and then look at two simplification steps.

The conventional implementation requires rather extensive source code that can be confusing for beginners, because you already need to understand (or ignore) classes, visibility modifiers, arrays, static methods, and (unused) method parameters, as well as the reference to `System.out`:

```java
public class OldStyleHelloWorld
{
    public static void main(String[] args)
    {
        System.out.println("Old Style Hello World");
    }
}
```

As a first step, based on the above variant, we derive the following clearer short form called Instance Main Method, which already omits a few things and is reduced to the essentials:

```
class HelloWorld
{
    void main()
    {
        System.out.println("Instance Main Method Hello World");
    }
}
```

Finally, this can be simplified once again using a `main()` method without an explicit, surrounding class definition—referred to as Unnamed Class in Java 21 LTS, Implicitly Declared Class since Java 22, Simple Source File since Java 24, and Compact Source File since Java 25 LTS:

```
void main()
{
    System.out.println("Simple Source Files Hello World");
}
```

These simplification steps have already brought us quite far. Only the reference of `System.out` to the static element `out` of the class `System` from the fully qualified method call could still be slightly disruptive. Below, we will examine the respective changes in modern Java (described in detail in Sect. 11.4.2) that also address this minor imperfection.

11.4.1   New Features in Java 22 to 25 LTS

While the version of the program shown above represented a so-called Unnamed Class with a `main()` method in Java 21 LTS, this changes in Java 22. An implicitly named class (or implicitly declared class) is created, whose name is determined by the name of the Java file. This eliminated the need for separate tooling.

Example

Let's use the last variant of the console output shown in the preliminary considerations again within the following simple `main()` method:

```
void main()
{
    System.out.println("Simple Source Files Hello World");
}
```

Suppose these lines are saved as a file named `CompactSourceFiles-HelloWorld.java`. In that case, they can be executed using direct compilation (see Sect. 15.5) and this call:

```
$ java CompactSourceFilesHelloWorld.java
```

Alternatively, you can compile with `javac` to recognize that the name of the generated class is determined by the name of the Java file:

```
$ javac CompactSourceFilesHelloWorld.java
```

This creates a file `CompactSourceFilesHelloWorld.class`, whose contents can be inspected using the `javap` tool integrated into the JDK:

```
$ javap CompactSourceFilesHelloWorld.class
Compiled from "CompactSourceFilesHelloWorld.java"
final class CompactSourceFilesHelloWorld {
  CompactSourceFilesHelloWorld();
  void main();
}
```

Special Feature: No Package Specification for Implicitly Declared Classes

You cannot use package specifications in implicitly declared classes:

```
package jep512_compact_source_files; // ATTENTION: incorrect

void main()
{
    System.out.println("Hello, World!");
}
```

This results in a compilation error:

```
Package statement is not allowed for implicitly declared class
```

Package Specifications for Instance Main Methods In the case of instance main methods, however, package specifications are possible:

```
package jep512_compact_source_files;

class InstanceMainMethodExample
{
    void main()
    {
        System.out.println("InstanceMainMethodExample");
    }
}
```

Simplified Rules for Detecting `main()`

Theoretically, multiple `main()` methods can now exist in a class. To determine which `main()` method to execute, Java 21 LTS has quite complex, four-step rules. The procedure has been simplified in Java 22. Now, if there is a method named `main()` with a `String[]` parameter, this method is called. Otherwise, the parameterless variant is called. This procedure is unambiguous, since a class is not allowed to define a static method and an instance method with the same name and signature.

Identifying the appropriate `main()` method is thus significantly easier, and one only needs to remember the mnemonic "parameter first," in contrast to the substantially more complex rules of the previous JEPs:

```java
class InstanceMainMethodExample
{
    void main()
    {
        System.out.println("InstanceMainMethodExample");
    }

    static void main(String[] args)
    {
        System.out.println("Static main");
    }
}
```

Here, the static `main()` method is executed, and the following is output:

```
Static main
```

Let's remove the parameter from the static `main()` method and add it to the non-static `main()` method:

```java
class InstanceMainMethodExample2
{
    void main(String[] args)
    {
        System.out.println("InstanceMainMethodExample");
    }

    static void main()
    {
        System.out.println("Static main");
    }
}
```

Then, as expected (and according to the mnemonic "parameter first"), the "normal," non-static `main()` method is executed. This results in the following output:

```
InstanceMainMethodExample
```

Reminder: Two `main()` methods without parameters, one static and one non-static, are syntactically not allowed and result in a compilation error.

11.4.2   Further Innovations in Java 22 to 25 LTS

In addition to the enhancements described, you get these significant innovations:

- **Interaction with the Console Using the Class `java.lang.IO`**: Implicitly declared classes, like other classes, can directly use all possible types residing in package `java.lang`. To simplify interaction with the console, Java 23 introduced a class `IO`. As of Java 25 LTS, it is now located in the package `java.lang`.
- **Automatic Module Import from `java.base`**: Implicitly declared classes automatically import the module `java.base` (see Sect. 9.4). It means that all public types (especially classes and interfaces) of the packages exported by the `java.base` module are directly accessible, such as the functionalities from the Stream API or the Date and Time API.

> **Hint: Modules in Java**
> With Java 9, the JDK was split into individual, smaller building blocks, known as modules. Modules bundle thematically related functionalities. Similar to the class `Object` as the basis of all classes, there is also a module called `java.base`, which serves as the basis for all other modules and bundles all essential and commonly used packages.

Interaction with the Console

When starting in programming, you often develop small programs that output values to the console or accept input from it. If you are at the beginning of your programming career, it would be desirable if this could be implemented directly with a simple method call. In fact, however, this has been somewhat complicated in Java up to now. Even for output, you have to use a rather unreadable call to `System.out.println()`. For experienced developers, however, this is not really a problem. Novice programmers, on the other hand, repeatedly stumble over this construct and, depending on their level of knowledge, ask themselves: What is `System`, what is `out`, and what are the dots for?

While these details can be easily ignored, reading from the console is even more complex, as shown below:

```java
try
{
    var reader = new BufferedReader(new InputStreamReader(System.in));
    String line = reader.readLine();
    // ...
}
catch (IOException ioe)
{
    // ...
}
```

A slightly better variant of reading in is offered by the class `java.io.Console` (not provided as a listing) or, as shown below, the use of the class `java.util.Scanner`, which makes the implementation shorter and a little easier to understand—in particular, there is no exception handling:

```
try (var scanner = new Scanner(System.in))
{
    String line = scanner.nextLine();
    // ...
}
```

Again, experienced developers will hardly be bothered by this, but it's certainly not ideal. For beginners, however, the construct is peppered with advanced concepts, such as exception handling and I/O streams, the lesser-known class `Scanner`, as well as try with round brackets—along with new, `var`, and `System.in`. At least one of these questions is bound to come up: What are `try` and `catch` used for? Why does it need both `java.io.BufferedReader` and `java.io.InputStreamReader`? What is a `java.io.IOException`? Or what is a `Scanner` and why do you write `try` with round brackets and without `catch` in the second case?

The `java.lang.IO` Class As a Remedy As briefly mentioned earlier, the `IO` class has been added to the JDK. It provides the following three methods to simplify the creation of small, interactive programs:

```
public static void println(Object obj);
public static void print(Object obj);
public static String readln(String prompt);
```

Conveniently, these methods can be used directly in any implicitly declared class without having to write an import.

Based on this, the `main()` method can be written even more concisely as follows:

```
void main()
{
    IO.println("Shortest and Python-like 'Hello World!'");
}
```

Even simple interactions can be designed to be highly readable, understandable, and pleasant for beginners:

```
void main()
{
    var name = IO.readln("Please enter your name: ");
    IO.println("Hello " + name);
}
```

The trick behind this is that every implicitly declared class can automatically access the types from `java.lang`. You only need to specify the class name `IO`, which is easier to understand than `System.out`. This simplification is a big help, especially for beginners, and is reminiscent of the elegance offered by Python.

But it gets even better: for anything that goes beyond such simple programs and uses, for example, lists, streams, or the Date and Time API, all public types from the `java.base` module are automatically available. Let's take a look at that now.

Automatic Module Import from `java.base`: Using Additional JDK Functionalities

As you gain experience, you will often want to implement more complex things, namely, those that go beyond simple gimmicks and interactions with the console. Let's imagine, for example, that you want to manage the inputs in a list or save them in a file for later use. The JDK offers various useful methods for these tasks. Until now, you had to explicitly include lists using `import java.util.*`. This can be confusing for beginners. Additionally, the package hierarchy and the location of various interfaces and classes are not always known. This is even more true when implicitly declared classes are created using only a text editor, rather than within an IDE.

For the purpose of demonstrating this, we will store a few first names in a list and allow the user to enter their name. In a loop, this will then be compared with those from the list, and if there is a match, a message will be displayed:

```java
void main()
{
    var name = IO.readln("Please enter your name: ");

    for (var authorName : List.of("Tim", "Tom", "Mike", "Michael"))
    {
        if (name.equalsIgnoreCase(authorName))
            IO.println(name + " you are registered as author!");
        else
            IO.println(authorName + ": " + authorName.length());
    }
}
```

As a reminder: Oracle decided to make the first steps in Java easier by automatically importing the module `java.base` for every implicitly declared class. This means that all essential and popular APIs from commonly used packages, such as `java.io`, `java.math`, and `java.util`, are directly usable, including `java.util.List` above.

I have already explained the advantages of this, such as the simplification of file interactions, in the context of JShell in Sect. 9.4.4. Now, I would like to illustrate it again here in a similar form:

```
void main() throws IOException
{
    var name = IO.readln("Please enter your name: ");
    var age = Integer.parseInt(IO.readln("Please enter your age: "));
    var today = LocalDate.now();

    var info = """
                Hello, %s!
                Today is %s
                Your current age is %d
                """.formatted(name, today, age);
    IO.println(info);

    Path infoFile = Paths.get(name+".txt");
    Files.writeString(infoFile, info);

    String content = Files.readString(infoFile);
    Stream<String> asStream = content.lines();

    List<String> lines = asStream.toList();
    IO.println(lines);
}
```

11.4.3   *Step-by-Step Development of a Program*

A program realized as an implicitly declared class allows you to focus more on
implementing the desired task. Anything irrelevant can be omitted (at the start).
Nevertheless, all things work in the same way as in a regular class.

To convert the implicitly declared class shown above into a regular class, we
add the imports and the class definition, including the name as a bracket around the
`main()` method:

```
package jep512_compact_source_files;

import java.io.IOException;
import java.nio.file.Files;
import java.nio.file.Path;
import java.nio.file.Paths;
import java.time.LocalDate;
import java.util.List;
import java.util.stream.Collectors;
import java.util.stream.Stream;

public class GrowingClass2
{
    void main() throws IOException
    {
        var name = IO.readln("Please enter your name: ");
        var age = Integer.parseInt(IO.readln("Please enter your age: "));
        var today = LocalDate.now();

        var info = """
        Hello, %s!
        Today is %s
        Your current age is %d
        """.formatted(name, today, age);
        IO.println(info);
```

```
        Path infoFile = Paths.get(name+".txt");
        Files.writeString(infoFile, info);

        String content = Files.readString(infoFile);
        Stream<String> asStream = content.lines();

        List<String> lines = asStream.toList8);
        IO.println(lines);
    }
}
```

However, it is worth noting the number of imports required and the difficulty in manually listing them all. Conveniently, IDEs nowadays usually take care of preparing the `import` statements. Apart from that, the advantage of module imports is that they provide a much better overview and a much shorter list of imports. The above lines with imports can be replaced by the following one-liner:

```
import module java.base;
```

Finally, it should be noted that, interestingly, the `main()` method remains unchanged, but is just framed within a class definition.

If necessary, a simple program can evolve into a more complex one, incorporating multiple classes, through step-by-step development that is clear and understandable.

11.4.4 Conclusion

Not so long ago, Java had a rather steep learning curve. It tended to discourage newcomers and is one of the reasons why many novice programmers, as well as students and lecturers, preferred other programming languages, such as the currently extremely popular Python, over Java when starting.

This JEP lowers the barriers for learning Java, making it more enjoyable and easier to dive into the world of Java. In particular, it is now possible to create smaller programs that focus on the essentials and require significantly less knowledge of advanced concepts, such as classes and visibility modifiers. Knowledge is built up gradually through experimentation. If necessary, an implicitly declared class can then gradually evolve into a larger application with multiple classes.

The best thing about it is that no Java dialect had to be developed for this easier introduction. Instead, the simple programs shown are standard Java. It means that the IDEs and tools that have been tried and tested for years, including build tools such as Maven and Gradle, can still be used. Additionally, everything can grow on demand.

Three things are essential for these improvements:

- **Optional Class Definition**: The ability to omit explicit class definition and perform it implicitly simplifies things considerably. Initial programs do not need the concept of object orientation for getting started, but it can be added later if needed.

- **Simplification of `main()`**: A `main()` method now requires neither visibility modifiers nor parameters nor the specification of `static`. This simplification makes it more comfortable to get started because the whole thing is easier to read, more understandable, and has fewer hurdles, such as knowing how `static` works.
- **Introduction of the `java.lang.IO` Class**: The provision of three static methods for input and output, and the fact that these are automatically available in an implicitly declared class, simplifies the first steps.

11.5 Miscellaneous

In addition to the changes discussed in detail, there are several JEPs that address minor issues or internal matters and their improvements. Depending on their potential relevance, I will describe these briefly or, for the sake of completeness, in just one or two sentences.

JEP 475: Late Barrier Expansion for G1

In garbage collection, so-called barriers provide the opportunity to execute specific instructions before and/or after accessing Java objects.[1] Until now, this has been done for G1 in the form of bytecode instructions.

It allows logging references and ensures that objects continue to be addressed correctly when they are moved, for example, when memory areas are compacted to turn Swiss cheese back into a more orderly memory image with larger contiguous regions.

With this JEP, the actions are specified not using bytecode, but in the form of machine code, which should ensure optimized processing.

Incidentally, the ZGC (Z Garbage Collector) has been using late barrier expansion since its introduction.

JEP 479: Remove the Windows 32-bit x86 Port

In the last LTS release, Java 21 LTS, the 32-bit Java version for Windows was marked as "deprecated for removal." It means that support will be removed in the future. This step is only logical, as there is hardly any practical need for 32-bit support for Windows anymore. Furthermore, it only affects Windows 10, as there is no longer a 32-bit version of Windows, starting with Windows 11.

With this JEP 479, the port was removed, which also simplifies the further development of the JDK. Additionally, some features were not implemented for the 32-bit version, such as virtual threads.

---

[1] Somewhat similar to aspect-oriented programming.

JEP 483: Ahead-of-Time Class Loading and Linking

The feature "Ahead-of-Time Class Loading and Linking" aims to reduce the startup times of Java applications by compiling various classes in advance into machine language. The program parts optimized in this way are stored in caches. To fill these caches, applications are monitored during execution. Appropriate optimizations are stored in the cache for subsequent runs.

JEP 490: ZGC: Remove the Non-generational Mode

Let's take a quick look back: the Z Garbage Collector (ZGC) was not originally a generational garbage collector. Such a generation-oriented mode has been introduced and tested for the ZGC for several Java versions.

With this JEP, the non-generational mode of the ZGC was scheduled for removal. Initially, this was the only mode available until a generational mode was added with Java 21 LTS.

To prevent misuse, the non-generational mode of the ZGC can no longer be activated with `-XX:-ZGenerational` as before, but instead results in an error message similar to this: "OpenJDK 64-bit Server VM warning: Ignoring option ZGenerational; support was removed in 24.0."

JEP 491: Synchronize Virtual Threads without Pinning

Virtual threads are a helpful innovation for starting a large number of threads, allowing for the thread-per-request approach in a server environment. With many blocking I/O actions, virtual threads enable the execution of other tasks instead of waiting for the I/O to complete and blocking the current thread.

However, until Java 24, there was still an inconvenience for `synchronized` methods in combination with blocking calls. Although it was possible to use them in virtual threads, this meant that the virtual thread was then bound to its carrier thread, and no other virtual threads could be processed with this carrier thread.

This restriction drops with the introduction of this JEP. Since Java 24, it has been possible to detach the virtual thread from the carrier thread when entering a synchronized block or method and then use it to process other tasks from other virtual threads. This increases scalability.

JEP 493: Linking Run-Time Images Without JMODs

This JEP 493, entitled "Linking Run-Time Images without JMODs," aims to reduce the size of the JDK by around 25 % by removing the tool `jlink`'s dependence on the JDK's JMOD files when creating custom runtime images. The motivation behind this initiative lies in the increasing importance of cloud solutions and the potential savings in terms of data transfer and smaller container images.

What is the background: This optimization is only possible because a JDK consists of a runtime image (the executable Java system) and a collection of module files in the `jmod` directory. The latter were previously necessary for the `jlink` tool to create standalone runtime images. Java applications themselves, on the other hand, rely on the modules from `lib/modules`.

With this JEP, `jlink` is now being adapted to use the module information from the current Java runtime image instead of explicitly the module files from the `jmod` directory.

JEP 501: Deprecate the 32-bit x86 Port for Removal

This JEP marks all 32-bit x86 ports for removal. The Windows port has already been removed with JEP 479. Only the Linux 32-bit x86 port remains in the JDK and will be removed in Java 25 LTS.

JEP 503: Remove the 32-bit x86 Port

With Java 25 LTS, the cleanup work from JEP 501 was finalized and completed. It means that there are now no more 32-bit x86 ports of the JDK.

JEP 514: Ahead-of-Time Command-Line Ergonomics

This JEP addresses improvements in the creation of ahead-of-time (AOT) caches, which accelerate the startup of Java applications.

JEP 515: Ahead-of-Time Method Profiling

This JEP enables specific optimizations to be performed more efficiently. For this purpose, method execution profiles are created for relevant parts of the application and made available for later execution. Based on this, the HotSpot optimizer can generate native code directly.

JEP 518: JFR Cooperative Sampling

The work on this JEP enhances the stability of the JDK Flight Recorder (JFR), particularly for the asynchronous processing of thread stacks.

JEP 519: Compact Object Headers

Compact Object Headers represent an optimized variant of Java object storage, particularly their object headers. This feature was introduced experimentally as JEP 450 in JDK 24 and has now become a final feature.

JEP 520: JFR Method Timing and Tracing

This JEP extends the JDK Flight Recorder (JFR) with functions for measuring the time and tracing methods using bytecode instrumentation.

JEP 521: Generational Shenandoah

As mentioned a few times in the context of garbage collectors, it is a very good idea to support a generation-oriented approach. This also applies to the garbage collector called Shenandoah. The previously experimental feature is now being finalized for this purpose.

Chapter 12
Exercises on the Features in JDK 22 to 25 LTS

The following exercises are intended to deepen your understanding of the new features in JDK 22 to 25 LTS. Sample solutions can be found in Sect. 12.2.

12.1 Exercises

✍ Exercise 1: Markdown Comments ✍

Since Java 23, you can use Markdown to define JavaDoc comments, which allows you to express things more precisely. Experiment a little with Markdown to describe a to-do list, a shopping list, or a baking recipe, for example. Headings allow structuring and are specified with `# Level 1`, `## Level 2`, etc. There are no limits to your creativity in this task. You are also welcome to include various font changes (such as bold or italic) in the documentation.

✍ Exercise 2: Standard Stream Gatherers ✍

Learn about the stream gatherers predefined in the JDK based on the `Gatherer` interface as a basis for extending intermediate operations with its capabilities.

Complete the following program snippet to calculate the product of all numbers in the stream. To do this, use one of the new predefined gatherers from the `Gatherers` class. As a second part, you should divide the input data into groups of three elements:

```java
void main()
{
    var crossMult = Stream.of(1, 2, 3, 4, 5, 6, 7);
    // TODO
    IO.println(crossMult); // Optional[5040]

    var values = Stream.of(1, 2, 3, 10, 20, 30, 100, 200, 300);
    // TODO
    IO.println(values); // [[1, 2, 3], [10, 20, 30], [100, 200, 300]]
}
```


M. Inden, *Java 25 and Beyond*, https://doi.org/10.1007/979-8-8688-2385-5_12

_____________✍ **Exercise 3: Gatherer to Process Information** ✍_____________

(a) Coordinate Information A stream with individual values for x, y, and z is to
be converted into corresponding 3D coordinates. The following record is used for
modeling:

```
record Point3D(int x, int y, int z) {}
```

Please start with the following program fragment:

```
void main()
{
    var coordinates = Stream.of(0, 0, 0, 10, 20, 30, 100, 200, 300,
                                1000, 2000, 3000).
                          gather(null /* TODO*/)
                          /* TODO */;

    IO.println("coordinates: " + coordinates);
}
```

The following results are expected:

```
coordinates: [Point3D[x=0, y=0, z=0], Point3D[x=10, y=20, z=30], Point3D[x
    =100, y=200, z=300], Point3D[x=1000, y=2000, z=3000]]
```

(b) Temperature Jumps Based on a time series with temperature data, those
adjacent value pairs should be collected for which there were temperature variations
of 20 degrees or more:

```
void main()
{
    var temps = Stream.of(10, -7, 20, 0, 12, 17, 20, 40, 10, 20, -2).
                // gather(/* TODO */).
                // filter(/* TODO */).
                toList();

    IO.println("temp jumps: " + temps);
}
```

The following results are expected:

```
temp jumps: [[-7, 20], [20, 0], [20, 40], [40, 10], [20, -2]]
```

_______✍ **Exercise 4: `DistinctBy` Gatherer, Removing Duplicates** ✍______
A separate gatherer `distinctBy()` is to be created. It should remove duplicates
based on a criterion and works as shown below:

```
void main()
{
    var values = Stream.of(1, 2, 3, 4, 5, 1, 2, 3, 4, 5, 1, 2, 3, 4, 5);
    IO.println("distinctBy(n -> n): " +
            values.gather(distinctBy(n -> n)).toList());
    // => distinctBy(n -> n): [1, 2, 3, 4, 5]
}
```

```
    var names = Stream.of("Maik", "Mike", "Jim", "Tim", "Tom", "Jim",
                          "Jim", "John", "Sophie", "Joelle", "Stefan",
                          "Anne", "Lili", "Michael", "Andreas");
    IO.println("distinctBy(String::length): " +
            names.gather(distinctBy(String::length)).toList());
    // => distinctBy(String::length): [Maik, Jim, Sophie, Michael]
}
```

___✍ **Exercise 5: Scoped Values As an Alternative to `ThreadLocal`** ✍___
In this exercise, it's your task to convert information passing implemented via
parameter transfer to the usage of scoped values. This involves simulating request
processing with a multi-layered call hierarchy using simplified `Controller` and
`Service` classes. The starting point for the calls is the class `ScopedValues-`
`Example`, which is to define two scoped values to provide information about the
logged-in user and the time of the request. Currently, the information is still passed
on as parameters:

```
public class ScopedValuesExample
{
    // ...

    void main()
    {
        // Simulate requests
        for (String name : List.of("ATTACKER", "ADMIN"))
        {
            var user = new User(name, name.toLowerCase());
            controller.consumingMethod(user, ZonedDateTime.now());
            // TODO: Conversion of consumingMethod() without parameters

            controller.consumingMethod(user, null);   // no time passed
            // TODO: Conversion of consumingMethod() without parameters

            String answer = controller.process(user, ZonedDateTime.now());
            // TODO: Conversion of process() without parameters
            System.out.println(answer);

            String answer2 = controller.process(user, null);   // no time
                passed
            // TODO: Conversion of process() without parameters
            System.out.println(answer2);
        }
    }
}
```

Your task is to convert the above program fragment using scoped values, fill them
with appropriate values, and implement their propagation in the call chain from
`ScopedValuesExample` via `Controller` and `Service`. The information
should then be accessed in both classes without being passed as parameters in the
method calls.

✍ Exercise 6: Primitive Type Patterns, `instanceof`, and `switch` ✍

Before Java 23, apart from a few numeric literals, that is, fixed values such as 10, 20, or 30, it was impossible to use `switch` with primitive types—single `char`s were also allowed. However, `long` numbers were not.

Simplify the following source code utilizing primitive type patterns. Enable preview features to eliminate boxing and utilize pattern matching with conditions:

```java
void main()
{
    int value = 42;

    Integer boxedValue = value;
    switch (boxedValue)
    {
        case Integer i when i > 0 && i < 10 -> log(i + " is lower than 10");
        case Integer i when i >= 10 && i < 40 -> log(i + " is lower than 40");
        case Integer i when i >= 40 && i < 70 -> log(i + " is >= 40");
        case Integer i -> log("Some unexpected value is perfect: " + i);
    }
}

void log(final String str)
{
    System.out.println(str);
}
```

✍ Exercise 7: Experiments with the Vector API ✍

The Vector API allows performing SIMD calculations. In this exercise, it is your task to convert an implementation specified as a scalar calculation to one using the Vector API. Given is this implementation of the scalar calculation of the formula $a_i * b_i + a_i * b_i - (a_i + b_i)$:

```java
public float[] scalarComputation(float[] a, float[] b)
{
    float[] c = new float[a.length];

    for (int i = 0; i < a.length; i++)
    {
        c[i] = a[i] * b[i] + a[i] * b[i] - (a[i] + b[i]);
    }

    return c;
}
```

Modify the program fragment to utilize the appropriate calls from the Vector API. Experiment a little:

1. What happens if the loop is not correctly mapped to all iterations?
2. How can the formula be simplified? May a scalar multiplication, that is, using a fixed value, be beneficial?

________________ ✍ **Exercise 8: Flexible Constructor Bodies** ✍ ______________

Discover the elegance of the new syntax for constructors, which allows actions to be executed before calling `super()`. For the `Rectangle` class shown below, this new feature should be used to validate parameters before constructing the base class:

```java
public Rectangle(Color color, int x, int y, int width, int height)
{
    super(color, x, y);

    if (width < 1 || height < 1)
        throw new IllegalArgumentException("width and height " +
                                           "must be positive");

    this.width = width;
    this.height = height;
}
```

________________ ✍ **Exercise 9: Flexible Constructor Bodies** ✍ ______________

In this exercise, the parameter of the subclass `StringMsgOld` has a different type than that of the base class. This is where the trick with the helper method for argument checking and conversion comes into play:

```java
public StringMsgOld(final String payload)
{
    super(convertToByteArray(payload));
}
```

In addition, we assume that complex actions are still performed in the helper method—here only indicated as an example by `switch` and the method call of `heavyStringTransformation()`.

The task now is to convert the whole thing to the new syntax in a more readable way—what are the other advantages of the modern variant?

```java
private static byte[] convertToByteArray(final String payload)
{
    if (payload == null)
        throw new IllegalArgumentException("payload should not be null");

    var transformedPayload = heavyStringTransformation(payload);
    return switch (transformedPayload)
    {
        case "AA" -> new byte[]{1, 2, 3, 4};
        case "BBBB" -> new byte[]{7, 2, 7, 1};
        default -> transformedPayload.getBytes();
    };
}

private static String heavyStringTransformation(String input)
{
    return input.repeat(2);
}
```

_______________________✍ **Exercise 10: Module Imports** ✍_______________________

Imagine a program with several import statements for various types from the JDK, as follows:

```java
import javax.swing.*;
import java.awt.*;
import java.io.*;
import java.time.LocalDate;
import java.util.List;
import java.util.Map;
import java.util.function.Function;
import java.util.stream.Collectors;
import java.util.stream.Stream;
```

Simplify these individual imports by using appropriate module imports and consider and handle potential ambiguities.

_______✍ **Exercise 11: Special Features of Structured Concurrency** ✍_______

In addition to the joiner `awaitAllSuccessfulOrThrow()`, which stops all other calculations when an error occurs, structured concurrency also offers the joiner `anySuccessfulResultOrThrow()`. This allows multiple calculations to be started, and once one has delivered a result, all other subtasks can be stopped. How can this be useful? Let's imagine various search queries where the fastest one should win.

The task is modeled as establishing a connection to the mobile network in the variants 5G, 4G, 3G, and WiFi. Fill the following program snippet with life:

```java
record NetworkConnection(String type)
{}

void main() throws InterruptedException
{
    var joiner = StructuredTaskScope.Joiner.<NetworkConnection>
                                    anySuccessfulResultOrThrow();
    try (var scope = StructuredTaskScope.open(joiner))
    {
        // TODO
        StructuredTaskScope.Subtask<NetworkConnection> result1 = null;
        StructuredTaskScope.Subtask<NetworkConnection> result2 = null;
        StructuredTaskScope.Subtask<NetworkConnection> result3 = null;
        StructuredTaskScope.Subtask<NetworkConnection> result4 = null;

        NetworkConnection result = null;                 // TODO

        System.out.println("Wifi " + result1.state() +
                        "/5G " + result2.state() +
                        "/4G " + result3.state() +
                        "/3G " + result4.state());
        System.out.println("found connection: " + result);
    }
}
```

The following helper methods are also given:

```
private static NetworkConnection tryToGet3g() throws InterruptedException
{
    sleepRandomlyUpToOneSec();
    return new NetworkConnection("3G");
}

// ...

private static void sleepRandomlyUpToOneSec() throws InterruptedException
{
    Thread.sleep((long) (1000 * Math.random()));
}
```

12.2 Solutions

✍ Solution 1: Markdown Comments ✍

For example, if you want to create a shopping list with Markdown that contains
different sections for the supermarket and hardware store, you can do so as follows:

```
/// # Shopping list
///
/// ## Supermarket
/// - Bread
/// - **Milk**
/// - Eggs
/// - Fruits:
///    - Strawberries
///    - Bananas
///
/// - Vegetables:
/// - ***Tomatoes***
/// - **Organic cucumber**
/// - Bell peppers
/// -
/// ## Hardware store
/// - **Shower curtain**
/// - Paintbrush
public static void shoppingList()
{}
```

✍ Solution 2: Standard Stream Gatherers ✍

In this exercise, you should use predefined gatherers from the class `Gatherers` to multiply all elements and subdivide them into lists of length three. To do this, use the two gatherers `fold()` and `windowFixed()` as follows:

```java
void main()
{
    var crossMult = Stream.of(1, 2, 3, 4, 5, 6, 7).
                          gather(fold(() -> 1L,
                                      (result, number) -> result * number)).
                          findFirst();
    System.out.println("crossMult: " + crossMult);

    var values = Stream.of(1, 2, 3, 10, 20, 30, 100, 200, 300);
    List<List<Integer>> result = values.gather(windowFixed(3)).toList();
    System.out.println("windowFixed(): " + result);
}
```

For simplicity, both are imported statically:

```java
import static java.util.stream.Gatherers.fold;
import static java.util.stream.Gatherers.windowFixed;
```

The result is this output:

```
crossMult: Optional[5040]
windowFixed(): [[1, 2, 3], [10, 20, 30], [100, 200, 300]]
```

✍ Solution 3: Gatherer to Process Information ✍

(a) Coordinate Information The stream given below, with individual values for x, y, and z, is to be converted into corresponding 3D coordinates. This record is used for modeling:

```java
record Point3D(int x, int y, int z) {}
```

The predefined data must now be subdivided into sections of three values. This is the task of `windowFixed(3)`, which returns a list of three values. Using `map()` and a constructor call, these three values built up a `Point3D` object. For this purpose, the coordinates are determined by index access and passed to the constructor:

```java
void main()
{
    var coordinates = Stream.of(0, 0, 0, 10, 20, 30, 100, 200, 300,
                                1000, 2000, 3000).
                           gather(Gatherers.windowFixed(3)).
                           map(window -> new Point3D(window.get(0),
                                                     window.get(1),
                                                     window.get(2))).
                           toList();

    System.out.println("coordinates: " + coordinates);
}
```

As expected, the result is a list of points consisting of three coordinate values:

```
coordinates: [Point3D[x=0, y=0, z=0], Point3D[x=10, y=20, z=30], Point3D[x
    =100, y=200, z=300], Point3D[x=1000, y=2000, z=3000]]
```

(b) Temperature Jumps Based on a time series with temperature data, the adjacent temperature values that show variations of 20 degrees or more should be found. Because this requires a pairwise comparison of values, `windowSliding(2)` is helpful in this context. To identify the relevant temperature fluctuations, we implement a helper method `isRelevantTempDiff()` based on the list of two values provided by `windowSliding(2)` as follows:

```java
static boolean isRelevantTempDiff(List<Integer> window, int threshold)
{
    return Math.abs(window.get(0) - window.get(1)) >= threshold;
}
```

After using `windowSliding(2)` to divide the stream of values into two-element lists, we now use the previously created detection method in a call to `filter()` to determine the relevant temperature jumps:

```java
void main()
{
    var temps = Stream.of(10, -7, 20, 0, 12, 17, 20, 40, 10, 20, -2).
                      gather(Gatherers.windowSliding(2)).
                      filter(window -> isRelevantTempDiff(window, 20)).
                      toList();

    System.out.println("temp jumps: " + temps);
}
```

The expected result is determined for the specified sample data:

```
temp jumps: [[-7, 20], [20, 0], [20, 40], [40, 10], [20, -2]]
```

______ ✍ **Solution 4: `DistinctBy` Gatherer, Removing Duplicates** ✍______
A gatherer `distinctBy()` should be implemented to remove duplicates based on a specific criterion. For this purpose, the methods of the `Gatherer` interface must be implemented appropriately. Additionally, state management is required:

```java
static <TR, R> Gatherer<TR, ?, List<TR>> distinctBy(Function<? super TR, ?
    extends R> selector)
{
    class State
    {
        List<R> uniqueMappedValues = new ArrayList<R>();
        List<TR> uniqueValues = new ArrayList<TR>();
    }

    return Gatherer.ofSequential(
            State::new,

            Gatherer.Integrator.of((state, value, downstream) ->
            {
```

```
                     var mappedValue = selector.apply(value);

                     if (!state.uniqueMappedValues.contains(mappedValue))
                     {
                          state.uniqueMappedValues.add(mappedValue);
                          state.uniqueValues.add(value);
                     }
                     return true;
               }),

               (state, downstream) -> {
                   // Passing the different values
                   for (var value : state.uniqueValues) {
                       downstream.push(value);
                   }
               }
            }
        );
}
```

This gatherer could be used as follows:

```
void main()
{
    var values = Stream.of(1, 2, 3, 4, 5, 1, 2, 3, 4, 5, 1, 2, 3, 4, 5);
    System.out.println("distinctBy(n -> n): " +
                       values.gather(distinctBy(n -> n)).
                              toList());

    var names = Stream.of("Maik", "Mike", "Jim", "Tim", "Tom", "Jim",
                          "Jim", "John", "Sophie", "Joelle", "Stefan",
                          "Anne", "Lili", "Michael", "Andreas");
    System.out.println("distinctBy(String::length): " +
                       names.gather(distinctBy(String::length)).
                              toList());
}
```

The result is the following output:

```
distinctBy(n -> n): [1, 2, 3, 4, 5]
distinctBy(String::length): [Maik, Jim, Sophie, Michael]
```

✍ Solution 5: Scoped Values As an Alternative to `ThreadLocal` ✍

The goal of this exercise was to convert a program's information forwarding, which
was traditionally implemented by parameter passing, to scoped values. Instead of
direct method calls, these are now called in `run()` or `call()`. Beforehand, one
or more calls to `where()` are used to define the required value assignment or
parameterization of the scoped values for which the actions then take place:

```
void main()
{
    // Simulate requests
    for (String name : List.of("ATTACKER", "ADMIN"))
    {
        var user = new User(name, name.toLowerCase());
        ScopedValue.where(LOGGED_IN_USER, user).
                where(REQUEST_TIME, ZonedDateTime.now()).
                run(controller::consumingMethod);

        // just user no time
        ScopedValue.where(LOGGED_IN_USER, user).
                run(controller::consumingMethod);

        String answer = ScopedValue.where(LOGGED_IN_USER, user).
                        where(REQUEST_TIME, ZonedDateTime.now()).
                        call(() -> controller.process());
        System.out.println(answer);

        String answer2 = ScopedValue.where(LOGGED_IN_USER, user).
                        call(() -> controller.process());
        System.out.println(answer2);
    }
}
```

✍ Solution 6: Primitive Type Patterns, `instanceof`, and `switch` ✍

With Java 25 LTS, you can use not only all primitive types in `switch`, but also,
in addition to older Java, numeric literals of type `long`, `float`, and `double` and
even literals of type `boolean`, as well as primitive type patterns, provided you
have enabled preview features. This eliminates the need for boxing, which was often
necessary in the past. This simplifies the query from the task as follows:

```
void main()
{
    int value = 42;

    switch (value)
    {
        case int i when i > 0 && i < 10 -> log(i + " is lower than 10");
        case int i when i >= 10 && i < 40 -> log(i + " is lower than 40");
        case int i when i >= 40 && i < 70 -> log(i + " is >= 40");
        case int i -> log("Some unexpected value is perfect: " + i);
    }
}
```

✍ Solution 7: Experiments with the Vector API ✍

The Vector API allows you to perform SIMD calculations. The scalar calculation
specified in the task for the formula $a_i * b_i + a_i * b_i - (a_i + b_i)$ can be implemented
using the Vector API as follows:

```
public float[] vectorComputation(float[] a, float[] b)
{
    VectorSpecies<Float> SPECIES = FloatVector.SPECIES_PREFERRED;
    float[] c = new float[a.length];

    int i = 0;
```

```
for (; i < SPECIES.loopBound(a.length); i += SPECIES.length())
{
    var va = FloatVector.fromArray(SPECIES, a, i);
    var vb = FloatVector.fromArray(SPECIES, b, i);

    var vc = va.mul(vb).add(va.mul(vb)).sub(va.add(vb));
    vc.intoArray(c, i);
}

for (; i < a.length; i++)
{
    c[i] = a[i] * b[i] + a[i] * b[i] - (a[i] + b[i]);
}

return c;
}
```

In fact, the formula can be simplified to $a_i * b_i * 2 - (a_i + b_i)$. This results in the following call to the Vector API:

```
var vc = va.mul(vb).mul(2).sub(va.add(vb));
```

Try this out using the following `main()` method:

```java
import jdk.incubator.vector.FloatVector;
import jdk.incubator.vector.VectorSpecies;

void main()
{
    float[] a = {1, 2, 3, 4, 5, 6, 7, 8, 9, 10, 11, 12, 13, 14, 15};
    float[] b = {2, 3, 4, 5, 6, 7, 8, 9, 10, 11, 12, 13, 14, 15, 16};

    float[] result1 = scalarComputation(a, b);
    System.out.println("result using scalar calculation: " +
                    Arrays.toString(result1));

    float[] result2 = vectorComputation(a, b);
    System.out.println("result using Vector API: " +
                    Arrays.toString(result2));
}
```

The result is the following output:

```
result using scalar calculation: [1.0, 7.0, 17.0, 31.0, 49.0, 71.0, 97.0,
        127.0, 161.0, 199.0, 241.0, 287.0, 337.0, 391.0, 449.0]
result using Vector API: [1.0, 7.0, 17.0, 31.0, 49.0, 71.0, 97.0, 127.0,
        161.0, 199.0, 241.0, 287.0, 337.0, 391.0, 449.0]
```

When starting the program, remember that you must include the appropriate incubator module and specify `--add-modules jdk.incubator.vector`. Otherwise, you will receive error messages like this:

```
Error: Unable to initialize main class ch10_api_java_22_25.jep508_vector_api.
        FirstVectorExample
Caused by: java.lang.NoClassDefFoundError: jdk/incubator/vector/Vector
```

✍ Solution 8: Flexible Constructor Bodies ✍

The syntax innovation of Flexible Constructor Bodies makes it possible to execute actions before calling `super()`. This allows you to move the argument check before the constructor call:

```java
public Rectangle(Color color, int x, int y, int width, int height)
{
    if (width < 1 || height < 1)
        throw new IllegalArgumentException("width and height must be positive
            ");

    super(color, x, y);

    this.width = width;
    this.height = height;
}
```

✍ Solution 9: Flexible Constructor Bodies ✍

The use of Flexible Constructor Bodies improves the readability and comprehensibility of the construct shown in the exercise. Neither the `null` check nor the processing call should be executed in the conversion method. However, this could not be avoided previously. Now, the `null` check can be called first in the constructor, followed by the processing and conversion. The final step is then the base class constructor call:

```java
public class StringMsgNew extends PlainByteMsg
{
    public StringMsgNew(final String payload)
    {
        Objects.requireNonNull(payload, "payload should not be null");

        final String doubledPayload = heavyStringTransformation(payload);
        final byte[] convertedPayload = convertToByteArray(doubledPayload);

        super(convertedPayload);
    }

    private static byte[] convertToByteArray(final String payload)
    {
        return switch (payload)
        {
            case "AA" -> new byte[]{1, 2, 3, 4};
            case "BBBB" -> new byte[]{7, 2, 7, 1};
            default -> payload.getBytes();
        };
    }

    private static String heavyStringTransformation(String input)
    {
        return input.repeat(2);
    }
}
```

After this refactoring work, everything is now in the right place and has the appropriate granularity in the form of methods that can be combined as needed. This also improves testability.

✍ Solution 10: Module Imports ✍

The following list with some individual import statements for various types from the JDK was given as an example:

```java
import javax.swing.*;
import java.awt.*;
import java.io.*;
import java.time.LocalDate;
import java.util.List;
import java.util.Map;
import java.util.function.Function;
import java.util.stream.Collectors;
import java.util.stream.Stream;
```

Instead of listing these imports individually, module imports simplify and clarify the process. The above imports originate from the modules `java.base` and `java.desktop`. The original list of imports can therefore be shortened and made more concise with two module imports. However, there is an ambiguity regarding the type `List`, which is why an explicit import is required to ensure clarity:

```java
import module java.base;
import module java.desktop;

// resolve ambiguity
import java.util.List;
```

✍ Solution 11: Special Features of Structured Concurrency ✍

This exercise involves using the joiner `anySuccessfulResultOrThrow()` once. It terminates the active subtasks if a substep has already been successful. The states of the individual calculation steps are accessible by invoking `state()`. Since the scope may contain only one result, it is provided by calling `join()`:

```java
void main() throws InterruptedException
{
    var joiner = Joiner.<NetworkConnection>anySuccessfulResultOrThrow();
    try (var scope = StructuredTaskScope.open(joiner))
    {
        var result1 = scope.fork(() -> tryToGetWifi());
        var result2 = scope.fork(() -> tryToGet5g());
        var result3 = scope.fork(() -> tryToGet4g());
        var result4 = scope.fork(() -> tryToGet3g());

        NetworkConnection result = scope.join();

        System.out.println("Wifi " + result1.state() +
                        "/5G " + result2.state() +
                        "/4G " + result3.state() +
                        "/3G " + result4.state());

        System.out.println("found connection: " + result);
    }
}
```

Part IV
Outlook and Summary

Chapter 13
Outlook: What's New in Java 26

This chapter provides an overview of the new features planned for Java 26. At the time of writing, in January 2026, Java 26 has entered the feature-freeze phase, meaning that no additional functionality is expected to be introduced and the existing features are considered finalized, subject only to stabilization and final adjustments. The official release of Java 26 is scheduled for mid-March 2026 and is expected to include a total of ten JEPs (JDK Enhancement Proposals). As is typical for a non-LTS release, the number of entirely new enhancements not based on earlier previews or incubator features is relatively small.

The new features of Java 26 are listed below; preview, incubator, and experimental features are marked in italics—they represent further iterations rather than brand-new introductions and are being refined and resubmitted for final review.

Each JEP is presented in its own section. In particular, those JEPs that provide the greatest practical benefit to software developers are discussed in greater detail. Less application-focused topics, such as JEP 504, JEP 516, and others, are covered more concisely in a dedicated summary section.

- JEP 500: Prepare to Make Final Mean Final
- JEP 504: Remove the Applet API
- JEP 516: Ahead-of-Time Object Caching with Any GC
- JEP 517: HTTP/3 for the HTTP Client API
- JEP 522: G1 GC: Improve Throughput by Reducing Synchronization
- *JEP 524: PEM Encodings of Cryptographic Objects (Second Preview)*
- *JEP 525: Structured Concurrency (Sixth Preview)*
- *JEP 526: Lazy Constants (Second Preview)*
- *JEP 529: Vector API (Eleventh Incubator)*
- *JEP 530: Primitive Types in Patterns, instanceof, and switch (Fourth Preview)*

M. Inden, *Java 25 and Beyond*, https://doi.org/10.1007/979-8-8688-2385-5_13

13.1   JEP 500: Prepare to Make Final Mean Final

As is well known, the keyword `final` prevents a variable from being reassigned. More precise: After the first value assignment, no further assignments via "=" are possible. For primitive types, this means a constant value. For reference types, however, `final` refers exclusively to the reference itself and not to the state of the referenced object.[1]

It is important to note that `final` was never intended to make objects immutable. `final` merely guarantees that a variable cannot be reassigned after its initial assignment; it makes no statement about the mutability of the object itself.

Let's return to the purpose of the keyword `final`. A glance at the JEP title shows that `final` has not been able to enforce this assignment guarantee in all cases so far. Reflection provides a mechanism for inspecting classes and their attributes at runtime and, in certain cases, for modifying them. Usually, even with reflection, attempts to change a variable marked as `final` fail at runtime. A special case is deep reflection, which has so far allowed this protection to be bypassed by calling `setAccessible(true)`. Even simple reflection violates information hiding and encapsulation, but deep reflection goes a step further.

While this behavior may be acceptable within our programs, it allows unrestricted access to all attributes from outside the project and is generally undesirable.

13.1.1   Introductory Example

To begin, let us define two simple data containers—one implemented as a class and the other as a record:

```java
public class DataContainer
{
    /* private */ final int fixedValue;    // any visibility

    public DataContainer(int fixedValue)
    {
        this.fixedValue = fixedValue;
    }

    public int fixedValue()
    {
        return fixedValue;
    }
}

record RecordDataContainer(int fixedValue) {}
```

---

[1] If reference variables refer to a mutable data structure, such as an `ArrayList<E>`, the content, more precisely, the elements, is modifiable—often unexpectedly.

We now want to use deep reflection to access the internal components of both types. For this purpose, we define a method for each type, shown here only for the class as an example; the variant for records works in the same way:

```
static void accessAndChangeValue(Class<?> clazz) throws
                                        NoSuchFieldException,
                                        IllegalAccessException
{
    DataContainer obj = new DataContainer(13);
    IO.println("DataContainer ctor: " + obj.fixedValue());  // Prints 13

    // Make final field mutable
    java.lang.reflect.Field field = clazz.getDeclaredField("fixedValue");
    field.setAccessible(true);

    // Mutate the final field in the object
    field.set(obj, 666);
    IO.println("after set(): " + obj.fixedValue());  // Prints 666

    // Mutate the final field in the object
    field.set(obj, 1313);
    IO.println("after 2nd set(): " + obj.fixedValue());  // Prints 1313
}
```

We implement the following `main()` method for trying out the above modifications using reflection:

```
void main() throws NoSuchFieldException, IllegalAccessException
{
    accessAndChangeValue(DataContainer.class);
    accessAndChangeRecord(RecordDataContainer.class);
}
```

The output of the lines above modifying the class is as follows—please pay attention to the warning messages:

```
DataContainer ctor: 13
after set(): 666
after 2nd set(): 1313
WARNING: Final field fixedValue in class reallyfinal.DataContainer has been
    mutated reflectively by class reallyfinal.ReallyFinalExample in unnamed
    module @72ea2f77 (file:/Users/michaelinden/IdeaProjects/Java26Examples
    /target/classes/)
WARNING: Use --enable-final-field-mutation=ALL-UNNAMED to avoid a warning
WARNING: Mutating final fields will be blocked in a future release unless
    final field mutation is enabled
```

Attempting to modify a record initialized with the value 777 using reflection results in an initial output of the passed value and afterward an exception as follows:

```
Record ctor: 777
Exception in thread "main" java.lang.IllegalAccessException: Can not set
    final int field reallyfinal.RecordDataContainer.fixedValue to java.lang
    .Integer
    at java.base/jdk.internal.reflect.FieldAccessorImpl.
        throwFinalFieldIllegalAccessException(FieldAccessorImpl.java:132)
    at java.base/jdk.internal.reflect.FieldAccessorImpl.
        throwFinalFieldIllegalAccessException(FieldAccessorImpl.java:136)
    at java.base/jdk.internal.reflect.MethodHandleIntegerFieldAccessorImpl.
        set(MethodHandleIntegerFieldAccessorImpl.java:107)
```

```
at java.base/java.lang.reflect.Field.lambda$set$0(Field.java:909)
at java.base/java.lang.reflect.Field.setFinal(Field.java:1452)
at java.base/java.lang.reflect.Field.set(Field.java:909)
at reallyfinal.ReallyFinalExample.accessAndChangeRecord(
    ReallyFinalExample.java:43)
at reallyfinal.ReallyFinalExample.main(ReallyFinalExample.java:9)
```

This example illustrates that, while final fields in regular classes can still be mutated via deep reflection—albeit with warnings—records strictly enforce their immutability and reject such modifications outright. This behavior reflects the direction planned for the future of classes as well, where reflective mutation of final fields is expected to be increasingly restricted to provide stronger guarantees of data integrity. Let us now explore how Java 26 advances in this direction.

13.1.2 New Features in Java 26

While the actions shown above—using deep reflection to modify classes—could be performed without issues in Java 25 LTS, the situation changes with Java 26. It introduces stricter checks to prevent unintended or unsafe modifications. As a result of JEP 500, the following warning messages are now emitted in this example:

```
WARNING: Final field fixedValue in class reallyfinal.DataContainer has been
    mutated reflectively by class reallyfinal.ReallyFinalExample in unnamed
      module @5b2133b1 (file:/Users/michaelinden/IdeaProjects/Java26Examples
      /target/classes/)
WARNING: Use --enable-final-field-mutation=ALL-UNNAMED to avoid a warning
WARNING: Mutating final fields will be blocked in a future release unless
    final field mutation is enabled
```

The warning refers to a new JVM startup parameter, `--enable-final-field-mutation=<module-name>`, which can be used to permit deep reflection for specific modules and, if necessary, suppress these warnings.

In the long term, Java will further restrict deep reflection. Instead of issuing warnings, future releases will throw exceptions when illegal mutations of final fields are attempted. Currently, this behavior can already be controlled via the JVM option `--illegal-final-field-mutation=<level>`:

- `allow`: Behavior as in Java 25 LTS, that is, no warning messages for changes made by deep reflection.
- `warn`: Standard behavior in Java 26, where warning messages are issued for the first change made using deep reflection.
- `debug`: Tightening of the standard with warning messages for all changes made using deep reflection. The warning messages also log this stack trace:

```
Final field fixedValue in class reallyfinal.DataContainer has been mutated
    reflectively by class reallyfinal.ReallyFinalExample in unnamed
      module @77459877 (file:/Users/michaelinden/IdeaProjects/
      Java26Examples/target/classes/)
  at java.base/java.lang.reflect.Field.postSetFinal(Field.java:1534)
  at java.base/java.lang.reflect.Field.setFinal(Field.java:1449)
```

```
    at java.base/java.lang.reflect.Field.set(Field.java:909)
    at reallyfinal.ReallyFinalExample.accessAndChangeValue(
        ReallyFinalExample.java:21)
    at reallyfinal.ReallyFinalExample.main(ReallyFinalExample.java:7)


Final field fixedValue in class reallyfinal.DataContainer has been mutated
    reflectively by class reallyfinal.ReallyFinalExample in unnamed
    module @77459877 (file:/Users/michaelinden/IdeaProjects/
    Java26Examples/target/classes/)
    at java.base/java.lang.reflect.Field.postSetFinal(Field.java:1534)
    at java.base/java.lang.reflect.Field.setFinal(Field.java:1449)
    at java.base/java.lang.reflect.Field.set(Field.java:909)
    at reallyfinal.ReallyFinalExample.accessAndChangeValue(
        ReallyFinalExample.java:25)
    at reallyfinal.ReallyFinalExample.main(ReallyFinalExample.java:7)
```

- `deny`: Represents the final stage of development and prevents final attributes from being altered via deep reflection. Trying to do so results in the following exception:

```
Exception in thread "main" java.lang.IllegalAccessException: class
    reallyfinal.ReallyFinalExample (in unnamed module @5b2133b1) cannot
    set final field reallyfinal.DataContainer.fixedValue (in unnamed
    module @5b2133b1), unnamed module @5b2133b1 is not allowed to mutate
    final fields
    at java.base/java.lang.reflect.Field.preSetFinal(Field.java:1504)
    at java.base/java.lang.reflect.Field.setFinal(Field.java:1447)
    at java.base/java.lang.reflect.Field.set(Field.java:909)
    at reallyfinal.ReallyFinalExample.accessAndChangeValue(
        ReallyFinalExample.java:21)
    at reallyfinal.ReallyFinalExample.main(ReallyFinalExample.java:7)
```

If a modification is still required, the JVM option `--enable-final-field-mutation=<module-name>`, described above, must be specified accordingly.

Beyond providing greater control and reliability, preventing changes to `final` fields also has a performance benefit. The JVM can apply an optimization called constant folding, which improves runtime efficiency by inlining constant expressions.

13.2 JEP 517: HTTP/3 for the HTTP Client API

This JEP extends the `HttpClient` API to support HTTP/3, the modern version of HTTP introduced in 2022. The extension integrates seamlessly into the existing, well-structured design of the `HttpClient` API, as will become clear after a brief introduction.

13.2.1 Introduction to HTTP/2 API (Java 11 LTS)

HTTP (Hypertext Transfer Protocol) is the standard Internet protocol for transporting content, most notably web pages. Until 2015, the HTTP/1.1 standard adopted in 1997 was still widely used. Today, many websites rely on the newer HTTP/2. HTTP/2 is based on the binary SPDY protocol (SPDY stands for "speedy"), which was originally developed by Google. In contrast to the text-oriented transmission model of HTTP/1.1, the binary format of HTTP/2 enables significant performance improvements while still preserving backward compatibility with HTTP/1.1.

Since Java 11 LTS, HTTP/2 support has been available in the JDK via the `java.net.http.*` package. The programming model is centered around well-defined HTTP communication components, such as requests and responses. This clear terminology makes the API both intuitive and easy to use.

Introductory Example with the HTTP/2 API

Accessing the Java 26 website and retrieving its content as a string can be implemented in a concise and readable way using the HTTP/2 API, as shown in the following example:

```java
static void readJava26WithHttpJdk11Api() throws IOException,
                                        InterruptedException
{
    try (var httpClient = HttpClient.newHttpClient
    {
        var uri = URI.create("https://jdk.java.net/26/");
        var request = HttpRequest.newBuilder().uri(uri).GET().build();

        var asString = HttpResponse.BodyHandlers.ofString();
        var response = httpClient.send(request, asString);

        printResponseInfo(response);
    }
}

private static void printResponseInfo(HttpResponse<String> response)
{
    IO.println("Status:  " + response.statusCode());
    IO.println("Body:    " + response.body().substring(0, 1000));
    IO.println("Headers: " + response.headers().map());
}
```

A `java.net.http.HttpRequest` is created using methods such as `newBuilder(URI)`, along with `GET()` or `POST()`. To process the response data, an instance of `java.net.http.HttpResponse.BodyHandler` is required. Some of these handlers are predefined and can be created using the factory methods of the inner class `java.net.http.HttpResponse.BodyHandlers`, such as `ofString()` for processing textual response data.

An instance of the class `java.net.http.HttpClient`, created via the factory method `newHttpClient()`, is the starting point for HTTP communication.

Since Java 21 LTS, `HttpClient` implements the `AutoCloseable` interface, making it possible to use try-with-resources to manage and release resources automatically.

The communication can then be started synchronously by calling `send()` — asynchronous processing is also possible.

The returned `java.net.http.HttpResponse` provides, in particular, the two methods `statusCode()` and `body()`. The first allows access to the HTTP status code, and the second allows reading the response content. In addition, the `headers()` method returns a `java.net.http.HttpHeaders` object that provides information about the header values of the response.

Alternative Data Formats As an alternative to the string-based representation used in the example above, a `BodyHandler` can also be created for other result formats. For this purpose, the methods `ofLines()`, `ofByteArray()`, `ofFile()`, and `ofFileDownload()` are available; each produces a result corresponding to the format implied by its name.

Downloading a Website As a File

We now use the `BodyHandler ofFile()`, mentioned above, to download the Java 26 website—which was previously retrieved as a string—and store it as a file named `java26-overview.html`:

```java
void main() throws IOException, InterruptedException
{
    var uri = URI.create("https://jdk.java.net/26/");
    var downloadPath = Path.of("java26-overview.html");

    downloadFile(uri, downloadPath);
}

static void downloadFile(URI uri, Path downloadPath)
        throws IOException, InterruptedException
{
    try (var httpClient = HttpClient.newHttpClient())
    {
        var request = HttpRequest.newBuilder(uri).GET().build();

        var asFile = HttpResponse.BodyHandlers.ofFile(downloadPath);
        var response = httpClient.send(request, asFile);

        if (response.statusCode() == 200)
        {
            IO.println("Content written to file: " +
                    downloadPath.toAbsolutePath());
        }
        else
            IO.println("Download unsuccessful: " + response.statusCode());
    }
}
```

Listing 13-1 Executable as "**HTTP2DOWNLOADEXAMPLE**"

13.2.2   New Features in Java 26

Java 26 adds support for HTTP/3, the latest version of HTTP. To use this version, the preferred protocol must be explicitly specified in the request, as HTTP/2 remains the default:

```
var request = HttpRequest.newBuilder(uri).
                          version(HttpClient.Version.HTTP_3).
                          GET().
                          build();
```

This configuration attempts to use HTTP/3 for the given request. If the target server does not yet support HTTP/3, the client automatically falls back to HTTP/2.

Alternatively, HTTP/3 can be enabled globally for all requests by configuring the HTTP client accordingly:

```
var httpClient = HttpClient.newBuilder()
                           .version(HttpClient.Version.HTTP_3)
                           .build();
```

With HTTP/3 support, Java 26 enables applications to benefit from reduced latency, improved multiplexing without head-of-line blocking, and more resilient connections—especially on mobile or unreliable networks. Thanks to automatic fallback to HTTP/2, these advantages can be adopted incrementally without sacrificing compatibility or robustness. For more details, please refer to the corresponding JEP 517 (https://openjdk.org/jeps/517).

13.3   JEP 525: Structured Concurrency (Sixth Preview)

Let us briefly recap the key points discussed in detail in Sect. 10.6. Structured concurrency greatly simplifies multithreaded programming by allowing tasks to be cleanly decomposed into subtasks, executed in parallel, and their results merged in a well-defined manner. It also makes it straightforward to cancel subtasks—for example, when their results are no longer required—and to propagate errors in a controlled way. We looked at examples such as the following:

```
static Response handleStructuredTaskScope(long userId)
    throws InterruptedException
{
    // waits for all subtasks to complete successfully or propagates errors
    // var joiner = StructuredTaskScope.Joiner.awaitAllSuccessfulOrThrow();
    try (var scope = StructuredTaskScope.open())
    {
        Subtask<String> userSubtask  = scope.fork(() -> findUser(userId));
        Subtask<Integer> orderSubtask = scope.fork(() -> fetchOrder(userId));

        scope.join(); // Merge both actions
```

```
        // Both branches were successful here; merge results
        return new Response(userSubtask.get(), orderSubtask.get());
    }
}
```

13.3.1   New Features in Java 26

As part of this JEP, several enhancements and adjustments have been introduced. If you have already experimented with structured concurrency, most of these changes require only minor modifications to existing source code. Together, they simplify everyday usage and provide greater flexibility.

The most important changes are outlined below:

- The joiner `allSuccessfulOrThrow()` no longer returns a stream of `Subtasks`. Instead, it now returns a list containing the results of the subtasks directly, which significantly simplifies result handling. The following example illustrates this change; the previously required stream-based variant is now reduced to a single line of code:

```
// Similar results => allSuccessfulOrThrow()
var allSuccessful = StructuredTaskScope.Joiner.allSuccessfulOrThrow();
try (var scope = StructuredTaskScope.open(allSuccessful))
{
    scope.fork(() -> fetchProposal1());   // String
    scope.fork(() -> fetchProposal2());   // String

    // var results = scope.join(). // Stream<Subtask<String>>
    //                     map(Subtask::get).
    //                     toList();
    var results = scope.join(); // List<String>
    IO.println("Results: " + results);
}
```

- The joiner `anySuccessfulResultOrThrow()` has been renamed to `anySuccessfulOrThrow()` for consistency with the naming of other joiners.
- The `Joiner` interface now includes an `onTimeout()` method, which by default throws a `TimeoutException` when a timeout occurs. The method has a `void` return type and is intended to be overridden in custom `Joiner` implementations. This allows applications to react to timeouts—for example, by discarding any results collected so far and supplying a default value instead. As an illustration, the following example demonstrates a `Joiner` that collects all successful results; if a timeout occurs, these results are discarded and the underlying data structure is populated with a default value.

Two aspects should be considered when implementing this behavior:

1. The method `onComplete()` can be called by multiple threads in parallel. Your own implementations of a `Joiner` must therefore be thread-safe. For this reason, a `ConcurrentLinkedQueue<E>` is recommended, as it is

designed for concurrency and allows results to be collected in a thread-safe manner.

2. The `result()` method of the standard implementations of the predefined joiners always returns immutable results lists. You should also base your own implementations on this behavior to avoid unintended side effects.

With these two points in mind, we implement our own joiner as follows:

```java
static class AllSuccessfulOrDefaultOnTimeout<T>
       implements StructuredTaskScope.Joiner<T, List<T>>
{
    private final Queue<T> allSuccessfulResults =
                            new ConcurrentLinkedQueue<>();
    private final T defaultValue;

    public JustSuccessfulWithTimeoutDefault(T defaultValue)
    {
        this.defaultValue = defaultValue;
    }

    @Override
    public boolean onComplete(StructuredTaskScope.Subtask<T> subtask)
    {
        if (subtask.state() == StructuredTaskScope.Subtask.State.SUCCESS)
        {
            // If subtasks may return null values, this must be handled
            // explicitly, as ConcurrentLinkedQueue does not permit
            // null elements and will throw a NullPointerException
            // when attempting to add them.
            allSuccessfulResults.add(subtask.get());
        }
        return false; // do not cancel
    }

    @Override
    public void onTimeout()
    {
        allSuccessfulResults.clear();
        allSuccessfulResults.add(defaultValue);
    }

    @Override
    public List<T> result()
    {
        return List.copyOf(allSuccessfulResults);
    }
}
```

- Since Java 25 LTS, the signature of the method `onComplete(Structured-TaskScope.Subtask<T> subtask)` no longer has a wildcard parameter. This simplifies the implementation of custom joiners.
- The static method `open()`, which accepts a `Joiner` and a way to change the default configuration, now uses a `UnaryOperator` instead of a `Function`.

Note

Structured concurrency was first introduced as a preview feature in Java 21 LTS. Subsequent releases made incremental refinements, followed by a more substantial API revision in Java 25 LTS. Java 26 continues this evolution with additional improvements.

As structured concurrency represents a major step toward simplifying multi-threaded programming, it is highly desirable for the feature to reach final status in the near future.

13.4   JEP 526: Lazy Constants (Second Preview)

This JEP continues and refines the preview feature originally introduced as *Stable Values*. It provides an API for initializing values exactly once—at the latest when they are first needed—and then keeping them unchanged afterward (see Sect. 10.5).

The JVM may treat such special values as constants and apply corresponding optimizations; the new name "Lazy Constants" reflects this capability more accurately. Lazy Constants offer greater flexibility than `final` fields, which must be initialized in a constructor or during static initialization.

Introduction: Typical Application Scenario

Let us revisit the typical application scenario previously introduced for Java 25 LTS. In the following example, we define several components that are used throughout the application. For the sake of simplicity, these components are intentionally grouped into a single class. In a real-world application—such as one based on Spring—controllers, services, and repositories would be distributed across multiple application classes rather than being centrally bundled:

```java
public class OldStyleApplication
{
    private final OrderController ORDER_CONTROLLER = new OrderController();
    private final ProductRepository PRODUCT_REPO = new ProductRepository();
    private final UserService USER_SERVICE = new UserService();

    public OrderController orderController()
    {
        return ORDER_CONTROLLER;
    }

    static void main()
    {
        var application = new OldStyleApplication();
        IO.println("Orders: " + application.orderController().orders());
    }

    // ...
}
```

Let's just briefly and exemplarily look at the implementation of the `OrderCon-troller`—both other components follow the same pattern, and `UserService` also simulates a heavier initialization by some time sleeping:

```java
public class OrderController
{
    public OrderController()
    {
        IO.println("OrderController constructed");
    }

    public List<String> orders()
    {
        return List.of("Order 1", "Order 2", "Order 3");
    }

    // ...
}
```

If we now execute the `main()` method of the `OldStyleApplication` class, we observe that all components are instantiated eagerly. As a result, they may execute actions during construction, which is reflected in the following console output:

```
OrderController constructed
ProductRepository constructed
UserService start construction
UserService constructed
Orders: [Order 1, Order 2, Order 3]
```

From a design perspective, this behavior is suboptimal. In general, component creation should be deferred until the component is actually needed. In this example, we pay the initialization cost of `ProductRepository` and `UserService` even though they are not yet required, resulting in unnecessary work.

Lazy initialization allows optional components to be initialized only on demand. However, lazy initialization introduces additional complexity and requires explicit checks, which can easily lead to subtle or careless mistakes.

13.4.1   New Features in Java 26

Java 26 tidies up and simplifies lazy constants, formerly known as stable values. Some rarely used, more technical methods have been removed to make the API clearer and easier to understand. Let's take a quick look at this.

Introduction: Lazy Constants API

Conveniently, lazy constants offer a simple and elegant way to perform lazy initialization, with an API built right into the JDK. This enables thread-safe, one-time lazy initialization. Better yet, the sometimes complicated calls of the Stable Values API introduced in Java 25 LTS (see Sect. 10.5) have been greatly simplified and are now much more natural and pleasant to use. Let's look at a modification of the above example using lazy constants:

```java
public class LazyConstantsApplication
{
    private final LazyConstant<OrderController> ORDER_CONTROLLER =
                LazyConstant.of(OrderController::new);

    private final LazyConstant<ProductRepository> PRODUCT_REPO =
                LazyConstant.of(ProductRepository::new);

    private final LazyConstant<UserService> USER_SERVICE =
                LazyConstant.of(UserService::new);

    public OrderController orders()
    {
        return ORDER_CONTROLLER.get();
    }

    public ProductRepository productRepository()
    {
        return PRODUCT_REPO.get();
    }

    public UserService userService()
    {
        return USER_SERVICE.get();
    }

    static void main()
    {
        var application = new LazyConstantsApplication();
        IO.println("Orders: " + application.orderController().orders());
    }
}
```

`LazyConstant.of()` creates a lazy constant that initially acts as a lightweight wrapper around the actual application component. The underlying objects—such as controllers, repositories, or services—are instantiated only when the `get()` method is invoked for the first time. The initialization logic provided to `of()` is executed exactly once, after which the computed value is permanently stored in the lazy constant. Thread safety is handled automatically by the API.

If we now execute the `main()` method of the above `LazyConstants-Application` class, we observe the benefits of introducing lazy constants: all components are instantiated lazily. As a result, only the needed `OrderController` gets initialized, which is reflected in the following console output:

```
OrderController constructed
Orders: [Order 1, Order 2, Order 3]
```

Hint: For practical use, it is important to note that lazy constants do not produce runtime overhead after initialization. Quite the opposite: The JVM optimizes repeated accesses, allowing lazy constants to behave much like regular constants during normal operation.

Lazy Lists und Lazy Maps

Sometimes, larger data sets also need to be initialized lazily. The method `List.ofLazy()` provides a way to pre-populate a lazy constant with, for example, a list of values. A fixed collection of 360 precalculated sine values, which is calculated when first accessed and remains unchanged thereafter, serves as an introductory example to illustrate the basic principle. As with individual lazy constants, initialization only takes place when first accessed—independently for each index position:

```
// 0..359 degrees -> sin(degree) (lazy per index, then stable)
static final List<Double> PRECALCULATED_SIN =
                    List.ofLazy(360,
                                  i -> Math.sin(Math.toRadians(i)));
```

In practice, lazy lists are preferred for storing values that are computationally intensive to calculate or for maintaining a pool of application components that are complex to construct. In addition to lazy lists, there are also lazy maps, in which individual map entries are initialized when they are first accessed.

Like lazy constants, lazy lists and lazy maps are thread-safe.

Recap of Changes in Java 26 The helper methods for creating lazy lists and lazy maps, as shown above, have been moved to where they most intuitively belong—directly into the `List<E>` and `Map<K,V>` interfaces. One could argue, however, that this design choice introduces awareness of lazy constants into these core interfaces, which may not be ideal from a purely architectural standpoint. That said, introducing a separate utility class as an alternative does not appear to be a clearly superior solution either.

It is also important to note that, for performance reasons, lazy constants, lazy lists, and lazy maps must not store `null` values. If an initialization or computation function returns `null`, a `NullPointerException` is thrown upon the first access to the lazy constant.

13.5   JEP 530: Primitive Types in Patterns, instanceof, and Switch (Fourth Preview)

Before examining the enhancements introduced in Java 26, let us briefly revisit primitive type patterns, which contribute to making Java a more complete and consistent programming language. Originally introduced in Java 23 as JEP 455 and later revised in Java 25 LTS as JEP 507 (see Sect. 9.3), this extension allows both type and value checks for primitive values to be expressed using `instanceof` and `switch`, whereas previously this was limited to reference types:

```
record LogLevel(int severity) {}

// ...

String msg = switch (logLevel.severity())
{
    case int severity when severity > 10 -> "high severity: " + severity;
    case int severity when severity >= 0 -> "normal";
    case int severity -> "Unexpected value: " + severity;
};
```

In this example, it is noteworthy that the pattern variable `severity` can be redefined and used in each `case` branch.

Type Checks

As we have already seen in Sect. 9.3.3, type checks must take into account not only pure value ranges but also other characteristics, such as values that cannot be represented precisely. To illustrate this, let us consider an example that checks which primitive types can be mapped based on a given `long` value:

```
static void checkMatchableTypes(long value)
{
    if (value instanceof byte b) IO.println("byte " + b);
    if (value instanceof short s) IO.println("short " + s);
    if (value instanceof int i) IO.println("int " + i);
    if (value instanceof long l) IO.println("long " + l);
    if (value instanceof float f) IO.println("float " + f);
    if (value instanceof double d) IO.println("double " + d);
}
```

Let us consider two examples. The value 7 fits within all primitive numeric types. By contrast, the value 22,222 cannot be represented as a `byte` or `short` due to their limited ranges.

A special case arises with the value `16_777_217`. One might assume it can be represented by `int`, `long`, `float`, and `double`. In reality, however, it cannot be represented exactly as a `float`—a nuance that is not apparent from a simple range check alone—please have a look at Sect. 9.3.3 to recap the specialities on numbers that cannot be represented exactly:

```
jshell> checkMatchableTypes(7)
byte 7
short 7
int 7
long 7
float 7.0
double 7.0

jshell> checkMatchableTypes(22222)
int 22222
long 22222
float 22222.0
double 22222.0
```

```
jshell> checkMatchableTypes(16_777_217)
int 16777217
long 16777217
double 1.6777217E7
```

If, instead, you want to check which primitive type corresponds exactly to a value, this can be expressed as follows:

```
static void checkTypeExact(long value)
{
    if (value instanceof byte b) System.out.println("byte " + b);
    else if (value instanceof short s) System.out.println("short " + s);
    else if (value instanceof int i) System.out.println("int " + i);
    else if (value instanceof long l) System.out.println("long " + l);
    else if (value instanceof float f) System.out.println("float " + f);
    else if (value instanceof double d) System.out.println("double " + d);
    else IO.println("No match");
}
```

Let's try it out:

```
jshell> checkTypeExact(7)
byte 7

jshell> checkTypeExact(22222)
short 22222

jshell> checkTypeExact(16_777_217)
int 16777217

jshell> checkTypeExact(22222222222222.22D)
double 2.222222222222222E13
```

13.5.1   New Features in Java 26

Let us now turn to Java 26 and recall that both the order of the `case` labels and their type patterns matter, as the so-called dominance check applies. What does this mean? If, for example, the order of `case int i` and `case short s` gets switched, the pattern `int i` dominates and shadows the `case short s`.

In this area, Java 26 introduces some further fine-tuning. For instance, the following source code compiles without errors in Java 25 LTS—although IntelliJ already flags potential issues or ambiguities:

```
void main()
{
    // case 1: float f dominates int constant
    int i1 = 1_000_000_000;
    switch (i1)
    {
        case float f -> IO.println("float " + f);
        case 16_777_216 -> IO.println("Special constant");
```

```
            default -> IO.println("Some default processing");
    }

    // case 2: int i dominates float f
    int someValue = 4711;
    switch (someValue)
    {
        case int i -> IO.println("int " + i);
        case float f -> IO.println("float " + f);
    }

    // case 3: short s dominates int constant f
    byte b = 42;
    switch (b)
    {
        case short s -> IO.println("short " + s);
        case 42 -> IO.println("The answer is 42!");
    }
}
```

With JEP 530, Java 26 further refines the dominance check. Firstly, it now correctly recognizes that a pattern such as `float f` dominates individual `int` constants, like `16_777_216`. Secondly, in the case of the pattern `float f`, the compiler detects that all possible `int` values are already covered by the previously declared pattern `int i`. Thirdly, similarly, for an individual numeric constant, the compiler recognizes that it is already handled by the earlier pattern `short s`.

As a result, the following error messages are produced:

```
$ javac --enable-preview --release 26 EnhancementDominanceCheck.java
EnhancementDominanceCheck.java:10: error: this case label is dominated by a
    preceding case label
            case 16_777_216 -> IO.println("Special constant");
                 ^
EnhancementDominanceCheck.java:17: error: this case label is dominated by a
    preceding case label
            case float f -> IO.println("float " + f);
                 ^
EnhancementDominanceCheck.java:23: error: this case label is dominated by a
    preceding case label
            case 42 -> IO.println("The answer is 42!");
                 ^
Note: EnhancementDominanceCheck.java uses preview features of Java SE 26.
Note: Recompile with -Xlint:preview for details.
3 errors
```

Note Pattern matching for primitive types was introduced as a preview feature in Java 23. Since no substantial changes have been made in subsequent releases, it is reasonable to assume that—following this latest clarification of the dominance check—the feature will be finalized in one of the upcoming Java versions.

13.6 Miscellaneous

In this section, I describe some minor innovations that were developed as part of JEPs. I also discuss a few deprecations and deletions.

JEP 504: Remove the Applet API

Applets have not been relevant in real-world use for years and are no longer supported by any modern web browser. Consequently, with Java 17 LTS, the Applet API was marked as deprecated for removal, after already being marked as deprecated in Java 9.

With Java 26, the Applet API, specifically the package `java.applet` and the class `javax.swing.JApplet`, will finally be removed from the JDK.

JEP 516: Ahead-of-Time Object Caching with Any GC

Ahead-of-time caching was introduced with Java 24 and speeds up application startup by preloading frequently used classes and storing them in a file. The next time Java starts, it can then scan this data. This can significantly reduce startup time (according to https://openjdk.org/jeps/516 in some cases by over 40 %). However, there is currently one (minor) limitation: the cache only works if the application is started with exactly the same garbage collector and VM settings as when the cache was created. Different settings render the cache unusable.

Java 26 introduces more flexibility to the ahead-of-time cache and addresses this limitation: the cache can now be created so that it works independently of the garbage collector used. Instead of transferring (mapping) the objects 1:1 to memory, they are gradually converted to a suitable format during loading and transferred to the heap. This allows the same cache to be reused in many more situations—even if GC settings or heap size differs.

This internal change allows for greater flexibility and fewer pitfalls, and you continue to benefit from shorter startup times—without having to change your own source code.

JEP 522: G1 GC: Improve Throughput by Reducing Synchronization

In Java 26, the G1 garbage collector has been further optimized to achieve higher throughput by significantly reducing synchronization overhead. Previously, G1 was required to synchronize certain internal data structures—known as card tables— between the application threads and the GC threads, an operation that incurred notable computational cost.

With Java 26, G1 employs a dual-card-table approach. While the application writes to one card table, the garbage collector can process the other independently. Once processing is complete, the two tables are swapped. This design removes much of the synchronization previously required and is conceptually similar to buffering techniques such as page flipping in graphics rendering.

In practice, this optimization typically improves throughput by approximately 5– 15 %. The change is entirely transparent to applications and does not require any source code modifications. The only trade-off is a minimal increase in memory usage to accommodate the additional card table.

Since the size of the card tables is proportional to the heap size, the additional overhead depends on the JVM configuration. In practice, however, this overhead is very small—typically only a few thousandths of the heap—and can therefore be considered negligible. JEP 522[2] states the following on this matter: "The second card table has the same capacity as the first, and uses the same amount of additional native memory. Each card table requires 0.2 % of Java heap capacity, corresponding to an additional 2 MB of native memory usage per 1 GB of Java heap capacity."

JEP 524: PEM Encodings of Cryptographic Objects (Second Preview)
PEM stands for Privacy-Enhanced Mail and refers to a format for storing cryptographic objects. For most developers, this topic is unlikely to be part of their everyday work, so here is just a brief, simplified explanation. If you want to delve deeper, you can find details at https://openjdk.org/jeps/524.

In the past, reading or writing PEM-encoded data in Java was quite cumbersome, often requiring many lines of source code. With Java 25 LTS, a new PEM API was introduced as a preview, significantly simplifying this work to just a few lines.

In Java 26, the basic principle remains unchanged. The API has been refined in only a few places: minor renamings and a few additional functionalities—overall, a sensible further development.

JEP 529: Vector API (Eleventh Incubator)
As already mentioned in Sect. 10.8, the Vector API enables platform-independent support for so-called vector calculations. Modern processors can, for example, perform addition or multiplication not only on two values, but on many values simultaneously (i. e., as a single operation). This execution model is also referred to as Single Instruction Multiple Data (SIMD).

Provided that appropriate hardware support is available, such calculations can be performed with high performance, since significantly fewer than n operations are required to process n values. The exact number depends on the vector width m, that is, the number of values that can be processed simultaneously, resulting in approximately n/m operations. In practice, m is typically between 8 and 32, while n is usually much larger.

Since this JEP does not introduce any substantial changes from previous versions of the Vector API, I would like to briefly discuss its further development.

This functionality is still provided as an incubator feature. Consequently, some patience is required before it progresses to preview status and eventually becomes a final feature. Further development of the Vector API depends on the availability of value classes—as an essential component of Project Valhalla—at least in preview form. This is because the Vector API classes are intended to be implemented from the outset as value classes, that is, as new types without their own object identity, providing a particularly lightweight and efficient data container.

---

[2] https://openjdk.org/jeps/522.

13.7   Modifications Without JEPs

Below, I describe a few minor innovations that were developed without JEPs. I also discuss one removal.

Support for Unicode 17

Java 26 supports Unicode 17, enabling classes such as `String` and `Character` to handle the characters introduced in this latest Unicode version. This enhancement improves internationalization (i18n) support, allowing Java applications to correctly process a wider range of global symbols. The change was implemented without a dedicated JEP and is documented solely as entry JDK-8346944 in the bug tracker (https://bugs.openjdk.org/browse/JDK-8346944).

Dark Theme for JavaDoc Documentation

Since Java 26, JavaDoc documentation can also be displayed in dark mode. There is a sun or moon icon at the top, as shown in Fig. 13.1.

Virtual Thread Unmounting During Initialization

Virtual threads, introduced in Java 21 LTS, enable high scalability by allowing many virtual threads to share a small number of platform (carrier) threads, making them well suited for I/O-bound or blocking workloads.

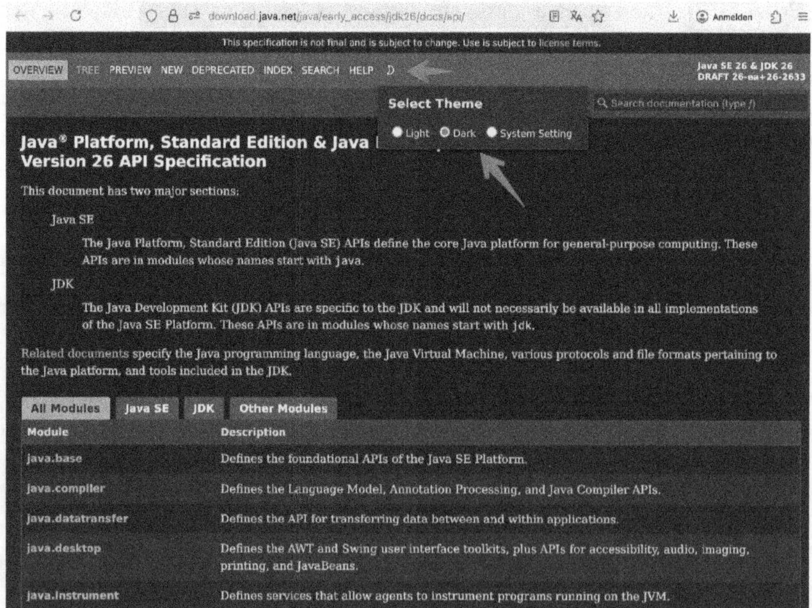

Fig. 13.1 JavaDoc documentation in dark mode

Until Java 24, a limitation existed: when `synchronized` was involved, a virtual thread could not be unmounted from its carrier thread during blocking operations. This was called pinning. JEP 491 solved this issue (see Sect. 11.5).

A related issue occurred when a virtual thread attempted to initialize a class that was already being initialized by another thread, causing it to block. This limitation was addressed in Java 26, as documented in JDK-8371412 (https://bugs.openjdk.org/browse/JDK-8371412).

Removal of `Thread.stop()`

The JDK originally provided the `stop()` method as a means of terminating threads. However, because its use can result in inconsistent program states, it has been deprecated since Java 1.2. With Java 18, it was further classified as *deprecated for removal*. To actively prevent continued use, invoking the method since Java 20 results in an `UnsupportedOperationException`.

The method was ultimately removed in Java 26. This change is not associated with a dedicated JEP; instead, it is documented solely through the bug tracker entry JDK-8368226 (https://bugs.openjdk.org/browse/JDK-8368226).

Adjusting the Default Heap Size

When starting a Java application, the minimum and maximum heap memory can be set using `-Xms` and `-Xmx`. If not specified, the JVM automatically allocates 1/64 of the physically available RAM. For a system with 48 GB, this amounts to roughly 750 MB—often more than necessary for lightweight or small-scale applications. This can also introduce additional overhead for garbage collection.

With Java 26, the default allocation has been reduced to 1/500. On a machine with 48 GB of RAM, this corresponds to just under 100 MB—adequate for many modest tasks.

This adjustment was implemented as part of JDK-8348278 (https://bugs.openjdk.org/browse/JDK-8348278).

13.8 Conclusion on the New Features in Java 26

From a developer's perspective, Java 26 does not introduce any groundbreaking innovations for everyday use. The implemented JEPs are helpful and welcome, but their impact on daily development work is limited. Under the hood, however, Java has improved significantly: it is now more stable, secure, modern, and performant—albeit without any significant "wow effect."

The finalization of structured concurrency and lazy constants would provide genuine momentum, and we eagerly await Java 27.

Chapter 14
Summary and Conclusion

So you've almost made it to the end of this book—congratulations! By now, you should have gained an overview of the many new features that have been added from Java 17 LTS to Java 25 LTS. The focus was particularly on useful syntax simplifications, practical extensions in the APIs, and improvements to the JVM. The examples and explanations presented should have given you a good impression of the further development of the language.

To deepen your understanding, I recommend working through the exercises and reviewing the sample solutions, and feel free to modify some of the tasks. Overall, there is a lot to discover—and the best way to learn is to experiment for yourself!

14.1 Thoughts on Migrating and Upgrading to Java 21 LTS or 25 LTS

Some companies are still relying on the ancient Java 8 LTS, released in 2014, even though Java 11 LTS, Java 17 LTS, Java 21 LTS, and, most recently, Java 25 LTS have been released. The reason for sticking with Java 8 LTS is explainable by the fact that, just as many companies were considering switching to Java 9, Oracle announced a biannual release strategy. In addition, many shied away from the complications introduced by the module system in Java 9. There were also other aspects, such as the expected effort, which was quite independent of the module system, of thoroughly rechecking the entire product after a Java version change to ensure that everything worked as before. Third-party libraries for which there was and is no support for Java 9+ also made the change more difficult. This also applies to removed APIs, in particular JAXB and JavaFX. Additionally, some customers refused to switch to a more modern Java version.

Uncertainty grew when Java 11 LTS introduced a new licensing policy, and Java (Oracle's JDK) has since been subject to a fee in production environments.

M. Inden, *Java 25 and Beyond*, https://doi.org/10.1007/979-8-8688-2385-5_14

Fortunately, this was corrected with Java 17 LTS, and this and later versions can now be used freely in production, but only until one year after the release of the next LTS release.

The biannual releases pose major challenges for both tool manufacturers and many companies, as they require a significant amount of effort to keep up with the new features. In product development, in particular, it is preferable to jump from LTS to LTS version, among other reasons, because these offer longer-term stability and the availability of security updates.

When switching, keep in mind that the included software and libraries may not have been updated to the latest LTS yet. Therefore, it's often a good idea to wait before switching to the newest version, so any possible initial problems have been resolved. However, it is not advisable to delay the switch for too long, as has happened at various companies in recent years. As mentioned at the beginning, there are indeed still projects based on Java 8 LTS—but many others have already switched to Java 11 LTS or Java 17 LTS. Keep in mind that Java 17 LTS is already several years old.

If a version change is imminent, it makes sense to switch directly to Java 25 LTS in the coming months. In addition to numerous technical improvements, you will also benefit from a noticeably better atmosphere in the development team.

If you are planning a new project, choose at least Java 21 LTS as your base; the latest Java 25 LTS would be even better. An intermediate step to Java 17 LTS, for example, would only incur additional costs—and dampen the enthusiasm of your developers, who will surely be eager to try out the latest language features after reading this book. :-D

14.2 Conclusion

Java 25 LTS combines the improvements from Java 21 LTS and Java 17 LTS, adding numerous practical innovations.

Syntax
The language enhancements include several notable changes—some as final features, some still as previews:

- **Unnamed Variables and Patterns:** Allow marking unused variables or record pattern parts with an underscore ("_").
- **Markdown Documentation Comments:** This feature is now officially available as a final feature.
- **Module Import Declarations:** Allow for clearer and tidier import sections at the beginning of a file.
- **Flexible Constructor Bodies:** Simplify initialization processes.
- **Primitive Types in Patterns (Preview):** Allow pattern matching for primitive types in `instanceof` and `switch`. It is still a preview feature.

Java 21 LTS also introduced `switch` expressions, pattern matching, and record patterns, which make complex queries significantly more compact and readable.

APIs

There are several highlights at the API level:

- **Stream Gatherers:** Facilitate user-defined intermediate operations in the Stream API.
- **Structured Concurrency:** Simplifies multithreading through clearly structured subtasks and flexible merging strategies. Unfortunately, this feature is still in preview state.
- **Scoped Values:** Make passing values in multithreading environments easier. Scoped Values provide an understandable alternative to the `ThreadLocal<T>` class.
- **Virtual Threads (Already Introduced in Java 21 LTS):** Simplify highly scalable server applications and ideally complement the feature Structured Concurrency.

JVM

Among other things, Launch Multi-File Source Code Programs has been implemented as a JVM improvement. It offers the possibility to execute multiple Java files directly without explicit prior compilation. In addition, Compact Source Files and Instance Main Methods make it easier to get started with Java. It allows smaller Java programs to be created much faster, with significantly fewer lines of code and without the terminology and concepts that are difficult for beginners, such as classes and visibilities.

Overall Assessment

The new Java versions are worthy successors that continue to make the language attractive for both beginners and experienced developers, as well as companies. Private users benefit particularly from the biannual releases, as almost every version offers new, useful features. The LTS cadence, which has been shortened to two years, is also likely to increase companies' willingness to update more frequently—supported by the fact that Oracle's JDK can once again be used free of charge in production, albeit only until one year after the release of the next LTS.

Looking ahead, Java 26 is currently in its feature-freeze phase and is scheduled for release in March 2026. Although it is not an LTS version, it introduces a number of refinements and enhancements that build on the improvements from Java 25 LTS. Among these are support for HTTP/3, Unicode 17, lazy constants and lazy collections, as well as further JVM optimizations. Exploring these upcoming features provides a preview of the platform's evolution and can help developers stay up to date with the latest capabilities of the Java ecosystem.

14.3   Final Notes

If you have read this book this far, then you have already taken an important step. In addition to learning about the many innovations in modern Java, you have also endured to the end, demonstrating curiosity and perseverance. These are qualities that distinguish good developers.

You may want to delve even deeper. In case you are familiar with German, my German book *Der Weg zum Java-Profi* [2] follows on from this book and introduces you to many exciting topics related to professional Java development. We were only able to touch on many of these topics in this book.

If you enjoyed the programming exercises, my book *Java Challenges* [3] offers a colorful mix of puzzles and tasks that are not only fun, but will also further hone your Java and programming skills.

No matter which path you choose, stay curious, try things out, and enjoy bringing your own ideas to life.

14.3.1   Personal Request

I have one personal request to conclude: If you enjoyed the book, please consider sharing your appraisal with others by recommending it to them. Of course, I would also appreciate a positive review on Amazon or another online retailer.

Feedback, suggestions for improvement, or requests for additions are always welcome. Please send them by email to `michael_inden@hotmail.com`.

There's only one thing left to say: I hope you enjoy modern Java and programming as a wonderful hobby and/or profession. With that in mind, happy coding!

Part V
Appendix

Chapter 15
Essentials from Java 8 LTS to 11 LTS

In this Appendix, we recapitulate essential extensions from Java 8 LTS up to Java 11 LTS, which should be present in the repertoire of any Java developer and which are especially crucial for understanding the innovations from the modern Java versions.

15.1   Getting Started with Lambdas

With lambda expressions (*lambdas* for short), JDK 8 introduced a language construct that many developers had eagerly awaited, which is already being used successfully in programming languages such as Groovy and Scala. Utilizing lambdas requires a different mindset to some extent and leads to a programming style that follows the paradigm of **functional programming**, which means that programs are composed of functions. These deliver an output based on inputs and a calculation, like in math $f(x) = x^2 + 7x - 2$. Lambdas help to express such functions.

A *lambda* is a container for source code similar to a method but without a name and without the explicit specification of a return type or thrown exceptions. A lambda has the following syntax allowing to express some solutions very elegantly:

```
(parameter list) -> { expression or instructions }
```

15.1.1   Lambdas by Example

A few simple examples of lambdas are the addition of two numbers of type `int`, the multiplication of a `long` value by a factor of 2, or a parameterless function to output a text to the console. These actions can be written using lambdas as follows:

M. Inden, *Java 25 and Beyond*, https://doi.org/10.1007/979-8-8688-2385-5_15

```
(int x, int y) -> { return x + y; }
(long x) -> { return x * 2; }
() -> { String msg = "Lambda"; System.out.println("Hello " + msg); }
```

This looks relatively unspectacular, and in particular, it becomes clear that a lambda is just a piece of executable source code that

- Does not have a name, but only functionality
- Thereby does not explicitly specify a return type
- And does not require or allow the declaration of exceptions

Lambdas in the Java Type System

We have seen so far that simple calculations can be expressed using lambdas. But how can we use and call them? First, let's assign a lambda to a `java.lang.Object` reference, just as it is possible with any other object in Java:

```
// Compile – Error :  incompatible types :  Object is not a functional interface
Object greeter = () -> { System.out.println("Hello Lambda"); };
```

The assignment shown is not supported and results in a compile error. The error message hints about incompatible types and points out that `Object` is not a functional interface. But what is a functional interface?

15.1.2   *Functional Interfaces and SAM Types*

A *functional interface* is a special kind of type. It represents an interface *with exactly one abstract method*, also called *SAM type*, where SAM stands for *Single Abstract Method*. This type of interface has been around for a long time—though it had no name before Java 8 LTS. Representatives of SAM types and functional interfaces are, for example, `Runnable`, `Callable<V>`, `Comparator<T>`, `File-Filter`, `FilenameFilter`, `ActionListener`, `EventHandler`, etc.:

```
@FunctionalInterface                    @FunctionalInterface
public interface Runnable               public interface Comparator<T>
{                                       {
    public abstract void run();             int compare(T o1, T o2);
}                                           boolean equals(Object obj);
                                        }
```

Looking at the `Comparator<T>` interface, the SAM characteristic does not appear to be present. Two methods are listed instead of one, and neither is marked with the keyword `abstract`: in fact, methods in interfaces without explicit marking are automatically `public` and `abstract`. Another special feature is that, in addition to the actual SAM method, methods from the `Object` class, such as `equals()`, may also be listed in a functional interface because they are always available in every class.

In addition, the listing shows the annotation `@FunctionalInterface` introduced with JDK 8 LTS from the package `java.lang`. This explicitly marks an interface as a functional interface. However, specifying the annotation is optional: any interface with exactly one abstract method (SAM type) is a functional interface even without explicit marking.

Implementing Functional Interfaces

An anonymous inner class can implement a SAM type or functional interface (even if they just existed conceptually in the past). Since JDK 8 LTS, however, lambdas are preferred for this purpose. The prerequisite for this is that the lambda expression can fulfill the abstract method of the functional interface, that is, that the number of parameters, their types, and the return type match. For clarification, let us first consider a general, somewhat abstract model for transforming previous realizations of a SAM type into a lambda expression using an anonymous inner class:

```
// SAM type as anonymous inner class
new SAMTypeAnonymousClass()
{
    public void samTypeMethod(METHOD-PARAMETERS)
    {
        METHOD-BODY
    }
}

// SAM type as lambda
(METHOD-PARAMETERS) -> { METHOD-BODY }
```

For short method implementations, which are common for SAM types, the ratio of payload code to boilerplate code (or noise) is quite poor. Using lambdas for such realizations allow to express with one line what would otherwise require five or more lines.

Example `Comparator<T>` The advantages of lambdas become obvious for the functional interface `java.util.Comparator<T>`. As a reminder: A comparison of two instances of the type `T` is expressed with a comparator. For this, the abstract method `int compare(T,T)` must be implemented appropriately and indicate the order of the values via its return value. If one wanted to sort two strings according to their length, conventionally, this would result in quite a lot of lines:

```
// Diamond operator is not possible for anonymous inner classes until JDK 9
Comparator<String> compareByLength = new Comparator<String>()
{
    @Override
    public int compare(String str1, String str2)
    {
        int length1 = str1.length();
        int length2 = str2.length();
```

```
        if (length1 < length2)
            return -1;
        if (length1 > length2)
            return 1;

        return 0;
    }
};
```

With JDK 7, class `Integer` has been extended by a method `compare(int, int)`, which possesses a comparator-compliant return value and thus significantly simplifies and shortens the implementation:

```
Comparator<String> compareByLength = new Comparator<String>()
{
    @Override
    public int compare(String str1, String str2)
    {
        return Integer.compare(str1.length(), str2.length());
    }
};
```

When using lambdas, the comparator can be crisply written as follows:

```
Comparator<String> compareByLength = (String str1, String str2) ->
{
    return Integer.compare(str1.length(), str2.length());
};
```

15.1.3   *Type Inference and Short Forms of Syntax*

The syntax of lambdas has some unique features to help formulating the source code compactly. In particular, the so-called *type inference* comes into play for lambdas: the compiler determines the appropriate types from the context of use. The previous comparator is written without type specification as follows:

```
Comparator<String> compareByLength = (str1, str2) ->
{
    return Integer.compare(str1.length(), str2.length());
};
```

The following rules can be used to further shorten the notation of a lambda:

1. If the piece of source code to be executed is an expression, the curly braces around the statements can be omitted.
2. In addition, the keyword `return` can then be omitted, and the return value corresponds to the result of the expression.
3. Furthermore, if only one input parameter exists, the braces around the parameter are optional.

This yields for the expressions

```
(int x, int y) -> { return x + y; }
(long x) -> { return x * 2; }
```

the following shorthand notations:

```
(x, y) -> x + y
x -> x * 2
```

Besides the apparent advantage of a compact notation, lambdas can be used more flexibly than strictly typed methods. For the calculations shown, it is possible to use them wherever the operator "+" or "*" is defined for the parameters, that is, for the types `int`, `float`, `double`, etc. In other words, ***anything that can be inferred may (and should) be omitted from the syntax***.

Effects on the Comparator Example   If we apply the above rules to the comparator, it can be written in an even more compact form. We use this in the following `main()` method:

```
public static void main(final String[] args)
{
    List<String> names = Arrays.asList("Peter", "Tim", "Andy", "Stefan");

    // Compact definition of the comparator (without brackets and return
    Comparator<String> compareByLength = (str1, str2) ->
                    Integer.compare(str1.length(), str2.length());

    names.sort(compareByLength); System.out.println(names);
}
```

Listing 15.1   Executable as "COMPARATORINTROEXAMPLE"

If we run the program COMPARATORINTROEXAMPLE, we get the following output, which clearly shows sorting by length:

```
[Tim, Andy, Peter, Stefan]
```

15.1.4   Method References

We have seen so far how lambdas can be used profitably. In addition, the use of method references introduced with JDK 8 LTS can help to increase the readability of the source code. The following syntax `class::methodname` is used and refers to

- **A Method**:[1] `System.out::println, Person::getName, ...`
- **A Constructor**: `ArrayList::new, Person[]::new, ...`

---

[1] Both instance methods and static methods are possible, such as `Integer::compare`.

This seems quite unspectacular. However, a method reference can be used instead of a lambda to simplify the notation:

```java
List<String> names = Arrays.asList("Max", "Andy", "Michael", "Stefan");

// Lambda
names.forEach(it -> System.out.println(it));

// method reference
names.forEach(System.out::println);
```

As you can see, the readability may improve. However, one should consider the following: Methods often receive parameters—as in the listing. Their values are passed automatically with the respective method call, but it's not that obvious when using method references.

Tips for Using Method References

In this section, we will briefly look at when to prefer method references and when it is better to use a lambda. I will illustrate the tips with an example and then provide a few rules of thumb.

When to Prefer Method References?

* A lambda only passes (one) parameter (`System.out::println`).
* For clear extractions/mappers (`Person::getName`).
* For static helper methods or comparators (`Integer::compare`).
* For constructor/array references (`ArrayList::new, Person[]::new`).
* If the method name clearly expresses the intention (`Objects::nonNull`).

When Are Method References Rather Disadvantageous and a Lambda Preferable?

* When additional logic is required (`str -> str.trim().toUpperCase()`)
* In case of ambiguity due to overloading or type ambiguities
* If arguments need to be fixed or reordered (`x -> foo(42, x)`)

Practical Examples   The above points can be illustrated with the following calls:

```java
// Good: clear mapper
var names = people.stream().map(Person::getName).toList();

// Good: comparator via method reference
people.sort(Comparator.comparing(Person::getLastName));

// Better use a lambda: additional logic
var ids = lines.stream().
                map(s -> s == null ? "n/a" : s.trim()).
                toList();

// Better use a lambda: additional argument when calling the method
buttons.forEach(btn -> enableComponent(btn, loggedInUser));
```

Rules of Thumb

- Use method references when they are shorter and clearer, and express exactly what a lambda would do.
- Switch to lambdas as soon as additional logic or actions are required.
- Prefer one style in pipelines: it's better to be consistently understandable than to use different notations.
- Performance is equivalent; decide primarily based on readability and risk of errors.

15.2 Streams at a Glance

JDK 8 LTS introduced the concept of *streams* for processing data. Therefore, the interface `java.util.stream.Stream<T>` plays a key role in this. Streams are an abstraction for *sequences of processing steps on data*. Furthermore, streams resemble both collections and iterators, where streams do not store data and can only be traversed once. Another analogy that can be used is assembly line processing.

For streams, we distinguish between three types of operations: *Create* (creation), *Intermediate* (calculation), and *Terminal* (result determination). This is shown schematically below:

$$\underbrace{Source \Rightarrow STREAM}_{Create} \Rightarrow \underbrace{OP_1 \Rightarrow OP_2 \Rightarrow \ldots \Rightarrow OP_{n-1}}_{Intermediate} \Rightarrow \underbrace{OP_n \Rightarrow Result}_{Terminal}$$

Introductory Example

The following listing illustrates the three types of operations without going into detail. For now, this is to get a first impression of streams and their processing. Therefore, let's look at a list of people called `persons`, filtered on all adults and returned as `List<Person>`:

```java
List<Person> adults = persons.stream().            // Create
                      filter(Person::isAdult).      // Intermediate
                      collect(Collectors.toList()); // Terminal
```

Besides all these (still unknown) implementation details, one can notice that concepts and the " what" are much clearer and that it's not the " how" (the details of the implementation of the functionality) that is in the foreground.

15.2.1 Create Streams: Create Operations

After the first example on streams, let's deepen our knowledge. In the following sections I will present some variants for creating streams.

Streams Based on Arrays and Collections

For arrays and collections the method `stream()` creates a `Stream<T>` object:

```java
String[] namesData = {"Karl", "Ralph", "Andi", "Andy", "Mike"};
List<String> names = Arrays.asList(namesData);

Stream<String> streamFromArray = Arrays.stream(namesData);
Stream<String> streamFromList = names.stream();
```

Streams for Predefined Value Ranges

In some cases, a fixed, predefined value range is to be mapped and processed via streams. There are special methods for this, such as `of()`, `range()`, and `chars()`:

```java
final Stream<String> names = Stream.of("Tim", "Andy", "Mike");      // String
final Stream<Integer> integers = Stream.of(1, 4, 7, 7, 9, 7, 2); // Integer

final IntStream values = IntStream.range(0, 100);                      // int
final IntStream chars = "This is a test".chars();                      // int
```

In addition to the generic interface `Stream<T>`, the listing above shows the interface `java.util.stream.IntStream` specific for the primitive data type `int`. Processing in this type of streams is done on values of primitive types and not on objects, like `Integer` with `Stream<Integer>`. To process the primitive types `long` and `double`, there are the classes `LongStream` and `DoubleStream` from the package `java.util.stream`. In addition to specialized, minimally higher-performance computations and conversions between them, you can also convert the streams to a stream of wrapper instances or any objects using `boxed()` or `mapToObj()`.

15.2.2 Intermediate and Terminal Operations at a Glance

Common use cases for the application of streams are filtering, transforming, and sorting values. For this purpose, so-called *intermediate operations* are used. These describe *processing steps* that can be easily connected in series. The remarkable thing about this is that, first, no calculations occur. Instead, only the sequences are described. There are **stateless** and **stateful** variants of processing steps. Filtering is a stateless action. This implies that for each element of the stream, this action can be executed independently of the others. This allows excellent parallelization of stateless operations. On the other hand, sorting is a stateful action that requires knowledge of the other elements in the stream (or at least some of them). Since streams do not cache data (or, for stateful operations, usually only a subset), they consume much less memory than collections. Thus, the design of streams often has little impact on memory requirements and execution time.

At some point, the **processing results** should be combined, output to the console, or processed differently. It is what **terminal operations** are for. Only a terminal operation actually causes the execution of the processing steps described by the intermediate operations to be performed.

15.2.3   *Intermediate Operations*

This section looks at various stateless intermediate operations and starts with filtering. We then move on to the extraction or mapping of values. After that, we will learn about two different stateful intermediate operations: sorting and eliminating duplicate entries.

Filtering: `filter()`

Filtering is a standard functionality that the JDK, unfortunately, did not provide before Java 8 LTS. Fortunately, this is changing with JDK 8 LTS.

For example, let's consider a list of `Person` objects. From this, we want to use `filter(Predicate<Person>)` to determine those `Person` objects that are adults by using the method reference `Person::isAdult` as follows:

```java
public static void main(String[] args)
{
    List<Person> persons = new ArrayList<>();
    persons.add(new Person("Micha", 43, Gender.MALE, "Zurich"));
    persons.add(new Person("Barbara", 40, Gender.FEMALE, "Hamburg"));
    persons.add(new Person("Yannis", 5, Gender.MALE, "Hamburg"));

    // Predicate<Person> isAdult = person -> person.getAge() >= 18;
    Stream<Person> adults = persons.stream().filter(Person::isAdult);
    adults.forEach(System.out::println);
}
```

Listing 15.2 Executable as "FILTEREXAMPLE"

The `isAdult` condition shown in the listing above can be written—as indicated in the comment—as a lambda or, alternatively, using a more readable method reference that points to the `isAdult()` method in the `Person` class (not presented here, but supplied in the companion resources). Thus, the FILTEREXAMPLE program produces the following output:

```
Person [name=Micha, age=43, gender=MALE, city=Zurich]
Person [name=Barbara, age=40, gender=FEMALE, city=Hamburg]
```

Multi-level Filtering   In practice, multi-level filtering according to different criteria is a frequent requirement. With the pipeline or assembly line analogy in mind, several filters can be connected in series, as shown in the following listing for three filter conditions:

```
Stream<Person> allAdultMikes = persons.stream().
            filter(Person::isAdult).
            filter(person -> person.getName().equals("Mike").
            filter(mike -> mike.livesIn("Zurich"));
```

In this way, we first identify all adults and then all those whose name is " Mike." Concerning this result set, we again keep only those who live in Zurich.

> **Opinion: Naming of Lambda Parameters**
>
> In general, it is advisable using descriptive names or standards like it for variables, and this also applies to parameters in lambdas—keeping programs as readable as possible. Just because an implementation is done functionally, there is no need to resort to name abbreviations like a, p, or x. Sometimes, however, identifiers with only one letter are suitable. This applies to mathematical calculations in the lambda, for example, x -> x + 1, and the parameter carries hardly any semantic meaning.

Mapping of Data, Extraction of Values: map ( )

Extraction of values is also a typical intermediate operation. Here, input data must be converted or mapped into a different format. For example, the attribute name or age could be extracted from a list of people. This is a mapping from one type to another: in the example, the type Person gets mapped to the type of the desired attribute, for example, String. For this purpose, one can use specializations of the interface Function<T, R> and implement the method apply(T) accordingly. The interface Function<T, R> is defined as follows:

```
interface Function<T,R>
{
    R apply(T t);
}
```

Let's say we need to extract the name from a Person object. We implement this using a lambda as follows:

```
Function<Person, String> extractPersonName = person -> person.getName();
```

With this prior knowledge, we implement the extraction of the name or the age for a list of people as follows:

```java
public static void main(String[] args)
{
    List<Person> persons = new ArrayList<>();
    persons.add(new Person("Barbara", 40, Gender.FEMALE, "Hamburg"));
    persons.add(new Person("Yannis", 5, "Hamburg"));

    // Mapping to name with lambda
    Stream<Person> adults = persons.stream().filter(Person::isAdult);
    Stream<String> namesStream = adults.map(person -> person.getName());

    // Mapping to age with method reference
    Stream<Integer> agesStream = persons.stream().map(Person::getAge).
                                    filter(age -> age >= 18);

    namesStream.forEach(System.out::println);
    agesStream.forEach(System.out::println);
}
```

Listing 15.3 Executable as "ATTRIBUTEEXTRACTIONEXAMPLE"

The ATTRIBUTEEXTRACTIONEXAMPLE program produces the following outputs:

```
Barbara
40
```

Eliminate Duplicates and Sort: `distinct()` and `sorted()`

The process of eliminating duplicate entries and sorting entries is described in the following listing by calls to the methods `distinct()` and `sorted()`. We first consider the execution of each method separately and then in combination:

```java
public static void main(String[] args)
{
    var distinct = createIntStream().distinct().
                                collect(Collectors.toList());
    var sorted = createIntStream().sorted().
                                collect(Collectors.toList());
    var sortedAndDistinct = createIntStream().sorted().distinct().
                                collect(Collectors.toList());

    System.out.println("distinct:          " + distinct);
    System.out.println("sorted:            " + sorted);
    System.out.println("sortedAndDistinct: " + sortedAndDistinct);
}

private static Stream<Integer> createIntStream()
{
    return Stream.of(7, 1, 4, 3, 7, 2, 6, 5, 7, 9, 8);
}
```

Listing 15.4 Executable as "SORTEDANDDISTINCTEXAMPLE"

Running the program SORTEDANDDISTINCTEXAMPLE removes duplicate elements and sorts the numbers. You get the expected output:

```
distinct:          [7, 1, 4, 3, 2, 6, 5, 9, 8]
sorted:            [1, 2, 3, 4, 5, 6, 7, 7, 7, 8, 9]
sortedAndDistinct: [1, 2, 3, 4, 5, 6, 7, 8, 9]
```

If you have looked very closely at the listing, you may have noticed the call to `collect(Collectors.toList())`. This is also a terminal operation, just like `forEach()`. A call to `collect(Collectors.toList())` transfers the data from a stream to a list. You can learn more about terminal operations directly below.

By the way, in more modern Java, it is easier to use the method `toList()` directly without first calling `collect()`. The improvement in the form of the method `toList()` is described in more detail in Sect. 2.7.2.

15.2.4   Terminal Operations

So far, we have used streams to perform various calculations, already using the terminal operation `forEach(Consumer<? super T>)` to produce console output. Let's now look at terminal operations in more general terms. Before that, let's remind ourselves that these lead to the processing of the pipeline and thus produce a result.

Let's now take a more general look at terminal operations. First, let's remind ourselves that these lead to the processing of the pipeline and thus produce a result.

Transfer Streams to Collections: `collect()`

With the help of `forEach()`, it is possible to iterate over the computation results, for example, to output them. For various use cases, it is necessary to store the data from a `Stream<E>` in a `Collection<E>`. Using `java.util.stream.Collector` instances, you can read data and transfer it to a list. Conveniently, the utility class `java.util.stream.Collectors` already provides several predefined methods that return matching `Collector` instances. This reduces the complexity of `Collector` provisioning, as shown below:

```java
List<Integer> ages = agesStream.collect(Collectors.toList());

List<String> names = namesStream.collect(Collectors.
                                 toCollection(ArrayList::new));
```

In the listing, we see the call to `toList()`, which is practical for many use cases. If you need more control over the type of the resulting data structure, you can call the method `toCollection()`, passing it the reference to the constructor of the desired collection, as shown in the second call.

The Methods `joining()` and `groupingBy()`

For joining strings as well as grouping data, the utility class `Collectors` provides several methods that can be profitably combined with the `collect()` method:

- `joining()`: Joins entries of type `String`. This is useful, for example, to implement a comma-separated representation.
- `groupingBy()`: Groups elements based on a criterion.
- `counting()`: Counts occurrences in combination with `groupingBy()`.

The usage of the above methods is illustrated in the following listing, where static imports enhance the readability. We employ various names as sample data, which we group by length, among other things, and count the occurrences as follows:

```java
import static java.util.stream.Collectors.counting;
import static java.util.stream.Collectors.groupingBy;
import static java.util.stream.Collectors.joining;

// ...

public static void main(final String[] args)
{
    List<String> names = Arrays.asList("Stefan", "Ralph", "Andi", "Mike",
                              "Florian", "Michael", "Sebastian");

    String joined = names.stream().sorted().collect(joining(", "));

    Function<String, Integer> strLength = String::length;
    Map<Integer, List<String>> grouped = names.stream().
                                    collect(groupingBy(strLength))
                                    ;
    Map<Integer, Long> counting = names.stream().
                              collect(groupingBy(strLength,
                                          counting()));

    System.out.println("joined: " + joined);
    System.out.println("grouped: " + grouped);
    System.out.println("counting: " + counting);
}
```

Listing 15.5 Executable as "COLLECTORSSPECIALEXAMPLE"

The program COLLECTORSSPECIALEXAMPLE produces the following output, which illustrates how the methods described above work:

```
joined: Andi, Florian, Michael, Mike, Ralph, Sebastian, Stefan
grouped: {4=[Andi, Mike], 5=[Ralph], 6=[Stefan], 7=[Florian, Michael], 9=[
    Sebastian]}
counting: {4=2, 5=1, 6=1, 7=2, 9=1}
```

15.3   Miscellaneous Extensions

Next, we look at some smaller enhancements in JDK 8 LTS through 11 LTS, such as additions to the `Comparator<T>` interface and the `Optional<T>` class, as well as the introduction of `var` also known as Local Variable Type Inference.

15.3.1   Extensions in Interface `Comparator<T>`

To sort objects, you can implement the interface `Comparator<T>` appropriately. Let's assume a list of people. It's obvious that there is a need to sort them by first or last name. For this purpose, we implement a `Comparator<Person>` in such a way that its `compare(Person, Person)` method takes the respective name component from the two passed `Person` objects and then compares them. Since JDK 8 LTS, this can be written concisely using a lambda:

```
Comparator<Person> compareByName = (person1, person2) ->
{
    return person1.getName().compareTo(person2.getName());
};
```

For further simplification the interface `Comparator<T>` has been extended by some useful methods:

- `comparing()`: Defines a comparator based on the extraction of two values that can be compared using the `Comparable<T>` interface.
- `thenComparing()`, `thenComparingInt()`/`-Long()` and `-Double()`: This enables the concatenation of comparators.

Comparators Based on `Comparable<T>`: `comparing()`

By invoking the static method `Comparator.comparing(Function<? super T,? extends U>)`, you create a comparator.[2] For this purpose, a so-called key extractor is passed as a parameter, which specifies how the desired attribute is retrieved from the instances to be sorted—in the example, from `Person` objects. The benefit here is that the fixed flow of the comparison, based on `Comparable<T>`, does not have to be implemented by you. Instead, only the variable part (the extraction) is passed as a parameter. The following example

---

[2] Here, you can find a useful example of a static method in an interface. However, it would have been possible to provide this through a separate utility class.

shows how to create a `Comparator<Person>` that extracts and compares the name component by calling `comparing()`:

```
// Variations with Comparator.comparing()
Comparator<Person> byName = Comparator.comparing(person -> person.getName());
Comparator<Person> byName2 = Comparator.comparing(Person::getName);
```

Concatenation of Comparators: `thenComparing()`

Often, sorting by only one criterion is not sufficient. For persons in particular, indeed, they sometimes carry the same last name. Thus, a second or even third sorting criterion is needed to achieve a unique order for people with the same last name. For this, we will execute several comparators one after the other. As basic building blocks, we first define different comparators for individual attributes and then combine them by calling the method `thenComparing(Comparator<? super T>)`:

```
// Comparators for a specific attribute
Comparator<Person> byFirstname = Comparator.comparing(Person::getFirstname);
Comparator<Person> byName = Comparator.comparing(Person::getName);
Comparator<Person> byAge = Comparator.comparing(Person::getAge);

// Combination of comparators
Comparator<Person> byNameAndFirstname = byName.
                                   thenComparing(byFirstname);
Comparator<Person> byNameAndAge = byName.thenComparing(byAge);
```

Often, you can avoid defining auxiliary comparators by using a " chain" directly:

```
Comparator<Person> byNameFirstnameAndAge =
                Comparator.comparing(Person::getName)592.
                        thenComparing(Person::5getFirstName).
                        thenComparingInt(Person::getAge);
```

Previously, we demonstrated how easy it is to execute comparators one after the other. However, in the first example, auto-boxing from an `int` to an `Integer` object occurs constantly for the age values, because `thenComparing()` creates a comparator based on `Comparable<Integer>`, but `getAge()` has the return type `int`.

For this case, one could define a comparator specialized to `int` as follows and use it as before:

```
Comparator<Person> byAge = Comparator.comparingInt(Person::getAge);
```

15.3.2 *The Class* `Optional<T>`

Sometimes, no result can be provided for calculations, such as in the case of an unsuccessful search or when determining the maximum of an empty set. This fact requires modeling of optional or nonexistent values. Until JDK 8 LTS, this was done in the form of `null` values or using the NULL OBJECT pattern. However, methods that potentially return `null` are problematic in handling. A caller may ignore or be not aware of the hint in the JavaDoc, which will eventually lead to a `NullPointerException`. Expressing and communicating optionality has become significantly easier since JDK 8 LTS by using the `Optional<T>` class, which represents a container for values of type `T` or `null`. This class allows optional values to be clearly expressed, and `NullPointerExceptions` can be avoided more easily.

Basics of the `Optional<T>` Class

Let's look at a search for a customer by name. A common variant returns a reference to a `Customer` instance if a matching customer is found. This can be implemented something like the following:

```
public Customer findCustomerByNameOldStyle(final String name)
{
    for (final Customer customer : customers)
    {
        if (customer.getName().equals(name))
        {
            return customer;
        }
    }

    // ATTENTION: potentially dangerous/unexpected
    return null;
}
```

Generally, this implementation is easy to understand. However, there is one drawback: the entire process becomes problematic if no matching customer is found. To express this special case, the value `null` is standard. However, more than just looking at the signature alone will be needed to determine how a nonexisting element gets communicated to a caller. Consequently, providing a corresponding JavaDoc comment is recommended.

Important Methods in the Class `Optional<T>`

Using the `Optional<T>` class helps make APIs more understandable and clarifies that sometimes no value can be returned. Therefore, in our example, however, we now need to convert a `Customer` instance or a `null` value into an `Optional<T>`.

The Methods `of()` and `empty()` When converting an object reference into `Optional<T>`, we must choose calling either the `of()` or the `ofNullable()` method. The latter suits better if a value to be converted may be `null`. If such a value is certainly `null`, it is a good idea to ivoke `Optional.empty()` directly, which models an empty result:

```java
public Optional<Customer> findCustomerByNameNewStyle(final String name)
{
    for (Customer customer : customers)
    {
        if (customer.getName().equals(name))
        {
            return Optional.of(customer);
        }
    }
    return Optional.empty();
}
```

The Methods `isPresent()` and `get()` Furthermore, as a caller, you are forced by the type system to work with the return type `Optional<T>` or, more precisely, have to make sure by various actions that a value is present. This is possible by calling `isPresent()`. If successful, with `get()` one accesses the stored value:

```java
Optional<Customer> optCustomer = findCustomerByNameNewStyle(name);

if (optCustomer.isPresent())
{
    Customer customer = optCustomer.get();

    doSomethingWithCustomer(customer);
}
else
{
    handleMissingCustomer(name);
}
```

The `ifPresentOrElse()` Method By using this method, the previous example can be written more concisely—in addition to specifying two actions, you especially benefit from the fact that the value is directly accessible in the positive case:

```java
public static void main(String[] args)
{
    Optional<Customer> optCustomer1 = findCustomerByNameNewStyle("Tim");
    optCustomer1.ifPresentOrElse(customer -> System.out.println("found: " +
                                 customer.getName()),
                                 () -> System.out.println("not found"));

    Optional<Customer> optCustomer2 = findCustomerByNameNewStyle("UNKNOWN");
    optCustomer2.ifPresentOrElse(customer -> System.out.println("found: " +
                                 customer.getName()),
                                 () -> System.out.println("not found"));
}
```

Listing 15.6 Executable as "OPTIONALIFPRESENTORELSEEXAMPLE"

Running the program OPTIONALIFPRESENTORELSEEXAMPLE produces the
following output:

```
found: Tim
not found
```

Differentiation: When to Use `Optional`?

Finally, please note the following: the class `Optional<T>` is not intended to
replace `null` in attributes or parameters, but was designed exclusively to explicitly
express the possibility of a missing result as the return value of a method.
    Therefore:

* Do not use as a type for attributes—not even in `records`.
* Do not use as a method parameter.
* Do not define as a static constant.

15.3.3   Syntax Extension `var`

Java 10 introduced the feature named Local Variable Type Inference, also known
as `var`, as a syntax extension. It allows omitting the explicit type specification
on the left side of a variable definition, provided that the compiler can determine
the concrete type for a local variable from the definition on the right side of the
assignment.

Examples

Let's look at some introductory examples of shorthand notation with `var` for
variable definitions:

```
var name = "Peter";                   // var => String
var chars = name.toCharArray();       // var => char[]

var mike = new Person("Mike", 47);    // var => Person
var hash = mike.hashCode();           // var => int
```

Especially in the context of generic containers, the Local Variable Type Inference
shows its advantages:

```java
// var => ArrayList<String>
var names = new ArrayList<String>();
names.add("Tim");
names.add("Tom");
names.add("Jerry");

// var => Map<String, Long>
var personAgeMapping = Map.of("Tim", 47L, "Tom", 12L,
                              "Michael", 47L, "Max", 25L);
```

Especially if the type specifications include several generic parameters, `var` helps make the source code much shorter and sometimes more readable. As an example, consider a nesting of types analogous to the following:

* `Set<Map.Entry<String,Long>>`
* `Map<Character, Set<Map.Entry<String,Long>>>`

In such cases, `var` saves quite a bit of typing—in addition, in this case, a static import of different collectors is necessary to increase readability:

```java
// var => Set<Map.Entry<String, Long>>
var entries = personAgeMapping.entrySet();

// var => Map<Character, Set<Map.Entry<String, Long>>>
var filteredPersons = personAgeMapping.entrySet().stream().
                                    filter(isAdult).
                                    collect(groupingBy(firstChar,
                                                       toSet()));
```

In the example, the following two lambdas are used to describe the grouping and for filtering:

```java
Predicate<Map.Entry<String, Long>> isAdult = entry -> entry.getValue() >= 18;

Function<Map.Entry<String, Long>, Character> firstChar = entry ->
                                    entry.getKey().charAt(0);
```

Isn't it desirable to abbreviate the type specification with `var` here too? Actually, yes! Why this is not possible, I explain in the following.

Special Case Lambdas and `var`

The compiler cannot determine the concrete type based on a lambda alone. Thus, no conversion to `var` is possible, but it leads to the error message " lambda expression needs an explicit target-type". If you insist on using `var` anyway, you would have to insert the following cast:

```java
var isAdultVar =
    (Predicate<Map.Entry<String, Long>>) entry -> entry.getValue() >= 18;
```

All in all, `var` is rather unsuitable for lambda expressions. This is a pity because, when possible, save some typing.

Differentiation: When to Use `var`?

Although using `var` can sometimes improve readability and minimize verbosity, it is preferable to choose `var` only when the abstracted type can be quickly understood by the user or is not particularly relevant for further usage.

Let's look at the following lines, each with an example where `var` provides simplification and greater clarity:

```
// repetitive
Map<String, Integer> mapping = new HashMap<>();
HttpRequest httpRequest = HttpRequest..newBuilder(). ...

// better
var mapping = new HashMap<String, Integer>();
var httpRequest = HttpRequest.newBuilder(). ...
```

Below we see a counterexample for the usage of `var`, because here you do not get any indication of the return type:

```
var result = doSomething();
```

Sometimes the type seems easy to understand, as here:

```
var users = userService.loadUsers();
```

However, it is not always that straightforward. In the example, the type could be one of the following:

- `List<User>`
- `Set<User>`
- `Stream<User>`

If the specific data type is semantically significant, that is, if you need to know whether it is a special type, then it is worth specifying an explicit type because it is immediately clear what it is. Below, we can see straight away that the result does not contain any duplicates and does not offer indexed access:

```
Set<User> users = userService.loadUsers();
```

15.4   Java + REPL => `jshell`

The command-line application JShell, which has been integrated into Java 9, is constantly being improved and has now become really useful. JShell allows for an interactive working style and the execution of small source code snippets, as is familiar from various other programming languages, in a similar form. This is also referred to as REPL (Read–Eval–Print–Loop) and makes it possible to write some Java source code and try things out quickly without having to start an IDE and create a project. During daily work as a software developer, you always have your IDE open anyway. You could achieve something similar with a `main()` method, but with the advantage of direct syntax checks and auto-completion. But JShell offers one advantage for smaller experiments: Java statements can also be executed without class and method definitions.

15.4.1   Introductory Example

Entering `jshell` on the command line opens the JShell:

```
$ jshell
|  Welcome to JShell -- Version 11.0.11
|  For an introduction type: /help intro
```

Then we are ready to try out some actions and calculations. A modification of a Hello World example serves as a starting point:

```
jshell> System.out.println("Hello JShell")
Hello JShell
```

Then we add two numbers:

```
jshell> 2 + 2
$2 ==> 4
```

From the output, we can see that the JShell automatically assigns the result of the calculation to a shell variable that begins with $, in this case $2—but only if we do not define a variable for the result ourselves:

```
jshell> int result = 2 + 2
result ==> 4
```

It is also possible to define your own methods as follows:

```
jshell> int add(int a, int b)
   ...> {
   ...>      return a + b;
   ...> }
|  created method add(int,int)
```

Conveniently, during method implementation, the JShell recognizes whether and when the statements are complete and whether further input is required in a subsequent line. This is indicated by `...>`. Ater the method implementation has been successfully completed, the message " `created method add(int,int)` " occurs.

After creating a method implementation, you can call it as expected and, as a special feature, also access the previously calculated and cached first result with $2:

```
jshell> add(3, $2)
$5 ==> 7
```

It is very convenient that the semicolon at the end of the line can be omitted (in some cases) and that you don't have to worry about handling exceptions, not even checked exceptions. The following statement

```
jshell> Thread.sleep(500)
```

demonstrates both: On the one hand, the semicolon can be omitted for statements in the JShell, and on the other hand, the InterruptedException triggered by Thread.sleep() does not need to be handled. More precisely, both only apply to commands in the JShell, but not when defining methods or classes there. In that case, a semicolon must still be used, and exceptions must be handled. We have just seen the semicolon in the method definition.

15.4.2   Additional Commands and Options

List Variables and Methods

The command /vars lists the currently defined variables:

```
jshell> /vars
|    int $2 = 4
|    int result = 4
|    int $5 = 7
```

The command /methods lists defined methods, in this case the method add() that was just created:

```
jshell> /methods
|    int add(int,int)
```

Command History

The JShell provides a command history, which is useful for viewing previous commands and repeating them if necessary. The last command can be restarted with /!. The /list command displays an overview from which the <nr>th command can be executed with /<nr>:

```
jshell> /list

   1 : System.out.println("Hello JShell")
   2 : 2 + 2
   3 : int result = 2 + 2;
   4 : int add(int a, int b)
       {
           return a + b;
       }
   5 : add(3, $2)
   6 : Thread.sleep(500)

jshell> /5
add(3, $2)
$7 ==> 7
```

15.4.3   More Complex Actions

In addition to simple actions, the JShell allows for more complex calculations and
even the definition of classes. Of course, loops are also possible:

```
jshell> for (var name : List.of("Tim", "Tom", "Mike", "Karthikeyan"))
   ...> {
   ...>       if (name.length() <= 3)
   ...>           System.out.println("Short name: " + name);
   ...>       else if (name.length() >= 10)
   ...>           System.out.println("Really long name: " + name);
   ...> }
Short name: Tim
Short name: Tom
Really long name: Karthikeyan
```

Special Features of Method Definitions

When experimenting in the JShell, it is helpful to be able to call methods that
have not yet been created when defining methods. This is referred to as forward
referencing. The JShell logs this appropriately and points out that the method just
defined cannot be called until the referenced method(s) has/have been defined:

```
jshell> int calc(int x, int y)
   ...> {
   ...>       checkBounds(x, 0, 10);
   ...>
   ...>       return x * y;
   ...> }
|  created method calc(int,int), however, it cannot be invoked until method
      checkBounds(int,int,int) is declared
```

Let's supplement the second method:

```
jshell> void checkBounds(int x, int lower, int upper)
   ...> {
   ...>     if (x < lower || x > upper)
   ...>         throw new IllegalArgumentException("x not in range " +
   ...>                                     lower + "--" + upper);
   ...> }
|  created method checkBounds(int,int,int)
```

To experience the testing functionality in action, we call up the following:

```
jshell> calc(42, 2)
|  Exception java.lang.IllegalArgumentException: x not in range 0--10
|        at checkBounds (#2:4)
|        at calc (#1:3)
|        at (#4:1)
```

Including Other JDK Classes

By default, only dedicated imported types from the `java.base` module (see the
following practical tip) are available in the JShell, but this is often sufficient for your
first steps in Java. By entering `/imports`, you will receive a list of the packages
available without further action, or, more precisely, the public types contained
therein:

```
jshell> /imports
|    import java.io.*
|    import java.math.*
|    import java.net.*
|    import java.nio.file.*
|    import java.util.*
|    import java.util.concurrent.*
|    import java.util.function.*
|    import java.util.prefs.*
|    import java.util.regex.*
|    import java.util.stream.*
```

Tip: Java Module System
With Java 9, the JDK was subdivided into individual, smaller building blocks,
known as modules. The modules bundle functionalities that belong together
thematically. Somewhat analogous to the `Object` class, which is the basis
of all classes and provides basic functionality, there is also a module called
`java.base`, which forms the basis of all other modules and bundles a lot of
essential and commonly used packages.

   If necessary, additional modules can be added when starting the JShell, or
even a class path can be specified:

```
$ jshell --class-path myOwnClassPath --enable-preview
```

If you want to use classes from the Date and Time API or Swing, for example, this requires corresponding imports, such as for the type `LocalTime` or `JFrame`. Try out a construction. Without the appropriate import, this will result in the following error messages:

```
jshell> LocalTime.parse("22:11")
|  Error:
|  cannot find symbol
|    symbol:   variable LocalTime
|  LocalTime.parse("22:11")
|  ^-------^

jshell> new JFrame("Hello World")
|  Error:
|  cannot find symbol
|    symbol:   class JFrame
|  new JFrame("Hello World")
|      ^----^
```

Therefore, we will now begin with the imports and execute the calls again:

```
jshell> import java.time.*

jshell> import javax.swing.*

jshell> LocalTime.parse("22:11")
$2 ==> 22:11

jshell> var jframe = new JFrame("Hello World")
jframe ==> javax.swing.JFrame[frame1,0,38,0x0,invalid,hidden ...
     tPaneCheckingEnabled=true]

jshell> jframe.setSize(200, 50)

jshell> jframe.show()
```

The second part of the above command sequence creates and displays a window measuring 200 × 50. It should look similar to Fig. 15.1.

Exiting the JShell

Finally, you can exit the JShell with `/exit`.

Fig. 15.1 Simple
Swing-Window started from
JShell

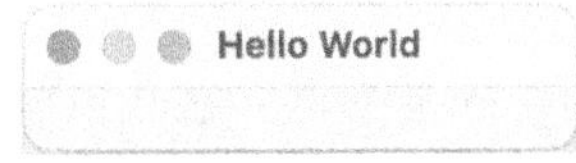

15.5   Launch Single-File Source Code Programs (Direct Compilation)

Since Java 11 LTS, it has been possible to compile and execute Java applications consisting of a single file directly in one step. This possibility saves a lot of work and means you don't need to know anything about bytecode or `.class` files.

As an alternative to the cumbersome expression " Launch Single-File Source Code Programs," we also refer to this as Direct Compilation. Because it can also be used to try out functionalities and preview features of newer Java versions, let's take a closer look at it.

15.5.1   Introductory Example

First, we will create a simple class `HelloWorld` in a file `HelloWorld.java`:

```
package direct.compilation;

public class HelloWorld
{
    public static void main(final String[] args)
    {
        System.out.println("Hello Execute After Compile");
    }
}
```

In the directory where the class is located, enter the following on the console:

```
$ java ./HelloWorld.java
```

Thereby, the above class is compiled under the hood and then the `main()` method is executed, and we get this output:

```
Hello Execute After Compile
```

This is particularly useful for executing smaller Java files as scripts and for getting started with Java.

This example also shows that there is no explicit call to `javac` required. Moreover, the package specification is ignored, and you don't have to worry about the package hierarchy matching the directory hierarchy in the file system.

This new feature replaces the significantly more complicated command sequence with a correctly set class path:

```
$ javac ./HelloWorld.java
$ java -classpath . direct.compilation.HelloWorld
```

15.5.2 *Special Feature: Shebang Script*

Unix-like operating systems have a feature called shebang execution. What does this mean? You can create a script with any name (it must not end with `.java`, but is entirely independent of the class name) as a text file. This script begins with the characters followed by the command to be executed. The rest of the file is then used as input for this command. To ensure that the file is actually executable, the appropriate executable flags must be set, for example, with `chmod +x`.

If we now put two and two together, we can specify a reference to Java in the first line, including the parameter `--source`, and the desired source code to be executed in the lines that follow.

Let's use this knowledge to recreate a simple directory listing:

```
#!/usr/bin/java --source 11
import java.nio.file.*;

public class DirectoryLister
{
    public static void main(String[] args) throws Exception
    {
        var dirName = ".";
        if (args == null || args.length < 1)
        {
            System.err.println("Using current directory as fallback");
        }
        else
        {
            dirName = args[0];
        }

        Files.walk(Paths.get(dirName)).forEach(System.out::println);
    }
}
```

Let's assume we named this file `DirLister`, assigned it the appropriate permissions, and called it as follows:

```
$ ./DirLister .
```

Then the output would be something like this:

```
.
./HelloWorld.java
./PalindromeChecker.java
./DirLister
```

By the Way ...
Unfortunately, shebang does not work on Windows systems. However, there is a trick—create a `.bat` file and call the `java` command there just as you would type it on the command line, for example, as a file `DirLister.bat` with the following content:

```
@ECHO
?%JAVA_HOME%\bin\java? com.example.inden.DirLister %*
```

Then you can execute `DirLister` or other commands based on Direct Compilation in the same way as on Unix systems.

References

1. Bloch, J.: Effective Java, 3 edn. Addison-Wesley (2017)
2. Inden, M.: Der Weg zum Java-Profi: Konzepte und Techniken für die professionelle Java-Entwicklung, 5 edn. dpunkt.verlag (2020)
3. Inden, M.: Java Challenges: 100+ Proven Tasks that Will Prepare You for Anything. APress (2021)

Index

GPSR Compliance
The European Union's (EU) General Product Safety Regulation (GPSR) is a set
of rules that requires consumer products to be safe and our obligations to
ensure this.

If you have any concerns about our products, you can contact us on

ProductSafety@springernature.com

In case Publisher is established outside the EU, the EU authorized
representative is:

Springer Nature Customer Service Center GmbH
Europaplatz 3
69115 Heidelberg, Germany